Recreational Fisheries

William F. Sigler and
John W. Sigler

Recreational Fisheries

Management, Theory, and
Application

University of Nevada Press
Reno and Las Vegas

The paper used in this book meets the minimum requirements of American National Standard for Information Sciences—ANSI Z39.48—1984. Binding materials were selected for strength and durability.

Library of Congress Cataloging-in-Publication Data

Sigler, William F.
   Recreational fisheries : management, theory, and application / by
William F. Sigler and John W. Sigler.
      p.   cm.
   Includes bibiographical references.
   ISBN 0-87417-139-3 (alk. paper)
   1. Fishery management.   I. Sigler, John W., 1946–   . II. Title.
SH328.S55   1990   89-21512
333.95′6—dc20   CIP

University of Nevada Press, Reno, Nevada 89557 USA
Copyright © 1990 William F. Sigler and John W. Sigler
Designed by Kaelin Chappell
Printed in the United States of Ame
2 4 6 8 9 7 5 3 1

Contents

Preface

It is a privilege to write the preface for a book whose senior author initiated my career in fisheries. A book coming from such a renowned fisheries scientist adds stature to the fisheries profession, and what a wonderful gift it is for these authors to leave their years of experience, dedication, and hard work to younger professionals.

There are over 60 million people in the United States who participate each year in freshwater recreational fishing. The continuous dramatic increase in the numbers of anglers has constantly made it more difficult for the nation's waters to produce both the product and the recreation users demand. Consequently, recreational fishery managers have little choice other than to intensify the management and use of the nation's waters so they produce more and better fishing. This increasing demand for recreational fishing, which continues to outstrip the nation's population growth, occurred during times when many recreational fishing stocks were actually decreasing. The nation often failed to treat its waters with needed respect, and a few centuries of heavy impact have taken their toll. Additional waters have been created to help balance this loss. The end result, however, is that the nation's waters cannot begin to produce the amount of high-quality recreational fishing so much in demand. This book will play its role in solving this dilemma by educating and building the awareness needed by the public and the fisheries specialist to keep fisheries research and management moving ahead.

This book is aimed at the younger biologist just entering the field, the researcher who needs an overview to produce payoff results, the experienced fishery professional who needs a constant reference, and the administrator who seldom has the time or facilities to obtain guidance from scattered research papers. With the increasing number of colleges and universities offering fishery courses, I would also hope that this book will be adopted as the text for fishery management classes. This will allow the student to grasp the real problems and solutions they will eventually be facing in their profession. This book should also be on the desk of those recreational anglers who are not only interested in the catching, but must also be aware and fight for the habitat conditions that make their recreation possible.

The first part of this book presents a philosophical and historical discussion of fishery management, including nongame species, and provides a step-by-step description of procedures for collecting, recording, and interpreting data relative to the management objectives associated with sport and ecologically important fishes. The second part presents concepts for management.

Each chapter has been written to stand alone. For example, one chapter discusses the basic assumptions that must necessarily be made when using bony material as an aid to ageing. Various ageing techniques are suggested so the researcher can determine the reliability of a concept when applied to a particular species or population. A corollary of this is the need for a biologist to determine his or her own objectivity and consistency when processing data.

Several ways of presenting data are suggested since no fisheries investigation is complete until the data have been arranged in a form that meets stated objectives. Adequate presentation of data may help establish such needed management information as the presence of dominant-year classes, rate and time of growth, and movements and migrations. Today's fishery biologist may be responsible for management, research, or program administration. In any event, he or she needs to understand fish population dynamics, know how to manipulate the environment and the fish population, and have a grasp of the sociopolitical and socioeconomic problems involving the fishing and nonfishing public.

The experience of the authors in teaching and management comes through in this book in their selection of topics and the many methods presented. Their experience will stimulate the interest necessary for tackling the large array of problems related to recreational fishing. Unlike engineering and mathematics, recreational fishery solutions will not come in simple formulas and given angles. The book, therefore, gives a great variety of methods and solutions, with much latitude for deep thinking and personal judgment. The book covers the subject from the past to the future. I invite you to explore this comprehensive text and use it continuously. I started my fisheries work reading William F. Sigler's books *Fishes of Utah* and *Wildlife Law Enforcement*. How timely it is that I now can refer to this new book. I invite you to explore this great work; the need is urgent, and this work will fulfill it for a long time to come.

William S. Platts
Boise, Idaho
Past President, American Fisheries Society

Acknowledgments

We acknowledge the review, assistance, and helpful contributions of the following:

Richard O. Anderson, Director, National Fish Hatchery and Technology Center, U.S. Fish and Wildlife Service, San Marcos, Texas.

Nancy Banks, Library Research Assistant, Corvallis, Oregon.

Robert J. Behnke, Associate Professor of Fish Biology, Department of Fishery and Wildlife Biology, Colorado State University, Fort Collins.

David H. Bennett, Associate Professor, and Larry K. Dunsmoor, Graduate Research Assistant, Department of Fish and Wildlife Resources, University of Idaho, Moscow.

Eric P. Bergersen, Assistant Unit Leader, Fish and Wildlife Research Unit, U.S. Fish and Wildlife Service, Department of Fishery and Wildlife Biology, Colorado State University, Fort Collins.

Theodore C. Bjornn, Assistant Unit Leader, Fish and Wildlife Research Unit, U.S. Fish and Wildlife Service, Department of Fish and Wildlife Resources, University of Idaho, Moscow.

Carl E. Bond, Professor Emeritus, Department of Fisheries and Wildlife, Oregon State University, Corvallis.

Kenneth D. Carlander, Professor Emeritus, Department of Animal Ecology, Iowa State University, Ames.

David L. Carlson, Planning Specialist, Developmental Center for Handicapped Persons, Utah State University, Logan.

Steven E. Clyde, Attorney at Law, Clyde & Pratt, Salt Lake City, Utah.

John A. Coates and John Blum, Makah Tribe, Neah Bay, Washington.

Joseph Coffelt, President, Coffelt Electronics Company, Inc., Englewood, Colorado.

Blair Csuti, Regional Zoologist, The Nature Conservancy, San Francisco Office, Rocky Mountain Natural Heritage Program, Denver, Colorado.

Gretchen P. Davis, Secretary/Editor, WFSAI, Logan, Utah.

James Deacon, Professor, Department of Biological Sciences, University of Nevada-Las Vegas, Las Vegas.

Fred H. Everest, Research Fishery Biologist, U.S. Forest Service Pacific Northwest Forest and Range Experiment Station, Corvallis, Oregon.

Harry Everhart, Head (Emeritus), Department of Fisheries and Aquatic Sciences, Cornell University, Ithaca, New York.

Stacy V. Gebhards, Area Director, Idaho Department of Fish and Game, Boise.

William H. Geer, Former Director, Utah Division of Wildlife Resources, Salt Lake City.

Bruce C. Giunta, Federal Aid Coordinator, Utah Division of Wildlife Resources, Salt Lake City.

Lois Gunnell, Secretary, Logan, Utah.

Thom Hardy, Associate Research Professor, Civil and Environmental Engineering Department, Utah State University, Logan.

Ronney D. Harris, Professor, Electrical Engineering Department and Center for Atmospheric and Space Sciences, Utah State University, Logan.

William T. Helm, Associate Professor (Emeritus), Department of Fisheries and Wildlife, Utah State University, Logan.

B. L. Jensen, Hatchery Manager, Dexter National Fish Hatchery, Dexter, New Mexico.

Keter Publishing House Jerusalem Limited, Jerusalem, Israel.

George W. Klontz, Professor, Fishery Resources, Department of Fish and Wildlife Resources, University of Idaho, Moscow.

Stephen P. Malvestuto, Assistant Professor, Department of Fisheries and Allied Aquaculture, Auburn University, Alabama.

James K. Mayhew, Fisheries Superintendent, Iowa Conservation Commission, Des Moines.

Thomas E. Moen, Biologist (retired), U.S. Fish and Wildlife Service, Arkadelphia, Arkansas.

James W. Mullan, Project Leader, U.S. Fish and Wildlife Service, Fisheries Assistance Office, Leavenworth, Washington.

John M. Neuhold, Professor and Assistant to the Dean (Emeritus), College of Natural Resources, Utah State University, Logan.

Harold Olson, Director (retired), New Mexico Game and Fish Department, Santa Fe.

Sydney Peterson, Editorial Assistant, Logan, Utah.

William S. Platts, Research Fisheries Biologist (retired), U.S. Forest Service, Boise, Idaho.

Eric D. Prince, Fisheries Research Biologist, National Marine Fisheries Service, Southeast Fisheries Center, Miami Laboratory, Florida.

James B. Reynolds, Leader, Fish and Wildlife Research Unit, University of Alaska, Fairbanks.

Temple Reynolds, Director (retired), Arizona Game and Fish Department, Phoenix.

Rosalie A. Schnick, Technical Information Specialist, U.S. Fish and Wildlife Service, National Fishery Research Laboratory, La Crosse, Wisconsin.

William B. Scott, Senior Scientist, Huntsman Marine Laboratory, St. Andrews, New Brunswick, Canada.

Margaret B. Sigler, Secretary/Editor, WFSAI, Logan, Utah.

Donald V. Sisson, Professor, Mathematics and Statistics Department, Utah State University, Logan.

Ralph Swanson, U.S. Fish and Wildlife Service, Endangered Species Office, Portland, Oregon.

Robert C. Summerfelt, Professor, Department of Animal Science, Iowa State University, Ames.

Tom Wesche, Watershed Specialist, Wyoming Water Research Center, University of Wyoming, Laramie.

Roy A. Whaley, Supervisor, Reservoir Research Unit, Wyoming Game and Fish Department, Casper.

James Williams, U.S. Fish and Wildlife Service, Endangered Species Office, Washington, D.C.

Larry J. Wilson, Director, Iowa State Conservation Commission, Des Moines.

Gar W. Workman, Fish and Wildlife Extension Specialist, Department of Fisheries and Wildlife, Utah State University, Logan.

Illustrations are by Beth Walden, Specialized Information Systems, Logan, Utah.

1. Historical Perspectives

It can reasonably be stated that recreational fisheries management involves almost as much art as science. This statement is not a disparagement of fishery managers but rather reflects the current state of fishery management in North America.

In 1870, no unified or uniform fisheries management structure existed at either the federal or state level. Citizens and scientists had expressed some concerns for the resource by this time (Thompson 1970), but little had been accomplished to effectively manage any fishery. Prior to 1870, fishery management and related activities consisted only of some regulatory efforts by state commissions, exploitation of marine and inland stocks (much of which had been ongoing for over 350 years), and limited commercial fish culture. It can be fairly stated that prior to 1870 or perhaps 1900, fisheries management was simply the planting of fish (Thompson).

Scientists and citizens alike had noted declines in various fish populations, particularly Atlantic coast trout and salmon stocks. These declines were attributed to pollution, soil erosion, dam construction, and habitat impairment (Thompson 1970). It was assumed, however, that depleted stocks could be replaced or replenished in the fisheries with stocks from the existing commercial species.

Bennett (1962) points out that fish management can be defined as the art and science of producing sustained annual crops of wild fish for recreational and commercial uses. He notes that fish culture and management can be divided into three time periods for historical perspectives. The first period stretches from the earliest development of fish culture and management in the pre-Christian era to approximately A.D. 1900 and is characterized by what could be described as classical fish culture. The second time period, which roughly covers from 1900 into the 1930s, represents attempts to manipulate wild populations. The third period began in the 1930s and extended somewhere into the 1960s or 1970s, or possibly to the present.

The Beginnings of Fish Culture

Fish culture, which started in the United States as early as 1853, was providing a substantial income to several individuals by 1865. Seth Green, perhaps the first successful American fish culturist, established a hatchery for brook trout in 1864 near Caledonia, New York, intending to sell them on the food market. The demand for eggs and small fish was so great, however, that few of his fish reached the food market. Prices for products were high. One thousand eggs sold for $8 to $10, while an equal number of fingerlings and two-year-old fish sold for $40 and $250, respectively (Bowen 1970). Fish culture activity during the 1860–65 period centered mostly in New York and New Jersey. Pioneers in fish culture included E. C. Kellog, D. W. Chapman, S. H. Ainsworth, T. Norris, and J. H. Slack.

Fish culture was probably the first tool of fishery management in North America, even earlier than regulations. As early as the 1870s, federal policy makers with the U.S. Commission of Fish and Fisheries determined that depleted marine fish stocks could be rehabilitated through stocking programs.

The American Fish Culturist's Association was formed at a meeting in New York on December 20, 1870, by individuals actively involved in fish culture. It met to fix prices on fish and fish eggs. The association was formed "to promote the cause of fish culture; to gather and diffuse information bearing upon its practical success; the interchange of friendly feeling and intercourse among the members of the association; the uniting and encouraging of the individual interest of fish culturists" (Thompson 1970). Seth Green, evidently not in attendance at the initial meeting, was the first chairman of the association's executive committee in 1872 (Bowen 1970). In 1878, to reflect the broadening area of interest and to attract members not directly involved in fish culture, the members voted to call themselves the American Fish Cultural Association. In 1884, following a lively debate, the name was changed again to the American Fisheries Society (Thompson). Prior to the establishment of various fish health and fish cultural sections in the parent society in recent years, emphasis on fish culture began to wane; in the interim, managerial and research-oriented biologists became involved with the society, a trend now somewhat ameliorated by the increased numbers of specialized sections.

The Natural History Era

Fisheries management apparently evolved as a sideline of natural history observations designed to record the presence of the varied fauna of the newly settled North American continent. Observations of both live fish and collected specimens spurred speculation and subsequent research into habitat requirements and life stages of species of interest. Prior to 1800, however, almost nothing of a truly scientific nature was contributed to North American zoology by North Americans.

Gonzolo Fernandez de Oviedo should perhaps be credited with the initial observance of fish in America (Myers 1964). He documented the presence of freshwater sharks in Lake Nicaragua, only twenty-five years after Columbus's last voyage.

Catesby's *Natural History of Carolina, Florida and the Bahama Islands* (1731–43) was the single most descriptive work of North American natural history until early nineteenth-century works by Rafinesque, Soy, Le Sueur, and others (Myers 1964).

Soon after 1800, William Maclure and others had begun to discuss the "natural sciences" and by 1812 had founded the Academy of Natural Sciences of Philadelphia (Myers 1964). Two scientists associated with the academy, Constantine Samuel Rafinesque and Charles Alexandre Le Sueur, can be credited with initiating North American freshwater ichthyology, mostly along the Ohio and Wabash rivers. Samuel Latham Mitchill, a New York physician responsible for describing and classifying some 166 fish species near New York City in the late 1700s, presented much information on North American marine and freshwater ichthyology during the same period with his publication *The Fishes of New York* (Myers).

In 1850, David Humphries Storer published *Synopsis of the Fishes of North America*. In the same year, Louis Agassiz of Harvard University published *Lake Superior* (Hubbs 1964). By 1851, the only fish fauna in North America that had been discovered, named, and fully described was the coastal area of New England and New York (Hubbs).

Hubbs (1964) attributes to the period 1875–1900 the following: (1) a very intensive description of the fishes of North and Middle America, mostly by David Starr Jordan, and (2) the early development and rapid expansion of fish culture and related research.

Stephen A. Forbes began collecting fish on the Illinois River in the vicinity of Havana, Illinois, in 1876. The Illinois Biological Station was established at Havana in 1894. Forbes published *A Catilogue of the Nature of Fishes of Illinois* in 1883, and Forbes and R. A. Richardson published *The Fishes of Illinois* in 1920. The work on this section of the Illinois River continues today and represents the longest and probably the most intense study on any aquatic habitat in the United States.

David Starr Jordan and Barton W. Evermann, in addition to their other ichthyological works, produced their popular treatise *American Food and Game Fishes* in 1902. Jacob Ellsworth Reighard, after the turn of the century, studied the breeding behavior and development of fishes, partly in relation to fish culture (Hubbs 1964).

Dymond (1964) reports that natural history studies in Canada presented information on animals as early as 1771 and on fish as early as 1850 or 1852. By 1947 Canadian ichthyological publications included numerous "Fishes of" books, covering Toronto, eastern North America (Greenland to Georgia), Nova Scotia, Canada, and others. The by-product of all of these descriptive efforts was the accumulation of scientific information for biologists concerned with habitat, species requirements, and life history.

Past Trends

One beginning for a history of fishery research would be to observe that development of fishery science in America was shaped by the philosophy of Spencer Fullerton Baird and his immediate successors at the U.S. Commission of Fish and Fisheries, who placed great importance on hatchery culture as a solution to the problems of marine and freshwater fisheries (McHugh 1970).

In 1871, Baird directed the U.S. Fish Commission, the forerunner of the Bureau of Fisheries and the later U.S. Fish and Wildlife Service. The joint resolution of Congress which created the U.S. Commission of Fish and Fisheries on February 9, 1871, provided only for an inquiry into the decrease of food fishes, with a view of adopting any remedial measures that seemed necessary, and appropriated $5,000 for the effort (Bowers 1905). On July 3, 1903, the U.S. Commission of Fish and Fisheries was incorporated into the new Department of Commerce and Labor (Bowers).

Commissioner Baird steadily increased the scope of commission work even though he had only a small budget. Early commission inquiries led to the conclusion that artificial propagation was the most effective form of aid the federal government could render commercial fisheries (Bowers 1905).

Because the proclivity for fish cultural activities inhibited other aspects of fishery research and management, the federal government funded at disproportionately high levels a vigorous culture program from 1873 to about 1941. The result was the presence of seventy-three species on the propagation list (McHugh 1970). Scientific inquiry did not cease, however. Personnel at the Woods Hole Fishery Laboratory made important contributions to early scientific surveys on fishes, spawning, growth, distribution, and food habits. A research laboratory was founded at Beaufort, North Carolina, in 1901. In Canada, the Board of Management (for the first biological station) was created in 1898 and became the Biological Board of Canada in 1912. In 1937, the Biological Board became the Fisheries Research Board of Canada. In 1917, the California State Fisheries Laboratory was founded by W. F. Thompson as the first state laboratory. The Institute for Fisheries Research, founded by Carl Hubbs at the University of Michigan, and the Ontario Fisheries Research Laboratory, founded by B. A. Bensley and W. A. Clemens, were both opened in 1920 (McHugh).

Fishery research has its roots in ichthyology, making it at least as old as Linnaeus or Aristotle. Early fishery studies stressed age composition and rate of growth. Fluctuations in abundance (catch) of a particular stock, it was noted, were often accompanied by changes in size of fishes (Petersen 1894).

Just prior to World War II and immediately following, the science of population dynamics came into being. With it came the realization that if scientific fishery management were to succeed, it required an understanding of the dynamic relationships of total communities rather than restricted pictures of single species or stocks (McHugh 1970).

Significant Changes

While much has changed in fisheries and fisheries management in the last fifty years, three programs have had significant long-term effects on the overall philosophy and direction of both inland and marine fisheries management. These three programs are the original Dingell-Johnson Act (Federal Aid in Sport Fish Restoration Act), the Wallop-Breaux Act (expanded Dingell-Johnson funding), and the creation of the Cooperative Fishery Research Units.

As noted, prior to World War II, fisheries management consisted largely of stocking reared fish and law enforcement. Funding for state fishery agencies, based on license fees, was insufficient for complex management needs. The acts discussed below changed not only funding levels but basic philosophical approaches to fisheries management.

The Dingell-Johnson Act

In 1937 the Pitman-Robertson Act (Federal Aid in Wildlife Restoration Act) was passed, and in 1950 the Dingell-Johnson Act (Federal Aid in Sport Fish Restoration Act) was passed. The act was sponsored by Representative John Dingell of Michigan and Senator Edwin Johnson of Colorado. It provided for a 10 percent excise tax on fishing rods, reels, creels, artificial lures, baits, and flies. The tax is collected by the manufacturer or importer and paid to the states through the U.S. Treasury Department and the U.S. Fish and Wildlife Service. States are allocated funding based 60 percent on the number of licensed sport anglers and 40 percent on the land and water area of the state. No state may receive more than 5 or less than 1 percent of the total.

Dingell-Johnson funding has been used to construct new lakes, provide public access, improve aquatic habitat, protect fish from pollution and other adverse impacts, and develop or improve fisheries techniques through research (Mossmann 1975).

The Wallop-Breaux Act

In 1984 the Wallop-Breaux Act was passed by Congress, greatly expanding the effects of the original Dingell-Johnson program. The July 1984 Sport Fishing Institute (SFI) bulletin reported that the Wallop-Breaux Act would result in expenditures of over $1 billion, of benefit to 54 million Americans by 1995 (Anonymous 1984).

The Wallop-Breaux Act virtually rewrites the Federal Aid in Sport Fish Restoration Act. The act, named as was its predecessor in honor of its chief proponents, will dramatically alter sport fishery management. The authors, Senator Malcolm Wallop of Wyoming and Representative John B. Breaux of Louisiana, played vital roles in the passage of the respective legislation.

The new law, which was originally an effort to expand Dingell-Johnson in 1979, somewhat alters the process of funding. Major provisions include two accounts for monies collected: the Sport Fish Restoration Account and the Boat Safety Account. The first account receives monies from excise tax on tackle, yachts, etc., and excess over the first $46 million from the motor boat fuel tax. The first $45 million from the fuel tax goes to the Land and Water Boat Safety Account and $1 million goes to the Land and Water Conservation Fund. The main thrusts of the act are still to improve and foster recreational boating safety and use of all waters; coastal states must equitably allocate their funding between fresh water and salt water, and additional items are now taxable.

The most significant aspect of the Wallop-Breaux Act is that it is a user fee tax promoted by the users themselves, though a great deal of cooperative effort is still required.

Cooperative Fishery Research Units

By the 1930s, evidence of devastation in wildlife and agricultural systems in the United States was quite obvious. In concert with the ongoing economic depression, the persistent drought, and the general lack of organized efforts to alter any of these conditions, wildlife populations throughout North America suffered severely. At this time it became apparent that natural resources in the United States comprised the ultimate source of all wealth and that there is a subsequent associated limit to alterations which can be made in that natural inventory without severe adverse effects. During the middle to late 1930s, J. Norwood "Ding" Darling, more than any other individual, should be credited with promoting and establishing the framework and machinery to both halt encroachments on natural ecosystems and begin to reverse long-standing nationwide tendencies.

Ding Darling was a Pulitzer Prize-winning nationally syndicated political cartoonist. He was an extremely well-informed, outspoken, and wise individual regarding nature and natural resource issues. Darling is credited with the idea of creating cooperative research units at land-grant universities across the United States. Darling, along with others, promoted the programs of federal aid for fish and wildlife restoration (the Pitman-Robertson and Dingell-Johnson acts) and lobbied strongly for the creation of cooperative fish and wildlife units. Due primarily to the efforts of Darling and other naturalists, the first Cooperative Wildlife Research Unit was established in 1932 at Iowa State College (now Iowa State University) in Ames. The unit's first leader was Paul L. Errington, a recent PhD from the University of Wisconsin. In 1960, the cooperative wildlife programs were recognized by Congress and given statutory recognition as the Cooperative Research Unit Program under Public Law 86–686. This act was designed to "facilitate cooperation between the federal government, colleges and universities, the states and private organizations for cooperative unit programs of research and education relating to fish and wildlife and for other purposes."

The cooperative wildlife units had been so successful in the 1935–60 period that in 1960 the administrative framework for the Cooperative Fishery Research Units was established. The first unit was located at Utah State University in Logan. It was functional in early 1962, having been formally established in November 1961. The first leader was Donald Franklin. Several other units followed rapidly. The Missouri unit was established in October 1962, the Maine unit in November 1962, and the Louisiana unit in June 1963 (John Rogers, personal communication, 1985). Today, seven of the original nine units have been joined by seven more wildlife research units, nineteen fisheries research units, and ten combined fisheries and wildlife research units, a total of forty-three units in twenty-nine states. There is no question but that the units, both fisheries and wildlife, have far exceeded Darling's expectations when he initially set out to establish a mechanism to provide scientifically trained specialists to do professional fisheries and wildlife management research and administration. The unit programs have contributed to a large number of successful rehabilitation, research, and management projects over the years. These efforts have involved nongame as well as commercial and sport fishing species. Cooperative research units are involved in more than six hundred projects, ranging from short-term graduate student projects, to very sophisticated, long-term, interdisciplinary investigations with many participants and years of data collection, observation, and interpretation (Lendt 1984).

The cooperative units have aided the universities by helping provide a mechanism whereby graduate students, and to a lesser extent undergraduate students, can receive highly specialized training in management and research aspects of fishery biology. Without question, the creation and existence of the Cooperative Fishery Research Units have helped the universities have a profound and long-lasting effect on the course of inland fisheries research and management. With the continued existence of the units as a high-quality, federally funded and state fishery division and university-sponsored program, the units will continue to help produce well-trained fisheries biologists.

Some Thoughts

The roots of fishery management in early fish culture are still apparent. Concerns regarding the role of fish culture and hatcheries in fisheries management were voiced in 1985 (Abele 1985; Rosen 1985). The American Fisheries Society (AFS) held a plenary session at its 114th annual meeting in 1984 and published the results as "The Role of Fish Culture in Fishery Management: Politics, Policies and Future Directions—A Summary of the Plenary Session." AFS also sponsored a "Symposium on the Role of Fish Culture in Fishery Management" in the spring of 1985.

Royce (1984) notes that professionals of any kind are a special group in society, that aquatic scientists need to maintain high professional standards, and that all aquatic resources deserve the attention of individuals well trained and knowledgeable in all aspects of aquatic science. The focus then becomes personnel training requirements and certification as professionals.

Resource agencies have voiced concern over the amount, type, and applicability of training that fishery biologists and other aquatic scientists are receiving at academic institutions. The assertion is that graduates are inadequately prepared to deal with complex fishery resource questions and the everyday aspects of resource management. The complexity of the issue is reflected in the variety of subjects discussed in various "fishery science" and other publications (Nielsen 1981, 1984; Chapman 1979; Hester 1979).

Professional certification, the second area of concern, is not a new concept; even in fisheries it has been with us since 1961. In the early 1960s the society issued certificates to qualified members in professional and nonprofessional categories. The professional category required at least a B.A. or B.S. degree plus two or more years experience; the nonprofessional certificate required only experience (Benson 1970).

In August 1968, the society began awarding certificates to fishery scientists (Hutton 1970). Under this program, more than sixteen hundred fisheries biologists have been certified.

Since January 1985 the system has been two tiered: an entry-level associate fisheries scientist and a certified fisheries scientist, requiring a minimum of a B.S. or B.A. degree and five years applicable experience. Requirements for certification are being tightened, and AFS is examining the possibility of requiring periodic review of those people holding certification (Anonymous 1985).

Present Status

Assessing the present status of recreational freshwater fisheries management can be approached by compilations of statistics showing number of angler hours by state, the number of fish creeled, or the number of dollars spent for licenses and/or associated equipment, or by state or county statistics regarding the number of fishery professionals involved in managing recreational freshwater fisheries, comparing previous years or decades or by making projections into the future.

If all of these statistics and figures were cited, one thing would be readily apparent: recreational fishing in most of North America, particularly in the United States, is big business. Hundreds of millions of dollars are spent yearly for management of recreational fisheries. These funds come both from license sales and from legislative appropriations on both the state and federal level.

When all aspects of recreational freshwater fisheries are considered, it becomes obvious that the problems facing freshwater fisheries management are extremely complex. Hundreds of thousands of worker hours, millions of dollars, and a diversity of fishing needs and requirements are involved. This diversity includes the casual angler who spends one to two hours per season and the dedicated elitist who spends tens to hundreds of hours and thousands of dollars to catch, but not always creel, one or two trophy fish. The thought that emerges from all of this diverse information indicates that management of freshwater recreational fisheries is no longer simply a matter of placing or managing a few fish in selected streams within the boundaries of a management area and allowing people to catch those fish.

Another way to demonstrate the complexity of recreational fisheries management is to list all the tools and mechanisms used by fisheries managers. While many of the techniques used today were conceived many years ago, they have been improved by technology. Electroshockers are no longer devices constructed from scavenged parts of other equipment or put together to fill a short-term need; rather, they have become sophisticated devices with computer-controlled circuits and digital LED readouts. Fish scale-reading devices have been improved by computers, more sophisticated light projection, and better magnification. Computers are currently being used in hatcheries to program and project feed requirements and monitor growth and feed conversion ratios. This mechanism allows hatchery managers to more precisely utilize feed and physical facilities, thus providing a more tightly defined and predictable product. Computers are also being used to compile and integrate data in a fashion not possible ten years ago. The advent, popularity, and use of personal computers has provided a mechanism whereby all fisheries managers and researchers at every level can have immediate access to vast amounts of information as well as word-processing capabilities. More time is thereby freed for management of the resource.

If a summary paragraph were to be written regarding the status of fisheries management in North America, it would have to include a statement regarding its vastly increased complexity and an equally important statement regarding the growing technology available to fisheries managers for the latter part of the twentieth century. What can also be said in summary regarding the present status of freshwater fisheries management is that innovative programs specifically designed for a particular fishery or for filling the needs of a particular group of the fishing public will become not only more popular but more necessary in future years. Fisheries managers who explore all aspects of a problem should seek input and assistance from not only their peers and others in management departments but also from volunteer groups and other organizations eager to assist in habitat restoration or to improve fishing. General public awareness should not only be utilized but actually courted for assistance. The importance, from many aspects, of recreational fisheries and wise management of our fisheries resources is reflected in the development and publication of a "National Recreational Fisheries Policy" in 1988 (DOI 1988). The national policy, endorsed by over sixty concerned agencies, organizations, and departments, provides guiding principles and goals for management of recreational fisheries nationwide well into the twenty-first century.

Literature Cited

Abele, R. W. 1985. The AFS North American Fisheries Policy: Is It Relevant to Present and Future Policies and Directions for the Use of Cultured Fish in Fisheries Management? *Fisheries* 10(1):3.

Anonymous. 1985. Changes in AFS Professional Certification. American Fisheries Society News. *Fisheries* 10(1):22.

Anonymous. 1984. *The Wallop-Breaux Fund*. Washington, D.C.: Sport Fishing Institute. Bulletin 356. 8 pp.

Bennett, G. W. 1962. *Management of Artificial Lakes and Ponds*. New York: Reinhold Publishing Corporation. 283 pp.

Benson, N. G. 1970. The American Fisheries Society, 1920–1970. Pp. 13–24 in N. G. Benson, ed., *A Century of Fisheries in North America*. Washington, D.C.: American Fisheries Society. Special Publication 7.

Bowen, J. T. 1970. A History of Fish Culture as Related to the Development of Fishery Programs. Pp. 71–94 in N. G. Benson, ed., *A Century of Fisheries in North America*. Washington, D.C.: American Fisheries Society. Special Publication 7.

Bowers, G. M. 1905. Pp. 1–28 in *Report of the Commissioner*, 1903, Part XXIX. Washington, D.C.: U.S. Commission of Fish and Fisheries.

Chapman, D. G. 1979. Fisheries Education as Viewed from the Inside. *Fisheries* 4(2):18–21.

Department of the Interior. U.S. Fish and Wildlife Service. 1988. National Recreational Fisheries Policy. Washington, D.C. 20 pp.

Dymond, J. R. 1964. A History of Ichthyology in Canada. *Copeia* 1964(1):2–32.

Hester, F. E. 1979. Fisheries Education from the Federal Perspective. *Fisheries* 4(2): 22–24.

Hubbs, C. L. 1964. History of Ichthyology in the United States after 1850. *Copeia* 1964(1):42–59.

Hutton, R. F. 1970. The American Fisheries Society Today. Pp. 277–90 in N. G. Benson, ed., *A Century of Fisheries in North America*. Washington, D.C.: American Fisheries Society. Special Publication 7.

Lendt, D. L. 1984. *Fifty Years of Achievement—The Cooperative Research Unit Pro-*

gram in Fisheries and Wildlife 1935–1985. Washington, D.C.: U.S. Department of the Interior, U.S. Fish and Wildlife Service. 25 pp.

McHugh, J. L. 1970. Trends in Fishery Research. Pp. 25–56 in N. G. Benson, ed., *A Century of Fisheries in North America*. Washington, D.C.: American Fisheries Society. Special Publication 7.

Mossmann, W. H. 1975. *25 Years of Federal-State Cooperation for Improving Sport Fishing. Accomplishments under the Federal Aid in Fish Restoration Program 1950–1975*. Washington, D.C.: U.S. Fish and Wildlife Service. 37 pp.

Myers, G. S. 1964. A Brief Sketch of the History of Ichthyology in America to the Year 1850. *Copeia* 1964(1):33–41.

Nielsen, L. A. 1981. Accreditation in Fisheries—To Be or Not to Be. *Fisheries* 6(1): 9–11.

———. 1984. Undergraduate Curricula of Inland Fisheries Schools. *Fisheries* 9(2): 5–7.

Petersen, C. G. J. 1894. On the Biology of Our Flatfishes and on the Decrease of Our Flatfish Fisheries, Appendix V. On the Labelling of Living Plaice. *Report of the Danish Biological Station*, 4:140–43.

Rosen, R. A. 1985. The Role of Fish Culture in Fishery Management: Politics, Policies, and Future Directions—A Summary of the Plenary Session. *Fisheries* 10(1):2–4.

Royce, W. F. 1984. A Professional Education for Fishery Scientists. *Fisheries* 9(3):12–17.

Thompson, P. E. 1970. The First Fifty Years—The Exciting Ones. Pp. 1–12 in N. G. Benson, ed., *A Century of Fisheries in North America*. Washington, D.C.: American Fisheries Society. Special Publication 7.

2. Fish and Water in Today's World

"As America has grown out of its colonial background, we have carried with us a national irreverence for our natural resources, born of our ancestral need to conquer the wilderness." Our forefathers considered the wilderness a challenge, something to subdue. Moreover, the resources—water, fish, game, forests, and soils—were considered inexhaustible, or nearly so. How then could one abuse them? Only in the last forty-five years have we recognized that there is a limit to our essential resources and that existence rests upon humanity's ability to equalize resource use on the one hand with stewardship of them on the other (Gottschalk 1971). Since the early 1970s, greater emphasis has been placed on good stewardship and wise management of our natural resources. Much remains to be accomplished.

We have occasional water crises today, but we may be in continuous water crisis by the turn of the century. Competitive situations will exist between communities and various recreational pursuits, including fishing (Gottschalk 1971). Both floods and droughts create problems in fishery management. Both require that water be moved from areas of surplus to areas of relative shortage. It is obvious that we must, in the near future, develop both a philosophy and a policy of long-range water priorities and management if we are to minimize conflict between potential water users while maximizing use. Additionally, we should evaluate the costs of abuse of aquatic resources.

Resources on the Public Domain

The public domain of the United States is an immense area of varied natural resources, including aquatic resources. Many species of wild animals exist within the confines of the public domain, the vast land holdings belonging to the people of the United States. A number of America's finest trout streams head in areas controlled by the U.S. Department of Interior Bureau of Land Management or the U.S. Department of Agriculture Forest Service. Many public marshes produce warmwater game fish as well as some of the world's finest waterfowl habitat. All of this points to the vast reservoir of resources harbored and protected on the public domain—all for the benefit of the people of the United States.

The history of the public domain partially explains the attitudes and behavior of the people who use the public lands today and sheds some light on the manner in which natural resources on these lands are presently managed. In 1763, England acquired all land in North America east of the Mississippi River by defeating France in the Seven Years' War. In 1783, with the signing of the Treaty of Paris, the original thirteen American colonies won British rights to those lands. Thus a vast new empire, including all of the future public domain lands of the United States, passed to a newly independent nation. An empire had been ceded, but ownership remained in doubt. When Maryland refused to ratify the Articles of Confederation until all such claims were ceded through Congress, creation of public domain, land owned by the national government, became a prerequisite to forming the nation. The articles were ratified and a new nation with public domain as its patrimony was created (Zimet 1966).

The subsequent history of the public domain coincides with that of U.S. expansion. Of the major domestic and foreign problems that have confronted this nation, many have been directly concerned with, or closely related to, matters of governing, acquiring, and disposing of public lands in the expanding west (Zimet 1966). While the western frontier was expanding, public lands in the East, then in the Midwest, were quickly passing from public to private ownership. Yet today, nearly one third of the nation, primarily in the western states, is still public lands (Public Land Law Review Commission 1970). Now, more than two hundred years after the creation of the original public domain, its management philosophies and practices are far from settled. Questions constantly arise as to the need or advisability of disposing of public lands, as exemplified by the sagebrush rebellion, and what the uses of them should be. Development versus preservation and the establishment of wilderness areas which have previously been utilized by interests other than recreationists are constantly in the news. The public lands, principally in the West, have consistently generated conflicts between users: Indians and settlers, cattlemen and sheepmen, stockmen and homesteaders, mineral interests/timber operators and conservationists, and finally, the most recent addition to the field, and the most powerful in point of numbers, the recreationist. These latter-day entrants first became interested in the public domain because it appeared to them to be a vast, unexploited, free recreation resource. They soon discovered that other people had preceded them and that their use, if not their very presence, was resented or at times forcibly objected to. The real problem was access. The land was there; it was public, but some of it, and in some places much of it, was accessible only by passing through private land. Lack of public access to some lands was the focal point of many conflicts (Munger 1968). In some areas, fishing and hunting access is still limited. Many states have purchased rights-of-way to streams and hunting areas through private land to open areas previously closed to the public.

States, in addition to purchasing rights-of-way, are asserting that a public right to access exists for navigable waterways within the state. Under state law (rather than federal law which is tied to commerce), streams have been defined as navigable if they are capable of floating a six-inch log. States, such as Idaho, have held that a natural stream, navigable under state law, running through private land is accessible across that private land as a result of a public easement. These easements include public right to use of the stream, up to the high water mark, for uses to which the stream is suited (e.g., boating, swimming, fishing, and portage rights around obstructions) (*Southern Idaho Fish and Game Association v. Picabo Livestock Inc.*, 96 Id.360.528 P 2d 1295 [1974]). As long as the public is able to gain access to the stream without trespassing across private land, a stream may be used for recreational purposes. This rule applies even though the streambed is owned by the riparian landowner. With regard to access for sports enthusiasts, the overriding criteria is whether the public can lawfully gain access to the water body (Steven Clyde, personal communication, 1986).

Western livestock men had sought and won the use of unappropriated public lands long before the government established a system for administering the acreage. This use was gained to some extent by the ownership of strategic tracts of land acquired by homesteading and by other methods, some of them quite devious. This hard-won usage of federal range lands was interpreted by stockmen as an implied proprietary interest in public domain land—an interest that they have vigorously defended over the years.

The sharp rise in the demand for outdoor recreation of all forms following World War II soon outstripped the supply of readily accessible land. Additionally, "the wilderness experience," which required solitude, became a part of the growing use of public land. Alarmed landowners began to restrict access to and across private lands, complaining about the irresponsible acts of sports and outdoor enthusiasts, who, on the other hand, countered that they were denied the use of public lands (Munger 1968). By the late 1950s this situation had attracted national attention. Articles on the subject began to appear in newspapers and sports magazines. Criticism was directed at the Bureau of Land Management and other public land management agencies. Studies released pointed out how many million acres of public land were blocked to free public access legally or otherwise. In short, the land crunch was on.

The overall problem was further complicated by the fact that unpatented mining claims were, and still are, not open to the public, although title to these lands rests with the federal government. These claims can, and often do, block access to other public lands. Additionally, the development of mining claims which have been dormant for decades has given rise to protests about development of mines in areas near or within proposed or existing wilderness areas. The legal authority of the federal government to acquire public rights-of-way through condemnation procedures is inherent in the federal government powers but is rarely used exclusively for acquiring rights-of-way.

Public responsibility and authority, however, are not created solely by laws, executive directives, or court decisions. Other social institutions, less formal but no less powerful, often are important determinants of public land management policies. This situation explains why the federal government is in the business of providing recreational services in the first place and why it is likely to continue in this line of activity. It also explains why the controversy over public access for recreational use of public land carries with it the threat of major political repercussions (Munger 1968). Nowhere was this better demonstrated than at Earth Day activities of the early 1970s. Political action had become a part of the out-of-doors movement.

Water—A Diminishing Resource

Top-quality water is becoming scarce in many parts of the United States. Use of water has become not only extremely competitive, but increasing demands are being put on a limited resource which must serve a growing population and industrial base. Fishery management is intimately related to water resource use. Streams that are dewatered regularly for irrigation, or are subject to large-scale flow fluctuations, or reservoirs which are subject to drawdowns cause special problems for fishery managers.

Water Law—A Brief Overview

To the uninitiated, the water laws of the various states, complicated by federal laws and interstate compacts, are complex to say the least. While water law can be subdivided into two basic categories (riparian and appropriated), the interrelationships, precedence, and complexity when all aspects are considered are many tiered. Below is a very brief outline of the major aspects of water law, each of which has different implications for the fishery manager.

An appropriated water right may be acquired only for a beneficial purpose (traditionally considered to be irrigation, domestic, storage, stock watering, and industrial), must be diverted from the watercourse, and must also be reasonable in light of other demands for water. Riparian rights exist by virtue of the location of lands adjacent to water courses and do not require any diversion or application of the water to a beneficial use (Public Land Law Review Commission 1970).

Vested rights exist when an appropriated right has been applied to beneficial use and from that point constitutes a protected property right. Riparian rights are vested without any positive human action.

Riparian Water Rights

The theory of riparian water law is grounded in the principle that all riparian proprietors have equal rights to use the water, providing others with equal rights are not deprived. Two theories are applied. The natural flow theory holds that each riparian proprietor has a right to have the body of water maintained in its natural state, not diminished in quantity or impaired in quality. The reasonable use theory holds that each proprietor is free from any unreasonable interference with his or her use of the water (Trelease 1967).

While interpreted differently by state and federal courts, riparian ownership, if not altered by federal mandates regarding navigability and interstate commerce, may be interpreted to mean not only the banks of the stream or lake, but the bed and channel as well. This interpretation may prevent public access to stream sections, where surrounding land is in private ownership. The water, however, generally remains the property of the state. As a result, legal interpretations have established the right of the public to use the water (fishing, boating, etc.) and included incidental use of the privately owned stream bank as necessary for public enjoyment of the water (Trelease 1967).

Appropriated Water Rights

The doctrine of appropriated rights (prior appropriation) developed in the United States when settlers (primarily miners) found the riparian systems of water rights incapable of dealing with problems found in the arid West. The concept of priority of rights was established to protect the vested rights of those first on the stream. In times of shortage, junior rights were curtailed (Clyde 1982). Appropriated rights were limited to use of the amount of water originally taken (generally based on the size of the ditch) and required use (beneficial use) to retain them. Thus a landowner (originally miners) could take water from a stream, divert it to an area out of the watercourse, and use it on property away from its point of diversion. Failure to use the water resulted in its loss. This system of appropriation was much more effective in the arid West than the system of riparian rights (Trelease 1967).

The federal government (prior to 1866), as proprietor of the western lands, in effect agreed to their occupation by not preventing occupation. The acquisition and use of water, and water rights, were left to local custom, and the water rights were protected by due process of law. Specific appropriation laws were not devised until much later and had little real impact on development or function of early western water law, serving mainly to improve administrative process and water distribution (Clyde 1982).

New water rights are approved if unappropriated water exists which can be used without infringement on existing rights. Permit systems now in use evolved over many years and served only to formally control the appropriation process. Applications under the permit systems of most western states are rejected if no unappropriated water is available or if the proposed use would interfere with an existing right. Applications can also be denied if they are deemed to interfere with a more beneficial use, are contrary to the public interest, or would unreasonably affect public recreation or the natural stream environment (Clyde 1982).

Social recognition of other than traditional beneficial values and uses is resulting in an increasing movement to protect values of water not covered by traditional water law. Uses such as fish propagation, recreation, and aesthetics, and values such as minimum stream flows are gaining judicial and legislative support (Clyde 1982).

Public Trust Doctrine

The Public Trust Doctrine, also known as the Mono Lake Decision, is based on a decision by the California Supreme Court that held the Public Trust Doctrine not only authorized but required the state to regulate water rights for the protection of the public trust values (*National Audubon Society v. Superior Court*, 33 Cal.3d 419 [1983]). These values commonly include navigation, commerce, and fisheries. This doctrine is gaining wide support and has been upheld in decisions of the supreme courts of Idaho and Montana. The expanded use of the Public Trust Doctrine, previously regarded only as a basis for state ownership of lands lying beneath navigable waters, can clearly work to the benefit of fisheries and other natural resource values (Steven Clyde, personal communication, 1986).

Federal Water Rights

The federal government has two roles with respect to water law. The first role relates to its sovereignty and the exercise of powers granted by the U.S. Constitution. The second role, generally more applicable in the western United States where it owns much of the land and water, is that of a proprietary owner. The federal Endangered Species Act and the Wild and Scenic Rivers Act, as well as state-sponsored instream flow legislation, are the areas in which states, citizens' groups, and other organizations have the greatest potential for protecting and developing fisheries and other aquatic resources.

Federal Proprietary (Reserved) Rights

The federal government controls much land as a proprietary owner and, as such, is free to dispose of that land, and its waters, like any other proprietor. While the federal government gave up its rights to control appropriation of western water in the Desert Land Act of 1877, it did not surrender either its sovereign powers, including regulation of commerce and control of navigation, or its proprietary rights as a landowner (Clyde 1984).

As a proprietor, the federal government may use any unappropriated water or land it controls for a federal purpose. This reserved right theory has been used to provide water for Indian reservations and has been extended to other federal installations as well. The priority of the reserved right is generally taken to be the date of the establishment of the federal reservation, not the date on which the water is first used (Clyde 1984).

Interstate Rights—Equitable Apportionment

Application of the theory of equal apportionment of water between states is based on the principle that while states may regulate and legislate water matters within their borders, they may not legislate water matters affecting other states. The legal aspect of equitable apportionment between states centers on the principle that one state may not use or threaten to use more than its equitable share of a stream (Trelease 1967). Equitable apportionment can render appropriated rights of one state invalid in an effort to ensure that another state on interstate waters receives its share. Equity, of course, may have more than one perspective. Strict priority rights may not be an applicable theory if economics or other considerations weigh heavily.

Equitable apportionment is accomplished in one of three ways. Interstate compacts, agreed to by the participants and Congress, are the most common vehicle. It can also be accomplished by judicial decree or congressional fiat. Apportionment serves primarily to quantify each state's right to develop (use) water which is part of an interstate system. Apportionment is subject to treaties and other sovereign federal powers. Allocations within a state which exceed that state's share of water under an apportionment are void when the terms of the compact are violated (Clyde 1982).

Interstate Commerce Clause

Interstate commerce, regulated by the federal government, is a use of waters in the United States that generally takes precedence over state use. Waters affected by interstate commerce have generally been considered to be limited to those waters defined as navigable. The concept of navigability is, however, linked by definition to a water's use for interstate commerce.

The interstate commerce clause is intended to allow and foster economical movement of trade goods and other commodities from one area to another. Hindrance of this movement, construed to be against the public good, may result in federal intervention on those waters deemed necessary for interstate commerce. While the historical and traditional handling of interstate commerce and water has been related to navigation on interstate waterways, U.S. Supreme Court and other judicial decisions shifted the focus in the early 1980s. Federal regulation of interstate commerce has, based on several court opinions, severely eroded states' rights to manage waters if they were attempting to restrict movement of this scarce resource (Steven Clyde, personal communication, 1986). The commerce clause of the U.S. Constitution, Article 1, Section 8, Clause 2, grants the U.S. Congress authority to regulate commerce among the states. Any state law or regulation that interferes with interstate commerce is voided. In assessing the validity of state regulations, the legitimacy of the local purpose of the regulation, the severity of the effect of this regulation on interstate commerce, and the purpose of the regulation are factors for consideration (Clyde 1982, 1984).

Wild and Scenic Rivers Act

The federal Wild and Scenic Rivers Act, as amended, was passed as Public Law 95–625 in November 1978. This act established as policy of the U.S. government that "certain selected rivers of the Nation, which with their immediate environments, possess outstandingly remarkable scenic, recreational, geologic, fish and wildlife, historic, cultural or other similar values, shall be preserved in free-flowing condition, and that they and their immediate environments shall be protected for the benefit and enjoyment of present and future generations."

The act instituted a federal system of national wild and scenic rivers and prescribed methods and standards by which additional components could be added to the system. Values to be associated with each designation (wild, scenic, or recreational) were included in the act. Individual states in which federally designated rivers existed or which chose to include additional areas have subsequently passed legislation establishing policies and management objectives.

Fundamentally, both the national and individual state laws prohibit alteration of the free-flowing status of the rivers by impoundment, diversion, or other means. The state and federal laws provide some measure of protection for fish and other aquatic organisms by retaining flows at least similar to natural flows.

Endangered Species Act

Federal endangered species legislation was passed in 1973, with amendments in 1978 and 1979. Many states also have regulations protecting species of importance in their state.

The federal act and amendments require that all federal agencies and federal monies spent through state or local governments consider and mitigate the impact of their actions on listed species. Projects or actions which could alter or destroy ecosystems or habitat are subject to interagency review and consultation to eliminate or reduce the effects of federal actions. Under federal or state endangered species regulation, it is at times possible to promote some aspects of recreational fishing in concert with protection of the species of concern. Chapter 6 discusses practical and philosophical considerations of protecting rare species of fishes.

Other Federal Mandates

Other legal or legislative avenues exist to enhance environmental and/or aesthetic values. The U.S. Army Corps of Engineers has sweeping responsibility in issuing permits for dredging and/or filling in wetlands and waterways (particularly navigable waters). These so-called Section 404 permits may be withheld until imposed conditions, designed to increase or maintain fisheries or minimum stream flow values, have been met (Clyde 1985). This process and other federal regulations can, at times, be used to achieve necessary instream or fishery and recreational values.

Instream Flow Legislation

Many states have in place or are investigating instream flow requirements and are attempting to reserve a minimum level in the streambed year around. Legislative mandates enforce instream flows at a time when selling water for premium prices is not universally popular. Nowhere is this conflict more apparent than in the arid western and southwestern states. Hopefully it will be resolved. It is obvious that in order for a fishery to exist, there must be a water resource with acceptable quality and quantity to support it. Fisheries managers at all levels must be aware of potential water development and the impact it will have on fishery resources in their areas. Additionally, economic and other types of data must be developed that will support the use of at least a portion of the water for fishery purposes.

State versus Federal Government in Resource Management

Management of resources remaining within the boundaries of a state (or nearly so) are managed by state agencies. Those species which roam across many states, such as waterfowl, are generally managed by federal authority. State fish and game departments, particularly those in the West, have shown increasing concern in recent years over what they consider the too active role of the federal government in the management of nonmigratory game, as well as nongame species. This concern extends to threatened and endangered species, which includes many species of fish not generally well known to the public. State management agencies have been especially concerned with a number of statements made by the Public Land Law Review Commission (PLLRC), which was established by Public Law 88–606 and still carries considerable weight more than fifteen years after publication. The PLLRC report, *One Third of the Nation's Land*, deals with direct and indirect management impacts on the nation's lands as related to the fish and wildlife resources.

The Public Land Law Review Commission (1970) has said, "State policies which unduly discriminate against non-resident hunters and anglers in the use of public lands through license fee differentials in various forms of non-fee regulations should be discouraged," but it does not define undue discrimination. The commission report also states, "a federal land-use fee should be charged for hunting and fishing on all public lands open for such purposes." This latter proposal has aroused the concern if not the ire of most western fish and game administrators who view this as a scheme for license fee splitting in which they are bound to lose. Many residents of midwestern and eastern states hold entirely different views. A partial refutation of the findings of the PLLRC has been published by the International Association of Game, Fish and Conservation Commissioners (1971).

The final chapter in the dispute between federal or state management may not be written for years or decades, but it is essential that an interim policy or philosophy be established allowing use of public domain lands without undue degradation or destruction. The depth of the requirement of this policy can be better understood when one realizes that it must address many issues. Some of these are: development of privately owned recreational facilities on public land, game animal harvesting (killing), tree harvesting, and reclamation. Also, should development of resources on public lands of special interest such as national parks be totally restricted or decided on a case-by-case basis? Many other complex questions can be asked.

Trends in Outdoor Recreation

Fishing and hunting account for a substantial share of the leisure and travel time of the nation's citizens as well as a significant portion of their disposable income. In the United States 33 percent of the men fished (11 percent of the women), and 20 percent of the men hunted (1 percent of the women) as of 1970 (USDI 1972). In 1980 women accounted for 31 percent of the fishing effort and 8 percent of the hunting effort (USDI and USDC 1982). This demand is directly related to population growth and to increasing income and leisure time.

In 1970, almost 55 million people in the United States, nine years old or older, spent 779 million recreational days either hunting, fishing, or both. This means that one third of the people in the United States either hunted or fished, despite the supposed adverse conditions. In 1970, 7 million bird watchers spent 432 million recreation days, and 5 million wildlife photographers spent 40 million recreation days in their respective endeavors. Increases in the five-year period from 1965 to 1970 in substantial sports enthusiasts (that segment accounting for at least 95 percent of the effort and expenditure) included over 3 million anglers and hunters, $3.1 billion in expenditures, 201 million recreation days, and 7.7 billion passenger miles. In 1980, 99.8 million Americans sixteen years of age and older participated in one or more wildlife-associated activities; 42.1 million fished, 17.4 million hunted, and 83.2 million engaged in nonconsumptive activities. Total participation for fishing was in excess of 857 million days. An additional 11.8 million youths (age 6 to 15) fished and 2 million hunted. Total expenditures were $41 billion, of which $17.3 billion was for fishing, $8.5 billion for hunting, and $14.8 billion for nonconsumptive activities (USDI and USDC 1982).

Anglers and hunters pay their way, for the most part, to maintain resources for their activities. Sports enthusiasts bear the cost of excise taxes on fishing tackle and sporting arms and ammunition (Wallop-Breaux Act for fishing and Pitman-Robertson Act for hunting). As well, they pay use and license fees to federal and state agencies and contribute directly to conservation programs that increase fish and game. During the severe winter of 1983–84, feeding programs were established in many western states for deer and elk herds that may otherwise have suffered record starvation. While contributions for feed came from many states and from hunters as well as nonhunters, much of the distribution effort was made by people with a direct interest in the resource. Many states have instituted programs whereby portions of state income tax returns can be devoted to nongame animals. These funds to some extent help finance research and restoration efforts on species (including fish) not otherwise provided funding.

Although some people are not overly concerned with what they catch as long as it is a legal game fish, many anglers are acutely aware of the status associated with capturing socially acceptable species. Unless an angler is fishing for food, he or she is not likely to brag about the numbers of suckers or carp caught on a fishing expedition. Rather, status is achieved in his or her own eyes and the eyes of other anglers when either a trophy-sized or a highly prized game fish is caught. Regionally, people who capture largemouth bass, muskellunge, northern pike, cutthroat trout and brown trout, as well as steelhead trout and chinook salmon have achieved some status. An additional concern of anglers fishing for food is taste and palatability. This extends also to the difficulty associated with preparing the fish and such considerations as intramuscular bones. Some anglers are not interested in catching fish that take too much time to clean and prepare.

The Fishery Resource

It is generally understood that the world's fish stocks are not inexhaustible, but they do sometimes offer a relatively unexploited source of food and protein supplement. This is especially true in Africa, South America, and in some developing nations of the world where there is adequate water but limited harvest effort. In the United States, game fish are sometimes underexploited due to inaccessibility or overly protective laws, while many food fish are ignored because they are not sporting or are socially unacceptable (e.g., the common carp and many suckers). This situation could become detrimental since the United States seems committed to creating more and more large impoundments with their inevitable and stable populations of predominantly nongame species.

Several aspects of reservoir fisheries are worthy of mention. A substantial data base exists which supports the hypothesis that many, if not most, reservoir sport fisheries are doomed to drastic decline three or four years after initial filling (Jenkins 1979; Leidy and Jenkins 1977; Hall 1971). Exploitation of the top carnivore (e.g., a game species) in a system may result in a dramatic increase in the number of prey species lower on the food chain. Exploiting these nongame species may be necessary to control numbers and/or biomass. Reservoirs are artificial environments. As such, the habitat is one in which species have not evolved, leading to successional changes and drastic increases in numbers of primary consumers. The dramatic increase in numbers of primary consumers may be followed by like increases in numbers of secondary consumers if habitat and other life history requirements are met. Reservoir ecosystems "planned" by fishery managers have met with only mixed success, particularly in the West.

Many nutritionally acceptable nongame fish should be appearing in the marketplace. The resource is unused and people are going hungry. These fish are often one step down from the top of the food pyramid and are therefore more productive than predacious game fish. The amazing reproductive potential of some fish is illustrated by the Atlantic Coast alewife in Lake Michigan. This fish has been estimated to have increased from a few specimens in 1949 to between 300 million and 1 billion pounds in 1966 (Cable 1971).

It is recognized that an acre of properly managed water in units such as freshwater ponds may produce more pounds of usable protein than a nearby acre of land. Utah, an arid state of 82,073 square miles, produced, in 1967,

3.8 million pounds of wild fish in addition to the hatchery-reared fish sold directly to the consumer (Sigler 1969). In 1983 total annual hatchery production was 8,663,000 fish weighing 788,000 pounds, which included a 15 percent reduction due to fiscal constraints (John Leppink, personal communication, 1985).

The United States has long been a fishing nation. The fish and shellfish which have been abundant along our shores were among the first natural resources used by early settlers. From coast to coast, as new areas were settled, resources available in lakes and streams sustained the pioneers when other resources were not available or when crops failed. Fishery products were an important article of commerce during the nineteenth and the first half of the twentieth centuries; trade in these commodities led to the development of the United States as one of the leading shipping and fishing nations of the world. However, this has changed drastically since 1960 (Power and Peck 1971).

Fish stocks may be adversely affected by such factors as overfishing, loss of year classes, pollution, and the effects of introduced species. For example, two saltwater species, the parasitic sea lamprey and the Atlantic Coast alewife entered the western Great Lakes through Lake Ontario and the Welland Canal and depleted Great Lakes fish stocks for many years (Cable 1971). In other areas, introduced species have resulted in the decimation of native fish, many of which are unable to compete or survive the parasites and diseases accompanying stocked species.

As the United States has shifted increasingly from an agricultural to an industrial economy, population pressures and industrial development have changed aquatic habitats. Over 75 percent of the people in the United States live in areas bordering the sea, the Great Lakes, and major rivers. While this picture is changing, large population centers are still located near substantial river courses or other large bodies of water.

Today, industrial and domestic wastes are of extreme concern. Since the days of the pilgrims, rivers, lakes, estuaries, and even coastal waters have been used for waste disposal. Fish habitat has been lost through construction of power, navigation, and flood-control structures, and by housing developments on major rivers and estuaries. In certain areas, such as along much of the Snake River in Idaho, dams prevent fish from reaching their ancestral spawning grounds. Along portions of the Columbia River, much of the historical spawning grounds of salmon and steelhead trout are inundated by water backed up by power-generation dams. In addition to blocking spawning runs and preventing easy migration of smolts, dams have sometimes created thermal pollution barriers and nitrogen gas poisoning (Power and Peck 1971). Many of these problems have only recently been addressed. Modifications to the spillways now reduce nitrogen gas saturation at many dams, and special ladders allow adults to pass upstream. Downstream migrants are sometimes collected and transported via barge or truck past dams. However, these alterations have not eliminated the negative impact of dams on the anadromous stocks in the Columbia River Basin.

The widespread use of herbicides, insecticides, and detergents continues to have an impact not only on aquatic life, but on human beings who use the aquatic resource as food or for recreation. Since the passage of the 1972 Amendments to the Water Quality Act, water quality has improved in many major drainages. There are still significant problems with many waters, but since 1975 water quality and game fish habitat have generally improved.

Control of pesticides, once considered especially harmful since they accumulate in some food fishes, has been improved. The detrimental effects of DDT have been much reduced. New threats, however, are rising from chemicals such as PCBs (polychlorobiphenyls), a major problem in some drainages.

Fish Culture—Its Benefits and Problems

The private sector of the fish culture industry (aquaculture) likes to refer to itself as the fastest growing segment of agriculture. Its strong preference for agricultural affiliation can be attributed almost entirely to the fact that it does not want to follow the disease control rules established by state and federal fish disease specialists. This stand is taken even though most privately grown fish are reared either in public waters or where the effluent reaches public waters. Body wastes, excess food, antibiotics, and even dangerous and contagious fish diseases may be the by-products of a fish production facility. It is, therefore, reasonable to expect public waters and the fishery resource to be protected from these problems. In the United States, state agencies establish water quality guidelines (including hatchery effluent standards) under criteria and guidelines established by the Environmental Protection Agency.

Many species of fish are used in fish culture in the United States today, but only four groups merit special attention. They are salmonids, baitfishes, catfishes, and species used for bioassay tests or as pets. Actually, only three species of fish, one from each of the first three groups, make up the bulk of the fish culture industry. They are the rainbow trout, the golden shiner, and the channel catfish. Fish used for bioassay tests or as pets comprise a considerably smaller group which reach the wild but still must be dealt with by fishery managers. In terms of gross dollar yield for the first three groups, the catfish industry is probably the largest, with baitfish next and trout third. It is interesting to note that the trout industry is the oldest and the catfish the youngest. Though large, the exact magnitude of the pet fish industry is unknown.

In recent years, the practice of salmon ranching or ocean farming has boomed. Fish are hatched and partially reared in commercial hatcheries, then released to the sea to return two or three years later. The ocean growth is at no cost to the hatchery; however, the mortality factor is. This practice has been developed in Alaska and potentials for Washington and Oregon are currently being developed. The future of this industry is viewed with mixed feelings by many fishery managers and some salmon ranchers.

Fish culture is intimately tied to certain wild (put-and-take) fishery management requirements for two reasons: (1) the waste residues from commercial and agency-operated fish-rearing operations often reach public waters, and (2) fish from the first three groups of reared fish are stocked in large numbers in public waters at one time or another. Pet fish, either intentionally or accidentally, have been introduced into restricted habitats of native fish species with disastrous results. From the walking catfish in Florida to guppies in Nevada, many examples exist of introduced species decimating populations of native species, often to the point of extinction. Additional native populations have been destroyed by the transplanting of game fish by well-meaning individuals or groups, who, without benefit of understanding the ecology of small aquatic habitats, have released predacious fish into areas where no competitors have existed for thousands of years. The fishery manager must, therefore, be aware not only of direct problems created by fishery production operations, but of effects of intentional or accidental introductions of nonnative species.

Summary

Fishery management is a complex business. Increased public fishing includes not only more opportunity but a more varied opportunity. Water uses require both treatment to retain acceptable quality and establishment (or retainment) of a fishery as a valid use of instream flows. As leisure time increases, fishery managers and researchers must continue to develop new and more efficient (cost-effective) ways to provide quality fishing experiences for an increasingly demanding public (USDI and USDC 1982). These trends continue to grow (USDI 1988).

Literature Cited

Cable, L. E. 1971. Inland Fisheries. Pp. 324–58 in Sidney Shapiro, ed., *Our Changing Fisheries*. Washington, D.C.: U.S. Department of Commerce, National Oceanic and Atmospheric Administration, National Marine Fish Service.

Clyde, S. E. 1982. State Prohibitions on the Interstate Exportation of Scarce Water Resources. *University of Colorado Law Review* 53(3):529–58.

———. 1984. Legal and Institutional Barriers to Market Transfers and Reallocation of Water Resources. *South Dakota Law Review* 9(Spring):232–57.

———. 1985. Trading 404 Permits for Enhanced Fish Habitat. *Natural Resources and Environment* 1(1):37–41.

Gottschalk, J. S. 1971. Good, Bad or Indifferent? Pp. 439–51 in Dan Saults, ed., *Sport Fishing U.S.A.*. Washington, D.C.: U.S. Department of the Interior, Bureau of Sport Fishing and Wildlife.

Hall, G. E., ed. 1971. *Reservoir Fisheries and Limnologies*. Washington, D.C.: American Fisheries Society. 511 pp. Special Publication 8.

International Association of Game, Fish and Conservation Commissioners. 1971. *Public Land Policy Impact on Fish and Wildlife*. Washington, D.C.: International Association of Game, Fish and Conservation Commission. 80 pp.

Jenkins, R. M. 1979. Predator-Prey Relations in Reservoirs. Pp. 123–34 in H. Clepper, ed., *Predator-Prey Systems in Fisheries Management*. Washington, D.C.: Sport Fishing Institute.

Leidy, G. R., and R. M. Jenkins. 1977. *The Development of Fishery Compartments and Population Rate Coefficients for Use in Reservoir Ecosystem Modeling*. U.S. Department of the Interior, U.S. Fish and Wildlife Service, National Reservoir Research Program, Fayetteville, Arkansas, for Office, Chief of Engineers, U.S. Army. Vicksburg, Miss.: U.S. Army Engineer Waterways Experiment Station. 225 pp.

Munger, J. A. 1968. *Public Access to Public Domain Land—Two Case Studies on Landowner-Sportsman Conflict*. U.S. Department of Agriculture, Economic Research Service, Miscellaneous Publication 1122. 64 pp.

Power, E. A., and W. L. Peck. 1971. The National Picture. Pp. 2–18 in Sidney Shapiro, ed., *Our Changing Fisheries*. Washington, D.C.: U.S. Government Printing Office.

Public Land Law Review Commission. 1970. *One Third of the Nation's Land*. Washington, D.C.: U.S. Government Printing Office. 207 pp.

Sigler, W. F. 1969. *Utah's Wildlife Resource*. Utah Science Agriculture Experiment Station 30(4):105–8.

Trelease, F. J. 1967. *Cases and Materials on Water Law*. St. Paul: West Publishing Company. 364 pp.

United States Department of the Interior, Bureau of Sport Fisheries and Wildlife. 1972. *1970 National Survey of Fishing and Hunting*. Washington, D.C.: U.S. Government Printing Office. 108 pp.

United States Department of the Interior, Fish and Wildlife Service, and United States Department of Commerce, Bureau of the Census. 1982. *1980 National Survey of Fishing, Hunting and Wildlife Associated Recreation.* Washington, D.C.: U.S. Government Printing Office. 156 pp.

United States Department of the Interior, Fish and Wildlife Service. 1988. *1985 National Survey of Fishing, Hunting, and Wildlife Associated Recreation.* Washington, D.C.: U.S. Government Printing Office. 167 pp.

Zimet, S. 1966. *The Public Domain.* Washington, D.C.: U.S. Department of the Interior, Bureau of Land Management. 15 pp.

3. Fisheries Management

Part One—Approaches

This nation was colonized and developed around its water resources, which in turn were modified, altered, polluted, dammed, diverted, and otherwise changed in many unforeseen ways. The face of this nation's waters has the imprint of industry, municipalities, agriculture, energy development, and recreation (including fishing) indelibly stamped on it. All of these aspects of change influence the capabilities of these waters to provide viable recreational fisheries. Water resource status and use change yearly, as streams and lakes are continually being appropriated. Some are degraded or changed by such forces as acid rain, hydroelectric dams, and municipal and agricultural uses, while others are restored as productive fisheries. The construction of more dams is now widely accepted by a large segment of the general public as inevitable even when they are not always ecologically or economically satisfactory.

In the twenty years or so following World War II, the cornerstone philosophy of recreational fisheries management was maximum sustained yield (Larkin 1977). From the 1920s to the 1970s refinements were made on the methodologies and concepts surrounding the theory of maximum sustainable yield. Handbooks such as Ricker (1975) and Gulland (1969) became standard texts, and nonbiological precepts began to influence fisheries management (Larkin 1980).

Anderson (1975) argues convincingly that management of recreational fisheries is more involved than attempting to obtain a maximum (or perhaps even optimum) sustained yield. Fisheries management now and for the remainder of this century must explore multiple options for fisheries management and include considerations other than harvest in determining yield and value for recreational fisheries. Sustaining and improving the quality of fishing, as perceived by anglers, is a major management responsibility.

Management of recreational fisheries is a complex issue, having biological, social, political, and economic aspects. This chapter presents approaches to dealing with the multitude of issues and problems confronting managers and is divided into two parts. The first part presents ideas, philosophies, and methods for collecting and assembling data needed for effective management. Goals are defined and methods of setting goals are presented, data needs for a fishery management plan are discussed, as are habitat and habitat enhancement, classification, and habitat suitability indices. These aspects are then related to the development and completion of a program to establish or improve a fishery. While some of the materials in the first part could be discussed in other chapters, the information is presented together for continuity.

The second part discusses concepts for managing fisheries under the Zone Management Concept, and under the topic of Urban Fishing, a management scheme whose time has come.

Recreational Fishery Management and Its Goals

Simply stated, recreational fishery management is the utilization of fish stocks and their habitats to provide opportunity for any and all anglers to catch a reasonably acceptable size and number of a satisfactory and/or popular species. Management involves manipulation of dynamics (rates of reproduction, recruitment, growth, and mortality), habitat, and availability in order to achieve benefits—food, gross national product, memories, and quality of life.

The main goal of fishery management is to satisfy and sustain the expectations of success for a broad spectrum of anglers. The magnitude of the goal becomes apparent when the fishing public is described. It includes all ages, almost all degrees of personal health, and a wide array of individual and regional beliefs of what is desirable. A five year old may be happy with 4- to 6-inch sunfish as long as they come often and someone else handles the tedious end of things. A purist angler fly fishing for cutthroat trout may be distressed if there is anyone in sight using bait or hardware or, in some cases, just anyone in sight. He or she may also be quite happy to catch only one or two fish of good size which will be released. From another perspective, anglers may be considered to fall into categories of casual, active, or expert, each with varied expectations.

Fish caught (and perhaps released) must be socially acceptable, an aspect that varies both geographically and by individual. Carp, for example, may be either unacceptable or highly prized for both food and sport, depending on the locale and the individual. In some areas salmonids are the only acceptable fish of the elite, or sometimes even the majority of anglers. Some people fish only for food, some only for sport, but the majority of anglers seek both. The old saying that people go fishing to catch fish is still true; the level of intensity from casual to dedicated expert may vary. Spaulding (1970) lists seven attributes anglers would miss if they had to stop fishing: (1) experiencing the euphoria-tension feeling, (2) catching fish, (3) involvement with some aspect of the environment, (4) interpersonal relationships, (5) aesthetic attributes of the environment, (6) experiencing transition in situations, and (7) personal integrative responses. Recreationists who fish in Utah's Uinta Mountains consider fishing only one part and not necessarily the most important part of their wilderness experience. These anglers indicate their motivation is to get away into a natural setting. Only a few come primarily to catch trout (Kennedy and Brown 1976). Driver and Knopf (1976) believe that while anglers would not fish in waters known to have no fish, satisfaction derived goes considerably beyond the taking of fish. They suggest a rather long list of reasons why people fish including being out of doors, developing skills, pitting wits with the fish, being with friends, sharing skills with other people, change and relaxation, exploration, a learning experience, exercise, food, trophy value, testing and use of new equipment, and escape from everyday pressures. Many anglers look at water quality, natural beauty, and privacy first, with the size of fish caught, weather conditions, and access being of lesser importance. However, number and/or size of fish caught are generally associated with most memorable angling experiences. Many anglers rated support facilities of little importance (Moeller and Engelken 1972). In a somewhat unusual experiment in 1973, the Utah Division of Wildlife Resources stocked about 49,000 albino rainbow trout in three Utah rivers. A survey indicated that 12 percent of the anglers preferred no albinos in their limits of eight, 66 percent preferred one to four, and 22 percent preferred five or more (Kennedy and Wood 1977). Management philosophies associated with the notion that people fish for food have prevailed since the end of World War II. When modern fisheries management developed, a new philosophy was espoused by both managers and anglers alike: catch-and-release. A catch-and-release (or nonconsumptive fisheries) philosophy is based on the belief that capture is the desired end; subsequent release does not detract from the excitement of capture. This mind-set will be of increasing importance in future management to anglers and managers alike, particularly on heavily used bass and trout fisheries. The level of hooking mortality should be considered in all cases. Clark (1983) presents data on the potential effect of catch-and-release programs on recreational fisheries.

Trophy anglers are often willing to fish for a week or more for one fish, but it must be large and the right species. Quite a number of these sophisticated anglers seek only large sport fish, and they travel far and wide to satisfy their desires. Examples include largemouth bass, muskellunge, striped bass, flathead catfish, sturgeon, steelhead trout, brown trout, lake trout, and salmon.

Bond and Whittaker (1971) state many recreational skills are established before the age of six and fully 90 percent before the age of fourteen. The average age of anglers sampled was forty, and the average number of years fished was twenty-six. Ninety-three percent participated in these activities in their youth. Anglers began fishing alone at age thirteen. Seventy percent were introduced to fishing by a parent or other relative, and 68 percent said they had spent most of their childhood in a rural environment.

How Fishery Management Goals Are Set

Goals set in broad, general terms, such as providing optimum sustainable yield, are not always meaningful. Objectives should be set to meet goals. The logical way and perhaps the simplest for a manager or a management agency to make objectives meaningful is to isolate them into manageable segments using habitat types (e.g., ponds, trout streams, etc.). For example, a three-acre pond may produce catchable sunfish and medium-size largemouth bass. Some high, cold streams may produce trout or grayling. Large cool streams may produce northern pike, smallmouth bass, or trout, and slow, warmwater streams may yield catfishes and largemouth bass. Larger lakes or impoundments may produce trout, walleye, largemouth bass, and striped or white bass. These varied habitats will not be managed identically, nor will the objectives at each area be the same. Established objectives should take into consideration the capacity of the habitat, the fish populations, the desires of anglers, the nearness to centers of population, and the limitations imposed by time or funding.

Objectives set to provide a fishery for one segment of the public, or to protect an existing stock of fish, must consider the myriad aspects of maintaining a particular species in a habitat subject to one or more pressures. Modification of objectives is often required over a period of years. To deal with the political, social, economic, and species requirements necessary to successful fishery management requires considerable data integration and interpretation. The fishery manager must be cognizant of and assess all the factors that can have a negative impact on the resource and what the effect of each factor will be, separately and in concert with other factors. Based on their assessment, managers must then define problems, propose solutions, and set objectives.

Good fish habitat has the water quality and physical attributes that meet the need to sustain a balanced fish population. Balanced populations have numbers and sizes of fish to meet management objectives. For example, an ideal high mountain trout stream in central Idaho must have cold water, pools for hiding, and riffles for spawning and feeding; much of it must be fast flowing and relatively clear of barriers. Muskellunge in Minnesota need a large lake with an abundance of prey species and weedy deltas or small, weedy, stump-ridden backwater areas or slow-flowing streams in which to spawn. Urban ponds in New York City or Los Angeles may be warm with a low water exchange rate and support catfish or sunfish quite well. Unfortunately, what fish need and what is available are often at variance. Waters that do not meet minimum criteria for selected species can often be modified (within the resources available to the management agency) to provide a useful fishery of an alternate type. Management objectives must recognize the status and potential of existing habitat.

Fundamental Approaches

Application of a fisheries management technique to a specific portion of a fishery minimally requires a knowledge of the species involved, the nonbiological (sociopolitical) realities, and the capabilities of the habitat to support the decision (carrying capacity, productivity, lotic or lentic). Approaches or solutions to a particular problem can be addressed in the following questions.

Question one: What is the present status of the fishery, i.e., what do we have now? This question incorporates biological, habitat, and sociopolitical (e.g., angler preference) information pertinent to the population or stock.

Question two: What benefits can be provided within existing biological, habitat, and sociopolitical constraints? This question requires information on the structure of populations, existing habitat, water quality, and angler acceptability. Angler acceptability is related to kinds, densities, and sizes of fish.

Question three: What can be done and how do we accomplish it? This question addresses solutions to the problems identified. Potential management techniques fall into seven broad categories: fish stocking, law enforcement, regulations, habitat improvement, predator/competitor removal/reduction, refuges, and opportunity.

Determining Existing Status

No useful goal can be achieved without data to define both desired and existing conditions. Determining the status of existing stocks is an essential first step in preparing a fishery management plan. The mechanism chosen to assess the existing status of a fishery is as important as the collection of the information itself. Anderson (1980) points out in reference to fishery management plans that no planning is necessary if objectives are poorly defined, and that planning is difficult at best if models are weak or information is inadequate. Identification of the real problems is the most significant aspect of planning a research or management investigation. The best method of stock assessment, the best index of productivity, the most accurate cost-benefit assessment approach are all keys to the most effective management of a fishery.

The Fishery Management Plan

Management plans are written in a wide variety of disciplines. There are financial management plans, personnel management plans, and wildlife and fisheries management plans. All have a common goal of presenting and formalizing information necessary to manage resources adequately.

A fishery management plan incorporating information from all appropriate disciplines can be lengthy or short, specific or broad in nature. It should not, however, be so broadly written that it is meaningless in a particular instance, or so specific that it is inflexible and artificial. A fishery management plan should do what the name implies: provide information on all aspects of a particular fishery and aid in achieving the stated objectives to fit management goals. More to the point, a plan lists specifics of fishery management policy (state, regional, or provincial) and formalizes in writing the policies and goals pertinent to that particular fishery. It also establishes the basis for that fishery's relationship with other benefits provided by the system (e.g., water use, boating, livestock, timber) and with other fisheries.

In order to write a management plan, it is first necessary to define and/ or describe the management units to be included. Management units may be defined by fish species, by a designation as either wild (spawned and reared in the wild) or hatchery stocks, and by geographic units such as lakes, streams, or drainages. The most useful definitions of management units are those that can be applied across the state (or other unit area) and have few exceptions or variations.

A group of fish can be treated as a management unit (stock) if possible differences within the group and interchanges with other groups can be ignored without making the conclusions reached depart from reality to an unacceptable (significant) extent (Gulland 1983).

A fisheries management plan is not limited to use by its author. A plan, and the information known about a fishery, is written to be used and should formalize the decision-making process regarding a particular system. A management plan, while including species information, should be written on systems. It should be written in such a prognostic fashion that it can be reliably used for several years and by new personnel. A plan should be updated or modified when new data become available.

Stock Assessment and Status

Management of a particular fish stock requires biological information regarding when the species is vulnerable to fishing and when or if it should be protected from fishing during periods of concern, such as during spawning. The level of information required in a stock assessment varies considerably. Secondary considerations would include nonbiological aspects of stock assessment (social and political) which are reflected in such esoteric factors as species and size preference, type of fishing preferred (e.g., bait, fly, catch-and-release), duration and expense involved in reaching a fishing area, and time of year for a particular geographic area when most fishing occurs.

Once a management class has been defined and described (e.g., wild trout streams), management units, such as a river reach, must be selected. It is essential to determine the biological status of the stock or stocks which comprise the unit. This requirement includes a biological and physical description of the unit and a discussion of its potential. For sport fisheries, this description must be related to both harvest and yield potential and optimum levels of effort.

Stock status or assessment can be considered in light of at least ten characteristics: (1) abundance (numbers or weight), (2) recruitment, (3) food habits, (4) movement, (5) age composition and growth rate, (6) structure or mortality rate (including diseases, parasites, and stress), (7) yield, (8) size (length frequency, condition), (9) reproduction, and (10) relative catch/effort.

Abundance

Either direct counts, estimates, or indices may be used to determine abundance. Direct counts, such as at dams (Everhart and Youngs 1981), weirs (Gulland 1983), traps, or in limited access fisheries, theoretically count all of the fish at a particular point and time (e.g., above a dam), but in reality are only estimates based on direct count information. Direct counts are most useful where stocks must migrate past a particular point or control structure to enter the fishery.

Other population estimators include single- and multiple-census techniques. Estimates based on the Peterson or Lincoln single-census mark recapture techniques (Everhart and Youngs 1981) depend on the validity of at least four assumptions: (1) marked fish retain marks and can be distinguished when recaptured, (2) there is no change in vulnerability between marked and unmarked fish, both are identically available to the gear, (3) there is no change in mortality between marked and unmarked fish (e.g., marks cause no mortality), and (4) chances of capture for both marked and unmarked fish are random and equal (i.e., marked fish are randomly distributed among the population). The general form of the equation for single-census population estimates is $N = MC/R$, where N is the estimated number, M is the number of individuals marked, C is the number of individuals captured on subsequent efforts (both marked and unmarked), and R is the number of marked fish recaptured.

Marking and recapture are done concurrently in multiple-census methods such as the Schnabel method (Everhart and Youngs 1981) when either mark or recapture numbers are predicted to be low. These models assume: (1) no recruitment occurs, (2) no mortality occurs, (3) the marked and unmarked fish are equally likely to be caught, (4) marked fish are recognized (i.e., marks not lost), and (5) the marked fish are randomly distributed among the population.

Other population estimation techniques include the Jolly method (Jolly 1963, 1965), which classifies recaptures according to last marking, and the removal method (Southwood 1966; Zippen 1958), which requires: (1) fishing must not change probability of fish being caught, (2) there is no recruitment, mortality, or migration, (3) fish catches are independent of one another, and (4) catch is random (i.e., chance of being caught is equal for all fish).

Other estimators include the two-catch or Seber method (Seber and LeCren 1967). A review of all techniques is not essential to understanding or utilizing abundance estimators. Investigators must determine what procedure or technique fits their data requirements, physical location, gear availability, and fiscal constraints.

Indices are used when direct and indirect counts are impractical or infeasible. Redd counts and echo sounding evaluations (Gulland 1983), as well as tow net catches, are estimating techniques which have been used successfully.

One of the most successful methods of obtaining information on relative abundance is catch or catch-effort data evaluation. Either the Leslie or DeLury method is used if effort is variable and the Moran or Zippen method if effort is known to be constant (Everhart and Youngs 1981).

Recruitment

Recruitment is defined as that process (with an inherent point in time implied) whereby young fish previously inaccessible to the fishery become, as a result of growth to a catchable size, change of behavior, or movement into an area of fishing pressure, vulnerable to the gear being fished (Gulland 1983). Factors that regulate the number of recruits to a fishery include: (1) stock abundance and fecundity, (2) environmental and other factors influencing spawning and hatching, (3) survival as influenced by predators, habitat, and water quality, and (4) growth as influenced by availability and abundance of food and other factors.

Gulland (1983) notes that the stock-recruitment process seems to lie at the heart of the control of fish populations and to be the main mechanism in determining how populations maintain themselves at the observed levels. Stock-recruitment curves, presenting the number of spawners (horizontal axis) versus the number of recruits (vertical axis), are available for a variety of fish stocks and innumerable hypothetical situations. Two general curves exist (figure 3.1).

The dome-shaped curve is appropriate when cannibalism by adults on young provides a significant regulatory mechanism, or when the result of greater density is an increase in the time needed for young to grow past a vulnerable size range, or when high adult density reduces fecundity or spawning success.

Reproduction curves can theoretically be based on census data taken at any time, but for recruitment curves the data are based on spawners versus recruits (Ricker 1975). Reproduction curves can be defined as data dealing with young-of-the-year or fingerlings (or some other life stage), while recruitment curves incorporate data regarding when a fish enters the fishery (stock size). The stock size may include two or more year classes depending on the population. Recruitment is best considered as a rate (e.g., number/year). One spawning group may provide recruits for two or more years. Both recruitment and reproduction can be estimated with difficulty as rates (number/acre/year or number/stream mile/year). Curve fitting is discussed in detail by Ricker and Gulland (1983).

Ricker (1975) lists some general characteristics of recruits (R) plotted against parental stock (P): (1) the curve should pass through the origin so that no parental stock equals no reproduction; (2) there should be no point at

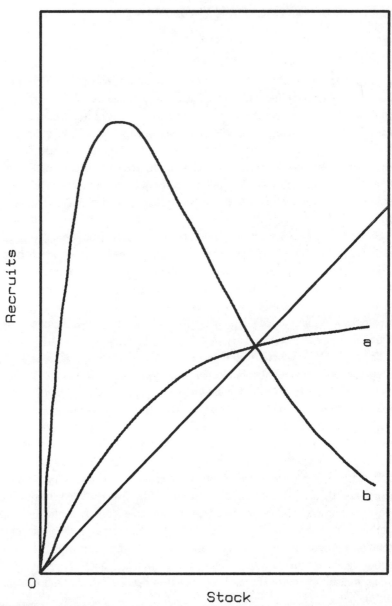

Figure 3.1. Stock recruitment curve (45-degree line represents replacement, a and b represent different stocks).

which reproduction is completely eliminated by high stock densities; (3) the recruitment rate (ratio of R/P) should decrease with increasing parental stock (e.g., fewer recruits per parent with greater stock numbers); and (4) recruitment must exceed parental stock over some part of the range of numbers of P for the stock to persist.

Food Habits

Food and feeding habits are studied primarily to determine the impact of a group of animals on their environment (Hiatt 1947) and if food is a limiting factor. In the context of stock assessment, food and feeding habits are studied to determine the relationship between a fish and prey organisms. The presence and availability of food, both quantitative and qualitative, has management implications and needs consideration. If data indicate food is limiting, it may be possible to introduce species of prey. If habitat is limiting, habitat enhancement may be in order. Methods and procedures for studying and documenting food and feeding habits as well as theoretical considerations are presented in chapter 12. Feeding is discussed in chapter 14.

Movement

Individual fish may move only short distances in their lifetime, such as inland stocks of trout or sunfishes, or may migrate hundreds, or in some cases, thousands of miles. Movement may be related to daily or annual feeding migrations (e.g., some trout populations), to movement from summer to winter areas, or to reproductive migrations involving movement from one habitat to another within a stream or from fresh to salt water and back. Fish may also move in response to environmental changes such as pollution, altered habitat, or in response to changes in predator-prey relationships. Fish may move following growth, migrating from juvenile rearing areas to establish adult territories. Knowledge of when and why a species moves, as well as the extent of that movement, allows managers to incorporate changes in location into management plans.

Age and Growth

Age and growth data are not always considered as part of a stock assessment. Both age (mortality) and growth can be addressed as rates and can be discussed separately. Age and growth studies are a significant portion of a fisheries study and are presented in chapter 11.

Mortality Factors: Diseases, Parasites, and Stress

In its simplest form, a mortality estimate is based upon knowing the number of fish alive at the beginning and end of a designated time period, usually one year. Total mortality is a function of numerous factors, each of which can vary temporally or with size classes.

Gulland (1983) provides a simple mathematical formula for factors comprising total mortality: $N_1 = P + D + O + C + N_2$, where N_1 and N_2 are the numbers of fish alive at the first and second points in time respectively. Losses to predation are represented by P, while D and O represent numbers lost to disease and other causes. Losses to the population by harvest (catch) are represented by C. Gulland notes that these values, when expressed mathematically (e.g., annual predation rate $= P/N$), are easily understood but not of great use in population dynamics studies.

Instantaneous rates, applied over a short period of time, are unaffected by deaths from other causes (a complicating factor), and can be combined so that they are proportional to the total nonfishing mortality (natural mortality M) and total instantaneous fishing mortality F.

Mortality can be estimated from catch curves. In a single sample taken at a given moment, each age-group will have been exposed to one more year's mortality than the preceding one and their ratio will approximately equal annual survival, the reciprocal of annual mortality. Gulland (1983) and Ricker (1975) provide detailed mathematical formulas for these determinations. Theoretical problems associated with the use of catch curves to estimate mortality include changes in recruitment and catchability, both of which can result in misinterpreted mortality data.

Population size composition is related to total mortality in that the lower the mortality, the more older, larger fish there are present. This general relationship can be used to approximate mortality rates if age-composition data are unavailable (Gulland 1983).

Cohort analysis, catches of the same year-class in successive years, may be used to estimate mortality rates. This technique is valuable in fisheries with a large number of age-groups but requires a long series of age composition data.

Diseases, parasites, and stress from such causes as handling or pollutants can adversely affect fish stocks. Knowledge of the types of diseases or parasites present and the vectors of infection, effect of infection, and potential for spreading to other species is useful in making management decisions regarding a stock. While many pathological events are similar in fish hatchery and wild fish populations, diseases are often ignored in the wild and treated with variable effectiveness in hatcheries. Diseased hatchery populations can really only be disposed of in one of two fashions: either plant (stock) the fish in a "suitable" drainage or bury them and sterilize the hatchery. All of the problems of hatchery disease are relative, however, to the extent and nature of the disease in the affected population.

Simply stated, disease is literally a lack of ease (Warren 1983). It is a morbid condition deviating from the normal. Diseased fish and pathogens in an ecosystem create special problems for fish and their managers, and most likely indicate a source of stress, such as pollution or water quality problems. Both should be identified and categorized as to prevalence, distribution, and the hazards they impose on the fish. Often these conditions are infectious in nature and capable of inducing long-term losses ranging from minor annoyance to catastrophic devastation which may eliminate an entire population. On the other hand, the stock may not show losses but may have carriers with latent infections (Goede 1986). These carrier fish are the Typhoid Marys of the fish world. Managers should be aware of and consider these potential problems before stocking fish in a drainage. When fish are stocked without considering the ultimate risk of disease or pathogens in the environment, the results may range from slight or unknown loss to almost complete loss of fish to the creel.

Disease Problems. Bullock and Wolf (1988) document the detection, diagnosis, and control of historically significant fish diseases (pre-1950) and highlight newly recognized diseases (post-1950), their problems, and control. According to Goede (1986), one of the reasons that disease control programs fail is that traditional fishery managers tend to place fish diseases in a black box and consider them only vaguely as causing mortality. The reasons for this are many, but they generally fall into one or more of four categories: (1) hard-nosed, dollar-conscious administrators may find it too difficult to order large numbers of fish destroyed when they presumably could be planted and hopefully caught by enthusiastic (satisfied) anglers; (2) administrators may not believe that a long-term hazard to the environment and to the fish truly exists; (3) both administrators and managers may consider disease control programs as a nuisance to be shrugged off; or (4) there may be no fish health specialists available to recognize diseases and plead the case for the long-term effects and costs (Goede). Today, even though the need for this specialist is great in hatchery and stocking programs, the position may be given a low budgetary priority or assigned to a biologist with less than adequate training in diseases. The result may be a hidden but very high cost. The days when a country doctor approach to fish health problems was adequate are long gone. Today it is a highly sophisticated field.

Fish culturists often feel their responsibilities end when the fish are planted, believing that after stocking the fish become the manager's problem. Often the manager may not even be aware of the problem, or know what to do about it. In general, the impact of diseases and their inherent stresses in biological populations is poorly understood by dominant core professionals and are therefore given inadequate consideration.

In the early days of fish rearing, inadequate amounts of food were a limiting factor. With the advent of manufactured food (in the mid to late 1950s), disease control (assuming adequate water quality and quantity) became the number one problem in hatcheries. As the efficiency of transporting fish and fish products nationally and internationally increased, so did the spread of disease. Disease control was no longer a local concern. Many virulent pathogens were introduced into environments where native fish had no natural immunities. This problem has, for example, created serious problems for many of the small nongame threatened or endangered fishes of the western Great Basin, especially, the killifishes (Hardy 1987; Hardy 1982). World demand for high-protein food and increased sport fishing has stimulated intensive hatchery production, and inherent in this are the problems of crowding, decreased water quality, and increased handling, all of which are conducive to disease (Souter 1983).

Causes of Stress. Most people know they are more susceptible to colds or flu after they have been stressed by fatigue, cold weather, or some other cause. The pathogen that causes the disease is often there, but it is unable to strike effectively until the body is in a weakened condition. The same is true of fish. Fish under such stress conditions as crowding or low oxygen are most susceptible to virulent pathogens. Stressors in the wild include environmental degradation such as organic and inorganic pollution, rapid water temperature changes, low oxygen levels, drastic reduction of habitat, or reduction of the habitable zone by decrease of oxygen or increase/decrease of temperature. In some reservoirs, fish remain healthy until the upper layer of water becomes too warm and the bottom layer in the reservoir is depleted of oxygen, which sometimes leaves the fish with no more than a band of 6 to 8 feet of habitable water. It is at this time that parasites are able to easily find a host (Wolf 1988).

Wild stocks are generally free of epizootic diseases. Serious outbreaks are associated with intensive culture in the hatchery (Griffiths 1983). Diseased fish in the hatchery have already been subjected to stress and they satisfy the necessary components of a disease epizootic. They are further stressed in the process of handling and stocking (Goede 1986). Goede cites the work of various investigators, noting that recovery from these stressors may take as long as two weeks. The disease organisms themselves are also stressors which further add to the problem. An early sign of disease may be mortality from an unidentified source. There are three factors that result in disease: a susceptible host, a virulent pathogen, and an environment that brings these two together. A virulent pathogen may be defined as a microbe capable of causing disease. However, lack of certain items, such as necessary vitamins, can also cause disease. Chemical agents such as aflatoxins can cause disease or they may be passed on to the egg, resulting in the death of sac fry (Warren 1983). Multicellular organisms or biological agents can be the causative agent of infectious diseases.

Stress may be induced by a number of factors varying with time, place, and species. For example, Snieszko (1957) found that common carp were more stressed by handling in the spring on a rising temperature than when handled later in the year.

In the early days of fish hatcheries when the manager was confronted with a disease problem, he or she usually had two options: the use of antibiotic prophylaxis or destruction of all stock—neither a pleasant choice. Recently the use of vaccines has emerged (Souter 1983). Prevention, however, is still the cornerstone of any fish health program (Warren 1983).

Fish diseases are generally not caused by a single event, but are the result of interactions of etiological agents, along with the fish and the environment (Wedemeyer, Meyer, and Smith 1976). Many disease organisms exist in populations of fish without causing losses but provide a ready source of infection and disease (Goede 1986). This potential can be a serious problem if it is not recognized. It also means that any stress situation may turn a healthy population into a diseased one. The real problem in this case, according to Goede, is greatest in systems with significant fish reproduction and the possibility of vertical transmission (from parent to progeny) of intracellular pathogens, such as the viruses. In this case a system may be contaminated for a very long time. Another factor to consider is that a diseased fish may not die, but may have a very reduced performance. For example, they may grow much slower than healthy fish. They also may move slower and therefore be more vulnerable to predation.

Yield

Strictly defined, yield is the total amount of fish tissue harvested by a fishery (Liss and Warren 1980). Absolute yield may be measured in terms of weight per unit of time per unit area (e.g., 500 pounds/acre/year). Relative yield per recruit to the fishery is also a useful concept, and although primarily of value in commercial fisheries, it can be applied to sport fisheries (Gulland 1983; Ricker 1975).

Yield can be measured by complete enumeration in a fishery where access control exists or where all harvest must be reported (e.g., small lakes/streams, limited access fisheries which facilitate creel checks, or use of catch cards). Yield can also be measured by estimates from samples of the fishery users (see chapter 13). These samples may be based on mail or phone surveys (systematic or indiscriminate) or surveys of select groups (e.g., a fly fishing club).

Maximum sustained yield (MSY) can be simply defined as the greatest amount of fish which can be harvested from a fishery by a given effort for a long duration without adversely affecting the biological capability of that stock to produce that yield.

Maximum sustained yield was the basis for fisheries management from about 1946 to 1966 (Larkin 1977). A graphic expression of this principle is shown in figure 3.2. On a stock/recruitment basis, once the shape of the curve is known (figure 3.1), MSY can be approximated with a straight line from the 45-degree (stock replacement) line to the highest point of the curve.

While the definition and theory of MSY are relatively simple, application of its principles are complex and varied, leading to heated debates and discussion about its usefulness. By the mid-1970s, MSY was viewed by many experts as being too narrow and confining a principle for application to all but a few specialized fisheries (Roedel 1975a). Other authorities remained concretely behind MSY, dismissing other concepts such as optimum sustainable yield (OSY) and net economic yield or maximum economic yield (MEY) (Roedel 1975b).

Optimum sustainable yield (OSY) was promoted as early as 1968 (Anderson 1975) as a means of achieving more effective fisheries management. Roedel (1975b) provides the following definition of optimum sustainable yield in an effort to incorporate the input from economists, sociologists, and the political realities under which fishery management must function: "a deliberate melding of biological, economic, social and political values designed to produce the maximum benefit to society from stocks that are sought for human use, taking into account the effect of harvesting on dependent or associated species."

Larkin (1977) points out that while MSY has some redeeming characteristics, the principle was developed, advocated, and utilized at a time when many of the world fisheries were in serious trouble from exploitation. It provided the basis or foundation for order and subsequent principles. It is not now, however, a functional principle for either sport or commercial fisheries because it cannot be adequately defined or controlled and has some inherent serious risks incorporated in its use (e.g., lack of a method to rapidly reduce harvest in the event of recruitment failure).

Larkin (1977) also criticizes the principle of optimum sustainable yield

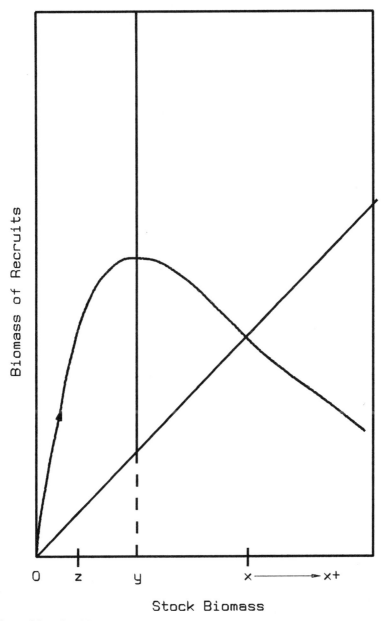

Stock Biomass

Figure 3.2. Graphic representation of MSY. The 45-degree line represents replacement. MSY can be approximated by drawing a line from the replacement line to the highest point of the curve. x = carrying capacity; $x+$ = over carrying capacity; $y = 0.5\,x$ = stock biomass to sustain MSY; $z = 0.2\,x$ and may reflect stock with recruitment problems.

(OSY) as lacking a means for providing an operational basis for making management decisions. Larkin indicates this lack is related to the fact natural (biological) systems are diverse and complex, precluding the use of a single, simple method for regulating harvest from a fishery.

Clearly a concept or technique of measuring and/or assessing yield and associated benefits is necessary in recreational fisheries. To include all of the areas of concern (e.g., maximizing food production, preserving ecological balance, allocating access optimally, providing for economic viability and growth, optimizing distribution and minimizing instability in returns, insuring prior recognition of economic and social impact of technological change, minimizing dependence on paternalistic industry and government, and protecting national security and sovereignty) is to attempt to optimize too many things at the same time, a practice doomed to failure (Larkin 1977).

Anderson (1975) notes that while yield and harvest are often used synonymously, yield broadly implies all benefits to society and in recreational fishing includes not only numbers and weight of fish harvested, but dollars, personal gratification, and memories. If optimum is defined as most favorable or most acceptable, all of the above factors must be included in defining a fishery's yield. Anderson points out that while optimum yield in commercial operations is related to net return or profit, in a recreational fishery it is a function of fishing quality.

Anderson (1975) notes that since quality fishing means different things to different people, fishery managers must incorporate societal values into management programs. Production capabilities of aquatic ecosystems are related to their organic base and production efficiency and, along with a balance among fish communities, are considered to be important aspects of management. Carlton (1975) reinforces the variety of societal requirements of quality fishing by noting that in addition to fisheries (biological) considerations, management plans must include the value of recreation and the use of natural resources by society, both of which are difficult to define.

Yield is an important biological concept in fisheries management. In recreational fisheries, however, its definition and application must go beyond the poundage or number of fish landed. Yield must include (for management purposes) aspects of varied regional species preferences, aspects of the fishing experience (e.g., location, isolation, natural beauty), number of fish kept, and values of associated experience (e.g., camping, hiking, family outings, etc.).

Length-Frequency Indices. Indices based on length-frequency distributions of populations are a relatively new concept for stock assessment (Anderson and Gutreuter 1983). Representative samples describing size distributions reflect the results of rates of reproduction, recruitment, and growth and mortality over the life-span of year classes present in the sample. The indices were originally derived from analyses of populations of largemouth bass and bluegills (Wege and Anderson 1978; Anderson 1976). Predefined minimum total lengths for stocks, quality, preferred, memorable, and trophy-size groups have been presented by Gabelhouse (1984) and Anderson and Gutreuter. Fish of stock size are at or near maturity; fish of quality size and larger are those desired by anglers. Size designations for largemouth bass are: stock 20 cm (8 in.); quality 30 cm (12 in.); preferred 38 cm (15 in.); memorable 51 cm (20 in.); and trophy 63 cm (25 in.).

The index Proportional Stock Density (PSD) is the proportion of fish of quality size in the stock.

$$PSD = \frac{number \geq minimum\ quality\ length}{number \geq minimum\ stock\ length} \times 100$$

If in a sample of 100 largemouth bass greater than 20 cm long, 40 fish were longer than 30 cm, the PSD would be 40. If populations contain young fish or fish with slow growth and/or high mortality, PSD values may be less than 20; when recent and successive year classes are weak or absent in a population, PSD may be higher than 75. Populations of game fish and panfish with satisfactory rates of reproduction, growth, and mortality may exhibit PSD values from 20 to 70 (Anderson 1980; Anderson and Weithman 1978; Weithman, Reynolds, and Simpson 1980).

The index Relative Stock Density (RSD) is the proportion of any designated size group in the stock, RDS-P being the proportion of preferred size and longer. Sequential RSD values can describe the proportion of fish in a size range. RSD-SQ is the proportion less than quality size.

Reproduction, Relative Catch Effort, and Other Considerations

Reproduction can be discussed in terms of rate. Often reproductive success is related to numbers of progeny versus number of adults. For stock assessment, it is important to relate reproduction to fishing harvest. Reproduction is discussed in chapter 14.

Catch per unit of effort, in concert with other stock assessment data, often reflects the status of the stock. Capture (creel) survey methods are discussed in chapter 13.

In order to fully understand the ecological requirements of a stock, it is necessary to understand not only the organism but the environment in which it lives, feeds, reproduces, and competes. Ecological considerations which can be used to more fully understand a particular species are discussed in chapter 14. Taxonomic and genetic information are also useful in developing a more complete understanding of the requirements or differences between species or even strains that are closely related. Chapter 15 deals with life history data and how to present it.

Status of the Habitat

Habitat Classification Systems

Fisheries literature from the late 1970s and early 1980s contains many references to the need for a uniform stream and lake classification system, allowing managers to uniformly document both structure and form of various segments of habitat. Fisheries management techniques could then be routinely applied based on information gained. For analyses, a uniform system would be beneficial but would not solve all habitat classification problems.

The complications of fishery habitat classification are pointed out and discussed by Platts (1980) who indicates that the lack of a classification system for fisheries habitat makes planning and management difficult. Platts points out that in numerous cases fishery inputs to such documents as environmental impact statements were found by the legal system to fail to meet the requirements of the National Environmental Policy Act. Platts believes that there are several reasons why fisheries are often involved in court proceedings, including the lack of a uniform classification system. These reasons are: (1) the fishery is often totally neglected, (2) the fishery biologist is absent or in a minority on an interdisciplinary team, and (3) most of the other life science disciplines have a better (existing) classification system for integrating their information and interpretations into the planning and management processes. Platts notes that classification, in the strictest sense, means ordering or arranging objects into groups or sets on the basis of their similarities or relationships and that classification in natural resources management usually includes identification, mapping or regionalization, and taxonomy. A classification system which is simple, and yet all encompassing, will likely be self-defeating because of the complex nature of natural ecosystems. Is it, therefore, more reasonable to first develop a satisfactory fishery classification system and later integrate it into a natural resources classification system when it has been proven, or to attempt to develop a system that integrates well with nonaquatic parameters? No easy answers prevail.

Many positive steps have been taken toward establishing a usable fishery habitat classification procedure. What is now needed is a unified effort by fisheries biologists, in concert with other natural resource managers, to first develop a fisheries habitat classification system in such a fashion that it can be (or is) integrated into an overall natural resources classification system, or develop the system as an integral part of either an existing or an evolving natural resources classification system. This effort will require assistance from state as well as federal fisheries managers and research biologists, but it is something that must be accomplished if we are to incorporate concerns for fisheries and the aquatic habitat into local, regional, and national policy-making, legal, and decision-making processes.

Habitat Evaluation Systems

Habitat evaluation and classification are related, but not equal, concepts. Classification involves arranging things into categories; evaluation means assessing what is present.

A thorough discussion of fisheries literature on habitat evaluation techniques is beyond the scope of this review. A conservative estimate would be that there are in excess of thirty techniques presently in use attempting to evaluate aquatic habitats and instream flow conditions. Several good review articles exist but are not generally available, making individual evaluation difficult.

Wesche (1983) provides a broad overview of evaluation techniques used in the western United States. Platts, Megahan, and Minshall (1983) provide a detailed review of methods for evaluating not only stream but riparian and other biotic conditions. Anyone interested in detailed theoretical and/or practical application data is directed to the series of reports by the U.S. Fish and Wildlife Services, Fort Collins, Colorado, Cooperative Instream Flow Group (Bovee 1974, 1982; Bovee and Cochnauer 1977; Bovee and Milhous 1978; Lamb 1989). These publications do not provide a complete review of existing techniques and the various modifications by federal regions or state agencies, but they do provide an adequate starting point for research into assessment methods. Fausch and Parsons (1986) provide a review of models to predict standing crops of stream fish from habitat variables.

The two techniques proffered below are not presented as final answers to instream flow research but rather as examples of methods available, usable, and currently accepted by at least portions of the fishery research community.

The first technique is the Instream Flow Incremental Methodology (IFIM) of the U.S. Fish and Wildlife Service's Instream Flow Group for assessing current status and projecting it against proposed changes. The technique involves measurement of width, depth, and velocity, and the use of a computer model that simulates changes. IFIM is specifically designed for simulating and quantifying impacts of changes of flow, channel morphology, or water quality, resulting from water management or stream and channelization activities, on fish, invertebrates, and instream recreational activities (Bovee 1982; Grenney and Kraszewski 1981; Milhous, Wegner, and Waddle 1981).

The IFIM data base includes publications dealing with probability-of-use criteria for salmonids (Bovee 1978), development and evaluation of weighted criteria for probability-of-use curves for instream flow assessment (Bovee and Cochnauer 1977), and hydraulic simulation in instream flow studies, both theory and techniques (Bovee and Milhous 1978).

The second technique, Habitat Evaluation Procedures (HEP), is published by the Division of Ecological Services of the U.S. Fish and Wildlife Service. The HEP are designed to quantify habitat values and document impacts of habitat changes on fish and wildlife resources in both aquatic and terrestrial ecosystems (U.S. Fish and Wildlife Service 1980a, 1980b). This technique consists of information manuals designed to acquaint the user with procedures for preparing determinations of habitat suitability and explanations of their use. The procedure manuals are: "Habitat Evaluation Procedures," "Standards for the Development of Habitat Suitability Index Models," and "Human Use and Economic Evaluation." In addition to the basic manuals, numerous habitat suitability index models are available for both freshwater and coastal fish species. This information is preceded by an introduction to the use and usefulness of the habitat suitability index models. The basic use of the manuals is to provide habitat information for evaluating impacts on both fish and wildlife habitat resulting from water or land-use changes. The habitat suitability index model series concentrates on quantitative relationships between key environmental variables and habitat suitability for a particular species. In each case the information in the series publications is synthesized into explicit habitat models which can be utilized in quantitative assessments. This mechanism provides fisheries managers with a tool whereby they can correlate proposed changes with existing habitat status for fish populations of importance. Suitability index models provide graphic, text, and mathematical information as well as a discussion of relationships among variables and the components of the system being studied.

Armour, Fisher, and Terrell (1984) document the differentiating features and recommend uses of the IFIM and HEP techniques for environmental assessment. IFIM and HEP are similar in that they both provide information about habitat changes over time. Both provide a means of comparing impacts of alternative management practices on fish habitat and combine habitat quality and quantity for indexing. Both make use of suitability relationships between habitat variables and habitat quality, and both are computerized. Differences between the two include the fact that HEP is a technique usable in both terrestrial and aquatic habitats; IFIM is restricted to flowing water situations only. IFIM includes simulation models for predicting changes in the important physical variables of velocity, depth, substrate, cover (microhabitat and water temperature and quality), and macrohabitat. IFIM is primarily used for in-kind mitigation of stream flow; HEP is a more generalized method for mitigation evaluations. IFIM models always contain velocity, depth, substrate, and cover variables and require development and use of suitability index curves for each variable; in HEP the use of suitability index curves is not required. Armour, Fisher, and Terrell provide guidelines on how to determine which of the two techniques to use and, in fact, point out that in some situations it may be beneficial to utilize both the IFIM procedure and the HEP techniques.

The overriding consideration for all stream habitat evaluation techniques, as well as subsequent riparian zone or instream structure modification, should be, first, the prognostic accuracy of the evaluation techniques, and second, the reliability of the resource decision made and the resulting improvement of fish habitat. Platts, Megahan, and Minshall (1983) summarize both the needs and the techniques available to adequately design, complete, and report on studies to document physical and biological attributes of aquatic habitat. They point out that only through constant refinement of present methods, incorporation of additional attributes, and standardization of techniques will fisheries managers be able to develop a practical means of obtaining information of use to resource managers. Platts, Megahan, and Minshall cover a broad spectrum of biological and abiotic factors necessary for evaluating stream, riparian, and other aquatic ecosystems. Among those which should be considered on a stream are: water column, channel morphology, stream bank, and stream. In the riparian zone, streamside cover, vegetation use by animals, herbage production and utilization, vegetation overhang, and habitat type should be documented. To evaluate fish populations, they discuss the use of electrofishing, toxicants, explosives, direct underwater observation, and macroinvertebrate analyses. They present sampling strategies, methods, processing, data interpretation, and biological indices useful in determining the amount and quality of feed available for fish.

Habitat Suitability Index Models

Habitat Suitability Index Models (HSI), essentially management-oriented life histories (see chapter 15), provide species-specific information on the requirements of all life history stages of a species. These models have been used with varying degrees of success to predict the consequences of identifiable actions on habitat. Terrell (1984) provides information presented at a

workshop symposium on fish habitat suitability index models. A summary
of two species models are presented: cutthroat trout and largemouth bass.
Both game and nongame species are presented in the habitat suitability index
model series. Data in the models provide a starting point for habitat/species
planning. The data can be used to assist managers in assessing impacts on
a specific population. Applicability of the models with tested data should be
done (and verified) for each particular population or habitat type before making
management decisions. Verification has been difficult where attempted.

Habitat Suitability Index Model: Cutthroat Trout. Information in the habitat
suitability index model for cutthroat trout (Hickman and Raleigh 1982) includes habitat use data described under the general headings of age, growth and
food, reproduction, anadromy, and specific habitat requirements. Under the
topic of habitat suitability index models, the subjects include model applicability, model description-riverine, suitability index graphs for model variables,
riverine model, lacustrine model, and interpreting model outputs. A final section deals with additional habitat models that can be utilized depending on the
situation encountered. Descriptions included in the above-mentioned headings
include the differences among geographically distinct forms and the scientific
names associated with the various forms throughout the western part of North
America. Both general and specific statements on maturity and feeding habits
of cutthroat trout are included as is a general description of reproductive characteristics. For this particular species, discussion of the forms of anadromy are
also provided. Specific habitat requirements of cutthroat trout are discussed regarding both chemical and physical characteristics to include clear, cold water
with a silt-free fine-sediment, rubble-gravel rock substrate, riffle/pool ratios of
1:1, appropriate water velocities, cover, and the availability of adequate overwintering habitat. Specific information for adults, embryos, fry, and juveniles
are discussed with regard to water velocities, water temperature, and space
requirements. The model is then keyed to geographic areas to which it can be
or has been applied.

Graphics presentations for variables studied for this species include average
maximum water temperature during the warmest period of the year (data are
provided for adult, juvenile, and fry), average maximum water temperature
during embryo development, minimum dissolved oxygen, depth during late
growing season, average velocity over spawning areas, percent cover, average
size of substrate, percent substrate size class, dominant substrate type, percent
pools during late growing season (low-water period), average percent vegetation, average percent rooted vegetation, annual maximal and minimal pH,
average annual base flow, pool class rating during late growing season (low-
flow period), percent of fines in riffle/run and spawning areas, and percent of

stream area shaded between 1000 (10:00 A.M.) and 1400 (2:00 P.M.) hours. The model does not consider catastrophic events such as floods or ice flows, nor of major factors such as overfishing or predation. Predictive capabilities of the model have not been fully evaluated.

Habitat Suitability Index Model: Largemouth Bass. Information in the habitat suitability index model for largemouth bass (Stuber, Gebhart, and Maughan 1982) includes habitat use data described under the headings of general; age, growth, and food; reproduction; and specific habitat requirements. The habitat use information presents a general overview of the largemouth bass, including information that it is native to the eastern United States, excluding the northeastern states, and has been introduced throughout the United States. Two subspecies are generally recognized—the northern and the Florida subspecies. Age, growth, food, and reproduction are discussed briefly.

Specific habitat requirements indicate that a lacustrine environment is preferred and optimal conditions are in extensive shallow areas supporting submergent vegetation. Water must be deep enough to allow successful overwintering. Habitat requirements include the information that the growth of largemouth bass is reduced when dissolved oxygen levels are below 8 mg/l.

What Fisheries Can Provide

Determination of the status of the existing fishery and habitat must be closely paralleled by (or preceded by) determination of what anglers desire and what can be provided within the existing framework. Examples include put-and-take trout or channel catfish (stream) fishing, gear-restricted quality areas, catch-out ponds or streams (single or mixed species), trophy-only fishing, slot length-only fishing, and catch-and-release fishing. Questionnaires or surveys of anglers in the area affected and open meetings are effective data-gathering tools.

Example 1—Georgia Public Fishing Area Plan

Georgia's Public Fishing Area (PFA) Plan is one facet of the fisheries management section's effort to provide quality recreational fishing to Georgia's 1.16 million anglers (Quintrell, Young, and McSwain 1981). In 1973, surveys of the fishing public indicated that more public areas for fishing was the most needed improvement in Georgia's recreational fisheries. Good access and high success rates were secondary factors.

In response to the perceived need and with the realization that fewer new waters were being created in the 1980s, the Georgia Department of Natural Resources identified three options for meeting the need for additional public fishing lakes. These options are: (1) more intensive management of existing, state-owned waters; (2) lease private lakes for public fishing; and (3) construct new lakes on state land.

Through surveys, public involvement, and planning, Georgia identified a need for 6,684 bass/bluegill pond acres and 2,716 catfish pond acres to satisfy growth in their use regions in the near future. Implementation of the solutions to the problem may face fiscal constraints, but the need and possible solutions have been identified should funding be available.

Example 2—The St. Joe River Cutthroat Study

Cutthroat trout abundance and size declined in the St. Joe River, Idaho, during the 1950s and 1960s. Rankel (1971) attributed this decline to overfishing, perhaps overharvest by current definition.

In 1973 the Idaho Fish and Game Commission closed Reeds, Bond, Trout, and Mica creeks to angling. These closures had been requested by local anglers to increase trout abundance in the main stem St. Joe River. To evaluate effects of the closures on populations of westslope cutthroat trout in the main stem and tributaries, studies were initiated to assess species composition, abundance, and movement in closed and open tributaries and in tributaries with trophy fish regulations from 1973 to 1977. Angler survey data on effort, harvest, and opinions on the fishery were also developed. Protective regulations (closed tributaries) increased abundance of cutthroat trout larger than 7.9 inches (200 mm) in accessible stream segments. Reduced angling mortality was reflected in increased abundance after a three-year closure period (Thurow and Bjornn 1978).

The rapid response of cutthroat trout populations to restrictive regulations has been noted by several researchers (Johnson and Bjornn 1975; Chapman, Pettit, and Ball 1973; Lowry 1966). Trout over 6.7 inches (170 mm) respond fastest to restrictive regulations (Gowing 1975; Alexander 1971; Chrystie 1965), and the increased abundance of juveniles is probably a direct result of more spawners (Thurow and Bjornn 1978).

Thurow and Bjornn (1978) conducted angler preference surveys and concluded that a majority of the fishing public would be in favor of and support restrictive regulations if the fishery would benefit. While some disparity existed between anglers who fished tributaries in regard to closing tributaries to improve main stem St. Joe River fishing, the public generally supported the regulations. Thurow and Bjornn concluded that with public involvement, separate regulation of upper and lower tributary reaches would be acceptable to anglers and result in increased trout abundance.

Public participation, innovative regulations, and understanding of the dynamics of the fish population are necessary in order to achieve results such as those reported for the St. Joe River and its tributaries. Restrictive regulations must be based on sound biological data and in addition have the support of the angling and recreation public.

Program Establishment and Follow-Through

When provisions to manage a fishery under existing conditions have been completed and the determination has been made that additional fishing areas or types are required, it is necessary to provide for changes in the existing system. Seven mechanisms exist for managing changing fisheries: (1) fish stocking, (2) regulations, (3) law enforcement, (4) habitat improvement, (5) predator/competition control/removal, (6) refuges, and (7) opportunity. Most of these tools (e.g., fish stocking and law enforcement) can be used in managing existing fisheries. They are presented here as a unit only for continuity.

A sound understanding of what is to be done, based on biological data, must be developed before the initiation of any program involving stocking, habitat improvement, or predator/competition removal. Each option is expensive and should be planned to meet needs defined in preceding investigations. Law enforcement activities or regulations may require less capital outlay but should also be carefully planned. An ill-conceived enforcement or regulation program is just as detrimental to good fisheries management as a poor biological program.

Refuges for other than limited areas or for species with special status (e.g., threatened/endangered) are of limited value because of the inherent biological and sociological problems associated with their operation. Additionally, they are expensive to develop and maintain.

The options discussed below are all independent, but in a well-planned management unit will be coordinated and designed to maximize benefits.

Fish Stocking

The use of fish hatcheries in the production of a cold-, cool-, or warm-water fishery has been and will continue to be an integral part of management. Stocking to increase fishing success is an important aspect of management in most states. In general, fish are stocked either to be caught shortly, or to produce offspring that will be caught. Fingerling plants incorporate the concept of put-grow-and-take fisheries.

In situations where a new species is stocked, a careful assessment should be made as to the effects of this stocking on other species in the system. It is essential when a fish is introduced into a new environment that documentation regarding food supply, water temperature, spawning grounds, competitors, and effects on native fishes be completed.

Brood stocks are planted in lakes or streams where either disaster or reclamation projects (with toxicants) has eliminated the original stock, or where a new species is to be introduced. In some cases, prey fish, such as cyprinids, shad, and smelt, are stocked to provide food for game fish.

Stocking for the creel should be carefully assessed before a species or size is selected. Use of stocks genetically related to either existing stocks or consideration of the requirements of the fish in its native habitat are recommended.

Coldwater Fishes

Coldwater fishes are species that prosper best at 38° to 62°F. Although some of these species grow more rapidly at higher temperatures, they are then more prone to stress and disease. These fishes are most abundant in the northern latitudes and high altitudes, although they are present and even abundant in some areas of the far south at median to low elevations. They are held in high esteem by anglers for their fighting ability, beauty, and palatability. Their growth is relatively slow, maturity is later in life, and longevity is greater than cool- or warmwater fishes. The number of eggs produced per year is low. Productivity, as measured by pounds per acre, is generally low, sometimes only a few pounds. In some instances, however, such as in the South Platte River of Colorado, production may reach 500 pounds/acre (Robert Behnke, personal communication, 1986). The number of species in a given habitat is few. Some species fare best in a monoculture (e.g., grayling and golden trout).

Salmonids stocked to provide offspring for eventual capture are not necessarily the same species or strains as those stocked in a put-and-take fishery. Even when fish are stocked to be creeled in a few days or weeks, some may live to reproduce. One example is the various strains of rainbow trout used for put-and-take fisheries in many cool or cold waters. Catchable size (7 to 10 inches) rainbow trout are stocked, particularly in the western states, either just before opening day, or on holidays, where a high angler effort is expected. In other areas, particularly in the eastern United States, fish, principally trout, are stocked in waters that will support them for only a limited time (paucity of available resources).

Since it is costly to rear these fish, it is desirable that a high percentage be caught. They should not be used in situations where they will be fished lightly with the remainder being lost to natural mortality. Additionally this type of stocking should not be done on top of abundant wild fish stocks of either the same or competing species.

In habitats where it is possible for trout to overwinter, avoid predators, and grow to catchable size, it is feasible to stock fingerling or a subcatchable size. Fingerlings can be stocked much more economically and can utilize the natural food to achieve the desired size. From species to species grow-out time may vary from one to several years. This aspect should be considered in planning for from two to five years ahead of expected harvest.

Grayling may be stocked as fingerlings, preferably in a monoculture in lakes or streams. When they are stocked in streams, the strain should be from stream stock (considered by Williams [1981] as threatened). Grayling sometimes survive under quite adverse conditions. Escapees from the Utah Wildlife Division Fisheries Experiment Station at Logan moved down a small ditch into the Logan River, then several miles upstream through rather warm, sometimes polluted waters where several were caught by surprised anglers.

Brook and brown trout are generally able to reproduce and provide a fishable population once an adequate brood stock is established. Brook trout tend to stunt unless they are fished heavily and are therefore not as popular with managers or anglers as most other salmonids. A slot-length regulation of 7 to 10, 7 to 12, or 8 to 12 inches may be appropriate. Lake trout grow slowly and to a large size, but they do not reproduce readily in many waters outside their native range. They are generally held in a hatchery for one or two years before planting. They are also much more difficult to raise than rainbow trout. Dolly Varden and bull trout are raised in hatcheries infrequently. In many states the hatchery emphasis is on trout, particularly rainbow.

Stocking of one species may have adverse effects on another, desirable species. In the Logan River in Utah, above the mouth of Logan Canyon, cutthroat trout flourished in early times when the only other species there were mottled sculpin and mountain whitefish. Since the introduction of rainbow and brown trout, cutthroat prosper only in the higher and smaller reaches of the river.

Coolwater Fishes

Coolwater fishes are those species that live in both cold water and warm water, but are most likely to be successful in temperate waters (48° to 72°F). They range from the far north to south into Mexico. Some grow rapidly and to a large size and are long lived (e.g., muskellunge). Many are prized game fish that live in a wide range of habitats and with numerous other species, many of which are prey species (e.g., cyprinids and catostomids). The productivity is much higher than in coldwater habitats.

The most commonly stocked coolwater game fishes in North America are muskellunge, northern pike, walleye, and smallmouth bass. None of these is easy to raise nor inexpensive to stock. Muskellunge and northern pike are often stocked at a length of 8 to 10 inches; at this size their prey is almost wholly vertebrates. Walleye and smallmouth bass are sometimes stocked as fry, but more often as fingerlings. All four of these fish are rather difficult to raise to a size larger than advanced fingerling.

Warmwater Fishes

Warmwater species live in the warm, much of the cool, and rarely the cold waters of North America. Although their range of temperature tolerance is wide, they thrive best in 58° to 82°F water. There are exceptions; one or more species of pupfish living in Death Valley, California, reproduce and prosper in water that at times is near 110°F. Warmwater fishes generally produce more pounds of flesh per acre, more eggs per pound of female, and grow more rapidly than fish in cooler waters. Their associates generally number several to many species. Perhaps the most widespread and sought after warmwater game fish is the largemouth bass. It is rarely necessary to stock largemouth bass where there is an adequate brood stock. When they are stocked in new or re-claimed waters, it is usually as advanced fry or fingerlings. Larger fish may be stocked to take advantage of a surplus of prey. The landlocked striped bass has increased considerably in importance as a game fish in the United States in the last twenty-five years. They have been stocked as fry and fingerling to establish them in relatively new habitat (e.g., Lake Powell on the Colorado River) and to supplement natural reproduction to improve an established fishery (e.g., Tennessee Valley waters). The channel catfish has been stocked, generally as fingerling, to establish a new fishery in many warm waters. At times it is also, unlike most warmwater species, stocked at catchable size.

Regulations

Regulations are not a new concept in fisheries management. As early as 1278, freshwater fisheries in the British Isles had restrictive regulations on the take or creel (Graham 1956). Laws in fisheries management are used to restrict and to spread out the harvest among anglers. The number of fish allowed to be taken in a particular situation may be as few as one or two (or none) if the fish are scarce or no surplus exists relative to objectives (e.g., stocked fish that will be caught in a matter of hours or days) or if the fish are trophy size. In the case of large numbers of fast-growing, short-lived fishes, high or unlimited numbers may be allowed (e.g., crappie). Length restrictions are either minimum length, maximum length, or range of length (slot lengths/limits, e.g., 14 to 18 inches protected, 18 to 30 inches legal, < 18 > 30 protected).

During the early years of fishery management the only consideration was minimum length limits, often ranging from 6 to 10 inches for trout and panfish, 8 to 10 or 12 to 18 inches for black basses, and 28 to 30 inches for muskellunge. Martin (1958) suggested the concept of protecting bass weighing 1 to 2 pounds. Andersen (1976) first tried a protected size regulation of 12 to 15 inches (36 to 38 cm) on bass. The intent of slot-length regulations in bass fisheries is: (1) to allow harvest of a surplus of suitable size bass age one and two, (2) to protect bass through age three and four, (3) to increase the number of bass age five and older or 15 inches or longer, and (4) to retain a balanced bluegill (prey) population (Anderson 1976). Basically, slot limits are used to reduce mortality on a particular size group. Many states now have or are considering slot limits (11- to 14-inch, 12- to 15-inch, 14- to 18-inch, and 15- to 20-inch) or minimum size limits from 12 to 21 inches. The purpose of minimum size limits is to help rebuild depleted stocks or to prevent depletion in new reservoirs (Novinger 1984). Prohibiting the harvest of less than minimum legal size should reduce fishing and total fish mortality and allow more fish to reach a legal size. On the other hand, a large number of small fish caught and released should generally survive, increasing the sport catch rate. Where there is an abundance of young fish and the adult or quality (median size) group is being depleted by fishing, then a slot limit may be initiated. This allows many small fish and the fewer quite large fish to be harvested.

In 1947 in northern Utah several spring-fed ponds had large populations of largemouth bass in the 15- to 18-inch class and moderate numbers of 5- to 8-pound fish. Following World War II there was a large influx of students to Utah State University, many of them avid bass anglers. In a relatively short time, the desirable size fish were largely eliminated from many ponds. Presumably a slot limit, assuming it was enforced, would have preserved this high-quality bass fishery, which was obviously fragile.

Anderson (1976, 1980), discussing regulation to manipulate fish population structure, points out that application of 12- and 14-inch minimum length limits on largemouth bass fisheries on small impoundments consistently results in a buildup of stock density. This positive aspect, however, is modified by a reduced harvest and few fish reach legal size. The problems of high natural mortality and slow growth are reflected in low PSDs, RSDs, and W_r (relative weight) of bass. In Philips Lake, Anderson noted that a slot-length limit of 12 to 15 inches was imposed in 1974. In two growing seasons, indices improved to the objective PSD range of 40 to 60 for bass. Slot lengths can be imposed to manage a fishery but must be utilized with care. The type of fishing regulation needed is determined relative to objectives and presence of a balanced fish community and is related to catch/effort and PSD for bass and panfish.

Other ways to reduce the take are by time closures (e.g., 9 P.M. to 6 A.M., December to May) and place (e.g., streams above 6,000 feet, specific lakes). Gear restrictions are also an effective means of limiting take. Restrictions to only hook and line (the most inefficient of all methods of taking fish), only one line and a limited number of hooks, no snagging, catch-and-release, in some areas no motorboats or no boats, and arguably no fish finders, all reduce the catch and harvest.

It is essential that fishing regulations be clearly written and readily available to the fishing public. When changes occur, modifying historic angling regulations, an intensive education and information program should be implemented. While more liberalized regulations are seldom a problem for the fishing public, regulations that are more restrictive on gear, bag limits, or other aspects may be either ignored or unknown.

Law Enforcement

Enforcement of the requirement for a proper license is one way to increase revenue to the department or division. Common license violations are no license, improper license (e.g., resident license for nonresidents), expired license, and claim of no license needed (e.g., a person fishing on their own property). Opinions vary widely as to how much revenue is lost by the use of improper license or fishing without a license, but the general agreement is that it is substantial.

The second type of loss from illegal fishing is to the resource. How many more fish would there be available for the legal anglers if there were no illegal activity? Again, precise agreement is lacking, but general agreement is that it is significant. Perhaps those that have the largest negative impact are illegal commercial anglers. These range from the lone efficient angler who sells to a local household clientele, to the highly organized group that sells to the food retail and restaurant industry (Bavin 1985). While the loss of revenue is nominal (a legal commercial license where one is available), the loss to the resource is considerable.

The primary consideration in the use of regulations that restrict the take is the effectiveness with which the law can be enforced. Law enforcement (conservation) officers are constrained by the same fiscal and hour limitations as are other management personnel; therefore, their activities must be on a best-use basis. All laws do not get equal time effort. To a certain extent, laws can be enforced least expensively at landing areas and other access points (roadblocks). The most economical and best public relations approach to law enforcement in fisheries management is to convince the fishing public that the laws are reasonable and valid—not an easy task—but public input when regulations are being considered is a very necessary ingredient of fishery management. This will, hopefully, reduce the number of violations and encourage a self-policing philosophy among individual anglers. Citizen involvement in such reporting programs as CAWT (Catch a Wildlife Thief) and toll-free 800 numbers to report poaching or other illegal activity have also been highly successful.

In general, in fisheries management as in other areas of natural resource management, enforcement should not be restricted to law enforcement officers, but rather should be considered important and aided by the entire user group. This necessitates laws that are considered to be both fair and equitable for everyone.

Habitat Enhancement

Improvement of the environment will receive increasing attention in future years. It may be the wave of the future. This includes control of point and non-point source pollution that occurs primarily at lower elevations (excluding acid rain) and in larger streams and lakes. Proper watershed management, including reduction of sheet erosion, control of fires, grazing, and riparian damage, should be intensively practiced.

Artificial habitat improvement is usually quite costly. It is therefore justified only when: (1) it is the central core for improvement of a larger area of habitat (when a direct improvement on a small area will make a larger area more usable); (2) it is the only way to provide a missing essential habitat factor for a species; and (3) it is needed to restore damage by human action or by catastrophic weather conditions and when natural restoration will not result within a reasonable period of time (Anonymous 1969).

The number of habitat enhancement techniques is large, but many fall into four categories: artificial reefs, riparian zone protection, instream structures, and instream flow allocation. In lentic ecosystems, destratification, vegetation control, and turbidity control may also be used. Stream habitat enhancement techniques include the use of barrier structures to create riffle-pool sequences or feeding areas, gabions or log dams, and very low head impoundment structures, increased cover, improved spawning or feeding areas, removal of obstructions, and creation of pools through the use of explosives. Almost uniformly, habitat enhancement procedures are expensive. Justification for their use must include a sound biological/economical basis, indicating, preferably in quantitative terms, the gain to be achieved.

Justification of habitat improvements should be on a biological/economical rather than a social or political basis. The criteria should include an analysis of what the alteration will do and how it will help the fish and/or the fishing. For example, if a single stream barrier can be removed, allowing access to several miles or even several hundred yards of stream for spawning or rearing, the cost-benefit ratio would likely be positive and in favor of the alteration. If, however, the alteration opens only a very short section of stream or allows access to a biologically unsuitable stream segment, the benefits are doubtful.

As a part of the need to effect stream rehabilitation or improvement, it is essential to carefully evaluate the objectives and potential results of any habitat improvement projects. Selecting correct enhancement options can be assured by conducting basinwide evaluations of available habitat, including spawning and rearing areas and habitat utilization (Everest and Sedell 1985). Everest and Sedell (1984) point out that planning for habitat improvements is complicated and often given inadequate consideration but is an essential step for both project success and cost-benefit analysis.

The need to both carefully preplan a habitat alteration and then evaluate its effectiveness cannot be overemphasized. Taking into consideration the complexity of aquatic ecosystems with a diversity of geology, topography, climate, hydrology, stream gradients and morphology, land use and treatment, differing seasonal requirements of individual species and regions, and local angler concepts of preferred species, a decision to complete a habitat alteration project should be well founded. A ready prescription or formula for identifying either the need for or the type of project to complete is unavailable and is not likely to appear in the near future. What is possible is to preplan projects on the largest possible conceptual scale, to include all the variables, and to compile and analyze in-depth species requirements. Following completion, it is then both necessary and prudent to evaluate, in detail, the probable level of success or failure of the project to perform as conceived and to document the reasons for either.

Evaluations of habitat improvements can be accomplished at three or more levels of intensity. An assessment can be made to determine whether physical changes have occurred after a project is completed. Assessment of anticipated changes in fish use is a second level, and completion of angler use and cost-benefit analyses can provide a more complete picture of cost effectiveness over the life of the project (Everest and Sedell 1984). Hall and Baker (1982), reviewing rehabilitation and enhancement of stream habitat, point out that many of the projects they looked at had not been evaluated at all, had not been adequately assessed, or had been assessed with a bias due to administrative requirements to publish only successful project reviews. They stress the need to evaluate and document all projects—valuable lessons can be learned from apparent failure. Hall and Baker, and Reeves and Roelofs (1982) emphasize that habitat rehabilitation is not and should not be a substitute for habitat protection.

Habitat improvement may also include such things as reserved stream flows. In many areas (principally in the western United States) reserved water flows in streams have not been considered a legally beneficial use of water resources; therefore, large sections of streams are annually dewatered, killing or stranding fish and degrading the habitat. The benefit to the habitat when flows are reserved is maintenance of a year-round aquatic ecosystem. Legislation to this effect has recently been enacted in some western states and is proposed in others. An extension of this methodology includes insuring sufficient stream flows at the proper time of year.

With limited water resources in most areas of North America, water must be used and reused wisely initially and subsequently. Habitat improvement procedures which allow for more than one beneficial use to prosper are becoming more economically attractive as fiscal demands tighten and resource values increase.

Habitat modification is a management technique that has been used for more than fifty years, but has gained popularity only in the last twenty. To some extent this is a reflection of the contention by some fisheries managers and angler groups that fish hatcheries are not providing a totally acceptable product, and where fish hatchery stocks are replacing natural stocks, they may be degrading both the quality of the fish and the fishery. Some states, such as Michigan, have gone as far as discontinuing stocking programs in selected streams, relying solely on reproduction by wild trout. A precursor to habitat improvement sufficient to allow wild stocks to maintain themselves must, however, be an analysis of that habitat.

Overall habitat enhancement can be made more precise by systematically delimiting aspects of the habitat. First, a determination if physical habitat rather than food is limiting should be made. If food is limiting, habitat alteration (e.g., providing riffles to promote growth of drift organisms) may be of value. If habitat is limiting, the aspect (spawning, rearing, overwintering, adult or juvenile cover, etc.) causing the limitation needs to be determined. An assessment of what can be done to improve the species limitation can then be attempted.

Presuming that a determination has been made regarding a species to be managed in a particular freshwater environment and regarding the available habitat, it is then necessary to match habitat requirements with the species. If habitat requirements are not met, determination must be made regarding the advisability of utilizing either instream or riparian zone modification to alter the habitat sufficiently to provide the necessary areas of shelter, feeding, rearing, and other characteristics required.

Artificial Reefs

The use of artificial reefs and the knowledge of the benefits afforded to fish, and subsequently anglers, are not new. Stone (1985) reports that artificial reefs for sheepshead in South Carolina were constructed as early as 1860, specifically to replace natural habitat destroyed by clearing and cultivation. While many initial efforts were related to offshore marine fisheries, freshwater artificial reefs or brush shelters, as they were originally called, were in use as early as the 1930s. Reports of the construction and use of experimental brush shelters or artificial reefs in Michigan lakes include publications by Hazzard in 1937, Hubbs and Eschmeyer in 1938, and Rodeheffer in 1938, 1939, and 1944 (Stone 1985). Increased interest in the use of artificial reefs in both marine and freshwater environments, principally to increase recreational fishing, was made more obvious in a lengthy book edited by D'Itri (1985). Radonski, Martin, and DuBose (1985) report a number of considerations for developing and siting an artificial reef either in fresh water or salt water.

Artificial reefs may range from simple tire reefs to the use of obsolete oil production platforms or ships (McGurrin 1989). In general, they have been designed and sited to create or improve spawning substrate or otherwise increase fish production, encourage fish to congregate in an area, and to increase species diversity in a particular area, generally for the benefit of anglers. An extremely wide variety of materials has been used including automobile bodies (Sigler and Workman 1967), construction rubble, tires, and other environmentally safe solid waste materials. The selection of materials usable in artificial reefs is limited only by cost, the fishery manager's ingenuity, and the constraint of environmental safety.

From a nonbiological perspective, artificial reefs should be sited in areas where they will be used by anglers, principally near population centers. In addition, considerations include the type of boats that will be used, the existing or subsequent location of launching ramps, the availability of fuel and/or bait and tackle items, as well as hotel accommodations and rental boats for nonresident anglers.

While artificial reefs are primarily designed to attract fish and help anglers, they may also be utilized to disperse anglers from areas of overuse, either on a particular water body or on a particular species of fish. While this may be less functional for freshwater than marine applications, diversity of structures in various areas should increase fishing potential. An additional consideration regarding artificial reefs includes the publicity programs generally associated with reefs in marine applications. While many western and midwestern states have specific policies discouraging media identification or publication of reports of hot spots or good fishing areas, the use of artificial reefs to attract fish and anglers may require a change in this philosophy. Radonski, Martin, and DuBose (1985) point out one additional aspect of artificial reefs of extreme importance in freshwater applications. Properly constructed artificial reefs (figure 3.3) can provide spawning habitat for some species in situations where optimal spawning habitat is unavailable. If excessive harvest depresses sport fishing in an area, greater numbers (through survival of progeny) may be provided by an artificial reef designed primarily to increase spawning. A factor in this approach is that sufficient prey species for growth of a sport fishery may be lacking and therefore be the limiting factor.

When artificial reefs are being considered, the ultimate benefit should be researched prior to commitment of funds or materials. Fisheries managers in an area where artificial reefs are proposed should take advantage of input and assistance from local anglers, fishing clubs, wildlife federations, and Boy Scouts.

Instream Modifications

The principal goal of instream flow modification is to provide or supplement a habitat characteristic that is degraded or insufficient. To be biologically cost effective, instream modifications must have permanence, affect the desired area, and have minimal adverse impact on the stream reach in which they are installed (e.g., siltation and migration barriers). The most important consideration in placing an instream modification is that it treats the actual fish-limiting factor (Platts and Rinne 1985). Many past efforts at stream rehabilitation have failed to achieve their stated objective. However, the reasons for failure have not been documented. Future efforts at instream modification or rehabilitation should be designed so that quantifiable documentation on the physical and biological effects can be obtained (House and Boehne 1985; Platts and Rinne 1985; Hall and Baker 1982; Reeves and Roelofs 1982). Historical (e.g., Gard 1961; Fearnow 1941; Davis 1934), as well as more recent evaluation and technique manuals (e.g., Rosgen 1985; Hall and Baker 1982; Reeves and Roelofs

Figure 3.3.   Artificial reef structure.

1982; Canadian Department of Fisheries and Oceans 1980; Ward and Slaney 1979; Maughan, Nelson, and Ney 1978), provide a basis for determining those techniques and procedures that have been successful and document what does or does not work in various streams. Habitat modification structures should promote or enhance the creation of areas usable by resident fish. All habitat alteration structures should be installed only after a careful appraisal of not only the site, but the particular structure.

Fajen (1981) reports that comparatively little research has been done to determine the potential value of instream structures in warmwater streams. Most bibliographies of stream improvement publications deal with coldwater streams. Since 1960 several studies have been directed toward development of methods for physical and biological improvement and maintenance of warmwater stream fisheries. Fajen also reports that warmwater stream habitat can be managed successfully if primary emphasis is given to optimizing natural riffle-pool development by restoring or maintaining an appropriate degree of sinuosity and adequate vegetational cover on the floodplain.

One of the options Fajen (1981) reported for warmwater stream habitat improvement includes the use of cover structures. He notes that they are costly and probably justified only in special circumstances, which include heavy angler use and stable channel conditions. Fajen also identifies a lack of habitat requirement information for warmwater stream species, thus preventing application of stream improvement tactics until sufficient information is available. Much of this information has been gathered in the last several years and is now available in the form of habitat suitability index models.

Gabions. A gabion is a wire basket (usually galvanized or otherwise treated) which can be placed, filled with rocks, and secured in a stream channel. They are often imbedded in the stream bank and are usually constructed in sets of two and sometimes more. Gabions can also be utilized along stream banks to add stability and prevent bank scouring (Canadian Department of Fisheries and Oceans 1980).

Gabion dams are effective under certain conditions. Baskets provide a basis for massive block-type structures which are well adapted to large, fast-flowing streams. Baskets themselves are highly flexible and allow structures to sag, bend, twist, or otherwise conform to the stream channel configurations without serious damage to the structure resulting (Anonymous 1969). Gabions may, under these conditions, last as long as fifty years.

Gabions have principally been used to stabilize banks and to alter or control channel grade in areas either naturally steep or impacted by human activity. Original designs used gabions placed directly perpendicular to stream flow (figures 3.4 and 3.5). More recently, a V-notched design has been utilized with mixed success (House and Boehne 1985; Reeves and Roelofs 1982). Klassen and Northcote (1988) report on the use of tandem V-shaped gabion wiers to improve spawning habitat for Pacific salmon.

Gabion dams are extremely useful in protecting stream banks and bottoms below culverts where there may be high-velocity discharges. Indigenous stream bank protection can also be used to create pools at culvert outlets to help pass fish.

Since unassembled gabion baskets and other materials are relatively light weight, they may be easily transported to remote areas either by helicopter or by horseback. Gabion structures are well adapted to remote stream sections where log materials are scarce and rock is abundant. In the process of constructing gabions, it is recommended that the successive layers or the entire structure be assembled together and stretched in place and then filled with rock. This allows the best positioning possible and greatly simplifies the process of fastening gabion baskets together. It is essential with gabions, as with other structures, that anchor sections extend 6 to 12 feet into the banks, depending upon what the bank is composed of. Maximum anchor lengths should be used when banks are unconsolidated material such as sand or gravel. The excavation area for anchor sections should only be as wide as the basket itself, thus minimizing loose fill along the wings. This will help retain the baskets in place during high flows.

Despite the convenience of machine assistance in making gabion structures, the best results are generally obtained by placing rocks in the baskets by hand. This is true because machines tend to increase fines, and small rock may cause sagging and collapse of individual units. The process of filling gabions, however, can be expedited by using machines or heavy equipment to place rock fill in a handy location.

Gabion basket lids should always be closed in the downstream direction to prevent floating debris or other material from snagging and tearing them apart. The structure should be watertight to facilitate fish passage in low-water periods. Additionally if the entire water flow filtrates through the structure, fish migration is blocked. Some type of material such as plastic sheeting can be placed on the inside face of the downstream wall of the gabion basket prior to filling with rock. This will result in a complete waterproofing. Use of other materials at hand such as straw are somewhat less effective for trapping fines and in making the dam watertight. The downstream side of the dam should have the rocks fitted together carefully. Overflow concentration can be achieved by arching the dam, that is, making it slightly deeper in the center. When the baskets are formed to the excavation there will be a depression in the center.

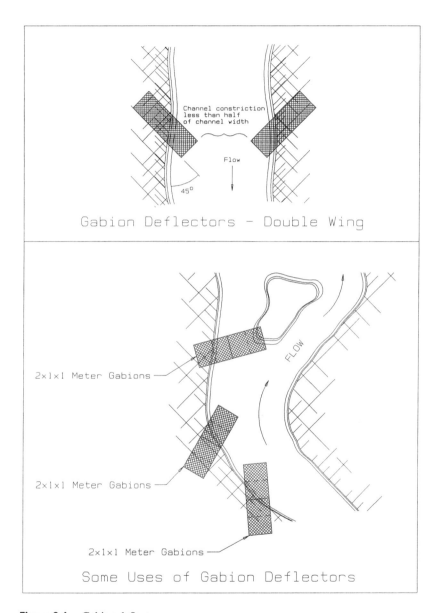

Channel constriction
less than half
of channel width

Flow

45°

Gabion Deflectors - Double Wing

2x1x1 Meter Gabions

FLOW

2x1x1 Meter Gabions

2x1x1 Meter Gabions

Some Uses of Gabion Deflectors

Figure 3.4. Gabion deflectors.

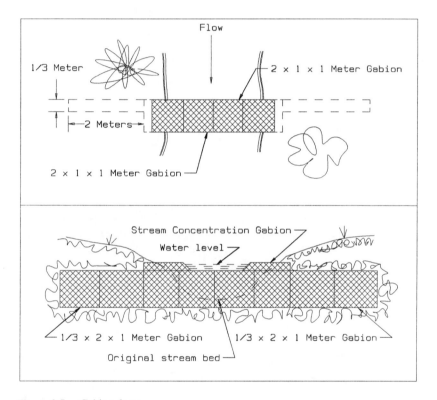

Figure 3.5. Gabion dams.

This does not weaken the structure because the baskets are flexible. Gabions have not been generally successful in low-gradient streams. End cuts weaken or cause total failure of the structure, at times resulting in a worse condition than existed prior to structure installation.

Dams. One of the primary purposes of dam construction of various types is the creation or improvement of pools. Pools provide resting space and shelter for fish and spawning areas for some species. There are several types of dams. Small stream improvement dams have in the past been visualized as creating a pool by impounding the stream flow. In many instances, however, in two or three years, a pool forms below the dam by the scouring action of water pouring over the dam during the flood period, and the area just above the dam is silted in. The lower pools are more stable and do not fill in with rubble or debris. Dams on small streams may fail because a pool below the dam becomes so steep that the streambed immediately above the dam is loosened and washed down under the dam (e.g., rock dams and log dams).

Special construction is necessary to stabilize the streambed on the upstream side of the dam. The K-dam (figure 3.6), so named because of the knee braces used at each end which when viewed from above give the dam the shape of the letter *K,* works well in many situations. To stabilize the structure, logs functioning as mud-retention cells are placed beneath the dam parallel to the stream flow to furnish the base on which the upstream face of the dam is constructed. After the mud cells and log dam are in place, woven wire can be stapled to the top of the log and pressed into place against the mud cells to which it is also stapled. Woven wire should extend up on the banks at least 3 to 4 feet and into the bank excavations at the ends of the dam. Rocks of a larger diameter than the openings in the woven wire should be layered carefully on to the woven wire. The entire structure is then filled with water-washed gravel which is carefully tamped around the ends of the logs extending into the bank excavation. Large rocks are placed on the gravel to provide a protective armor coat. When completed, the K-dam should have water running over the full length of the log between the knee braces. This not only provides a maximum amount of usable movement space, but also keeps the entire log wet and thus less subject to rot (Anonymous 1969).

A second type of dam is a board dam which is similar to the K-dam but uses board in place of mud cells and woven wire. For this reason board dams are somewhat more expensive than log K-dams. Generally speaking, any wood is suitable for construction of a board dam; however, green, rough lumber which is at least 2 inches thick is the preferred material. Dry lumber should

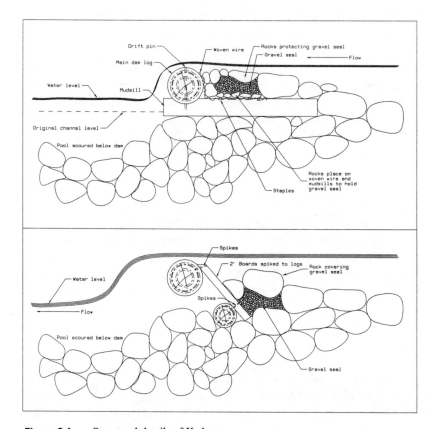

Figure 3.6a. Structural details of K-dams.

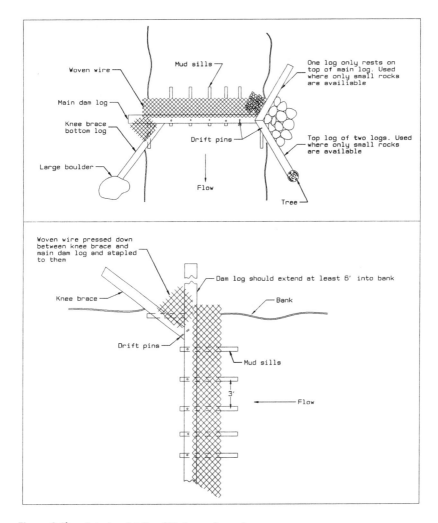

Figure 3.6b. Interior details of K-dams, from above.

be soaked before it is used; otherwise, expansion will result in buckling and displacement.

Rock dams may be efficiently constructed in areas where large rock is easily obtainable and if flooding is not severe. In areas where flooding is severe, rock dams may not last more than one or two years or until an extremely high flow. Generally speaking, rock dams are effective when they are restricted to streams less than 10 or 12 feet wide.

In constructing rock dams (figure 3.7), rocks at least 4 feet in length and oblong in shape should be used in the main section of the dam. They should be laid with their long axis parallel to stream flow. This convention results in scouring rather than rolling the rocks down the streambed. Wherever possible in the construction of a rock dam, the rocks forming the dam should be tied to those boulders or rocks already present in the natural stream. If boulders are not present in the stream, the rock dam should be constructed with an upstream arch which greatly strengthens the dam (Anonymous 1969). Rock dams should be low head to prevent destruction or movement by floods, and only one layer of rock is generally used. Building dams too high is a common mistake. The upper edges of rock dams may be sealed with small gravel and rocks. Streambeds should not be disturbed to any large extent, because the rocks and boulders already present should be used in the dam construction.

Deflectors. Deflectors can be used in habitat improvement to scour pools. This is accomplished by constricting the channel to protect eroding banks, or to divert flow from side channels which are no longer useful, or to direct flow to more suitable habitat. Where they can be used effectively, deflectors are preferred to dams, primarily because they are less disturbing to the stream bottom and are less subject to destruction than dams. Additionally, deflectors do not slow flow as much as dams and do not result in upstream material accumulation as dams do (Anonymous 1969). Deflectors may be used to protect banks either in a series of short ones or one long one, or they may be used in conjunction with protective vegetation established either in the riparian zone or nearby land. Deflectors can be constructed with gabions, which can be used to direct flow into or away from critical areas.

A sheet-piling deflector (figure 3.8), yet another type of deflector, is generally used in streams with sandy bottoms. Sheet-piling deflectors can be installed with a hydraulic jet cutting device, and are generally made of 1.25-inch lumber, 6 to 8 inches wide. The preferred lumber is tongue and groove with 0.50-inch-long tongues (Anonymous 1969).

Other types of deflectors include trash-catching deflectors, which can be

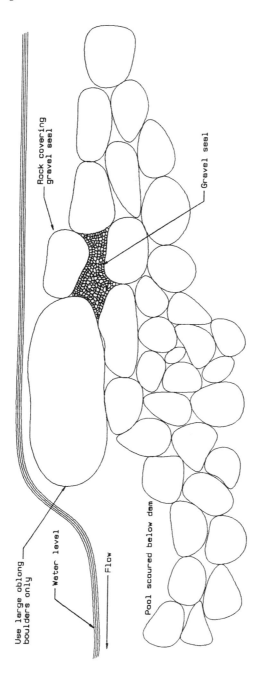

Figure 3.7a. Rock dams.

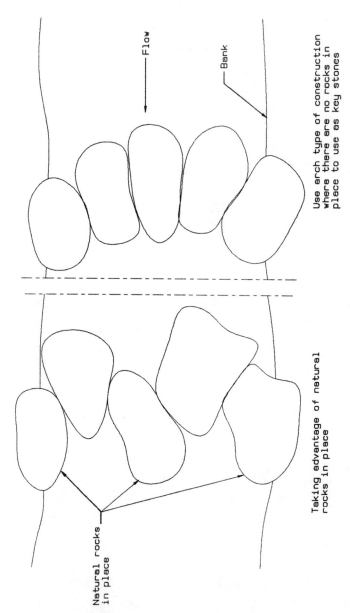

Figure 3.7b. Rock dams.

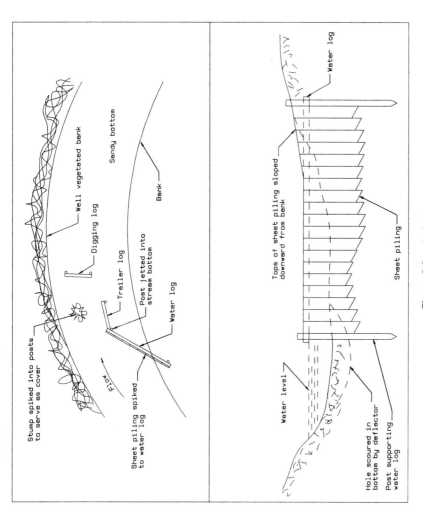

Figure 3.8. Deflectors.

made of wire mesh and posts, rock deflectors made of material obtainable from the stream area, and cabled tree deflectors, which are generally parallel to the bank with the butt of the tree pointing upstream. Limbs are left on in some cases to provide additional cover and deflection material. Care should be taken to install deflectors in such a fashion that high flows are not directed into unprotected banks.

Stream enhancement may also be achieved by random or staggered boulder placement (figure 3.9). Large, well-placed boulders are sometimes effective in producing pools and rest areas for fish, and they have the additional benefit of appearing natural. Placement cost may be relatively expensive, depending upon the size of boulder necessary to withstand seasonal flooding and the availability of material. Boulder placement should not be made in narrow channels or those with unstable banks. Boulder placement may not be necessary when the pool-riffle ratio exceeds 20 percent pools. Oblong boulders should be used and placed with the long axis at right angles to the stream flow for the best effect. This is similar to placement for rock dams but is not as great a concentration of material. A general rule of thumb is that the maximum number of boulders should not exceed 1 per 300 square feet of channel (Anonymous 1969). Boulders are also placed in clusters to increase the amount of cover. Planning, design, and placement of deflection structures should include input from either a qualified hydrologist or a hydraulic engineer.

Silt/Sediment Removal. If insufficient spawning area exists in a particular stream to obtain full seeding at either the juvenile or fry level, it may be possible to provide additional spawning gravel by cleaning existing gravel within the drainage. Improving spawning beds by cleaning fines from the gravel and rubble is accomplished by removing materials which are too small for spawning (e.g., one-eighth inch and less diameter for trout, one-fourth inch and less diameter for salmon) from potentially valuable areas. Removal of fine sediments from spawning beds is an especially beneficial technique if it can be assumed that additional fine sediment will not flow into the area. Prudence dictates establishing that the upstream fine sediment source has been reduced or contained before the expense of cleaning spawning substrate is incurred (Anonymous 1969). There are several mechanical gravel cleaners now being developed by various organizations and institutions across the country. Basically, the mechanical cleaners consist of a boat or other floating hull that is moved either by crawler feet, by propulsion of water jets, or by conventional prop. The device is moved across an area of stream where high-pressure water jets, coupled with dragging teeth to loosen the material, are blasted into the substrate. When the jets have loosened the fines or other material, a vacuum

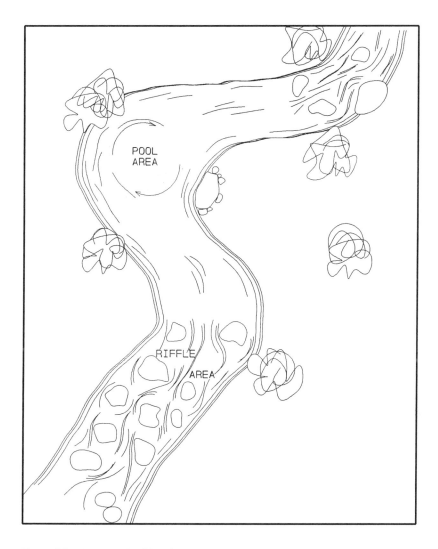

Figure 3.9. Random boulder placement.

cleaner-type device, located above the disturbed gravel, sucks in the floating sediment which is then pumped through an on-board pump and either dewatered and kept on board or sprayed up on the stream bank.

In addition to cleaning existing gravels which are of suitable size but fines embedded, it is also possible to establish additional spawning areas by placing gravel in the streams in usable areas. It is possible to do this either by trapping existing gravel in the watershed by low dams or deflectors or by introducing gravel into an area if no instream source exists. This can create a seminatural spawning habitat. Artificial spawning and hatching channels can also be established and in some cases sufficiently well controlled to reduce loss of fry and juveniles by predation. Construction of a spawning or hatching channel should be preceded by research that determines the level of need.

Barrier Removal. In an area where it may be necessary to remove a debris jam or barrier, it should be ascertained that the removal of the barrier will have a positive effect. If upstream waters are blocked, removal of a fish passage barrier may be beneficial. Removal of barriers may also permit scouring that removes silt and gravels deposited behind the jam. Each case should be assessed individually. Logjams prevent further sediment transportation and deposition downstream, but when they are removed, the debris and sediment will migrate downstream. Large debris barriers may play an important role in maintaining stream channel stability. An evaluation of the trade-offs is in order.

Fish Passage Facilities. Generally speaking, a fishway is a man-made structure designed to pass fish over a barrier. Solutions to passage problems can be achieved by blasting steps or pools in rock to modify natural barriers or the building of fish ladders to transfer fish over dams or other large barriers. Construction of fish ladders must be carefully engineered to insure that slopes are not too steep, resting areas are adequate, pools are large enough, other hydraulic conditions are satisfactory, and entrance or attractant water flows are acceptable. Generally speaking, constructed fishways are used only rarely in natural situations outside of dams or other man-made structures. There are, however, instances where fish passage devices are both necessary and cost effective. Fishways fall into several general categories: (1) pool and weir ladders, (2) Deneil, and (3) Alaskan steep pass.

Instream Flows. It is obvious that aquatic organisms require perennial water to survive. The diversion and drying up of stream segments, particularly in the West, annually result in the loss of millions of fish and potentially thousands of hours of angling enjoyment.

Many western states have developed, or are in the process of developing, instream flow legislation which allows water use to be defined as a beneficial use in the natural stream course (Reiser, Wesche, and Estes 1989). This circumvents the diversion requirement currently required by many western state water laws. Where possible, both state and federal agencies should work to obtain, either through purchase or lease agreements, rights to water that can be left in the natural stream channel, thus providing habitat for twelve months out of the year.

Riparian Zone Protection

Riparian stream vegetation is one of the most important aspects of fish habitat. Its improvement can be made by either manipulating less on existing vegetation or by planting desirable species. Plantings are generally made to increase the number or quality of existing plants or to replace those destroyed. Generally only native species are desirable. Introduction of new species should be carefully examined prior to their use (Anonymous 1969). The use of various species of willows has been highly successful (McCluskey et al. 1983). Fresh willow cuttings are obtained when dormant and planted immediately. These cuttings may be ineffective where large numbers of muskrats, deer, or cattle are present. Grasses can be used to stabilize stream banks and protect them from erosion. Again, native species should be used when possible, and exotics only when necessary. In most instances, riparian vegetation must be protected from destructive livestock grazing. A plant ecobiologist or a native plant specialist should be a part of revegetation efforts.

The riparian zone includes the area of stream bank and the floodplain. Vegetation here is usually that which is associated with the transition area between aquatic and terrestrial habitat. Ecologically a riparian zone is the interface, transition, or ecotone between the hydric (wet) and the xeric (dry) ecological community (Dasmann 1966). The benefits and importance of edge effect between two ecotypes is generally recognized as more favorable wildlife habitat than either type alone. Riparian zones are of limited size but provide important habitat components to both aquatic and terrestrial organisms. They are sensitive to impact and essential to maintaining diversity in the aquatic/terrestrial transition zone. Conditions of the riparian zones of streams are reflected in the quantity and quality of food for aquatic organisms, cover, water temperature, and sediment transport rate. The importance of riparian zones for both resident and anadromous fish is related to productivity and system stability. Streamside vegetation moderates water temperatures by reducing or limiting solar radiation, thus reducing the potential for lethal or suboptimal water temperatures.

Vegetation also reduces thermal loss during cold periods. Riparian zone vegetation provides habitat for terrestrial insects and detrital material for stream organisms. Streamside vegetation serves as a buffer zone to reduce sediment and debris loads moving into streams and regulates solar radiation affecting primary productivity (Meehan, Swanson, and Sedell 1977). Tree and shrub roots provide bank stability and overhanging cover habitat.

Concern for the condition of riparian zones has been increasing over the last ten years (Platts, Megahan, and Minshall 1983; Platts 1976, 1978, 1981; Duff and Cooper 1978). Principally in the West, cattle and sheep grazing and human-governed activities have had an impact on many areas of public land. Current research efforts to rehabilitate degraded habitat in riparian zones, identified in the early 1970s, stem from the need to mitigate or eliminate the adverse effects of degraded riparian zones both on those zones and the contiguous aquatic habitat. Several ways to protect riparian zones have been investigated. Among the options are (1) improve animal distribution, (2) change the season of animal use, (3) rest the area until recovery, (4) fence the riparian zone, (5) eliminate grazing, or (6) fence the stream corridor. Doing nothing and allowing continued degradation should not be considered a viable option.

Fenced Exclosures. Fences are used to prevent access to riparian zones by cattle and sheep. While fencing is effective, it is also costly. Platts and Wagstaff (1984) report costs of $6,000 per stream mile for two 100-foot corridors and $60 to $200 per stream mile per year for maintenance. In some areas of the West, estimates as high as $15,000 for a 100-foot-by-1-mile corridor and $500 per year maintenance are not uncommon. These high costs, in many cases, result in an unfavorable cost-benefit ratio, but where other options are unavailable, fencing may be required. Platts and Wagstaff estimate that fencing two 100-foot corridors on a stream would eliminate twelve animal unit months (AUMs) per stream mile. A careful analysis of the benefits that can be reasonably expected (e.g., increased angler days and subsequent catch) should be completed prior to any fencing project. Many test or research areas show the results obtainable with fencing. In many cases a direct relationship can be shown between fencing and increase in fishable populations (e.g., reduction of nongame species and increase in number of game species). Fencing may result in increased fish production, reduction of stream width, and increase in stream depth.

The No-Grazing Option. The option of eliminating or restricting (reducing) grazing has not been feasible in most areas. This is due primarily to economic and political considerations (Platts and Wagstaff 1984). Range users perceive grazing restrictions as a curtailment of their "vested rights" that they deem are associated with long and generally uninterrupted permit usage of the area (Nielsen et al. 1977).

No grazing (or fenced enclosures) offers the best mechanism for recovery of impacted areas and protection of riparian zones and associated aquatic habitat. However, when rest/rotation, deferred, or other grazing strategies will not achieve desired results, other alternatives must be examined.

Riparian Zone Planting. One of the more important functions of riparian zones is reduction of incident solar radiation and a subsequent lowering of summer stream temperatures. In areas where natural vegetation has been removed or degraded, plantings of various species of trees may provide increased shade and cover. Well-developed stands of trees provide direct cover from overhanging branches and indirect cover by shading. Root mosses may also provide additional cover within stabilized undercut banks (McCluskey et al. 1983). Substantial amounts of terrestrial insects and detrital material are contributed by riparian vegetation. This provides a direct food source and an indirect source of fish food through utilization by aquatic invertebrates (Reiser and Bjornn 1979; Meehan, Swanson, and Sedell 1977).

Plantings should be structured so as to promote project objectives. Gaps in the plantings left in riffle areas will increase diversity and promote solar penetration which increases macroinvertebrate populations. Open areas of more than 25 percent of total stream length will promote higher temperatures, potentially an adverse impact for coldwater or coolwater species. McCluskey et al. (1983) provide information on techniques for selecting, collecting, preparing, planting, and maintaining willow. Varied techniques for other species are reported by Hudak 1982 and Everett, Meeuwig, and Robertson 1978.

Cover and Cover Structures. Cover can be defined as those instream areas providing fish protection from the effects of high current velocities and predation (Wesche and Rachard 1980). Cover can be provided along a stream or a lake in a number of fashions. It may be by overhanging or submerged vegetation, submerged objects such as rocks and stumps, or undercut banks. Cover requirements and utilization varies by species and size. Requirements may also vary diurnally (Wesche 1973; Chapman and Bjornn 1969).

Overhead cover may be provided by plantings in the riparian zone. Instream structures are provided by boulder placement, the use of log weirs or half-log structures, or other structures. Use of half-log structures has proved successful in providing cover for resident trout in Wisconsin (Hunt 1978) and is being evaluated in areas in California (Reeves and Roelofs 1982).

Sufficient data exist to indicate that more fish will remain in a stream with cover than in a stream from which cover has been removed (Elser 1968; Peters and Alvord 1964; Boussu 1954). It is therefore important in stream reclamation projects to provide cover compatible with the size, number, and species of fish anticipated from the stream rehabilitation project.

Predator/Competitor Reduction/Removal

Complete removal of undesirable fish is generally attempted by using toxicants with Food and Drug Administration (FDA)-approved chemicals such as rotenone and, rarely, by drainage, which is practical only in small, specially constructed ponds or lakes. Toxicants are moderately expensive, rarely provide 100 percent kill, and their use may evoke the ire of environmentalists and some ichthyologists. There are, however, times when the use of toxicants appears to be the only answer to making a body of water productive for recreational fisheries. Partial or spot removal of undesirable fish by chemicals usually involves treatment of inlets and other areas that can be isolated. Selective toxicants such as squoxin, antimycin, and lamprecides have also been successful in some situations.

Cumming (1975) lists three principle reasons why fish are killed in management operations. The most prevalent rationale is removal of an existing fish population so that a different population, which will better meet public fishing demands, can be established. This may include removal of nonnative species to allow reestablishment of native species (e.g., cutthroat trout). Some managers stock different species, adjust species composition, or restore earlier endemic populations through selective, partial, or total fish kills. This mechanism allows the fishery manager to eliminate or at least reduce undesirable fish populations and replace them with more desirable ones. The second reason is the removal of unwanted fish by fish culturists in production ponds designed to raise only one species. This technique is also used to sustain a disease-free stock, without the effects of an introduced and unwanted second species. A third rationale for the use of fish toxicants is to remove undesired species in fish production ponds resulting in increased conversion from fish food to fish flesh or clean out previously used ponds in preparation for a new crop. Some southeastern states routinely treat and remove fish from sport fishing ponds prior to restocking with either the same or additional species. A more complete discussion of fish removal through the use of toxicants is included in chapter 8.

Mechanical removal techniques such as haul seines, gill nets, traps, and electric grids may remove large numbers of undesirable fish, but these operations often are quite expensive and have limited effect. In many cases it must be a continuous process if it is to be effective. Cost may be offset in part by the sale of the fish.

Before a removal program is instigated there should be sound biological evidence indicating that reduction or removal of the competitors or predators is feasible with the method proposed and of long-term benefit. Attempts to eradicate or markedly reduce large numbers of undesirable fish in large lakes or sections of large streams is both difficult and expensive. Commercial fishing operations have had somewhat limited success in some areas. Toxicants are almost never 100 percent effective and thereby leave a seed population. Before a fish is determined to be a serious predator or competitor of a desirable species, biological information should be gathered which strongly indicates that there is strong competition or predation. Only rarely are these facts obtainable to the degree that allows for a clear-cut decision. One example where this is true is the presence of sunfish or other centrarchids in commercial fee fishing or rearing ponds for channel catfish. In this instance it is possible to remove the undesirable fish by selective level poisoning with a toxicant such as antimycin at doses that affect only scaled fishes. Use of a species-specific toxicant such as squoxin may be indicated where squawfish are preying on salmonids.

Refuges

While refuges have been successfully used for terrestrial wildlife and waterfowl, only rarely are they used for fish. Refuges are used primarily for threatened and endangered species where areas can be set aside and fishing either eliminated or controlled. On occasion a fish normally considered a game fish needs sanctuary in some areas or some portions of its range (e.g., stream spawning grayling and spawning areas for steelhead trout or salmon). Law enforcement problems associated with maintaining refuges include all of the problems of law enforcement elsewhere plus either posting or building and maintaining physical barriers to restrict access to the refuge area. If the refuge is accessible to the public, the consideration of illegal taking of fish must be included in its management. A refuge for some twenty-five species and subspecies of nongame fish, plants, and invertebrates has been established in Ash Meadows, Nye County, Nevada, as a result of concern for the Devils Hole pupfish and other endemic species.

Opportunity

Opportunity fulfills the fishery management goal of providing fish for anglers to catch. Opportunity should be both varied over time and place and available to as large a number of anglers as is possible within the overall management plan. The concept of opportunity entails providing the most desirable fishing potential (from the angler's perspective) for the most anglers in all available waters. Opportunity is also related to total harvest and must therefore be modified to some extent by the biological considerations associated with the stocks being fished. This necessitates that some level of information be available on the amount of fishing a particular population can sustain. An additional consideration is what period or periods of the year would be most beneficial to the angler while still protecting the biological requirements of the species, such as spawning runs. Opportunity is thus related to knowledge of the stocks and habitats in which they exist and must be assessed through the use of fishery management techniques, such as electrofishing, and tools such as stocking and regulations.

Part Two—Concepts

The first part of this chapter presented distinctive individual actions that can be taken by managers and biologists or which can be used in a specific singular instance. The remainder presents two broad concepts under which the specific tools discussed can be incorporated or utilized. The first section, the Zone Management Concept, presents a theoretical procedure for managing fisheries within predefined geographic settings (zones) surrounding metropolitan areas. The second section deals with urban fisheries. Urban fisheries is a concept whose time has come. Increased recreational demands by intercity and metropolitan-area dwellers necessitates that fishing opportunities be provided in the immediate area of the population center. This can be achieved in various ways outlined below.

Both management concepts developed in this part rely on the management tools previously discussed as well as the data collection techniques covered elsewhere in this volume. Integration of these techniques and procedures into a management scheme for either a zone-managed fishery or an urban fishery will assist managers and research biologists in utilizing to the fullest the resources available within either a set of zones or within a developed urban area.

The Zone Management Concept

Realistically, a legal fishing entity, a state or province, should be zoned around two major points: centers of population and potential areas of fish production by species. In relation to production, it is obvious that the larger a fish, the more food it has eaten; and if it is piscivorous rather than an invertebrate herbivore, it has eaten still more biomass. This is reflected in food conversion estimates at 5:1 for fish, 10:1 for invertebrates, and 20:1 for plant material. A 20-pound northern pike or brown trout is quite a valuable item to anglers. They cannot reasonably expect to catch fish like this other than occasionally. Just as obvious is the fact that these fish will rarely be produced in heavily fished small farm ponds or urban fisheries. Rather they will be produced in areas at some distance from metropolitan areas. This takes us back to the theory of zoning.

Consider the following hypothetical example of a set of population centers and several zones around them (figure 3.10). In practice there will be several to many centers of population in a state, and the number and radius of zones will vary considerably and may in fact overlap. Logistics in the states of Delaware, Alaska, and Texas are different in the extreme.

Inner Zone

The inner zone is that area around, or closest to, the centers of population where there is not only the greatest density of anglers but also the largest number of people who can or will travel only a short distance to fish. The reasons for this limitation may range from age or health to economics to limited time. Those individuals close to easily accessible waters (within a 50-mile radius) should have large numbers of relatively easy-to-catch fish, warmwater panfish such as bluegill, crappie, and bullhead. There may also be yellow perch, pickerel, carp, and buffalo. The fish should be abundant enough to produce a high catch rate. The number of these fish that can be taken should be relatively high and the restrictions on gear and bait liberal. The open season for warmwater fish will normally be ten to twelve months; on temperate and coldwater species, it will sometimes be more limited. Where habitat and reared fish are available, a put-and-take fishery may be desirable. The catch limit of these fish will be low, perhaps two to four fish. Stocking densities and frequencies should be sufficient to sustain effort (determined by capture surveys). These fish, often trout, are eagerly sought by youngsters and adults alike. The obvious limitation is funding; there is also the avowed disapproval of "wild

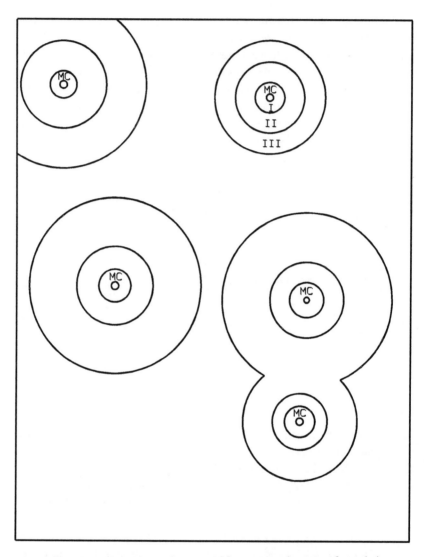

Figure 3.10. Zone Management Concept. MC represents the areas of population concentration; I = inner zone; II = median zone; III = outer zone which may have a radius greater than 200 miles.

fish only" anglers, but when fish are planted near populations centers, their protests are generally mild. In the back country, this may not be true.

Small impoundments where total catch can be managed by access limitations or catch restrictions often produce acceptable sport, especially for people willing to spend much time, but only limited money. All of this does not mean there may be no larger or more sought after fish in the inner zone. It simply means they will be something extra and not the mainstay of the zone fishery.

In addition to easy access, the inner zone may need special parking areas, fish-cleaning facilities, access for handicapped individuals, restrooms, launch ramps, and at times a public-relations-oriented conservation officer. Regulations should be posted and enjoyment of the sport emphasized. Whatever type of habitat is available will be, insofar as possible, adapted to these myriads of people. It is here that fishery biologists cater to the multitudes, not the elite.

Median Zone

The median zone (50 to 200 miles) will be more attractive to those anglers who have enough time, funds, and gear to travel to where there are fewer, but hopefully bigger or more prized fish. Travel may be distant, but not remote or inaccessible. This zone must sustain the fishery primarily by natural recruitment. The exception may be an occasional replenishment of brood stock or the introduction of a new species. Species predominantly sought will be brown trout, lake trout, steelhead trout, salmon, grayling, largemouth and smallmouth bass, northern pike, muskellunge, walleye, striped bass, and channel catfish. In general, large bodies of water will be open to year-round fishing. Small streams supporting coldwater fish may be the exception. Gear may be restricted and live bait prohibited. Catch rate will be low. Many median zone waters will be man-made, usually very large, reservoirs. Public facilities may be limited to parking areas and an occasional boat ramp. In national recreation areas facilities will be more elaborate. Trips to these areas will generally be for more than one day, and fishing may be combined with other recreational activities.

Outer Zone

The outer zone (more than 200 miles) is for those nomads who go where the fish are and stay until they are satisfied. They are looking primarily for a record-size fish, a fish that for some reason has a unique appeal, or for an experience that not everyone can participate in. These anglers require little or no assistance and are satisfied with their own effort. Stocking in these areas is only under disaster conditions or with the rare introduction of a new species. Fish species sought in this zone will include most of those in the median zone, but for various reasons the fishing experience will be more valuable. These areas may be wild rivers, wilderness areas, remote mountains, or large lakes and reservoirs. Seasons, except possibly for high-altitude country, are open most or all of the year. The number of trophy fish taken may be limited to one or two. Restrictions on fish as bait (particularly live fish) may be enforced. The catch rate for large fish may be as low as one or two per week and most of these will be released. Public facilities will be limited to loading ramps. In high or remote country, generally no public facilities are available. In this zone the biologist can point to these anglers' successes as his or her own, and neither will be unhappy for it.

The Urban Fishing Concept

Urban fishing is a segment of outdoor recreation that is in urgent need of attention and development, but it cannot be approached in the traditional manner. Millions of people, for economic or other reasons, can travel only short distances to fish. This includes children, senior citizens, carless households, unemployed, and low-income families. Their needs for recreation are in a sense greater than many others because often they have few alternatives. Duttweiler (1984) defines urban fishing as a program for residents of urban areas who do not otherwise have access to fishing. This, he says, is especially true for the poor, the elderly, some minorities, and the handicapped. The promoters of urban fishing believe there is an obligation to provide access to fishing for most or all members of society, and they think they are responding to what is considered fair. Social values support urban fishing over concerns about whether these programs can be economically justified (Botts 1984). These people are a human resource who can be helped with a natural resource that is vastly underused in many urban areas. The need and the resource are there, but bringing the two together is neither simplistic nor easy.

Local Support

At least the first and perhaps most urgent need is local support. Without this, most programs are doomed to early failure, or more likely, an inability to even get started. Preliminary work may, at best, take years of teamwork and broad-based support. The first requirement is support from top-level state fishery administrators. However, in some instances, urban fishing practices may be in conflict with state policy (Shupp 1980). Next and perhaps equal in support importance is the mayor and other city administrators and, in some cases, county administrators. City administrative support is needed at all stages. The city also needs to provide places to fish and at least partial funding. The city may eventually take partial or, ideally, complete control over the program. Fishing derbies and clinics are a major means of promotion and development of community support and involvement. (Special Olympics programs offer a model [Schedler and Haynes 1984]). Civic leaders should be brought into the program at its inception. They can form a citizens' committee that will advise, raise funds, coordinate other groups, and provide moral support. Industry should be called on to offer advice, funds, meeting facilities, and access to fishing areas. Other support can come from the Corps of Engineers, civic clubs, churches, youth clubs, Scouts, anglers' clubs, armed forces organizations, war and police veterans, local law enforcement agencies, and sea- and land-grant universities.

Urban fishing programs cannot be financed in the same way as traditional programs where a user-fee concept prevails and the programs are financed through licensing fees. Although there are no federal programs to provide direct funding for urban fishing, federal agencies such as the Fish and Wildlife Service have provided technical assistance and information (Jantzen 1984). The National Marine Fisheries Services also provides volunteer personnel and education programs (Gordon 1984). Dingell-Johnson funds have been used in several cases, and the Wallop-Breaux funds now available may also be used. Some federal programs for coastal zone management and urban renewal can provide indirect support. However, most urban fishing programs are initiated and financed by cooperation between state and local agencies. Corporate and business sources may provide support, but they must be approached in person and receive recognition for their contribution (Jones 1984).

A focus on fishing can result in a greater awareness for maintaining a healthy, productive environment, particularly for children. Annual workshops in the Washington, D.C., area supported by several federal agencies, local government, and representatives of private clubs have conducted successful workshops.

Manager Problems

Fishery managers must be people-oriented to succeed with urban fishing programs. They must have tolerance for cultural differences, understanding of the needs of the clientele, and a willingness to adapt the program to the needs of the people. In urban fishing, even the fish have to be people-oriented (Botts 1984). It must be understood at the outset that conventional approaches to fishery management are inadequate for urban fishing. A detailed short-term and a long-term plan should be drawn before contact is made with the target area. The plan of operation will include feasibility, scope, budgetary benefits and costs. Also to be considered are projected fishing sites in relation to centers of potential anglers, stocking policy including number, size, and species, and an evaluation of water quality including potential or known problems.

The manager may need to learn how to shape the program for education of clients with different needs from those of traditional anglers. Where they have been trained to develop a fishing program according to species, Ditton and Fedler (1984) say that urban fishing requires that fishery managers adopt a consumptive orientation that gives highest preference to anglers. Managers also need to learn how to work directly with anglers or to develop volunteers who will be able to work with them. In some cases, urban fishing may be conceived of as a means of teaching respect for private property and the rights of others. It can also be a means of teaching immigrants about the cultural values of North American society. Education rather than law enforcement may be used to teach them the views of their adopted society, while at the same time respecting their cultural background (Botts 1984). Angler problems include providing public transportation, so it is important to locate urban fishing sites near public transportation (Pulliam 1984). Breen (1984) urges fishery managers to approach urban developers and planning agencies about the need of access to fishing sites as a part of a waterfront development that she says is occurring in many major cities today. This, incidentally, appears to be borne out by numerous newspaper articles.

Erection of sanitation facilities at fishing sites is often needed, including fish-cleaning stations. There should be on-site safety devices in these areas, such as at piers, docks, bulkheads, and shore areas. Fishing skills and fish handling, sometimes including cooking, developing an interpretive program, fish identification and conservation, and broadly related social events should be taught. And last, but not least, angler satisfaction is an important consideration for fishery developers and managers.

Anglers may be expected to fish for fun or for food, and recognizing the difference is important. Even where recreation is the chief aim, sport and challenge are less important in urban fishing than the likelihood of success. Any fish is a trophy to a child as long as he or she catches it. Some urbanites fish to be out of doors and in a natural setting, but the prime motivation is still to catch fish. Urban fishing frequently involves bringing fish to where the people are instead of vice versa (Botts 1984).

Although an urban fishing program may be the work of several agencies, a single one must take the lead. Early site selection and planning are essential if the program is to succeed. Botts (1984) states that, in his view, the fishery manager must share responsibility for every aspect of urban fishing because the public does not distinguish between agencies in assigning responsibility or for assuring the fish caught are safe for consumption.

Aquaculture programs may, at times, be the keystone for the successful urban fishing program, but it should be recognized that the number of culturable species is limited. Nakamura (1984) states that the important groups include sunfishes, perches, pikes, minnows, and cichlids.

Mayo (1984) suggests a checklist of ten items that should be carefully considered when designing facilities for urban fishing. They are: (1) When the responsibility is passed to you, make sure you understand the scope of the work, the budget, the time frame, and get it in writing. (2) Select an in-house consulting firm that is in tune with the project's objectives and has at least some related experience. (3) When choosing consultants, concentrate on the projects that they have built and talk to those owners. (4) Know the site. (5) Make sure the project is carefully reviewed at the preliminary design stage. (6) Review preliminary plans for both the construction and function. (7) Check for such things as handicap access, parking, restrooms, fire protection, and zone compliance. (8) Go over your plans with other agencies which have done the same thing. (9) Since the projects are often small and sometimes nonstandard, prepare construction plans with special care. (10) Keep in mind who will be operating the facility, and keep maintenance simple.

Public Benefits

Fishing is recognized as a pastime that is both mentally and physically beneficial. This is especially true when it keeps young people off the streets and away from the temptation of crime. Senior citizens, low-income families, handicapped, and other people with no private transportation profit from this type of recreation. It may also supplement their food budget. The urban fishing program offers several opportunities for private enterprise. Wildlife resource departments profit from these programs by selling additional licenses and, more importantly, by projecting a positive public image.

Both communities and individuals can benefit from an urban fishing program in many ways. It can save energy in the metropolitan area by having sources of fishing close to home. Such things as close-in boat ramps can provide easy access to fishing. Youth and family fishing activities bring families closer together and help them enjoy these lifetime experiences (Gordon 1984).

According to Gordon, Chicago's police department is starting a youth program in cooperation with the American Fishing Tackle Manufacturer's Association and other corporate sponsors. Using a big brother approach, officers adopt a youth for the duration of the angler training program. This has, in many cases, resulted in a positive experience and relationship between youth and police. Reduction of crime and an increased awareness of the environment are two potential benefits.

Private Enterprise

There are substantial opportunities to sell bait, fishing gear, food, and fuel. Needed services include guides, party boats, charter boats, ground transportation, boat rental, and fee-fishing ponds. An aggressive urban fishing program can enhance the economy of the community and bring in new ventures, particularly with capital-improvement projects. When attention has been focused on the waterfront, the need for additional facilities such as boat ramps, bait and tackle shops, and marinas is recognized, and they can be built and operated by both public and private funds. As fishing increases, so do sales. An additional benefit is that as more people become intrigued with fishing, more seafood will be eaten. When this happens, both public and private organizations become interested in expanding the program. It is believed that many potential tourists would like to combine sightseeing with fishing. Since most tourists end up in major cities, the first step would be to provide them with an urban fishing experience (Gordon 1984).

Places to Fish

Places to fish in cities may be numerous, including shore areas, streams, lakes, canals, ponds, barrow pits, gravel pits, piers, jetties, bulkheads, fishing platforms, day fishing facilities, and occasionally portable pools (figure 3.11).

Sources of Fish and Species Stocked

Fish can be acquired from salvage operations, fish hatcheries, private industry, donations, or transferred from low to high fishing pressure areas.

Almost any species of fish that can be caught by hook and line may be stocked in urban fishing areas. The commonly used ones include sunfishes,

Figure 3.11. Fishing in an urban area (photograph by Dale Kerbs).

crappies, black basses, catfishes (generally channel catfish and black bullhead), trouts (mostly rainbow trout), common carp, and, occasionally, northern pike.

Discussion

The success of an urban fishing program depends on several obvious tangibles such as adequate fishing sites and public interest and support. There are less tangible, but equally important factors, such as angler satisfaction, catch rate, species composition of the catch, and the pleasure of the experience. Shupp (1980) lists as job objectives for the New York fishing program: making it an integral part of the park and recreational programs, obtaining funds, and helping mobility-restricted anglers. Citizen's committees that are incorporated as nonprofit organizations have several advantages including the ability to receive donations. The New York state urban fishing program uses comic books to stimulate interest in fishing and to develop skills (Shupp). Chicago, which initiated an urban fishing program in 1985, also uses a comic book promotion (Temple Reynolds, personal communication, 1985). Many potential anglers are turned off by pollution or litter in the water. Aesthetic appeal is eliminated by many negative factors. Pollution also raises concerns about the palatability and even the safety of eating these fish.

In one New York pond, anglers averaged 1.24 bullheads per hour fished. This was the best catch rate for any area. Ninety-six percent of the stocked bullheads were caught. The fishing pressure on this pond was 1209 hours of fishing per surface acre per year. The New York programs are publicized by television, radio, outdoor columnists, comic books, YMCAs, YWCAs, citizens' committees, slide shows, and school programs. The resource department biologists often act as coordinators rather than directors of the program.

Quintrell, Young, and McSwain (1981) summarize the use of publicly owned fishing or controlled areas in six southeastern states. These areas are almost always near the centers of population and are used heavily by people who often would not otherwise fish. Georgia operates six public fishing areas totaling 509 acres. Alabama operates or manages twenty-two public lakes, and a concession sells permits, bait, and tackle, and rents boats. South Carolina owns eleven public fishing lakes totaling approximately 1,300 acres and leases two additional ones. North Carolina manages about forty municipal water supply lakes owned by other agencies. Management options on these waters are quite limited due to priorities of the controlling agencies (e.g., drinking water). The small ponds owned by the state receive intensive management. Florida has twelve state-owned lakes ranging in size from 55 to 350 acres. The program also has sixty-five lakes, canals, and barrow pits ranging in size from

29 to 12,000 acres. Arkansas has twenty-five state-owned public fishing areas ranging in size from 60 to 6,700 acres.

The policy of the Colorado Division of Wildlife for the management of urban lakes consists of stocking salvaged warmwater fish. Species commonly used are bluegill, green sunfish, black basses, yellow perch, and both black and white crappies. Catchable rainbow trout stocking is limited to a few areas, principally Denver, which receives a large portion of all catchables stocked. In Barbour Pond, the minimum cost to the creel was $1.42/pound during a two-year period when salvaged fish were used. During the third year the cost increased to $1.90/pound. Cost per angler hour was $0.07 for the first two years and $0.17 for the third year. Hatching techniques were developed to rear fathead minnows and goldfish to be used as forage for bluegill and bass (Powell 1976).

Urban fishing pressure in some St. Louis lakes is incredibly high—in one instance 12,140 angler hours per acre per year. Catch rates in these urban lakes were low—0.176 pounds/hour. Angler preference was channel catfish and/or bullheads, followed by carp, largemouth bass, and bluegill. This is much different than the preference of most Missourians from other areas. Catching a preferred fish was an important component of an enjoyable trip as was the size and number of fish taken, an indication that urban angling in St. Louis is primarily for food fish (Alcorn 1981).

The Detroit area is unique in that it has potential for an almost unlimited variety of fisheries developments. Sites include piers, shorelines, docks, ponds, streams, and barrow pits. Emphasis is placed on stocking. Each year large numbers of trout and salmon are planted in the Detroit metro area. Education and interpretive services cover fishing, outdoor education, general fish and wildlife information, and nature centers. Private concessions add to the quality of the program (Fogle 1978).

An estimated 312,000 angler trips were made to forty-four fishing sites including piers, docks, and jetties in Puget Sound in 1981. The catch was 192,000 fish plus 5,500 pounds of herring and surf smelt. The annual catch per trip for all anglers was 0.62 fish. For all trips, 81 percent of the anglers caught no fish, 9 percent caught one fish, 3 percent caught two fish, and 5 percent caught more than two fish (Bargmann 1982).

Room for the Elitist

Somewhere in all of the varied management schemes and options must be a place for the elitist—the pure fly angler and the catch-and-release crowd who enjoy catching a fish and releasing it more than keeping it. Fish for these indi-

Figure 3.12.   Fishing in a rural area.

viduals must be truly wild. This generally means a remote mountain stream or section of stream is set aside with special regulations, such as catch-and-release or flies only. Generally these areas are in the median or outer zone, but occasionally they may be in the inner zone. The numbers of anglers are not great but their influence often is (figure 3.12).

In some instances, it may be possible to incorporate the needs of the elitist into urban or zone management concepts. The South Platte River near Denver supports a catch-and-release fishery of approximately 3,000 hour/acre/year (Robert Behnke, personal communication, 1986).

Literature Cited

Alcorn, S. R. 1981. Fishing Quality in Urban Fishing Lakes, St. Louis, Missouri. *North American Journal of Fisheries Management* 1(1):80–84.

Alexander, G. 1971. Dynamics of Brook Trout in Hunt Creek, Closed to Fishing. Pp. 103–8 in Michigan Project No. F–30–R–4. No. 1. 1 July 1969 to 30 June 1970.

Anderson, R. O. 1975. Optimum Sustainable Yield in Inland Recreational Fisheries Management. Pp. 29–38 in P. M. Roedel, ed., *Optimum Sustainable Yield as a Concept in Fisheries Management, Proceedings of a Symposium at the 104th Annual Meeting of the American Fisheries Society, Sept. 9, 1974, Honolulu, HI*. Washington, D.C.: American Fisheries Society. Special Publication 9.

————. 1976. Management of Small Warm Water Impoundments. *Fisheries* 1(6):5–7, 26–28.

————. 1980. Proportional Stock Density (PSD) and Relative Weight (W_r): Interpretive Indices for Fish Populations and Communities. Pp. 27–33 in S. Gloss and B. Shupp, eds., *Practical Fisheries Management: More With Less in the 1980's, Proceedings of the 1st Annual Workshop of the New York Cooperative Fishery Research Unit, Ithaca, New York*.

Anderson, R. O., and S. J. Gutreuter. 1983. Length, Weight, and Associated Structural Indices. Pp. 283–300 in L. A. Nielsen, and D. L. Johnson, eds., *Fisheries Techniques*. Bethesda, Md.: American Fisheries Society.

Anderson, R. O., and A. S. Weithman. 1978. The Concept of Balance for Coolwater Fish Population. *American Fisheries Society Special Publication* 11:371–81.

Anonymous. 1969. Wildlife Habitat Improvement Handbook. U.S. Department of Agriculture, U.S. Forest Service, FSH 2609.11. 252 pp.

Armour, C. L., R. J. Fisher, and J. W. Terrell. 1984. *Comparison of the Use of the Habitat Evaluation Procedures (HEP) and the Instream Flow Incremental Methodology (IFIM) in Aquatic Analyses*. Washington, D.C.: U.S. Fish and Wildlife Service, FWS/OBS–84/11. 30 pp.

Bargmann, G. 1982. *Recreational Angling from Piers, Docks and Jetties in Puget Sound, Washington During 1981*. State of Washington, Department of Fisheries, Technical Report No. 73. 37 pp.

Bavin, C. R. 1985. Management of Undercover Operations in Wildlife Law Enforcement. Paper presented at the Annual Business Meeting of the International Association of Fish and Wildlife Agencies, September 8–12, 1985, Sun Valley, Idaho.

Bond, R. S., and J. C. Whittaker. 1971. Hunter-Fisherman Characteristics: Factors in Wildlife Management and Policy Decisions. Pp. 128–34 in *Recreational Symposium Proceedings*. Upper Darby, Penn.: Northeastern Forest Experiment Station, U.S. Forest Service, U.S. Department of Agriculture.

Botts, L. 1984. Symposium Summary. Pp. 284–88 in L. J. Allen, ed., *Urban Fishing Symposium*. Bethesda, Md.: American Fisheries Society.

Boussu, M. F. 1954. Relationship Between Trout Populations and Cover on a Small Stream. *Journal of Wildlife Management* 18(2):229–39.

Bovee, K. D. 1974. *The Determination, Assessment, and Design of "Instream Value" Studies for the Northern Great Plains Region*. Northern Plains Resources Program. 204 pp.

———. 1978. *Probability-of-Use Criteria for the Family Salmonidae*. Instream Flow Information Paper 4. Washington, D.C.: U.S. Fish and Wildlife Service, FWS/OBS–78/07. 80 pp.

———. 1982. *A Guide to Stream Habitat Analysis Using the Instream Flow Incremental Methodology*. Instream Flow Information Paper 12. Washington, D.C.: U.S. Fish and Wildlife Service, FWS–OBS–82/26. 248 pp.

Bovee, K. D., and T. Cochnauer. 1977. *Development and Evaluation of Weighted Criteria, Probability-of-Use Curves for Instream Flow Assessments: Fisheries*. Instream Flow Information Paper 3. Washington, D.C.: U.S. Fish and Wildlife Service, FWS/OBS–77/63. 38 pp.

Bovee, K. D., and R. T. Milhous. 1978. *Hydraulic Simulation in Instream Flow Studies: Theory and Techniques*. Instream Flow Information Paper 5. Washington, D.C.: U.S. Fish and Wildlife Service, FWS/OBS–78/33. 130 pp.

Breen, A. E. 1984. Urban Fishing and Waterfront Development. Pp. 98–102 in L. J. Allen, ed., *Urban Fishing Symposium*. Bethesda, Md.: American Fisheries Society.

Bullock, G. L. and K. Wolf. 1986. *Infectious Diseases of Cultured Fishes: Current Perspectives*. U.S. Fish and Wildlife Service, Leaflet 5. National Fish Health Research Laboratory. Kearneysville, W.V. 13 pp.

Canadian Department of Fisheries and Oceans, British Columbia Ministry of the Environment. 1980. *Stream Enhancement Guide*. Vancouver: Salmonid Enhancement Program, Canadian Department of Fisheries and Oceans, British Columbia Ministry of the Environment. 82 pp.

Carlton, F. E. 1975. Optimum Sustainable Yield as a Management Concept in Recreational Fisheries. Pp. 45–49 in P. M. Roedel, ed., *Optimum Sustainable Yield as a Concept in Fisheries Management, Proceedings of a Symposium at the 104th Annual Meeting of the American Fisheries Society, Sept. 9, 1974, Honolulu, HI.* Washington, D.C.: American Fisheries Society. Special Publication 9.

Chapman, D. W., and T. C. Bjornn. 1969. Distribution of Salmonids in Streams, with Special Reference to Food and Feeding. Pp. 153–76 in *Symposium on Salmon and*

Trout in Streams, H. R. MacMillan Lectures in Fisheries. Vancouver: University of British Columbia.

Chapman, D. W., S. Pettit, and K. Ball. 1973. *Evaluation of Catch and Release Regulations in Management of Cutthroat Trout*. Annual Progress Report, Project F–59–R–4, Idaho Department of Fish and Game, Boise, Idaho. 18 pp.

Chrystie, E. L. 1965. Experiment in Fun. *The Conservancy* 19(6):2–4.

Clark, R. D., Jr. 1983. Potential Effects of Voluntary Catch and Release of Fish on Recreational Fisheries. *North American Journal of Fisheries Management* 3(3):306–14.

Cumming, K. B. 1975. History of Fish Toxicants in the United States. Pp. 5–21 in P. H. Eschmeyer, ed., *Rehabilitation of Fish Populations with Toxicants: A Symposium*. North Central Division, American Fisheries Society. Special Publication 4.

Dasmann, R. F. 1966. *Wildlife Biology*. New York: John Wiley and Sons, Inc. 231 pp.

Davis, H. S. 1934. The Purpose and Value of Stream Improvement. *Transactions of the American Fisheries Society* 64(1):63–67.

D'Itri, F. M., ed. 1985. *Artificial Reefs, Marine and Freshwater Applications*. Chelsea, Mich.: Lewis Publishers, Inc. 589 pp.

Ditton, R. B., and A. J. Fedler. 1984. Towards an Understanding of Experience Preferences of Urban Anglers. Pp. 55–63 in L. J. Allen, ed., *Urban Fishing Symposium*. Bethesda, Md.: American Fisheries Society.

Driver, B. L., and R. C. Knopf. 1976. Temporary Escape, One Product of Sports Fisheries Management. *Fisheries* 1(2):21, 24–29.

Duff, D. A., and J. L. Cooper. 1978. *Techniques for Conducting Stream Habitat Surveys on National Resource Land*. Technical Note 283. Denver, Colo.: U.S. Department of the Interior, Bureau of Land Management. 77 pp.

Duttweiler, M. W. 1984. Training Needs of Urban Fishing Planning and Management Personnel. Pp. 67–70 in L. J. Allen, ed., *Urban Fishing Symposium*. Bethesda, Md.: American Fisheries Society.

Elser, A. A. 1968. Fish Populations of a Trout Stream in Relation to Major Habitat Zones and Channel Alterations. *Transactions of the American Fisheries Society* 97(4):389–97.

Everest, F. H., and J. R. Sedell. 1984. Evaluating Effectiveness of Stream Enhancement Projects. Pp. 246–56 in T. J. Hassler, ed., *Proceedings of the Pacific Northwest Stream Habitat Management Workshop, October 10–12, 1984, Humboldt State University, Arcata, California*. American Fisheries Society, California Cooperative Fishery Research Unit, California Sea Grant, Humboldt State University.

Everest, F. H., and J. R. Sedell. 1985. Enhancing Enhancement Through Evaluation—Exposing New Options. Paper presented at the 1985 National American Fisheries Society Meeting, September 8–12, 1985, Sun Valley, Idaho.

Everett, R. L., R. Meeuwig, and J. H. Robertson. 1978. Propagation of Nevada Shrubs by Stem Cuttings. *Journal of Range Management* 3(6):426–29.

Everhart, W. H., and W. D. Youngs. 1981. *Principles of Fishery Science*. Second Edition. Ithaca and London: Comstock Publishing Associates. 350 pp.

Fajen, O. F. 1981. Warmwater Stream Management with Emphasis on Bass Streams in Missouri. Pp. 262–65 in *American Fisheries Society Warmwater Stream Symposium*.

Fausch, K. D., and M. G. Parsons. 1986. *A Review of Models that Predict Standing Crop of Stream Fish from Habitat Variables*. Fort Collins, Colo.: U.S. Department of Agriculture, U.S. Forest Service. 53 pp.

Fearnow, T. C. 1941. An Appraisal of Stream Improvement Programs of the National Forests of the Northeastern States. *Transactions of the North American Wildlife Conference* 6:161–68.

Fogle, N. E. 1978. *Michigan's Proposal for a Recreational Fishing Program*. Michigan Department of Natural Resources, Fisheries Division, Technical Report No. 78–2. 33 pp.

Gabelhouse, D. W., Jr. 1984. A Length-Categorization System to Assess Fish Stocks. *North American Journal of Fisheries Management* 4(3):273–85.

Gard, R. 1961. Creation of Trout Habitat by Constructing Small Dams. *Journal of Wildlife Management* 25(4):384–90.

Goede, R. W. 1986. Management Considerations in Stocking of Diseased or Carrier Fish. Pp. 349–55 in R. H. Stroud, ed., *Fish Culture in Fisheries Management*. Bethesda, Md.: American Fisheries Society.

Gordon, W. G. 1984. Promoting Urban Fishing Programs. Pp. 9–13 in L. J. Allen, ed., *Urban Fishing Symposium*. Bethesda, Md.: American Fisheries Society.

Gowing, H. 1975. *Population Dynamics of Wild Brown Trout in Gamble Creek, Subject to Angling, Then with No Angling*. Michigan Department of Natural Resources, Fishery Division. Fisheries Research Report No. 1824. 20 pp.

Graham, M. 1956. Concepts of Conservation. Paper presented at the International Technical Conference on the Conservation of the Living Resources of the Sea. Pp. 1–13. United Nations, New York.

Grenney, W. J., and A. K. Kraszewski. 1981. *Description and Application of the Stream Simulation and Assessment Mode: Version IV (SSAM IV)*. Instream Flow Information Paper 17. FWS/OBS–81/46. Washington, D.C.: U.S. Fish and Wildlife Service. 199 pp.

Griffiths, R. H. 1983. Stocking Practices and Disease Control. Pp. 87–88 in F. P. Meyer, J. W. Warren, and T. G. Carey, eds., *A Guide to Integrated Fish Health in the Great Lakes Basin*. Special Publication 83–2. Ann Arbor, Mich.: Great Lakes Fishery Commission.

Gulland, J. A. 1969. *Manual of Methods for Fish Stock Assessment* Part 1: Fish Population Analysis. Food and Agriculture Organization, Rome. *Manual of Fishery Science* (4) 154 pp.

————. 1983. *Fish Stock Assessment, A Manual of Basic Methods*. Somerset, N.J.: John Wiley and Sons. 223 pp.

Hall, J. D., and C. O. Baker. 1982. Rehabilitating and Enhancing Stream Habitat: 1. Review and Evaluation. No. 12 in a series by W. R. Meehan, ed., *Influence of Forest and Rangeland Management on Anadromous Fish Habitat in Western North America*. Portland, Oreg.: U.S. Department of Agriculture, Pacific Northwest Forest and

Range Experiment Station. General Technical Report PNW–138. 29 pp.

Hardy, T. B. 1982. Ecological Interactions of the Introduced and Native Fishes in the Outflow of Ash Springs, Lincoln County, Nevada. M.S. thesis, University of Nevada, Las Vegas. 79 pp.

————. 1987. Distribution and Status of Fishes in California, Colorado, Nevada, New Mexico, Texas, and Utah: A Relational Data Base Computer System. Engineering Experiment Station, Department of Civil and Environmental Engineering, Utah State University, Logan.

Hiatt, R. W. 1947. Food-Chains and the Food Cycle—Hawaiian Fish Ponds. Part I. The Food and Feeding Habits of Mullet, *Mugil cephalus*, Milkfish, *Chanos chanos*, and the 10-Pounder, *Elops machinata*. *Transactions of the American Fisheries Society* 74(1944):250–61.

Hickman, T. J., and R. F. Raleigh. 1982. *Habitat Suitability Index Models: Cutthroat Trout*. Washington, D.C.: U.S. Department of the Interior, U.S. Fish and Wildlife Service, Office of Biological Services, Western Energy and Land Use Team, FWS/OBS–82/10.5. 38 pp.

House, R. A., and P. L. Boehne. 1985. Evaluation of Instream Enhancement Structures for Salmonid Spawning and Rearing in a Coastal Oregon Stream. *North American Journal of Fisheries Management* 5(2B):283–95.

Hudak, H. 1982. A Technique for Establishing Woody Riparian Plants from Cuttings. In: *The Habitat Express*, 82-13, USDA Forest Service. Intermountain Region, Ogden, Utah.

Hunt, R. L. 1978. Instream Enhancement of Trout Habitat. Pp. 19–27 in K. Hashagen, ed., *Proceedings, National Symposium on Wild Trout Management, San Jose and San Francisco, California, February 3, 1977*. California Trout, Inc.

Jantzen, R. A. 1984. The Goal of the U.S. Fish and Wildlife Service in Urban Fishing. Pp. 14–16 in L. J. Allen, ed., *Urban Fishing Symposium*. Bethesda, Md.: American Fisheries Society.

Johnson, T. H. and T. C. Bjornn. 1975. *Evaluation of Angling Regulations in Management of Cutthroat Trout*. Job Performance Report, Project F–59–R–6. Idaho Department of Fish and Game. Boise, Idaho. 46 pp.

Jolly, S. M. 1963. Estimates of Population Parameters from a Multiple Recapture Data with Both Death and Dilution Deterministic Model. *Biometrika* 50 (Parts 1 and 2):113–28.

————. 1965. Explicit Estimates from Capture-Recapture Data with Both Death and Immigration-Stochastic Model. *Biometrika* 52 (Parts 1 and 2):225–47.

Jones, G. E. 1984. Urban Recreational Fishing—Sources of Funding. Pp. 77–80 in L. J. Allen, ed., *Urban Fishing Symposium*. Bethesda, Md.: American Fisheries Society.

Kennedy, J. J., and P. J. Brown. 1976. Attitudes and Behavior of Fishermen in Utah's Uinta Primitive Area. *Fisheries* 1(6):15–17, 30–31.

Kennedy, J. J., and D. B. Wood. 1977. Fisherman Reaction to the Stocking of Albino Rainbow Trout in Utah. *Progressive Fish-Culturist* 39(1):16–17.

Klassen, H. D., and T. G. Northcote. 1988. Use of Gabion Wiers to Improve Spawning

Habitat for Pink Salmon in a Small Logged Watershed. *North American Journal of Fisheries Management* 8:36–44.

Lamb, B. L. 1989. Comprehensive Technologies and Decision-Making: Reflections on the Instream Flow Incremental Methodology. *Fisheries* 14:22–29.

Larkin, P. A. 1977. An Epitaph for the Concept of Maximum Sustained Yield. *Transactions of the American Fisheries Society* 106(1):1–11.

———. 1980. Objectives of Management. Pp. 245–62 in R. T. Lackey and L. A. Nielsen, eds., *Fisheries Management*. New York and Toronto: John Wiley and Sons.

Liss, W. J., and C. E. Warren. 1980. Ecology of Aquatic Systems. Pp. 41–80 in R. T. Lackey and L. A. Nielsen, eds., *Fisheries Management*. New York and Toronto: John Wiley and Sons.

Lowry, G. R. 1966. Production and Food of Cutthroat Trout in Three Oregon Coastal Streams. *Journal of Wildlife Management* 30(4):754–67.

McCluskey, D. C., J. Brown, D. Bornholdt, D. A. Duff, and A. H. Winward. 1983. *Willow Planting for Riparian Habitat Improvement*. Technical Note 363. Denver, Colo.: U.S. Department of the Interior, Bureau of Land Management. 21 pp.

McGurrin, J., and the Atlantic States Marine Fisheries Commission Artificial Reef Committee. 1989. An Assessment of Atlantic Artificial Reef Development. *Fisheries* 14:19–25.

Martin, R. G. 1958. More Fish from Ponds. *Virginia Wildlife* 19(11):10–12.

Maughan, O. E., K. L. Nelson, and J. J. Ney. 1978. Evaluation of Stream Improvement Practices in Southeastern Trout Streams. Bulletin 115. Blacksburg: Virginia Water Resources Research Center. 67 pp.

Mayo, R. D. 1984. Facilities, Design and Construction. Pp. 103–5 in L. J. Allen, ed., *Urban Fishing Symposium*. Bethesda, Md.: American Fisheries Society.

Meehan, W. R., F. J. Swanson, and J. R. Sedell. 1977. Influences of Riparian Vegetation on Aquatic Ecosystems with Particular Reference to Salmonid Fishes and Their Food Supply. Pp. 137–45 in R. R. Johnson and D. A. Jones, eds., *Importance, Preservation, and Management of Riparian Habitat: A Symposium, July 9, 1977, Tucson, Arizona*. Fort Collins, Colo.: U.S. Department of Agriculture, U.S. Forest Service, Rocky Mountain Forest and Range Experiment Station. General Technical Report RM–43.

Milhous, R. T., D. L. Wegner, and T. Waddle. 1981. *User's Guide to the Physical Habitat Simulation System*. Instream Flow Information Paper 11. Washington, D.C.: U.S. Fish and Wildlife Service, FWS/OBS–81/43. 254 pp.

Moeller, G. H., and J. H. Engelken. 1972. What Fishermen Look for in a Fishing Experience. *Journal of Wildlife Management* 36(4):1253–57.

Nakamura, R. 1984. The Role of Aquaculture in Urban Fishing Programs. Pp. 106–17 in L. J. Allen, ed., *Urban Fishing Symposium*. Bethesda, Md.: American Fisheries Society.

Nielsen, D. B., E. B. Godfrey, M. Benson, W. A. Evans, L. Nelson, Jr., and G. A. Swanson. 1977. Socio-Economic Aspects of Livestock and Wildlife-Fisheries Interactions. Pp. 103–7 in J. W. Menke, ed., *Proceedings of the Workshop on Livestock* and *Wildlife-Fisheries Relationships in the Great Basin, Sparks, Nevada, May 3–5, 1977.*

Novinger, G. D. 1984. Observations on the Use of Size Limits for Black Basses in Large Impoundments. *Fisheries* 9(4):2–6.

Peters, J. C., and W. Alvord. 1964. Man-Made Channel Alterations in Thirteen Montana Streams and Rivers. *Transactions of the North American Wildlife Conference* 29:91–102.

Platts, W. S. 1976. Validity of Methodologies to Document Stream Environments for Evaluating Fishery Conditions. Pp. 267–84 in *Instream Flow Needs Procedures, Volume 2*. Bethesda, Md.: American Fisheries Society.

———. 1978. *The Effects of Livestock Grazing on Aquatic Environments, Riparian Environments, and Fisheries in Idaho, Utah, and Nevada—A Study Plan.* Boise, Idaho: U.S. Department of Agriculture, U.S. Forest Service, Intermountain Forest and Range Experiment Station. 100 pp.

———. 1980. A Plea for Fishery Habitat Classification. *Fisheries* 5(1):2–6.

———. 1981. Sheep and Cattle Grazing Strategies on Riparian Environments. Pp. 251–70 in *Proceedings of the Wildlife-Livestock Relationships Symposium, April 20–22, 1981, Coeur d'Alene, Idaho.* Moscow: University of Idaho Department of Wildlife Resources.

Platts, W. S., and J. N. Rinne. 1985. Riparian and Stream Enhancement and Research in the Rocky Mountains. *North American Journal of Fisheries Management* 5(2A):115–25.

Platts, W. S., W. F. Megahan, and G. W. Minshall. 1983. *Methods for Evaluating Stream, Riparian, and Biotic Conditions.* Ogden, Utah: U.S. Department of Agriculture, U.S. Forest Service, Intermountain Forest and Range Experiment Station. General Technical Report INT–138. 70 pp.

Platts, W. S., and F. J. Wagstaff. 1984. Fencing to Control Livestock Grazing on Riparian Habitats along Streams: Is It a Viable Alternative? *North American Journal of Fisheries Management* 4(3):266–72.

Powell, T. G. 1976. *Evaluation of Urban Lake Management Practices.* Work Plan III, Job 3. Project Number F–52–R. Job Final Report. Fort Collins: Colorado Division of Wildlife. 25 pp.

Pulliam, W. 1984. Involvement of Urban Legislators. Pp. 194–96 in L. J. Allen, ed., *Urban Fishing Symposium.* Bethesda, Md.: American Fisheries Society.

Quintrell, R. D., H. G. Young, and L. E. McSwain. 1981. *A Public Fishing Areas Plan for Georgia—Analysis of Supply and Demand.* Georgia Department of Natural Resources, Game and Fish Division, Fisheries Section. 59 pp.

Radonski, G. C., R. G. Martin, and W. P. DuBose, IV. 1985. Artificial Reefs: The Sport Fishing Perspective. Pp. 529–36 in F. M. D'Itri, ed., *Artificial Reefs, Marine and Freshwater Applications.* Chelsea, Mich.: Lewis Publishers, Inc.

Rankel, G. L. 1971. An Appraisal of the Cutthroat Trout Fishery of the St. Joe River. M.S. thesis. University of Idaho, Moscow. 55 pp.

Reeves, G. H., and T. D. Roelofs. 1982. Rehabilitating and Enhancing Stream Habitat:

2 Field Applications. Number 13 in a series by W. R. Meehan, ed., *Influence of Forest and Rangeland Management on Anadromous Fish Habitat in Western North America*. Portland, Oreg.: U.S. Department of Agriculture, Pacific Northwest Forest and Range Experiment Station. General Technical Report PNW–140. 38 pp.

Reiser, D. W., and T. C. Bjornn. 1979. Habitat Requirements of Anadromous Salmonids. Number 1 in a series by W. R. Meehan, ed., *Influence of Forest and Rangeland Management on Anadromous Fish Habitat in the Western United States and Canada*. Portland, Oreg.: U.S. Department of Agriculture, Pacific Northwest Forest and Range Experiment Station. General Technical Report PNW–96. 54 pp.

Reiser, D. W., T. A. Wesche, and C. Estes. 1989. Status of Instream Flow Legislation and Practices in North America. *Fisheries* 14(2):22–29.

Ricker, W. E. 1975. *Computation and Interpretation of Biological Statistics of Fish Populations*. Bulletin 191 of the Fisheries Research Board of Canada. Ottawa: Department of the Environment, Fisheries and Marine Service. 382 pp.

Roedel, P. M. 1975a. Preface in P. M. Roedel, ed., *Optimum Sustainable Yield as a Concept in Fisheries Management, Proceedings of a Symposium at the 104th Annual Meeting of the American Fisheries Society, Sept. 9, 1974, Honolulu, HI*. Washington, D.C.: American Fisheries Society. Special Publication 9.

———. 1975b. A Summary and Critique of the Symposium on Optimum Sustainable Yield. Pp. 79–89 in P. M. Roedel, ed., *Optimum Sustainable Yield as a Concept in Fisheries Management, Proceedings of a Symposium at the 104th Annual Meeting of the American Fisheries Society, Sept. 9, 1974, Honolulu, HI*. Washington, D.C.: American Fisheries Society. Special Publication 9.

Rosgen, D. L. 1985. A Stream Classification System. Paper presented at the symposium, Riparian Ecosystems and Their Management: Reconciling Conflicting Uses, April 16–18, 1985, Tucson, Arizona.

Schedler, T. R., and J. A. Haynes. 1984. Organization and Implementation of Fishing Derbies and Clinics. Pp. 165–68 in L. J. Allen, ed., *Urban Fishing Symposium*. Bethesda, Md.: American Fisheries Society.

Seber, G. A. F., and E. D. LeCren. 1967. Estimating Population Parameters from Catches, Large Relative to the Population. *Journal of Animal Ecology* 36(3):631–43.

Shupp, B. D. 1980. *New York State Urban Fishing Program Development*. Project Number FA–5–R. Albany: New York State Department of Environmental Conservation, Bureau of Fisheries. 80 pp.

Sigler, W. F., and G. W. Workman. 1967. Using Automobile Bodies as Fish Cover in Bear Lake. *Utah Science* 28(3):103, 107.

Snieszko, S. F. 1957. Natural Resistance and Susceptibility to Infections. *Progressive Fish-Culturist* 20(3):133–36.

Souter, B. W. 1983. Immunization with Vaccines. Pp. 111–19 in F. P. Meyer, J. W. Warren, and T. G. Carey, eds., *A Guide to Integrated Fish Health Management in the Great Lakes Basin*. Ann Arbor, Mich.: Great Lakes Fishery Commission. Special Publication No. 83–2.

Southwood, T. R. E. 1966. *Ecological Methods.* Methune and Company Limited, London. 391 pp.

Spaulding, I. A. 1970. *Variation of Emotional States and Environmental Involvement During Occupational Activity and Sport Fishing.* University of Rhode Island, Agriculture Experiment Station, Bulletin 402. 78 pp.

Stone, R. B. 1985. History of Artificial Reef Use in the United States. Pp. 3–12 in F. M. D'Itri, ed., *Artificial Reefs, Marine and Freshwater Applications.* Chelsea, Mich.: Lewis Publishers, Inc.

Stuber, R. J., G. Gebhart, and O. E. Maughan. 1982. *Habitat Suitability Index Models: Largemouth Bass.* Washington, D.C.: U.S. Department of the Interior, U.S. Fish and Wildlife Service, Office of Biological Services, Western Energy and Land Use Team, FWS/OBS–82/10.16. 33 pp.

Terrell, J. W., ed. 1984. *Proceedings of a Workshop on Fish Habitat Suitability Index Models.* Biological Report 85(6). U.S. Fish and Wildlife Service, Western Energy and Land Use Team. Fort Collins, Colo. 393 pp.

Thurow, R. F., and T. C. Bjornn. 1978. *Response of Cutthroat Trout Populations to Cessation of Fishing in St. Joe River Tributaries.* Bulletin No. 25. College of Forestry, Wildlife and Range Sciences, University of Idaho, Moscow. 35 pp.

U.S. Fish and Wildlife Service. 1980a. *Habitat as a Basis for Environmental Assessment.* ESM 101. Washington, D.C.: U.S. Fish and Wildlife Service, Division of Ecological Services. 31 pp.

———. 1980b. *Habitat Evaluation Procedures (HEP).* ESM 102. Washington, D.C.: U.S. Fish and Wildlife Service, Division of Ecological Services. 90 pp.

Ward, B. R., and P. A. Slaney. 1979. *Evaluation of Instream Enhancement Structures for the Production of Juvenile Steelhead Trout and Coho Salmon in the Keogh River: Progress 1977 and 1978.* Fisheries Techniques Circular No. 45. Vancouver: British Columbia Ministry of the Environment. 47 pp.

Warren, J. W. 1983. The Nature of Fish Diseases. Pp. 7–13 in F. P. Meyer, J. W. Warren, and T. G. Carey, eds., *A Guide to Integrated Fish Health Management in the Great Lakes Basin.* Ann Arbor, Mich.: Great Lakes Fishery Commission. Special Publication No. 83–2.

Wedemeyer, G. A., F. P. Meyer, and L. Smith. 1976. Book 5: Environmental Stress and Fish Diseases in S. F. Snieszko and H. R. Axelrod, eds., *Diseases of Fish.* Neptune, N.J.: T. F. H. Publications, Inc. 192 pp.

Wege, G. J., and R. O. Anderson. 1978. Relative Weight (W_r): A New Index of Condition for Largemouth Bass. Pp. 79–91 in G. D. Novinger and J. G. Dillard, eds., *New Approaches to the Management of Small Impoundments.* North Central Division, American Fisheries Society, Special Publication 5.

Weithman, A. S., J. B. Reynolds, and D. E. Simpson. 1980. Assessment of Structure of Largemouth Bass Stocks by Sequential Sampling. *Proceedings of the Annual Conference of Southeastern Fish and Wildlife Agencies* 33:415–24.

Wesche, T. A. 1973. *Parametric Determination of Minimum Streamflow for Trout.*

Water Resources Series Number 37. Laramie: University of Wyoming, Water Resources Research Institute. 102 pp.

————. 1983. Overview of Instream Habitat Evaluation Methods Currently Applied in the Western Region. Paper presented at the 1983 Western Division Meeting of the American Fisheries Society. 14 pp.

Wesche, T. A., and P. A. Rachard. 1980. *A Summary of Instream Flow Methods for Fisheries and Related Research Needs*. Eisenhower Consortium Bulletin No. 9. Eisenhower Consortium for Western Environmental Forestry Research, Cooperative Agreement No. 16–566–CA with the U.S. Department of Agriculture, U.S. Forest Service, Washington, D.C. 122 pp.

Williams, J. D. 1981. Threatened Desert Fishes and the Endangered Species Act. Pp. 447–75 in R. J. Naiman and D. L. Soltz, eds., *Fishes in North American Deserts*. New York: John Wiley and Sons.

Wolf, K. 1988. *Fish Viruses and Fish Viral Diseases*. Ithaca and London: Cornell University Press. 476 pp.

Zippen, C. 1958. The Removal Method of Population Estimation. *Journal of Wildlife Management* 22(1):82–90.

4. The Role of Administrators

Inland fishery management in most states is administered by either a section in the natural resources department or a division of the fish and game or wildlife department. The federal government's role in fishery management is limited to specific areas such as the operation of federal fish hatcheries, aiding Indian reservations, and input on federal lands. Federal funds also support disease control, nutritional research, and limited hatchery costs. Marine and/or anadromous fishery management may be housed in a separate state agency. Management recommendations are often initiated by field biologists and approved by the chief of fisheries. Generally this is done in consultation with the chief of law enforcement, along with other supporting sections where necessary. Final approval is given by the director and the policy-making board. In most states, the director of the wildlife agency is selected by a public board or commission appointed by the governor or as a direct appointment by the governor. Some states, such as Illinois, do not have a policy-making board. The director of the department of conservation has rule-making authority much like the secretary of the interior. Hence, the agency implements law through the administrative rule-making process directly.

The Director

It is the duty of the director to provide overall direction to the policies and goals of the department as defined by the board or other governing body. The director maintains contact with the governor's office and members of the legislature to apprise them of policies and their rationale, as well as financial and other general needs. In order to keep sport enthusiasts (individuals and organizations) reasonably happy and supportive (both morally and monetarily) of department policy, their needs sometimes demand special attention. All too many sports enthusiasts consider the state fish and wildlife agency the enemy, and the cause of poor fishing. These attitudes must be turned around if the department is to have the support it needs. The director may be, at times, in the untenable position of not moving fast enough toward stated goals to suit some department personnel, but moving much too fast for a large segment of the general public. Researchers may believe they see how a program can be quickly implemented and advanced to the benefit of everyone. However, it is quite often difficult to overcome public resistance to change. Some new ideas need to be put forth gently, hatched carefully, then hand fed over a period of months or years. People tend to be apprehensive of something new or different. But if it is laid out where they can see it and think about it, acceptance is more likely.

Today's natural resource departments do much more than manage animals for sport. The director must respond to the larger nonfishing public that is perhaps more interested in such functions as management of nongame, including threatened and endangered species, search-and-rescue efforts, and providing boating facilities, boating safety, and public conservation education. The director takes the lead in maintaining contact with other state and national leaders and being informed of their activities so the department's program can stay current with national activities and management trends. The director has an obligation to see that all pertinent personnel are informed of department policy, any changes in policy, and its rationale. All this is done in order to present a unified and positive front.

Leadership versus Administration

The distinction should be made between leadership and administration. They are not interchangeable, but practice sometimes make the differences unclear. Leadership relates to directing or moving an organization so as to achieve a purpose or serve certain values (Langton 1984). It means to go, to give directions, and it establishes goals and broad guidelines for reaching them. Leadership points to the goals, how to reach them, and attracts people to support and implement them.

Administrators are, in the most literal sense, housekeepers. Their duties are to maintain order over the resources and practices of the organization. Administrators plan, organize, supervise, and control. In an effort to accent the differences between leader and administrator, the annoying but apt terms agitator or bureaucrat are sometimes used. Another definition is that leaders are far-sighted dreamers, while administrators are committed to detail. Both types are necessary and must work together. Although the goals are the same for both, the functions differ, and, predictably, at times there is friction. The cause of this is often failure to understand another person's or group's viewpoint or problem, and it may occur at any organizational level. Langton (1984) makes five suggestions that may alleviate, but probably will not do away with, the problem: (1) hold an annual retreat for staff, (2) conduct regular staff meetings, (3) establish policies and procedures, (4) require administrative staff to review program proposals, and (5) require program staff to review administrative procedures.

Chief of Fisheries

Fishing regulations and the rationale for their proposal originate or are approved in the office of the chief of fisheries. The data base for regulations includes the status of the resource by management units, recommendations and wishes of anglers and in some cases nonanglers, budgetary constraints, especially those involving fish stocking (by size, place, and species). Also in most cases it is necessary to consider the political realities of the overall situation, including law enforcement problems. The chief of fisheries may hold public meetings, discuss problems with peer groups in the department and in other states, seek the sentiments of board members, and perhaps even consult legislators or the governor depending on department policy.

Budget proposals necessary to a successful recreational fishery program include the cost of fish hatchery operations including new facilities, added species, increased production, and fish distribution. Personnel costs include salaries, fringe benefits, proposed raises, and costs of new employees. Other internal items are office maintenance and travel. Field expenses include research and management equipment and operation, travel, and field office expenses.

Fishery personnel, both professional and support, are selected by the chief of fisheries in cooperation with the personnel department. Promotions and terminations are also initiated, with support information, in this office.

Other duties of the chief of fisheries include public relations with both the fishing and nonfishing public, writing and commenting on environmental impact statements involving aquatic resources, and consulting with personnel of other state and federal agencies.

Biologist

One of the principle functions of a fishery biologist is to gather information. In the process of gathering data, it is essential that biologists, in either a research or regional management situation, gather factual, accurate, concise, and complete information insofar as is possible within budget and personnel constraints. Information gathered by fishery biologists is a principal tool for the development of fishery management plans (see chapter 3). In their role as fact gatherers, biologists, like administrators, can strongly affect perceptions of both their superiors and the public by the mode of presentation and the material reported. In any given situation, factual information can be presented in such a fashion that while the facts are not altered, they are biased or slanted. It is here that fishery biologists must be aware of their own biases so as to limit their effect upon presentation of factual data. These biases must be taken into account when descriptions of fisheries stocks are made, when stock status is determined, when management alternatives are presented and discussed, and when the trade-offs or costs and benefits are provided for public discussion. Seeking public input, which should be included in any fisheries management plan, is part of the resource agency's job, and biases of fishery biologists should not sublimate this input.

Peyton and Langenau (1985), reporting on a comparison of attitudes toward animals held by Bureau of Land Management biologists versus the general public, note that the wildlife biologists have a different profile of attitudes toward animal resources than the general public. Biologists exhibit ecologistic, scientistic, and dominionistic attitudes (Kellert 1980) that are stronger and more varied than those of the general public. They also have much stronger naturalistic attitudes than the general public but exhibit similar variability. Biologists have a significantly lower score and less variability on the moralistic attitude scale than the general public, appearing to place importance on the humane and moral treatment of animals. They tend to reduce conflicts involving humane and moral issues to objective arguments.

Peyton and Langenau (1985) point out that goals established by administrators will reflect value priorities. If the administrators are unaware of value differences between themselves and the various publics, they may establish inadequate goals which can lead to considerable conflict. It is therefore essential that administrators and biologists recognize the existence and legitimacy of alternative value priorities. This should reflect both the understanding and the willingness of administrators to deal with priorities in their efforts to manage resources and communicate with the various publics. Peyton and Langenau point out that their study documents the need for value training in pre- and in-service educational programs for wildlife biologists and for public service agencies. They also note that university curricula generally omit this necessary training, focusing rather on scientific and technological components of resource management, and ignoring the fact that much of a public resource manager's or biologist's time is involved in dealing with people. Wildlife generally does well if people are managed. Managers and biologists who tend to impose their values upon a resource to the exclusion of public values can be reoriented by university instruction and in-service training.

Employee Management

Successful employee management is key to the effective operation of any organization. In fish and wildlife work this involves both agency personnel and the general public. Every organization, from large corporations, universities, and government agencies to small retail stores, must manage people to accomplish their objectives. Managers get work done through employee effectiveness. The pervasive view says that all managers are personnel managers, because they interact with people on a continual basis (Mathis and Jackson 1976). Key to the importance of this is that any organization should consider the wishes and needs of its employees, as well as requiring the employees to meet organizational needs and goals. This hopefully puts emphasis on activities more than on the person who performs them. Effective organization accounts for specific personnel activities in work analysis, staffing, compensation, appraisal, and development. Ultimately, an organization's effectiveness rests on the abilities of its people and the means employed to share information. There may be many good ideas in the subordinate work force that do not surface because they are not encouraged. When employees take part in the decision-making process, productivity is strengthened.

Management development may be limited by several factors, foremost being the lack of time and money. There may be a concern that once individuals are trained, they may go elsewhere. In a few cases top management does not want too much subordinate initiative or creativity (Mathis and Jackson 1976). Mathis and Jackson also believe that without a philosophy of professional management, developmental expenditures are largely wasted and in many cases much of the waste unrecognized. Administrative staffs, realizing they cannot own their human resources, may not be motivated to invest a great deal of money in them. However, many organizations and government agencies send administrators to professional training schools and to universities for short courses because such training is cost effective and enhances productivity and morale.

Most administrators, having made a major policy decision, find themselves wishing they had more or better information. Most have wanted more time to study an issue before deciding on a course of action. Difficult decisions made on complex issues within short time frames often preclude in-depth research. Policy making is never a straightforward process, seldom presents clear choices, and usually results in compromise among many options. Administrator policy decisions are often subject to intense review and scrutiny, not only by those immediately affected within the organization, but also by the public and media (Sonnichsen and Schick 1986).

Professional evaluation is a management (administration) tool that can help alleviate these problems and aid the decision maker (Sonnichsen and Schick 1986). Sonnichsen and Schick feel that in-house evaluation is more advantageous than using outside consultants. Evaluators can be used in three ways: (1) in a classic evaluation, reviewing major programs on a cyclic basis (e.g., every five years), (2) as policy analysts reviewing top management-selected topics with quick response times, and (3) review of specific, identified management problems with an attempt to identify the most effective/efficient ways of managing.

Before deciding on such an evaluation, Sonnichsen and Schick (1986) suggest a personal evaluation by a top manager directly involved with the problem or situation. Reflection by managers on their management and leadership style as well as office or department environment will help in making a decision about using the evaluation team technique. Sonnichsen and Schick suggest a nine-point review process for managers to ascertain if an evaluation group will be helpful:

1. Is information for major decisions of sufficient quantity and quality?
2. Is my knowledge of the major aspects of my area of responsibility sufficient that I can make informed decisions?
3. Are my current policies and programs being practiced or circumvented?
4. Are my programs effective/efficient and do I receive feedback on them?
5. Are units under my responsibility productive?
6. Are my subordinates performing adequately and do I have enough information to rate that performance?
7. Are potential top personnel identifiable under the promotion selection system?
8. Is a part of my organization responsible for program and/or organizational changes?

9. Would I solicit and use information from an evaluation group under my present managerial style?

Use of these techniques does not require a regimented following of the specifics outlined. Incorporation of the principles noted can, however, assist administrators in making more effective use of both their resources and personnel.

Loyalty to the organization for which one works and dedication to the resource should not be in conflict, but occasionally they are. Boards or other political entities may set goals and procedures that do not always coincide with an individual's idea of the best use of the resource. Individual perception of management direction and what one believes is good resource management may not concur. This disparity may go so far that the individual may feel it presses upon personal or professional integrity. When this is the case, internal conflict may result. There is no easy answer for the person in this position. Fortunately, it is rarely the case. There are times, though, when someone is asked to do something that appears illegal or not in the best interests of the resource. However, many of the principles some people hold to so tightly are idiosyncratic and sometimes nothing more than personal opinions. When opinions differ, the administrator's must have priority or order breaks down. Subordinates have fulfilled their obligation when they have stated their position, and when differences are apparently irreconcilable, the problem then often becomes personal as well as professional. However, administrative decision should be adhered to by the entire organization. If this proves unsatisfactory for the subordinate, the choices are clear—either fight, resign, or cooperate.

It may be small consolation to know you are not alone; hundreds in the business and professional world face this sort of problem every day. For example, a superior may, because of political pressure, order fish planted in a borderline habitat. The fish may not prosper, but politics are a fact of life in resource management. As another example, it may be suggested that an officer look the other way in an area where people are illegally spearing nongame fish. This tends to create disrespect for the law and special problems for the officer, since he or she is being asked to violate the laws he or she has sworn to uphold. Generally such problems can be resolved by changing the regulations or telling the people to stop spearing and explain why. This does not mean that officers should not use their judgment in any potential arrest situation. Rather, it means that violations cannot be tolerated because the resource will presumably prosper because of allowances (e.g., carp removal).

It appears at times that law enforcement officers and biologists disagree more than they should. Points of dissension include the importance of their relative positions to the resource, required level of responsibility, role in public relations, pay scale (including fringe benefits), hours worked, recommendations on unrealistic laws, and level of training. Biologists tend to believe they are closer to the resource and therefore more responsive to its needs than are law enforcement personnel. They believe inherent in their position is a higher level of resource responsibility. Law enforcement officers feel many biologists do not perceive, or cannot perform, the public contact needed to define and sell natural resource policies. Salaries, hours worked, and retirement benefits appear to be the heart of many enforcement-biologist conflicts. Salaries cannot be compared on a dollar basis alone. Duties and fringe benefits are generally not the same for biologists and enforcement officers with peace officer status. Unfortunately this complicates the problem. However, all of these issues may be secondary to the fundamental value orientations underlying these two professions.

Where comparable levels of education and numbers of working hours are required, conflict is minimized. However, policy makers often feel that management and especially research biologists should have at least a master's degree in fisheries or a closely related science, but that enforcement personnel need no more than a bachelor's degree in the natural sciences or, in some states, a high school diploma augmented by enforcement agency training. This almost inevitably leads to conflict. Biologists feel they should be rewarded for their advanced training; law enforcement officers point to the personal hazards faced in even routine enforcement. Enforcement personnel may believe that creel limits and other management regulations biologists make are unrealistic. The biologists' answer is that fine-tuned regulations are necessary for the welfare of the resource. An example of this could be requiring different daily creel limits and/or size restrictions for trout from two lakes in the same vicinity. Unless a heavy commitment of enforcement personnel can be made, such regulations are difficult or impossible to enforce and when enforced may not be cost effective. Best use of the resource dictates the more productive lakes be more liberally fished; one regulation for both lakes means one may be underfished or the other overfished. This is obviously an area where compromise is in order. Regulations tuned to the more productive lakes are suggested first. Fishing success on the less productive lake should eventually be lower and therefore self-leveling. If this procedure endangers the resource of the less productive lake, then it should be favored by more restrictive regulations.

Even the best administrators are at times faced with difficult employees. Glueck (1974) believes that in the disciplinary process communication of rules to employees is most essential. Unless employees are aware of the rules they cannot be expected to follow them. Closely related to this, Glueck believes, is the willingness to accept the rules and their enforcement. If employees or their representatives participate in rule formulation, their cooperation is more likely. However, they must be convinced that a rule is fair and related to job effectiveness. Glueck discusses difficult employees under three classes: (1) those whose personal problems off the job (alcoholism, drugs, money, or family strife) affect their job productivity, (2) those who violate laws on the job such as stealing from the organization or its employees or physical abuse of employees or property, and (3) those people whose quality or quantity of work is unsatisfactory due to their lack of ability, training, or motivation. The first behavior type is generally more widespread and much more difficult to deal with than the other two classes. The second behavior type is generally met with termination or prosecution if the employee persists. In the case of the third behavior type, where lack of ability or training is the problem, additional training or transfer to another job may be the answer. Lack of motivation may be considerably more difficult to resolve and may require individual in-depth analysis.

According to Graham (1985), quoting a Goodrich & Sherwood survey, administrators find terminating employees the most stressful part of their jobs. Additionally, if the employee is wrongfully terminated the manager may end up in court. Graham, quoting Goodrich & Sherwood, identifies six common termination mistakes: (1) inconsistency in reasons for termination, (2) lack of evidence, (3) failure to document evidence, (4) violations of laws, agreements, regulations, etc. by management, (5) terminating an employee with a high performance rating, and (6) terminating an employee without previous counseling and coaching. Termination should not come as a surprise to the affected employee. Avoidance of these mistakes may not make termination less painful, but it will make the process more fair.

First Amendment Rights

It sometimes happens that, regardless of the effort involved, disputes between administrators and employees end in litigation. When this happens, or before it happens, resource administrators should be aware of some of the general principles that determine whether the speech activity of public employees is constitutionally protected by the First Amendment. Schofield (1984) in analyzing the case of *Connick v. Myers* 103 S.Ct 1684(1983) makes some interesting observations. It should be pointed out that some of these statements may apply only to federal officers and that state laws regarding enforcement and nonenforcement personnel may differ, but the basic principles are valid. Public employees enjoy constitutional protection to speak on matters of public concern, but they do not always enjoy this same protection for work-related speech concerning only personal interests or grievances. If an employee's speech deals with a matter of public concern it is constitutionally protected, but only if its value to the public outweighs disruptions to government interest that may be caused by the speech. Some court decisions involve employees who have asserted a First Amendment right as justification for not accepting transfers, following a superior's directive, or adhering to the chain of command.

According to Schofield (1984) an employee's First Amendment rights can be violated by a punitive transfer or reassignment when it is based on protected speech activity. However, Schofield points out there is a judicial reluctance to interfere with the internal operation of law enforcement organizations. It is probable that personnel not in law enforcement have more leeway. Free speech claims must be viewed in light of the circumstances and in the context of all relative conditions existing at the time of the asserted free speech activity. Nor, Schofield states, can free speech rights be employed to provide immunity to actions that may merit condemnation or discipline.

Another area of interest is employee criticism of management decisions. According to Schofield (1984) employee criticism of decisions during working hours may be afforded less First Amendment protection than similar criticism directed to the public while the employee is off duty. Both employees and management should be guided by written policies that affirmatively encourage what is considered reasonable employee criticism, and it must also protect the legitimate interest of the department and its policy. If there are few or no written policies, employee latitude may be much greater in the matter of personal speech. There are restrictions that should be tailored to accommodate the needs of the department, such as the total protection of confidential personal information and the maintenance of on-duty discipline. There should be reasonable internal communication and stated grievance procedures where the employee understands the policy and the limitations. Good internal communications, according to Schofield, improves both morale and job satisfaction and assists management in identifying potential problems. In most cases this will prevent the employee feeling it necessary to go to court, but when he or she does, the department should be prepared for the occasion.

Selling the Program via Television and Video Presentation

The obstacles facing today's natural resource departments when they try to sell a program to sports enthusiasts, politicians, and the general public are formidable indeed. Getting and holding public attention is the first and most difficult step. Competitors for an individual's attention include many highly sophisticated television programs, well-produced television sports events, carefully orchestrated television news, and newspaper comics and sports pages. More important than might be suspected is an individual's desire to relax and be away from controversy and bad news, which can be accomplished by the flick of a switch. It is obvious to almost everyone that television is the most effective communication medium today.

Natural resource departments in the future will find themselves using television more, and typography and radio less, as a means of communicating. Natural resource departments can very successfully promote conservation, along with such unpalatable subjects as license increases and season closures, if they use the right script and project the proper image. But it takes much more than factually correct data and people who can remember their lines. Those two points may not even be a good beginning. The following discussion is intended to stimulate ideas for approach, content, and a feel for what it takes to project and hold a positive image in the minds of sports enthusiasts, politicians, and, perhaps to a lesser extent, the general public.

American children watch, on average, 5,000 hours of television before ever starting school and about 16,000 hours by the end of high school. These young people will have seen about 800,000 television commercials by the time they are twenty years old (Postman 1985). Considering this, Postman states that television is winning the competition with typography for the time, attention, and cognitive predispositions. All of us believe or say we believe we want to know what the truth is. A claim, whether true or false, must take the form of a proposition if it is to be challenged. If it does not take this form there is no challenge. Television advertisers rarely use propositions. According to Postman, the truth of advertising claims is not at issue. A fast food chain commercial, for example, is not a series of logical tests, but rather a drama of attractive people selling, buying, and eating hamburgers. This is not a claim, therefore it is neither true nor false. Postman believes that such questions do not apply to the world of visual images. He states that one can like or dislike a hamburger television commercial, but cannot refute it. And because this is so, the symbolic arena of advertising has changed and so has the province of politics and political information.

What does all this have to do with natural resource departments selling their program? Actually a very great deal. If hamburger chains, or political candidates, can present their product in an unchallengeable way, why can't natural resource departments do the same? The answer is obvious. They can. Today, through television, the visual image is our basic unit of communication in both politics and selling. Neither well-written communiques nor radio programs are much competition for television. Only a small group of people rely on typography, and the largest group of radio listeners are probably automobile travelers. According to Postman (1985), in the television age the ideas of political leaders are not, for the most part, expressed as subjects and predicates and are not, therefore, susceptible either to refutation or logical analysis any more than are hamburger chain commercials.

The picture that the speaker wants to remain in the viewer's mind is that of a virile, personable, sleek, outgoing, straightforward individual, with a sincere low-key sell. This prevails in both politics and advertising. Think back to recent U.S. presidential elections. Though integrity, character, experience, and accomplishments undoubtedly rated high with voters, all were second to television imagery. Both were needed to win; alone none could succeed. And consider the people who appear in television advertising. You cannot help but think that these are the kinds of people you would like to know, to have in your home. Many are celebrities solely because of the image they project on television. John Madden, for example, was for years a well-known professional football coach, but he became far better known after doing commercials.

Natural resources departments can sell their programs on television if they use such successful Madison Avenue techniques. Two oversimplified examples that natural resources might use are stocking fish and increasing law enforcement. Common sense tells the average angler that when more fish are stocked there are more to catch, and when there is an increase in law enforcement effort, there is less poaching. This is straightforward and unchallengeable. While they appear to be logical acts, they actually appeal largely to emotions. A television shot of a soaring eagle, a torrential river, and the many natural wonders and dramas of nature are noncontroversial and appealing. Around the turn of the century, many natural resource departments, in an effort to increase numbers in badly decimated deer herds, resorted to highly emotional appeals to sports enthusiasts. It became more than a misdemeanor to kill a doe. It was in some minds a terrible wrong, compounded by severe peer pressure. How well this campaign succeeded is known today to biologists in areas of the United States where they are trying to promote measures that maintain deer herds within the carrying capacity of the range by promoting either sex or doe hunts.

"What I am now saying," writes Postman (1985) in discussing selling and politics, "is that exposition, explanation and argument, those instruments normally considered of rational discourse, are less and less used as a means of expressing political (and other) ideas, and therefore the traditional means of educating people into critical thinking are less and less relevant." Complex and extended language is being replaced by gestures, images, and formats of the art of show business, toward which the news media, especially television, is at its best. Postman believes Americans no longer talk to each other; they entertain each other. They do not exchange ideas; they exchange images. They do not argue with propositions; they argue with looks, celebrities, parables, and possibly at times most of all with public opinion polls. Postman quotes the late Jessica Savitch, an NBC correspondent, as saying voters and viewers have come of age, "They now have a tremendous amount of visceral smarts." Postman believes the point to be insistent upon here is that the replacement of the brain by the viscera in political judgment situations was not anticipated by this nation's founders. Needless to say, he finds this present trend deplorable. He believes that Jefferson would have also found it so, since he saw universal education and the discipline of literacy as essential ingredients in the great American experiment.

Postman (1985) offers yet another facet of television technique that molds public opinion both for stands taken and to deter negative publicity. He believes that television and other modern media are to some extent degrading the meaning of information by creating a species of information that may properly be called disinformation. Postman notes that he is using this word almost in the same sense it is used by agents of the CIA or the KGB. Disinformation as used here does not mean false information, rather it means misleading information—misplaced, fragmented, irrelevant, or superficial information— information that creates an illusion of knowing something, but which in fact leads one away from knowledge or fact. In this sense Postman finds that almost all advertising is disinformation, and so are many other things on television, as far as serious social and political discourse is concerned. A not insignificant or irrelevant point should be made here. Almost all television programs have a musical theme, as a way of telling the audience what emotions are called for. This is a standard theatrical device and it is amazingly effective. Postman believes that in television panels, interruptions and questions by the participants slow down the tempo of the show and create a lack of certainty which tends to reveal people in the act of thinking. This, he believes, does not play well on television. Television does not direct our attention to sequential, slow-moving, abstract ideas. Rather, more often it directs us to respond to holistic, concrete, and simplistic images. Conservationists should learn how to use the system. This is particularly important for natural resource departments whose clientele are sometimes antagonistic, always well informed (in their opinion), and frequently emotional in response to what they believe will affect their favorite pastime.

An aspect of television that should not be overlooked in both educational and information transfer applications is the use of video tape presentations.

Use of television does not have to include live broadcast. Information specialists, conservation officers, and biologists involved in the use of slide-tape modules can effectively present natural resources management problems with this relatively inexpensive technique. Presentations of this type have several advantages: (1) while cost of the initial preparation may be moderate to high, numerous copies for wide distribution can be made at little added expense; (2) video tapes can be sent to schools, sporting groups, civic organizations, and other professional groups without the mandatory presence of an agency employee; (3) video tapes can be edited and tailored to either broad interest subjects such as enjoying the outdoors, or to narrowly defined topics such as special deer hunts in a particular area, or to the need to protect an endangered species; and (4) tapes can be modified to reflect changes in scientific data or department policy. All of these advantages can be put to use on television.

Selling One-on-One

Law enforcement people are one group of natural resource personnel that is in personal contact with the general public as much or more than any other. Because of this, law enforcement personnel bear a particular burden in projecting the desired image of the department and in selling programs. They are the ones who meet sports enthusiasts in the field in one-on-one situations, in meetings, in coffee shops, and in classrooms. Because they are known as individuals, they are more believable than others who are no more than a name on paper. Field biologists fit into this category, but perhaps to a lesser extent because their contacts are less of a demand nature and therefore less frequent. Because of the nature of their duties, conservation officers have a built-in problem. They must force their will on people who violate the law. They are viewed by some as wearing black hats, partly because they wear uniforms. Overcoming this image is difficult for many, impossible for some. It can best be done by presenting a low-key professional, compassionate, and understanding approach, such as: we are all in this together, we all want the resource to prosper so that each of us can have a fair share today, and there will be more tomorrow.

Although many people view a conservation officer as just another police officer, there are some sharp distinctions. Police see themselves as crime fighters, not social workers. Some even believe they are looked upon as social outcasts. Their job, they say, is to catch the crooks, not educate them (Empey 1982). Conservation officers, on the other hand, understand they are one of the department representatives whose job it is to sell first themselves then the department and its program. Their job, at times, is more prevention than arrest. Some duties appear to be only remotely related to law enforcement. As public-opinion molders at the grass-roots level, the conservation officer's and field biologist's role is indispensable. It does not conflict with mass media, but rather supplements it. Only a small percent of the public will ever be met face to face.

Young people present a special and sometimes very difficult challenge to conservation officers. It is important to meet this challenge because the youngsters are just embarking on an avocation that should be both law-abiding and satisfying. Since they are just testing their wings, their flight may not always be predictable or conventional. They may challenge authority to impress peers or to confront their elders. In other cases, they are conforming to the desires and behavior of their family and close friends. All of this presents the officer with an especially difficult task.

Good teachers from Socrates on have known that the intellect must be trained; one kind of training is in criticizing authority (Sabini and Silver 1985). Conservation officers, as natural resource authorities, can provide an area of practice for these young people. The conservation officer must learn to expect and respect criticism. He or she must also be a good listener, a rare trait these days.

It is perhaps more common in everyday life for young people to become entrapped by gradual increases in dubious commitments and find themselves engaged in acts outside the law. The proper course for them cannot be that of refusing to begin on any path which might lead to trouble, but rather, it should be to foresee where any given path is likely to lead, and then decide that these are points beyond which they will not go (Sabini and Silver 1985).

People who have broken the law may exhibit violent embarrassment when confronted by an officer. But, people who have committed themselves beforehand to disobey a law, may have developed countermeasures or rationalizations to lessen or eliminate the humiliation. This does not mean that all people who are not embarrassed by breaking the law have committed a premeditated act. Conservation officers must recognize that social pressures are forces in our lives whether we concede or even recognize them. Rational people who keep their actions in accord with their values, must learn to face or avoid those pressures when they tend to degrade their action, but they must also learn to employ the pressure of public commitment, the pressure implicit in making clear to others the value of what they believe and what they will stand by. Young people should be helped to recognize social pressures that affect them, and they should also learn how to use those pressures to support their own values. One reason we teach people to think critically is so they may take charge of their own creations (Sabini and Silver 1985).

The conservation officer's approach to public relations is the complete opposite of that used in mass media. Here, discussions are often one on one and put forth as propositions. The debate is pro and con, and the fine points of law are explained along with their rationale. The public relations aspects of law enforcement, in concert with preventive enforcement, are considered by many to be more important than arrest. The ultimate goal of law enforcement is to have the entire population completely law-abiding. Admittedly, this is unattainable, but any movement in that direction is progress. The conservation officer, who is much more than a person who arrests people, is a very important component in this program. On his shoulders rests a great deal of responsibility.

The Personal Computer

Natural resource directors and division chiefs of fish, game, and law enforcement may find using a personal computer a necessity. Owen Butler, chairman of Proctor and Gamble, and fifty-nine other chief executive officers listed in *Personal Computing*'s exclusive survey of Fortune 500 chief executives, now use personal computers for business, and some use them at home.

Let's look at some of the advantages of a personal computer as these CEOs see it. Owen Butler, at sixty-one, is an outspoken advocate of personal computing. He builds financial models and dabbles in programming (Fersco-Weiss 1985). He believes it is much more efficient to think through a problem at the same time you are working on it. Butler's case is especially interesting in that he has no data-processing background. John Curcio of Mack Trucks, Inc., finds a personal computer particularly valuable in writing speeches. He says that normally he would dictate a first draft of a speech so it would sound spoken, but after that it was a case of getting a draft and drawing lines in margins all over the place until his typist hardly knew how to recompose it. Now it is done more easily, efficiently, and quickly, and the end product is better. Several companies use computers for in-house memorandums, filing, room allocation, and calendar entries. Meeting arrangements are done in a matter of seconds rather than the old way which took as much as an hour and a half to get eight or ten busy executives together. Some of these CEOs use electronic mail for communication rather than the conventional telephone. A personal computer puts an administrator in instant communication with people in a field office. Robert Reuss of Centel, an independent telephone company, uses his personal computer to get financial information which enables him to run the company better than before, and he finds it much easier than digging around in the files (Fersco-Weiss).

Of primary importance, says Fersco-Weiss (1985), is the impact a computer has on personal productivity. In every case the people he talked to found a material improvement. Some talked of a new flexibility in their communication, some about sharper, more concrete approaches to problem solving, and others cited the ability to make clearer and faster decisions. In every case the advantages were positive.

If chief executive officers of large companies can make profitable use of computers, then natural resource administrators, who in the final analysis are only in a different kind of business, can certainly do likewise. One example is a natural resource administrator who has filed bibliographic information on each legislator and sporting group. These well-prepared individuals have a definite advantage when going before a sports group or legislators.

In any discussion of personal or micro-computers, it should be kept in mind, especially in light of disparaging remarks regarding these devices, that it is not generally necessary to know how a computer functions or is programmed to use one effectively. Comments such as "too complicated for an old-timer like me" and "these new things are beyond me" are not applicable to the new generations of user-friendly software and computers. The increased efficiency and effectiveness gained through the use of microcomputers more than offsets the time required for learning how to operate one.

Literature Cited

Empey, L. T. 1982. *American Delinquency, Its Meaning and Construction*. Homewood, Ill.: Dorsey Press. 540 pp.

Fersco-Weiss, H. 1985. Personal Computing at the Top. *Personal Computing* 9(3):68–79.

Glueck, W. F. 1974. *Personnel: A Diagnostic Approach*. Dallas, Tex.: Business Publications, Inc. 712 pp.

Graham, G., Knight-Ridder Newspapers. 1985. Mistakes Can Be Costly: Managers Find Firing Most Stressful Duty, Recent Survey Claims. P. 14B in *Salt Lake Tribune*, March 16, 1985.

Kellert, S. R. 1980. Contemporary Values of Wildlife in American Society. Pp. 31–60 in W. W. Shaw and E. H. Zube, eds., *Wildlife Values*. Institute Service Report 1. Tucson: University of Arizona, Center for Assessment of Non-Commodity Natural Resource Values.

Langton, S. 1984. *Environmental Leadership*. Lexington, Mass.: Lexington Books, D. C. Heath and Company. 160 pp.

Mathis, R. L., and J. H. Jackson. 1976. *Personnel: Contemporary Perspectives and Applications*. St. Paul, New York, Boston, Los Angeles, San Francisco: West Publishing Company. 438 pp.

Peyton, R. B., and E. E. Langenau, Jr. 1985. A Comparison of Attitudes Held by BLM Biologists and the General Public Toward Animals. *Wildlife Society Bulletin* 13(2):117–20.

Postman, N. 1985. Critical Thinking in the Electronic Era. *National Forum* 65(1):4–8.

Sabini, J., and M. Silver. 1985. Critical Thinking and Obedience to Authority. *National Forum* 65(1):13–17.

Schofield, D. L. 1984. Freedom of Speech and Law Enforcement: An Analysis of *Connick v. Myers*. *FBI Law Enforcement Bulletin* 53(12):17–23.

Sonnichsen, R. C., and G. A. Schick. 1986. Evaluation—A Tool for Management. *FBI Law Enforcement Bulletin* 55(2):5–10.

5. The Role of Hatcheries in Fisheries Management

In varying management situations throughout the coldwater, coolwater, and warmwater fisheries of North America and Europe, fish hatcheries are used to help achieve the goals of local or regional fishery management plans. Fish hatcheries are variously used to produce additional fish for put-and-take and put-grow-and-take fisheries, to supplement wild runs of fish for stock preservation, and to seasonally stock waters which do not support fish populations year around. To a limited extent, hatcheries are used to conduct feeding, rearing, disease control, and other fish culture experiments.

Fish hatcheries were probably the first tool of fishery management in North America. As early as the 1870s, federal policy makers at the U.S. Commission of Fish and Fisheries decided that depleted fish stocks (mostly marine) could be replenished through stocking programs.

The commission published "A Manual of Fish-Culture" in 1897 as an appendix to its annual report. Increased interest in artificial propagation warranted a new edition, and in 1900 it published a revised volume. Both editions of these early works included propagation information on a multitude of species, reflecting the level of involvement of the federal commission in fish culture activities. Each contained information on geographic distribution, habits, movements, size, growth, food, natural reproduction, and a technical description of each species. Since 1900, fish culture manuals have been published by the U.S. Fish and Wildlife Service and its precursors. Lynn Hutchens and Robert Nord authored a 1953 version, and in 1967 the service began publishing a series of several sections with J. T. Bowen as editor. In 1977, with the involvement of the American Fisheries Society and the service's associate director for fishery resources, G. L. Buterbaugh, efforts were renewed to complete publication of a new version (Piper et al. 1983; Bowen 1970).

Fish Hatchery Management was published in 1982 by the U.S. Department of the Interior and was reprinted in 1983 in cooperation with the American Fisheries Society. The editors, R. G. Piper, I. B. McElwain, L. E. Orme, J. P. McCraren, L. G. Fowler and J. R. Leonard, combined historical data with new techniques in six informative sections: hatchery requirements; hatchery operations; broodstock, spawning, and egg handling; nutrition and feeding; fish health management; and transportation of live fish.

Historical Overview

The beginnings of fish culture occurred in ancient China. This art has been practiced by the Chinese from time immemorial. Discovery of the technique of artificial impregnation of trout eggs is usually credited to Dom Pinchon, a French monk who lived in the fourteenth century and who was the first to employ a hatching box involving modern fish culture principles (Davis 1953).

Centuries passed with no progress in fish culture until 1763–64, when a series of papers by Lt. Steven Ludwig Jacobi, the owner of a large estate in southwestern Germany, described his experiments in the propagation of various kinds of freshwater fish. He presented in detail his methods of taking salmon and trout eggs and artificially fertilizing them by mixing the eggs and milt in water. After fertilization the eggs were buried in gravel which had been placed in a long wooden box with fine gratings at the top and ends. The box was then anchored in a stream with clear, running water, and the incubation of the eggs left to nature. Under Jacobi's direction, a number of fish farms were established. Advances in artificial fish culture then seem to have ceased for almost one hundred years.

Joseph Remy and Antoine Gehin, two anglers in the Vosges Mountains in eastern France, apparently rediscovered Jacobi's methods and put them into successful practice in 1842. When their claims were substantiated by scientists, the French government constructed a fish hatchery at Huningue in 1852. This hatchery was soon supplying eggs for all of Europe (Davis 1953).

Theodatus Garlick of Cleveland, Ohio, is generally credited with the first successful attempt at artificial propagation in the United States. In 1857 he published a treatise on his efforts, which were mostly concerned with brook trout. The technique of dry fertilization was developed in 1856 by Vrasski in Russia and by Atheni in the United States. Use of this procedure greatly increased the number of viable eggs produced (Davis 1953).

Fish culture started in America as early as 1853 and was providing substantial income to several individuals by 1865. Most states had established state fishery commissions by the mid-1800s. In 1856, the appointment of F. A. Chapman, Henry Wheatland, and N. E. Atwood to the Massachusetts Fish Commission and their report on European fish culture activities and conditions of state fishery resources drew attention to fishery restoration efforts. A second commission, under the direction of T. I. Lyman and A. A. Reed, investigated the habits of migratory fish, migration barriers, and improvement of fishways (Bowen 1970). This effort was undoubtedly one of the first attempts to discover the needs of fish in natural habitat.

The problems associated with early fish culture activities included fertilizing and hatching eggs, rearing young fish (especially during the first six months), food for all sizes of fish, disease, particularly fungus infections, and adequate water supplies of appropriate temperature.

Inland fishery resource declines were not understood, but the most logical solution was felt to be direct action to increase fish stocks and placate an aroused public. Destruction of inland fisheries was documented in only a few cases. Massive timber operations, in part to provide fuel for salt brine reductions (salted fish being a major American export as early as the 1790s) and iron smelters, had depleted much of the forests. Agricultural clearing procedures further reduced forests, increasing runoff and erosion into lakes and streams. Stream alteration by dams for power had destroyed an alewife run at Exeter, New Hampshire, by 1790. Overfishing had eliminated striped bass and sturgeon from the Exeter River by 1762 (Bowen 1970).

The need for fishery conservation was officially recognized with the creation of the U.S. Commission of Fish and Fisheries under Spencer Fullerton Baird in 1871. Baird accumulated collections of natural history specimens and impressive information while assistant secretary of the Smithsonian Institution. Through his own efforts and those of other natural historians, Baird developed extensive collections over a period of years. The first federal fishery investigation, funded at $100 in 1870 for an investigation into the decline of fish stocks, was conducted at Woods Hole, Massachusetts, by Baird (Bowen 1970).

The most significant change in the philosophy surrounding hatcheries in the last one hundred years is that the hatchery, once considered as an end in itself, is now only an important tool in fishery management. This change of attitude by fishery managers is reflected in public awareness that hatcheries are an essential part of fishery management, although not a cure-all. Research into methods for improving stocks and methodologies of hatcheries is an important aspect of fishery management and necessary to insure continued quality fishing and stock preservation.

Hatchery Aspects of Fishery Management

Fishery managers use hatchery fish for put-and-take and put-grow-and-take fishing, for supplementing wild stock or a run of fish, for preventing the loss of a stock, for population establishment, or for meeting management needs. Fish are also reared for experimental or research purposes.

Put-and-Take Fisheries

Put-and-take fisheries (those designed to place fish in a stream or lake for the sole purpose of recovery by angling in a short time) are common throughout the United States. These operations are often quite expensive. Utah, in the 1978–80 biennium for example, planted 3,570,337 fish weighing 1,100,774 pounds (8.5 to 9.2 inches or three to four per pound). These fish, mostly rainbow trout, were designated as put-and-take fish. This represented about a 4 percent increase in numbers over the 1970–72 biennium planting of 3,446,852 fish weighing 1,287,767 pounds. Minnesota is currently moving away from put-and-take salmonid stocking (principally brown trout) and using habitat restoration/improvement methods to assist natural reproduction and productivity. Only in streams where no other options are available are fish stocked for rapid creeling. Michigan terminated its catchable trout stocking program in the early 1960s and now manages all trout streams on a wild trout basis.

Georgia, primarily due to low habitat productivity, maintains a coldwater put-and-take program for rainbow, brown, and brook trout. Many 6-inch fish are planted, but 9-inch "catchable" fish are the program's goal. Over one million fish in this category were planted in fiscal year 1984. Over 40 percent of the fishing pressure in Georgia is on privately owned ponds. Georgia supplies, as fingerlings, striped bass, bluegill, redear, and channel catfish to private pond owners (Mike Gennings, personal communication, 1985; Fatora 1983).

These stockings reflect both changing demand and management philosophy concerning put-and-take fishing. In some states fish are reared to catchable size and stocked prior to opening day, legal holidays, or other special event days with high angler effort. These fish are expected to be caught soon and few reproduce. Because these fish are designated to be caught in a relatively short time, they do not have to be capable of competing with wild fish for food, shelter, or space. They do, however, need to be of suitable appearance, stamina, and edible quality to please anglers. Where possible, put-and-take fishery programs should be carefully examined to determine if other alternative management techniques are feasible (see also chapter 3).

Principal criticisms leveled at hatchery-reared fish are that after many generations in captivity (e.g., rainbow trout), fish have lost some of the sportiness of wild fish, such as fighting ability, and fish are less palatable, for example, lacking the pink meat color and firm flesh. These negative aspects, if true, must be balanced by the fishery manager against a gain of angler success and catch rate that generally accompanies supplemental planting. The definition of the product or uses to which the fish from the hatchery are to be put are discussed below.

Put-Grow-and-Take Fisheries

Put-and-take fisheries are expensive, primarily due to feed, maintenance, and personnel costs associated with maintaining fish to larger sizes. The concept of putting small fish (4-inch subcatchables) into waters that will sustain growth to a catchable size (8 to 9 inches) has been successfully utilized for several species.

This practice, where water productivity is sufficient to encourage it, has worked well primarily in lakes or reservoirs. Reservoirs or lakes from fifty to several hundred acres can be stocked with large numbers of 4-inch fish which are allowed to grow for a given period and then enter the fishery (regulations may be required on size limitation). The technique has been effective with trout and also with channel catfish. Minnesota is utilizing this type of program on many of its trout streams in concert with both habitat rehabilitation and put-and-take fisheries (Donald Wood, personal communication, 1985).

Where productive waters are available, put-grow-and-take stocking may be effectively used to return catchable-size fish to the creel without the costs associated with hatchery rearing.

Wild Stock Supplementation

Wild stock supplementation is necessary when a stock has been adversely impacted and can no longer sustain itself. As an example, by 1978, more than one hundred dams for hydroelectric power had been constructed or authorized on the Columbia River drainage in the Pacific Northwest (Netboy 1980). Construction and operation of the dams has severely limited or in some cases eliminated the spawning grounds of anadromous salmonids, particularly steelhead trout and chinook salmon. To counter the loss of spawning grounds and mitigate for subsequent loss of fish stocks, hatcheries were established throughout the Columbia River drainage. These hatcheries supplement the remaining wild stocks, or in some cases start new stocks in areas where there has been extirpation.

Chinook salmon runs on the middle Snake River, Idaho, have been so severely depleted in recent years that only a few hundred individuals migrated in the years 1979–80. To prevent the total loss of the genetic stock and uniqueness these fish represent, fish from this stock were collected during the spawning season, artificially spawned, and the progeny reared in hatcheries for release in more favorable locations. It is hoped that continuation of this effort over a period of years will result in a strong return of individuals to the release point and potentially the reestablishment of this stock in the middle Snake River. Without the increased survival rate obtainable in a hatchery and the increased survival of adults resulting from more favorable return points, this stock of fish would have ceased to exist.

Steelhead trout from the north fork of the Clearwater River, Idaho, historically contributed a significant portion of wild steelhead stock of the entire Columbia River drainage (Ted Bjornn, personal communication, 1977). When the gates of Dworshak Dam were closed in 1971, the spawning grounds of that stock and the possibility of adult returns to the spawning grounds were eliminated. To mitigate this loss, Dworshak National Fish Hatchery was constructed and is operated to supplement the remaining wild stocks of Clearwater River steelhead. Management of this mixed stock fishery is complex and involved due to the inherent differences in the numbers and behavior of the two stocks of fish (wild versus hatchery). Wild stocks currently will not sustain the levels of fishing pressure acceptable on the hatchery stock. As a result, fishing pressure on the wild stock must be reduced or it may suffer drastic loss. Hatchery stock is therefore utilized as a buffer, allowing anglers to land, either on a catch-and-release basis, or in some years, a catch-and-keep basis, substantial numbers of Clearwater River steelhead. The relationship between the two stocks is shown in figure 5.1. While hatchery stock can be fished heavily with little effect on the returning adult cycle, a reduction in the numbers of wild spawners can have a significant effect on the number of subsequent wild fish. Operational management of the hatchery is monitored and tailored to keep the hatchery stock phenotypically as near the wild stock as possible with regard to characteristics of interest, such as fighting ability, size, and palatability. This hatchery operation, therefore, serves two related purposes. It allows fishing on a stock that is highly prized by local, regional, and national anglers and thereby contributes

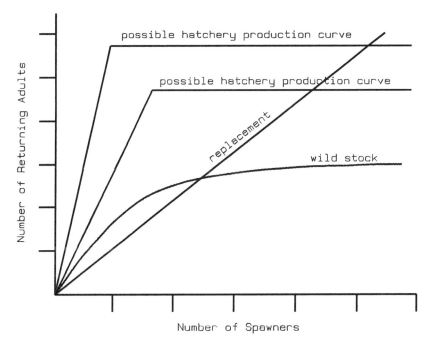

Figure 5.1. Representation of the level of effect on a hatchery stock and a wild stock if they are fished (harvested) at the same level of effort.

economically to nearby Clearwater River communities. By protecting the wild
stock that would otherwise be depleted or pushed to extinction, the gene pool
is preserved.

Population Establishment

Many waters, such as high mountain lakes, new reservoirs, ponds, lakes,
or streams chemically rehabilitated for sport fishing, and others, are essentially
barren of fish life. Once species suitability for the area has been determined,
fisheries management agencies can stock fish into these habitats. This use of
hatchery fish requires a knowledge of the species habitat requirements including food and spawning. Fish can be stocked either as fingerlings or catchables.

Experimental/Research Hatcheries

In the course of the last one hundred years, many significant advances have
been made in the science of genetics in fish rearing. These advances and the
science associated with them have allowed fish culturists and others to develop
useful strains of fish as well as other organisms. The most commonly stocked
strain of western rainbow trout is a result of generally unplanned genetic selection. Fish capable of assimilating massive amounts of food and growing
at extremely rapid rates provide some insight into the potential for protein
production. New treatments for disease or for increasing understanding of the
mechanisms of pathogen travel in the wild have been developed at experimental hatcheries. Mechanisms for controlling and treating fish diseases, which
can be applied in production hatcheries, have been developed. Testing of new
treatment chemicals, or chemicals to be used for unrelated purposes such as in
industry, have been accomplished and are use restricted based on the findings
of experimental hatcheries and research laboratories.

Hatcheries and Endangered Species Recovery

Hatcheries are currently being used as refuges or genome protection centers
for endangered species, a procedure which has evolved since the passage of
the Endangered Species Act of 1973 (Jensen 1986). Several federal facilities
exist that are partially or totally dedicated to holding, study, propagation, rearing, and reintroduction of federally listed species of fish. The Willow Beach

National Fish Hatchery, Arizona, pioneered the concepts involved in the use of hatcheries to aid in recovery of endangered species. Dexter National Fish Hatchery, New Mexico, now has responsibility for as many as twenty species at a time. A Devils Hole pupfish refuge exists at Hoover Dam, Nevada-Arizona. This refugium was established at a time when the Devils Hole pupfish was threatened with extinction due to groundwater withdrawals.

Five other federal hatchery facilities are involved in research to develop propagation and fish culture techniques for other listed species. The end product of each of these efforts will be development of a restocking/reestablishment program for the concerned species.

Research conducted at these facilities serves several purposes (Jensen 1986). Maintenance of a genetic stock in a stable environment with a tremendously reduced risk of impact increases a species' chances of survival. Techniques and methods to evaluate biological requirements of the species can be studied without jeopardizing its survival. A population of an endangered species can be held at the hatcheries while its life history requirements are investigated in natural conditions. Once suitable conditions are present, these fish can be used for reintroduction stock. Information on biological requirements (e.g., spawning temperatures) can also be collected at the facilities.

Hatcheries for endangered species are not an end in themselves, but rather serve to allow other mechanisms to function. Reintroductions of endangered species do not guarantee reestablishment of a population. Hatcheries can, however, help to prevent loss of species (and accompanying genetic information) and aid in preserving and enhancing their status. The program objectives at Dexter National Fish Hatchery, and to a large extent other similar federal facilities, are: (1) maintain a viable, protected gene pool of imperiled fishes, (2) develop techniques for culturing these species, (3) study biological requirements, (4) provide live and preserved fish to cooperating agencies and institutions, (5) provide an exchange of expertise and data on their culture and management, (6) publish findings of research conducted, and (7) implement a public information and education program regarding the status of and required recovery efforts for the species of concern (Jensen 1983).

Hatcheries as Fishery Management Tools

Historically, as well as under modern management plans, hatchery products were used in a variety of ways to advance management goals. These include increased fishing success in peak effort periods, higher productivity for selected lakes or streams which do not sustain year-round fish populations, and stock supplementation to insure complete seeding of a drainage or watershed with juvenile fish.

To effectively use the products of a fish hatchery, a biologist must first determine what is required. Product definition or the production of a fish suited to the use for which it is intended is the first step in a manager's approach to the use of a hatchery product. Product definition must include, at a minimum, the following considerations: survivability, reproduction, catchability, competitive ability, and angler acceptability (catch/challenge, status, and taste and palatability) (George Klontz, personal communication, 1977).

Survivability

Fish destined for put-and-take fishing do not necessarily need to be able to survive for long periods in the wild. Fish stocked prior to an opening day or holiday that will be creeled shortly do not need the survival capability of fish stocked for breeding. Fish planted as fry or fingerlings, however, must possess long-term survival capability. They must possess inherent genetic capabilities that will allow them to adjust to conditions in the wild and be physiologically suited for the environment.

Examples of fish used for quick creeling include rainbow trout, occasionally brook trout, and some warmwater species, particularly sunfishes and channel catfish. These fishes may have been subjected to severe hatchery crowding resulting in modified behavior and be incapable of competing in the wild. While they may have almost zero overwinter survivability they can satisfy the novice or casual angler.

Reproduction

Hatchery fish, used as brood stock, should be as genetically similar to existing wild stock as possible and should have been removed from the wild for as few generations as possible. The fish to be stocked should not carry any genetic characteristics (as far as is possible) that will detract from their survivability or create problems in the event of crossbreeding with the existing population. Fish destined to provide reproductive input into a fishery should also be examined for such characteristics as survivability and angler appeal.

Catchability

Sport fish are stocked for one of two reasons. They are either put there to be caught or to sustain the population. If a fish is to be captured shortly, it must not be too hard to catch. Thus, in a given area, it does no good to stock an elusive fish such as brown trout where there are only novice anglers. Conversely, if fish are being stocked as self-sustaining wild brood stock, it may be wise to choose a species that is harder to catch.

Competitive Ability

When a particular species is planted to be captured at a much later date, it must be able to compete and survive biotic and abiotic factors. This competitive ability should include considerations such as stocking size versus predators, food availability versus stocked size, water velocity, and depth and size of the water body. Numerous examples exist of fish stocked into waters where they did not survive because of poor productivity, inadequate food supply, competition from wild fish, or adverse water temperatures.

Angler Acceptability

Anglers fish, among other reasons, to catch fish. A particular angler may want a challenge and prefer an elusive fish with a catch rate of one per day, while another may prefer to catch five or six in an afternoon. What anglers want determines, to a large extent, what species of fish and what size are planted. Regionally, locally, and by individual preference, the status associated with catching certain species varies greatly (see chapter 2).

Economic Considerations

Biological and angler requirements aside, one of the most influential factors in hatchery stocking is cost. Economic considerations in most areas limit the numbers of fish which can be stocked. Both fishery biologists and hatchery managers must contend with budget constraints. A pound of trout can be raised for $0.30 to $0.50. It may be a temptation to plant many pounds of smaller fish, not necessarily the best management option. This necessitates a priority system that determines allocation of the available resources to producing the top two or three most needed hatchery products.

Social and Political Considerations

In addition to budgetary considerations, other nonbiological considerations include the pressure exerted by sports enthusiasts, legislative groups and lobbies, and others who have a vested interest in providing a particular kind of fish in a particular location. Present-day sporting groups are extremely powerful in many regions. These groups can, through lobbying and public relations, strongly affect biologically sound programs to obtain what they consider to be a reasonable fish-stocking program from a given hatchery. While biological considerations may be sound, it is necessary to deal with pressure groups in such a fashion as will hopefully appease their desires.

Purists (e.g., wild fish only) may demand areas for fishing in which bait-and-catch limitations are much too severe for the general public. Some elitists prefer that no other people be in the area that they have chosen to fish on a given day. While many elitist aspects are outside the control of either hatchery or fishery biologists and managers, it is generally desirable to provide these people with areas in which they can pursue their hobby.

If fish are stocked to be caught quickly, as is the case in planting before season openings and holidays, the question of having an opening day occurs. Some anglers fish only opening day or opening weekend and look forward to and plan for the event all year. If the season is open all year, there is no opening day and the effect of that event is lost. The needs of those anglers who fish only on opening day should be considered.

In the final analysis, fish and game commissions are governed to a large extent by that segment of the public which has an interest in their rulings. These groups include anglers, preservationists, water users, municipalities, engineers, land management agencies, ranchers, private land owners, and people who just want to know there are fish in a stream or lake. Pressure from these groups is applied to the governor and other elected officials, to state and federal wildlife officials, and at the polls. It may or may not be subtle, but it is almost invariably effective. This public input should not be viewed negatively. It is their resource and they are expressing their desires as to its use. People affected by commission rulings should have their needs recognized and followed where reasonable. Special interest groups present difficult problems, but commissions and administrations who do not listen to their constituents may have limited tenure.

6. Conservation of Threatened and Endangered Species

No matter how refined or developed modern technologies become, human livelihood is ultimately grounded in biological processes, intricately linked to ecological webs, and tied to other species. No one can prove that all existing species of fish are essential to our continued existence on earth. It is important to recognize, however, that in the last one hundred years, humanity has contributed to the extinction of numerous species of plants and animals.

Several species such as the June sucker and cui-ui, which are now protected by federal or state legislation, were at one time fished heavily to support local economies. Laws have been passed protecting designated species of fish, but they must be interpreted, and that interpretation may vary with personnel, species, habitat, and political climate. Factors that may bring about a threat to a species should be foreseen and avoided, but often this does not happen. Social, economic, and political factors need to be evaluated, each in its proper context. Ecological distortions and alterations caused by species extinction can have unforeseeable consequences. In addition to legal mandates, we have a moral and ethical obligation to protect and preserve those species with which we share habitat.

As long as humanity instigates changes in the environment, species will be at risk of extinction. This brings up the question of which species do we save or attempt to save in those situations where the habitat has or will be altered. Selection is both a moral and philosophical question founded in federal and state law. The social, economic, and political factors operate independently. Because threatened and endangered species are often discussed in the context of nonnative species, it is important that consistent terminology be applied to introduced organisms. The following terminology is suggested, based on Shafland and Lewis (1984):

introduced—a plant or animal moved from one place to another by man (i.e., an individual, group or population of organisms that occur in a particular locale due to man's actions). Introductions are in two categories:

exotic—an organism introduced from a foreign country or other discrete entity (i.e., one whose entire native range is outside the country where found), and

transplanted—an organism moved outside its native range but within a country where it occurs naturally.

Descriptive terms associated with introductions are:

established—an introduced organism with permanent populations (e.g., self-perpetuating) that cannot be practicably eliminated;

possibly established—reproducing but without permanent status, elimination would be impracticable;

localized—a reproducing but confined population that could conceivably be practicably eliminated;

reported—an organism collected without evidence of reproduction.

Philosophical Considerations for Species Preservation

Whether one views the earth's natural resources as a vast store of exploitable material to be used by humanity as it deems fit, or views natural resources as part of an ecological continuum of which humanity is but one part (albeit the part most capable of modifying ecosystems), it is reasonable to look at natural resources, whether as individual species or complex ecosystems, with four fundamental premises in mind. Ehrlich and Ehrlich (1981) present these four premises as arguments for preserving species—whether we understand their place or contribution to our well-being or not:

(1) Simple compassion demands preservation based on the argument that other products of evolution (other species) have a right to existence over and above the needs and desires of human beings.

(2) Species should be preserved because of their beauty, symbolic value, or intrinsic interest. Beauty, symbolic value, and intrinsic interest may all be in the eye of the beholder.

(3) Economics are to be considered also. Preservation of species (e.g., salmon and steelhead stocks) can be tied to direct economic value through harvest under a sustained yield principle. This theorem can be

extended to species man does not already harvest through the realization that undiscovered foods, drugs, or other useful products may be found when these species are researched and become more familiar to man.

(4) Indirect (not presently understood) benefits to mankind are also possible. Other species of living organisms are components of vital ecosystems whose existence provides humanity with free services, indistinguishably linked to our existence. The deliberate or unknowing extinction of species is an attack on man (and his possible extinction) or at least on his well-being.

The first two arguments are not something that an individual can be easily trained or pressured to acknowledge. Either a butterfly or a flower or any other species elicits one's compassion or it does not. Either a species is considered beautiful, symbolic, or as having intrinsic value, or it is not. Simply because we do or do not feel compassion or see beauty in regard to a particular species is not a very defensible position. Whichever way an individual feels, he or she is unlikely to change another's feelings based on these arguments.

The third argument, economics or direct benefits, can often be put in terms of dollars lost or gained based on either preserving (or at least failing to destroy without some consideration) or using a species. Myers (1983) provides a discussion of society's uses of corn products. Myers notes uses of corn ranging from the finish on book pages to ice cream to explosives, all utilizing corn products. The concept here is twofold: (1) industry, based on the use of this plant, is annually a multibillion dollar effort, and (2) without wild gene pools to provide for genetic modification to increase resistance to drought, blight, etc., the entire industry would fail (or at least be greatly reduced). Agriculture is one area of human endeavor where the benefits of being able to draw on wild, or recently domesticated, strains of crops are readily apparent.

Medical technology and cures or treatments based on wild species are also being discovered daily. The list includes treatments for Hodgkin's disease, malaria, chronic heart failure, and the discovery of new painkillers. The list is seemingly endless. A long list of both plant and animal species have been used to test products before human use or to provide basic information regarding genetics, embryology, birth defects, and cancer research, all helpful to people.

A valid argument is that species that are endangered or threatened are not often used in research, particularly fish species. The counterargument is that if a species became endangered or extinct before mankind is aware of potential uses and benefits, those uses and benefits will be sacrificed. Ehrlich and Ehrlich (1981) and Myers (1983) present valid arguments that ecosystem modification such as has occurred in North America in the last one hundred years and is presently occurring in the Amazon jungles and elsewhere, may result in the loss of entire ecosystems and species before the potential use of any of those species is understood. Certainly the argument that massive losses of genetic information results in reduced worldwide variability is valid.

The fourth argument, that of indirect benefits, that species or specie complexes provide mankind with benefits not noted or specifically cataloged, has merit. Waste disposal and nutrient cycling are completed by microorganisms both with and without human intervention or assistance (Ehrlich and Ehrlich 1981). Various plants and aquatic organisms provide mechanisms for monitoring air and water quality, radiation doses, and for pollution cleanup, all just through the fundamental process of life (Myers 1983). The example perhaps known to most people is that of oxygen production by green plants. Oxygen, essential to most species on earth and certainly essential to humans, is produced by most species of green plants as a by-product of their conversion of atmospheric carbon dioxide to usable sugars. Mankind does little to aid in this process and at times (air pollution) actively reduces it. Yet it should be abundantly clear to even the most environmentally insensitive individual that oxygen is not an ecosystem product that humanity can choose to be without. Aron (1982) succinctly summarizes the reasons for studying and preserving fish: "Unlike the compulsion to climb a mountain because it is there, it is not imperative to study fish because they are there, but because they and other living aquatic resources are linked to human activities!"

History of Species Extinction

One argument that always arises is that extinctions have always occurred, and therefore there is no reason to be concerned about them now. Laying aside the four postulates Ehrlich and Ehrlich (1981) presented and even accepting the theory that extinctions have always occurred, the number of extinctions caused by human intervention in natural ecosystems should be of concern. The rate of extinction of bird and mammal species between 1600 and 1975 has been estimated to be between five and fifteen times higher than it was prior to 1600. During the last decades of the twentieth century that rate may rise to forty to four hundred times "normal" (Ehrlich and Ehrlich).

Extinction, such as that of the dinosaurs, has been followed by development of other species—replacements such as mammals. Contemporary extinction may delete a far greater proportion of the world ecosystem's biological diversity and information than did historic extinctions, a problem made more serious by the fact that human-assisted (or at least not prevented) extinctions have the capability of removing entire groups of organisms at once, thus severely depleting regeneration (information) sources (Ehrlich and Ehrlich 1981).

Early fishes developed, evolved, and changed with changing climate and geology, and when either changed severely, some species could not cope and became extinct; for example, in early geologic times, the placoderms lived from the mid-Silurian to the mid- to late Carboniferous, about 115 million years ago, and the Anaspids from mid-Silurian through the Devonian, about 75 million years ago (Bond 1979). The present rate of accelerated extinction, however, is directly related to nonnatural changes resulting from human alteration of the environment and is occurring with increased frequency. For example, since about 1950 a dwarf lamprey has disappeared from Oregon, two or three species of cisco are apparently gone from the Great Lakes, several cyprinids and killifishes have disappeared from the western United States, and the blue pike is no longer present in Lake Erie.

Man-Made Changes

Humanity has been changing the environment for many thousands of years. These instigated changes undoubtedly will continue for as long as we pursue a livelihood on earth. Some of these manipulations will inevitably put certain species at risk and will likely result in the extinction of some species.

When our ancestors arrived in this country, settlement focused, of necessity, on the nation's waterways. With the advent of the industrial age, the damming, diverting, draining, and polluting of streams, lakes, and marshes were greatly accelerated. Fast rivers were made slow, shallow rivers deep, marshes into dry land, and lakes into sewage receptacles. Some of these changes created a fishery where there had been little or none before, but there was a price. For example, when Flaming Gorge Reservoir was created on the Green River, Wyoming-Utah, the habitat went from a turbid, fast stream to a deep, clear, cold impoundment. In the stream below the dam the water changed from warm and turbid to cold and clear. A salmonid fishery was created, but large numbers of some native cyprinids and one sucker were quickly depleted, first by an eradication program and later by an alien environment.

In the last seventy-five years many small spring-fed ponds in parts of Nevada have been partially or almost entirely drained to aid agriculture. Game fish were stocked in some areas, even pet fish were put in ponds to be later recovered. The native minnows, cyprinodontids, suckers, and trout which had evolved over thousands of years were poorly equipped to cope with a suddenly fluctuating habitat, predation, competition, and exotic disease. Some species did not survive, as will be discussed below.

What is important in the relationship between human activities and species endangered by those activities, is that consideration be given to all aspects of the ecosystem that is to be modified or altered. It is not enough to have good intentions, nor is it valid to assume that everyone uses the same philosophical basis for decision making.

Endangered Species Laws in the United States

Previous Laws

Various conservation and ecological organizations began efforts shortly after World War II to list those species of animals which were considered to be endangered. By 1963 over one hundred species and subspecies of fish in the United States, Mexico, and Canada had been listed by a joint endangered species committee under the auspices of the American Society of Ichthyologists and Herpetologists and the American Fisheries Society (Miller 1964). Early lists generated by both private and federal agency personnel were important in establishing initial legislation at the federal level. The 1966 passage of the Endangered Species Preservation Act called for the establishment of a list of endangered species by the secretary of the interior. It permitted the use of land and water conservation funds to acquire habitat for the protection of listed species. The U.S. Fish and Wildlife Service was at this time authorized to expend funds for management of listed endangered species. However, the 1966 act did not prohibit trading in or taking of endangered species and it also lacked provision for habitat protection.

In 1969 Congress passed the Endangered Species Conservation Act which required the establishment of two lists, one for foreign and the other for native endangered species. In addition, the 1969 act prohibited importation of those listed species without special permits (Williams 1981). This legislation, however, also lacked provisions for habitat protection.

The 1973 Endangered Species Act with its subsequent amendments is probably the most powerful legislation ever written to protect threatened and endangered species of plants and animals. The congressionally stated purposes of the Endangered Species Act of 1973 included conservation of the ecosystems on which endangered and threatened species depend, and provision for their conservation. One of the most encompassing aspects of this act was that it required all federal departments and agencies to seek to conserve endangered and threatened species and use their authority to further the provisions of the act. In addition it required the United States to live up to the international treaties and conventions on conservation to which it was a signatory (Williams 1981). The 1973 act also established two separate species categories. An endangered species was defined as any species in danger of extinction throughout all or a significant portion of its range. A threatened species was defined as one that was likely to become an endangered species throughout all or a significant portion of its range within the foreseeable future.

The determination of a species as endangered or threatened is presently, under the 1973 act and the 1978 amendments, based on one or more of the following factors: (1) the present or threatened destruction, modification, or curtailment of its habitat or range, (2) utilization for commercial, sporting, scientific, or educational purposes at levels that detrimentally affect it, (3) disease or predation, (4) absence of regulatory mechanisms adequate to prevent the decline of the species or degradation of its habitat, and (5) other natural or man-made factors affecting its continued existence (Williams 1981).

The concept of critical habitat was included in the 1978 and 1979 Endangered Species Act amendments. These requirements included delineation of critical habitat at the time of listing, and more participation by the public and relevant agencies. Congress clarified the term "critical habitat" in the 1978 amendments, stating:

> the specific areas within the geographical area occupied by the species, at the time it is listed in accordance with the provisions of section four of this act, on which are found those physical or biological features (1) essential to the conservation of the species and (2) which may require special management considerations or protection; and specific areas outside the geographic area occupied by the species at the time it is listed in accordance with the provisions of section four of this act, upon a determination by the Secretary that such areas are essential for the conservation of the species (Williams 1981).

The amendments also restricted critical habitat delineation by stipulating that it could not include the entire geographic area occupied by a threatened or endangered species except in circumstances determined by the secretary of the interior to be essential to the survival of the species.

Nonbiological Considerations

The statutes and legislation noted above do not allow one to simply make a determination regarding status of a species as threatened or endangered. The existence of regulations and laws requiring that species be protected does not alleviate the biologist's responsibility to accurately and scientifically determine if and when a species can be considered either threatened or endangered.

In addition to the biological considerations associated with determining status of the species as threatened or endangered, sociopolitical influences also exist. In well-documented instances, such as in the case of the Devils Hole pupfish in Ash Meadows, Nevada, the only established natural habitat of this species, it became obvious when the water table dropped and reproduction of these fish decreased that they were indeed endangered and threatened with extinction. The determination as endangered for this species, based on a 1967 finding of restricted habitat, was relatively clear cut from a biological standpoint. From a sociological standpoint, during the 1970 development effort, however, the developers who were causing the water table to drop may have felt that the loss of this species, if it would permit their project to go forward, was an acceptable loss. Another well-documented case is that of the snail darter, in which a large federal dam project in Tennessee was halted for almost a year. These matters cannot be decided on a biological basis alone but must include socioeconomic and sociopolitical considerations.

Mechanisms Leading to Threatened and Endangered Species Status

Two factors have together had an impact on more fish species than all other factors combined. The presence of exotic species and habitat degradation/destruction have, at times, worked together. Habitats were modified to contain exotic species stocked for a variety of purposes. Which factor has had the greatest impact in the past is academic, as both are responsible for losses of species. For future efforts, both should be carefully considered prior to any action. One note that should preface any discussion of extinction is that change, in either the physical or the biological environment, is the key (perhaps the common denominator) to extinction, or at least the precursor to extinction if change is not recognized and reversed.

The Presence of Exotic Species

The establishment of exotic species into habitats previously undisturbed or having a stable species structure, has led to the extinction of many species and subspecies of fish. Many instances can be cited, particularly in the isolated populations of the Great Basin desert in the western United States. Many species present in this area have evolved with no predation and very little or no competition. The presence of large predators such as the black basses rapidly and effectively removed most of these small fishes from many of the desert habitats in which they had lived undisturbed for thousands of years. In concert with the effect of predation by exotics was the establishment of many disease organisms with which the native fishes were not genetically able to cope. These diseases had been transported into these unique environments by exotics. Additional detrimental effects resulted from crossbreeding leading to genetic degradation and eventual species or subspecies loss.

Habitat Degradation/Destruction

A second critical cause of species endangerment results from changes in habitat. These changes can either involve modification such as stream channelization, reservoir construction on streams, or modification or destruction of the riparian zone. The other aspect is elimination of habitat required by a particular species through man-made changes in the environment. Examples include dams that block spawning or other migrations and the alteration of a stream ecosystem to that of a reservoir.

Any of the factors involved in chemically or physically changing an aquatic environment, including introducing new species, can result in an established species becoming threatened, endangered, or extinct.

Protection Requirements

Protection of a particular species by legislation or listing through existing legislative action is necessary in many cases to prevent decimation of a population by either man-initiated or a combination of man-initiated and natural events. This type of listing requires detailed documentation which necessitates an in-depth understanding of the particular species and its life history including ecology and environment.

Simply listing a species as threatened or endangered, however, is insufficient protection to prevent further decline or extinction. Management options must be exercised to provide specific conservation measures for a species or it will most likely continue to decline, eventually to the point of extinction. The mere fact that it is listed does nothing to prevent its extinction. In this light, the role of critical habitat becomes all important. It does no good to protect a threatened or endangered species and allow its habitat to be degraded or lost. The definition of critical habitat must, therefore, include sufficient geographic area and ecological diversity to allow the organism in question to complete its life cycle with a reasonable chance of perpetuation of the species. Critical habitat is defined in a documented study of the species proposed for listing as threatened or endangered and includes a mechanism to determine what geographic area is essential for its continued existence. For stream fishes, it is essential that watershed maintenance be addressed in critical habitat documentation.

Species Protection

In most instances of species listed under federal acts, the species is to be protected from commercial or sport harvest and is provided protection against incidental taking. The designation of threatened or endangered requires federal agency coordination and cooperation in all projects that could have a potential impact on the species.

States often provide protection to species not listed by the federal government. These designations provide for management consultation within a state where state or federal agency action may have an impact on a designated species.

A thorough consideration of the needs of a protected species must include management interactions involving not only sport fishing efforts but such considerations as hatchery stocking of potential competitors or predators; the spread of disease by any mechanism; control or mitigation of such impacts as pollution, including basin watershed management and water diversions; and plans and methods to move toward deletion of the species from the threatened and endangered list. Any propagation or reintroduction program should carefully document genetic consequences of the stocking program.

Protection of a species must include a level of knowledge of its life history sufficient to allow protection at all stages. Adequate protection is provided not only for adults, but for reproduction, young, and subsequent life history stages.

Habitat Preservation

Much of what can be said about protecting a species can be applied to protecting its habitat. A species protected from any direct harm will not survive if its habitat is altered beyond its ability to cope. In many instances, protection of the habitat is all that is required, in addition to preventing direct killing of the species, to insure survival.

It is important to remember that few fish species survive in narrow portions of their ecosystems and are able to cope with ecosystem-level changes outside of their areas of use. Changes in an ecosystem must invariably affect all species in that ecosystem, and to what magnitude and in what direction is often predictable before the changes occur. Transplanting common carp into North America is perhaps the best example of this relationship, the carp having altered numerous ecosystems with negative effects on the species dwelling there.

If the ultimate goal of listing a species is to improve its habitat or its living conditions (e.g., water quality, predator removal, etc.) so that it can be removed from listed status, habitat improvement must not only be a factor, it must be incorporated into the management and recovery plans from the initial planning stages. Often habitat preservation or improvement will require funding far in excess of simply listing or protecting a species from extinction (see chapter 3).

In order to adequately protect a species, habitat sufficient to allow completion of all aspects of the life history cycle must be provided. The provision must include both quantity and quality of physical habitat to insure species continuation.

The Use of Hatcheries in Endangered Species Recovery

The use of hatcheries as refuges or genome protection centers for endangered species has evolved since the passage of the Endangered Species Act of 1973 (Jensen 1986). Several federal facilities exist which are partially or totally dedicated to holding, study, propagation, rearing, and reintroduction of federally listed species of fish. These programs function to assist in recovering listed fish. The Willow Beach National Fish Hatchery, Arizona, was the first federal hatchery involved in recovery of listed species. Dexter National Fish Hatchery, New Mexico, now has responsibility for as many as twenty species at a time. The Devils Hole pupfish refugium exists at Hoover Dam, Nevada-Arizona. This refugium was established at a time when the Devils Hole pupfish was threatened with extinction due to groundwater withdrawals.

Five other federal hatchery facilities across the United States are involved in research to develop propagation and fish culture techniques for other listed species. The end product of each of these efforts will be development of a restocking/reestablishment program to assist in recovery and subsequent delisting of these species.

Hatcheries for endangered species are not an end in themselves, but rather function to provide research and data on recovery techniques. Reintroductions of endangered species do not guarantee their reestablishment and subsequent removal from listed status. Hatcheries can, however, help prevent species loss (and accompanying genetic information) and aid in preserving and enhancing the status of these species. The objectives of the program at Dexter National Fish Hatchery, and to a large extent the other similar federal facilities, are to: (1) maintain a viable, protected gene pool of imperiled fishes, (2) develop techniques for culturing these species, (3) study biological requirements, (4) provide live and preserved fish to cooperating agencies and institutions, (5) provide an exchange of expertise and data on their culture and management, (6) publish research findings, and (7) implement a public information and education program concerning the status of and required recovery efforts for the species of concern (Jensen 1983).

Guides for the Future

What fish species should we save? More specifically, what species, subspecies, or strains of fish should be protected from depletion of numbers or level or environmental degradation that will endanger their existence? This apparently simple question has two complex judgment-level problems: (1) Who determines what taxonomic level is applicable under the law? (The U.S. Fish and Wildlife Service has jurisdiction under the Endangered Species Act for all freshwater aquatic organisms.), and (2) How are the environmental hazards at various levels to be assessed? The experts submit their individual or collective opinions, but decisions are made administratively. In today's world, two factors complicate this apparently simple process: (1) strength of public opinion and (2) a propensity for going to court.

Underlying all decisions are the relative value factors or trade-offs. Straight-forward biological considerations are insufficient in and of themselves to justify any management alternative. Sociopolitical effects must always be considered and incorporated in the decision-making process. Industrialists may appear to environmentalists to support extremist viewpoints and vice versa. Final determination of the issue of an endangered species may be settled by any of the three branches of government, but not by an individual or an organization. It is the people who should make the final decision. It is therefore necessary that they be well informed and provided with sufficient information to make a reasonable, rational decision.

Because of this need for information, professionals, as well as concerned citizens, have an obligation to develop and project objective judgment. This is possible only after an in-depth, penetrating study has produced reasonable evidence that a proper course is being pursued.

A species of fish, independent of its impact upon society, cannot be considered. There must be a rationale for preserving a species. In today's world, that rationale must go beyond preserving the species simply because it exists.

How does the responsible state or federal employee respond to questions like these? The key is whether one becomes an advocate or remains an objective reporter. It appears quite obvious that a government employee has an obligation to remain objective since he or she represents the interests of the people as well as the resource. What is far less obvious is how and where to draw the line between advocacy and objectivity. Checks on objectivity are presumably maintained by such procedures as public hearings and review by superiors. The views given at public hearings for a number of reasons, however, may not be those of the general public. Superior review can be cursory or sometimes lacking in objectivity. Professionals are at times prone to present a united front against what they may consider outsiders or the uninformed. Emotional responses are at times a driving force which the professional cannot handle or may not even recognize. Resource scientists sometimes become so emotionally involved with the animal they are studying that objectivity is lacking. These scientists seek ways only to preserve and protect the species. They become so obsessed that they see only one side of an issue. This may seem unprofessional, but the fact remains that some very talented professionals do on occasion fall into this trap.

How should concerned citizens respond to these problems? If they want to be objective, they should make a reasonable effort to be informed regarding the pros and cons, including short-term trade-offs and long-term benefits, decide on a stand, and then pursue it. However, emotional responses to certain issues are sometimes high, resulting in a premature stand by some individuals or groups that becomes so strong that no amount of evidence can sway it. Sometimes there is no claim to objectivity. Factors that help form individual opinion include local culture, news media, family ties, economic interests, and peer opinion. These factors always have an effect on the decision-making process.

Where do the fish fit in all of this? While the fish species are obviously center stage in the debate, that simple fact may at times be largely obscured. Taxonomic experts are in reasonably good agreement at the genus and species level, but there is less agreement when defining subspecies, strains, or races. Although the American Fisheries Society does not publish lists of subspecies, there are many valid divisions of the species (Robins et al. 1980). For example, the steelhead is a subspecies of rainbow trout, and there are several recognized discrete strains of chinook salmon. The Lahontan cutthroat trout, a subspecies, is the world's largest cutthroat trout and currently listed under the Endangered Species Act as threatened. What constitutes a species is defined under the current Endangered Species Act legislation. A species includes that taxonomic level and under limited circumstances certain subdivisions of species.

None of this alters the fact that decisions, sometimes arbitrary ones, must be made before a fish can be declared endangered. To demand that participating scientists be totally and absolutely without bias is ridiculous and impossible. There is a degree of advocacy in any decision even for those making a concerted effort to avoid it.

The obvious factors that determine whether a fish shall be considered for threatened or endangered status are the current numbers of individuals, range or distribution of the species, condition of the habitat, and threats to the habitat. But there are other factors. There may be species of introduced or exotic fish that have a high negative value. It may be desirable to let them be extirpated. This should not be the case for any native species, but what of certain exotics? Consider the common carp, for example. It destroys game fish habitat over much of its range and is held in low esteem by many anglers, but there are areas where it is stocked and many more areas where it is fished as a sport fish. In addition, it certainly has the capability of producing large amounts of high-quality protein in what is often borderline habitat. Are we, as a nation, going to need this capability sometime in the future? The answer to the question, when it comes, will not be easy and it will not be contained in broad, sweeping statements. Each species must be considered in the light of its value as a unique biological entity, and its potential value to society now or at some future time. The social, economic, and political considerations encompass both the habitat and the fish. A very humbling thought is this: "Do we as inhabitants of this planet, have the right to destroy or allow to be destroyed an organism that nature, through thousands or millions of years, has put alongside us in this complex ecosystem?"

A Case Study—The Devils Hole Pupfish

The following scenario is based on Ash Meadows, Nye County, Nevada, and the Devils Hole pupfish. While the scenario is based on facts gleaned from a variety of sources, we have taken some liberties with time and events to present the points we feel are important. The basis for presenting this information is to let readers track events and at appropriate points reflect on what they would have done or what alternatives could have been pursued.

Prior to 1950, several fisheries biologists, as well as scientists from other disciplines, had produced sketchy but solid data that numerous endemic species and subspecies (fishes, plants, and others) existed in an isolated valley located in a remote region of Nye County, Nevada. Devil's Hole was designated as a national monument in 1952 by President Truman in recognition of the site's unique geology (Anonymous 1985). The Devils Hole pupfish was listed as endangered in March 1967 under the provisions of the Endangered Species Preservation Act and based on its restricted habitat. Subsequently it was discovered that Ash Meadows, Nye County, Nevada, is the sole habitat for approximately twenty-five species and subspecies of plants and animals endemic to the area. Ash Meadows is at 2,200 feet elevation in the Mojave Desert forty miles east of the Death Valley National Monument headquarters at Furnace Creek, California. It includes approximately 50,000 acres of desert uplands interspersed with spring-fed oases. Vegetation includes creosote bush (*Larrea tridentata*), salt grass (*Distichlis spicata*), mesquite (*Prosopis julifera* and *Prosopis juglans*), desert holly (*Atriplex hymenelytra*), salt bush (*Atriplex sp.*), and bur-sage (*Ambrosia damosa*) (Beatley 1971). Spring runoff provides some soil moisture in the lowlands, but higher elevations receive only minimal annual precipitation, averaging less than 3 inches. The annual evaporation rate is in excess of 8 feet (Anonymous 1985).

In the early 1960s, private land in the area was proposed for development in the form of a peat mining effort on several hundred acres.

As a federal or state fisheries biologist, what should your role be in protecting not only the endemic fishes, but also the critical habitat and the fragile ecosystem which exists in this area? How can the problem be approached? What are potential solutions? What are the foreseeable problems inherent in these solutions?

Prior to this time, little disturbance occurred in the Ash Meadows area. Approximately 1,950 acres of Carson Slough were destroyed by peat mining, disturbing a significant portion of the unique ecosystems in the area (Anonymous 1985). Following the peat mining operation, no development occurred for ten years. By the late 1960s, Spring Meadows Ranch had acquired, through purchase and trade with the Bureau of Land Management, some 11,700 acres to begin operating a cattle and alfalfa ranch. Ranch operations resulted in disturbance or modification of many springs, clearing of extensive acreage, and decreases in spring discharge due to pumping and diversion.

The Pupfish Task Force came into being in May 1969 and was composed of federal agency personnel representing the Bureau of Land Management (BLM), U.S. Geological Survey (USGS), National Park Service (NPS), and Bureau of Sport Fisheries and Wildlife (BSF&W). In 1970 the Pupfish Task Force funded a USGS study of the groundwater systems in Ash Meadows, and the Office of Water Resources funded a two-year study on Ash Meadows begun by the Desert Research Institute (DRI). The purpose of the DRI study was to analyze all existing hydrologic data on the study area and collect additional information where needed, and to develop a predictive model to analyze the most pressing groundwater production problems and the related possibility of irreversible threats to the environment (McBroom 1971).

On September 3, 1970, at the request of the Pupfish Task Force, the assistant secretary of the interior for public land management revoked the classification action of May 1968 by the state director (Nevada) of the Bureau of Land Management. This action reclassified 7,300 acres of public domain in the Ash Meadows area as inappropriate for disposal or exchange. This action halted all change in the status of these lands from public to private ownership (McBroom 1971).

In the spring of 1971, personnel from California Senator Alan Cranston's office contacted the Pupfish Task Force leaders. Their original proposal was to expand the Devil's Hole reservation, but the task force felt this would do little good. Instead, the establishment of a Desert Pupfish National Monument of 35,000 acres was proposed. Cranston introduced Senate Bill S.2141 on June 24, 1971, to promote this goal.

Action was now being taken to protect not only the Devils Hole pupfish, but also the other endemic species and their habitat. Spring Meadows Ranch was restricted from groundwater removal operations by a U.S. Supreme Court decision in 1976. This decision reflected the fact that a minimum allowable water level for Devil's Hole was considered to have been included in the reservation of the area under the initial listing in 1967. The Supreme Court decision did not concern pupfish other than those at Devil's Hole, nor did it apply to water uses besides agricultural (Schwartz 1984).

Following establishment of the minimum water level in Devil's Hole in 1978, Spring Meadows, Inc., put the ranch up for sale. The U.S. Fish and Wildlife Service was offered the land but did not purchase it. Preferred Equities Corporation, a Las Vegas, Nevada, real estate development company, purchased the ranch. Preferred Equities proposed to develop vacation homes, casinos, lakes, and golf courses. Subdivisions for 20,000 houses were approved by Nye County, and in 1981, road building, with its inherent modification of springs, pools, outflows, and other habitats, began (Schwartz 1984).

Development is now proceeding which will undoubtedly destroy most of the habitat of the twenty-five endemics and result in their extinction. To prevent this from occurring, what action can state and/or federal biologists and managers instigate? What legal options are available?

Completion of the planned development would drastically alter existing ecosystems. Although numerous organizations such as the Desert Fishes Council and the Ash Meadows Education fund had attempted to preserve portions of Ash Meadows by regulatory means, little other than Nature Conservancy's purchase of Big Spring in 1973 had been accomplished. By 1980 lawsuits were threatened by the Sierra Club and other environmental organizations.

In an effort to prevent further endemic extinction in the Ash Meadows area, Nature Conservancy, aided by a bill sponsored by Nevada's Senator Laxalt, purchased 12,613 acres of private land from Preferred Equities on February 7, 1984, for something in excess of $5.5 million and resold it to the U.S. Fish and Wildlife Service for the establishment of Ash Meadows National Wildlife Refuge on June 13, 1984. Additional public (BLM) lands adjacent to the refuge, as well as the purchase of private lands, will be added to the refuge to encompass some 23,000 acres of habitat occupied by endemics.

Restoration of the ecosystem and varied habitats in the Ash Meadows National Wildlife Refuge can now proceed. Management guidelines, public use, and species preservation activities will be planned and completed in subsequent years. The events surrounding this rescue effort are centered on the small Devils Hole pupfish, but have wide-ranging consequences. Most, if not all, would have been lost had development of the area been completed.

The current situation presents a rare opportunity not only to preserve one species of concern, but rather to preserve an entire ecological complex for study, research, and just plain watching. Reconstruction of the Ash Meadows ecosystem can proceed thanks to the Devils Hole pupfish, but it must proceed with all species in mind, preserving all aspects of this unique area.

As a biologist what plans can you propose to insure not only protection, but enhancement and eventual delisting of the species presently listed? How can this be accomplished in concert with protection and study of the other endemic species which are not currently listed? What management considerations need to be incorporated in the overall restoration project plans to insure not only protection but enhancement of the species and the physical habitat?

Literature Cited

Anonymous. 1985. Technical Draft, Ash Meadows Species Recovery Plan, June, 1985. Reno, Nevada: U.S. Fish and Wildlife Service, Great Basin Complex. 26 pp.

Aron, W. 1982. Fishery Science, Uncertainty and Responsibility. *Fisheries* 7(1): 6–8.

Beatley, J. C. 1971. Vascular Plants of Ash Meadows, Nevada. University of California, Los Angeles Laboratory of Nuclear Medicine and Radiation Biology, Atomic Energy Contract AT (04–1) GEN–12, Unpublished Report. 59 pp.

Bond, C. E. 1979. *Biology of Fishes*. Philadelphia, London, Toronto: W. B. Saunders Company. 514 pp.

Ehrlich, P. R., and A. H. Ehrlich. 1981. *Extinction: The Causes and Consequences of the Disappearance of Species*. New York: Random House. 305 pp.

Jensen, B. L. 1983. Culture Techniques for Selected Colorado River Imperiled Fishes. Pp. 178–89 in *Proceedings of the 34th Annual Northwest Fish Culture Workshop, December 6–8, 1983, Moscow, Idaho*.

————. 1986. The Role of Fish Culture in Endangered Fishes Recovery. Paper presented at the Bonneville Chapter, American Fisheries Society Meeting, March 5–6, 1986, Utah State University, Logan.

McBroom, J. T. 1971. Pupfish Task Force Report, Appendix 1971–5. *Proceedings of the Desert Fishes Council* III–IX:20–28.

Miller, R. R. 1964. Extinct, Rare and Endangered Freshwater Fishes. Pp. 4–16 in *The Protection of Vanishing Species, Proceedings of the International Congress of Zoology* 8.

Myers, N. 1983. *A Wealth of Wild Species: Storehouse for Human Welfare*. Boulder, Colo.: Westview Press. 274 pp.

Robins, C. R., R. M. Bailey, C. E. Bond, J. R. Brookes, E. A. Lochner, R. N. Lea, and W. B. Scott. 1980. *A List of Common and Scientific Names of Fishes from the United States and Canada*. Fourth Edition. Bethesda, Md.: American Fisheries Society. 174 pp.

Schwartz, A. 1984. Bright Future for a Desert Refugium. *Nature Conservancy News* 34(5):13–17.

Shafland, P. L., and W. M. Lewis. 1984. Terminology Associated with Introduced Organisms. *Fisheries* 9(4):17–18.

Williams, J. D. 1981. Threatened Desert Fishes and the Endangered Species Act. Pp. 447–76 in R. J. Naiman and D. L. Soltz, eds., *Fishes in North American Deserts*. New York: John Wiley and Sons.

7. Field Procedures and Preliminary Laboratory Techniques

Many field and laboratory procedures are routinely performed in fisheries work. They may vary from simple to complex and should be thoroughly documented for the circumstance under which they are to be implemented. The following chapter discusses techniques for accuracy in data accumulation and recording.

Field and Individual Data Sheets

Sampling results are only as good as the information recorded, and this in turn is frequently governed by field equipment and its use and attention to detail by the investigator. A description and discussion of equipment and collection techniques used in a study is generally reported in a separate section of the final report or it can be incorporated under appropriate headings in the body of a report or paper. The availability of computer-compatible field data-entry systems (data loggers) and simple yet sophisticated personal computer-based analysis systems (Bayley and Illyes 1988, Deventer and Platts 1985) has provided an alternative to written field notes and paper forms. The validity of the principle of collecting and entering accurate and complete field data remains unchanged.

A field data sheet is essential and should be made out for each fish or other field data collection as the occasion demands (see table 7.1). A new collection number is initiated whenever there is a change in either time or place. How fine these distinctions are is dictated by the use to be made of the data. For example, a series of collections around a large lake where there are discrete populations of fish probably should have individual collection numbers when

Table 7.1.   Fishery field data sheet.

1. Coll. No. _____ S 89 1 _____	2. Date _____ X 14 89 _____

3. Time of Coll. _____ 1400–1700 _____   4. State _____ UTAH _____

5. County _____ Cache _____   6. Drainage _____ Bear River _____

7. Township _____ 11 N _____   8. Range _____ 2E _____   9. Section _____ 30 _____

10. Locality _____ Logan River, 2.1 miles above junction HY 89 _____

11. Water Color _____ NONE _____   12. Turbidity (ppm) _____ 17.1 (Hach) _____

13. Velocity (f/s) _____ 2.1 _____   14. Flow (cfs) _____ 850 _____   15. Depth (average) ft _____ 4 _____

          (m/s) _____ 0.64 _____   (cms) _____ 24.1 _____   m _____ 1.22 _____

16. pH _____ 7.8 _____   17. Air Temp (F) _____ 82 _____   18. Water Temp (F) _____ 67 _____

19. Elevation (ft) _____ 4535 _____   (m) _____ 1382.6 _____   20. Weather _____ Overcast _____

21. Vegetation (%) Shore _____ Willow 80, Phragmites 20 _____

22. Vegetation (%) Aquatic _____ None _____   23. Bottom Type _____ Silt 92 Gravel 8 _____

24. Distance from shore (f/m) _____ 12/3.65 _____   25. Width of Coll. (f/m) _____ 30/9.1 _____

26. Capture Method _____ Electroshocker, 2 hrs. AC, 220V, 3000W, (1.5 v/f), cont. _____

27. Depth (capture—f/m) _____ 4 _____   28. Cover (%) _____ 0 _____

29. Pools (%) _____ A = 18, C = 51 _____   30. Shelter (%) _____ 15 _____

31. Fish Food _____ Not observed _____   32. Collectors _____ Sigler, Sigler _____

33. Fish Captured _____ RBT 27, 12–16"; BT 4, 17–21"; Mt. whitefish 106, 2–21"

          _____ Serial No. 1–10; carp 7, 18–29"; Utah chub 11, 4–7" _____

34. Fish Preserved: _____ Mt. whitefish, (10 2–3", TL) _____

35. Orign. Pres. _____ Formalin _____   36. Changed to _____ Alcohol XI–15–89 _____

37. Remarks: Length and weight of trout, Mt. whitefish (except preserved), carp, and Utah chub
    recorded in field and released. Ten whitefish returned to lab for length, weight, scales and
    stomach analysis (Serial No. 1–10).

these populations, as such, are of interest. In general survey work, or a study dealing with range or taxonomy, one collection number may be sufficient and time saving.

Observations for each of the thirty-seven items on the fishery field data sheet (table 7.1) should be standardized. All blanks should be filled with data or recorded as NO (not observed) or NA (not applicable). The collection number (item 1) is prefaced by a capital letter indicating the principal collector (S = Sigler), or it may denote drainage (BR = Bear River). The next two numbers indicate the year of the collection. The last number is an arbitrary one; generally, the first collection of the calendar year is number 1, and each year a new series of numbers is started. However, some collectors prefer to not duplicate this number and continue with one series year after year. This latter system eventually produces large numbers.

The month of the collection should be a Roman numeral followed by the day and year in Arabic numbers (item 2). The time of the collection (item 3) should be recorded as 0000 to 2400 (midnight to midnight). Listing times on a clock basis followed by A.M. or P.M. requires more space and is more susceptible to error in recording and reading. The locality, in addition to the legal description, should be an exact local description (item 10). A county road map and a state highway map are often useful, and topographical maps of the area are indispensable in some places.

True color of water should not be confused with turbidity, which is caused by filterable material or light refracting material (item 11). Care must be taken in utilizing various instruments to determine turbidity, as different instruments may be measuring different parameters (Hach 1972). If a U.S. Geological Survey color chart or some other color chart are not available, such descriptive words as tea, coffee, or cobalt colored may be used. The definition of these words should be decided in advance and understood and adhered to by all collectors. Turbidity (item 12) is best reported in ppm (parts per million) of silicon dioxide equivalents or as nephlerometric turbidity units (NTU). When this is not possible, a series of descriptive terms determined in advance may be used. Various turbidity meters and portable units are available. One meter or type of equipment should be selected and used for all field investigations or readings from other devices calibrated and converted to a selected unit.

Velocity of a stream in feet per second or meters per second may be recorded as a mean, or extremes may be given (item 13). Sophisticated digital or analog meters with calibrated depth measuring rods are available that allow precise determination of bottom, surface, and middepth velocities. When both velocity and average depth are estimated, the calculated flow in cubic feet per second or cubic meters per second may have a substantial error (item 14). Judgment for estimating flow is best gained by experience with velocity meters and weirs, but greater precision can be obtained by using meters and measuring tapes.

Shore and aquatic vegetation and bottom types are generally relative abundance estimates (items 21, 22, and 23). Bottom types may be arbitrarily designated as clay, silt (a mixture of organic and inorganic materials), sand, gravel, rubble, boulders, and bedrock. A more definitive system may utilize actual or estimated measurements for each of the size classes of material, such as:

Class	*Description*
Bedrock	virtually unbroken rock layer
Very large boulders	406–203 cm (160–80 inches)
Large boulders	203–102 cm (80–40 inches)
Boulders	102–51 cm (40–20 inches)
Small boulders	51–25 cm (20–10 inches)

Large cobbles	25–13 cm (10–5 inches)
Small cobble	13–6.4 cm (5–2.5 inches)
Very coarse gravel	6.4–3.2 cm (2.5–1.3 inches)
Coarse gravel	3.3–1.5 cm (1.3–0.6 inches)
Fine gravel	0.7–0.4 cm (0.3–0.16 inches)
Coarse sand	0.1–0.05 cm (0.04–0.02 inches)
Coarse silt	0.006–0.0031 cm (0.0024–0.0012 inches)
Muck	decomposed organic material
Debris	logs, brush, windblown material (Substrate under debris will be noted under one of the above groups.)

Innumerable techniques exist for rating or classifying substrate type. They range from extremely simple schemes with from six to eight categories to more complex ones with twenty or more categories. Platts, Megahan, and Minshall (1983) list twenty-four categories for rating substrate channel materials which range from very large boulders (160–80 inches) to very fine clay (0.5–0.24 microns). If the additional categories of silt, muck, and debris are added, one could list a total of twenty-seven bottom-type classifications.

To facilitate data comparison from one drainage or one geographic area with another, it is essential that a system of uniform descriptive terms and sizes be established. In a particular field situation it is not necessary to utilize all of the twenty-seven categories. What is important is that when a descriptive term is utilized (e.g., coarse gravel) that this term means the same thing in all reports (e.g., material 32–16 cm, 1.3–0.6 inches).

Net capture gear (item 26) should be described as to type, length, depth, mesh size, and number of passes made. In the case of electric equipment, voltage, amperage, or watts, frequency, alternating or direct current, continuous or pulsed flow, and time fished should be noted. The most meaningful electric data are volts and amperes per foot, that is, the actual amount of current flowing across a one foot or other designated gradient in the water rather than matching output.

The distance electrofished should also be recorded. In streams, upstream and downstream passes should be considered as a sampling unit due to efficiency differences in fishing upstream versus fishing downstream. Measured width and stream length should be used whenever possible. In lakes or reservoirs, at least an estimate of surface area should be made if measurements are not feasible (see chapter 10).

The amount of water that is shaded by vegetation, banks, and overhanging objects should be recorded as cover (item 28). Weather may be recorded as precipitation, percent of overcast, and direction and velocity of wind (item 20).

In addition to the percentage of the stream that pools occupy, the pools

Table 7.2. An example of relative abundance, by class, for one species of fish in a collection.*

Class I 1 to 10	Class II 1 to 100	Critique
1	1	Very rare, 1 or 2
2	2	Rare, more than 2
3	3–8	Uncommon
4	9–13	Not common
5	14–18	Common
6	19–25	Well represented
7	26–40	Extremely well represented
8	41–60	Abundant, most numerous
9	61–80	Very abundant outnumbering all others combined
10	81–100	Extremely abundant, dominating the collection almost to the exclusion of all others

* This is not in relation to numbers of other species in the collection, rather it relates to a hypothetical population of one species. Classes I and II have ten divisions; class II provides opportunity for additional breakdown within most divisions.

A Class I summary of relative abundance based on the collection in Table 7.1 would show RBT (27) Class I/6, BT (4) Class I/2, Mt. whitefish (106) Class I/9, carp (7) Class I/3, Utah chub (11) Class I/5.

may be described as grade A, B, C, D, or E, where A represents adequate area, depth, and cover for the population of fish present (or desired), B is 80 percent of A, C is 60 percent, D is 40 percent, and E is less than 40 percent (item 29). Shelter refers to below water level objects which provide fish protection (item 30) and can include a notation on the type of shelter (boulders, logs, or others).

Each species of fish should be recorded in either absolute or relative numbers (table 7.1, item 37, and table 7.2). Where hundreds or even thousands of fish are taken in a single collection, recording relative abundance on a scale of 1–10 or 1–100 is generally a necessity (table 7.2). When age and growth or food habits data are taken, serial numbers of these specimens are often recorded under remarks (table 7.1, item 37, and table 7.3). Items 1 through 36 of table 7.1 may be entered directly into a computer program. Item 37 may require separate entries. When data are taken on individual fish, the information should be complete enough to stand alone (table 7.3). A serial number is given each fish within a collection on which individual data are taken (table 7.3, item 1). Generally a new series of serial numbers is started with each collection, but one series of numbers may be used for a year or longer. (Catalog numbers are given only to museum specimens [table 7.3, item 3]). Scales or other bony parts used for age and growth and stomachs for food analyses are

Table 7.3.   Individual fish data envelope.

1.	Serial No.	1
2.	Coll. No.	S89–1
3.	Cat. No.	NA
4.	Species	Yellow perch
5.	Locality	Logan, River, 2.1 miles above junction HY 89
6.	County	Cache
7.	Township	11N
8.	Range	2E
9.	Sec.	30
10.	Stom.	Yes
11.	Sex	Male
12.	Age	Adult
13.	Gear	Elec

often taken along with other information. In practice, items 3, 5, 6, 7, 8, 9, and one or two of 11, 12, and 13 are often not recorded on each individual fish data envelope.

Types of Fish Collection Gear

The more common types of fish collecting gear are: (1) gill nets, commercial and experimental—list either as stretched or bar mesh measurement; (2) seines—list length, mesh size, size of bag, and depth; (3) hook and line—describe gear, lure, and method of use; (4) spear, gigs, etc.; (5) traps; (6) hand; (7) diversion or drainage of a stream; (8) chemicals (e.g., rotenone, sodium cyanide); (9) explosives; (10) miscellaneous nets (e.g., dip nets, throw nets); and (11) electric shock—generally 110 to 220 volts either AC or DC, cycles from 60 to 180, and capacity from 500 to 7,500 watts machine output—list all machine parameters and water conductivity if known. The amount of time fished should also be recorded to allow comparisons of the number of fish per unit of effort.

Gear Effectiveness

It is obvious that, in most cases, different types of fishing gear vary in effectiveness for a given habitat and fish size. To gain the best estimate of a fish population, more than one type of gear will normally be used. When only one method of collecting is used, the bias that it introduces should be known, that is, how does the sample collected vary in species and number from the actual population?

Gear Selectivity

Layher and Maughan (1984) report that in sampling a silty bottom stream in north central Oklahoma, rotenone collection of fish from a stream segment previously electrofished yielded mostly fish collected with electrofishing. The total numbers of fish collected with rotenone did not exceed the total numbers collected by electrofishing for four of the six species. In the case of mosquitofish and yellow bullheads, more fish that had not been collected by electrofishing were recovered with rotenone than had been collected by electrofishing. They conclude that depletion sampling with electrofishing (in this case a DC boom-shocker) was at least as efficient as rotenone except for mosquitofish and yellow bullheads.

Gear Selectivity: A Hypothetical Example

The discussion of an uncomplicated situation will demonstrate some variations in gear selectivity (table 7.4).

The inshore collection that employed 110 volts of alternating current was judged to be moderately effective on small fish. A higher percentage of the 4- to 7-inch group was taken than of the 0- to 3-inch group. It is speculated that the smallest fish were quite susceptible to electrical current but, due to their size, were more difficult to recover than the 4- to 7-inch group. Carp 8 to 22 inches in length were much less susceptible to this collection method than were the smaller fish. No fish over 22 inches in length was taken. Larger carp are more wary than the small ones, and in this case they may have been warned by the fringe of the electrical field. Electric current is judged to be effective for collecting small carp inhabiting shallow water but of relatively little value for estimating populations of large carp in this type of habitat. The marl bottom was a negative factor. Seining was moderately effective for those fish 8 to 28 inches long. The small fish could, and apparently did, swim through the net. The largest fish may have simply avoided the net.

The experimental gill net was the second most effective method of collecting larger fish. The net had too large a mesh size for the smallest fish and too

Table 7.4. A hypothetical example of the relative efficiency of five types of collecting gear on six size groups of carp in a twelve-acre midwestern pond.

Total length in inches						
0–3	4–7	8–12	15–22	23–28	29–34	Method of capture
(Percent of total in size group)						
23	29	2	1	0	0	110-volt alternating electrical current—oval electrodes (inshore)
0	0	21	14	1	0	200-by-5-foot drag seine—3-inch bar mesh
0	2	19	27	24	1	125-by-5-foot experimental gill net—¾, 1¼, 1¾, 2½, and 3½-inch bar mesh
0	2	12	11	1	0	24-by-4-by-4-foot trap net—50-foot wings, ¾-inch bar mesh
72	85	90	95	100	100	1 ppm—5 percent rotenone

Maximum depth 14 feet, water temperature 72°F, bottom soft marl, water conductivity 78 ohms/cmU, underwater obstructions none, water current none.

small a mesh for the largest fish. Net wariness may also have been a factor. Nevertheless, the experimental gill net catch did yield a reasonably reliable index of the carp population.

The trap net was only moderately effective for medium-size fish, probably because water current was lacking.

One part per million of 5 percent rotenone was the most effective collecting method used.

In summary, the use of 110-volt current was the only mechanical gear that took small- and medium-size fish. The seine was moderately effective on medium-size fish. The experimental gill net was the most reliable mechanical gear. One part per million of 5 percent active ingredients rotenone was reliable for all size groups. Rotenone has the obvious disadvantage of being nonselective. It is sometimes stated that all fish in a body of water are killed by an application of rotenone. Rarely, if ever, is this true.

Preservation of Material

Individual fish data should be taken shortly after death. When it is impossible to do this, fish should be stored in a cool, dry place. Digestion of stomach contents continues slowly even at near freezing temperatures. Fish should not be frozen, however, before individual lengths and weights are recorded, since both are often changed in the freezing process. The most common initial fish preservative is 10 percent formalin (100 percent formalin is labeled 37 percent formaldehyde), which for a collection to be used for any purpose but gross examination should be buffered with sodium salts. Buffering is essential if any tissue or histopathological examination is contemplated. A formula for the preparation of neutral pH, buffered formalin is provided in appendix C. Fish slated to be examined in detail for pathological purposes should be preserved in Bouins Solution. This is generally used for preservation of tissue but can be used for whole fish as an expedient in the field. A formula for the preparation of Bouins Solution is included in appendix C. Paraformaldehyde is also used as a preservative (Taube 1965) but is not as readily available as formalin. Specimens preserved in formalin may be transferred to 70 percent alcohol for long-term storage. This keeps them soft and avoids the health hazards associated with extended exposure to formalin-preserved specimens. Formalin in preserved specimens is at times (and with individual sensitivity) toxic to the skin or lungs of people handling fish extensively. A procedure for deformalinizing specimens for study purposes is advised for lengthy or repeated exposures. Formalin is considered a toxic chemical and should be disposed of properly. The procedure is based on salts of sodium and is included in appendix C.

Specimens destined for the museum or for further species identification efforts should be dropped in the preservative alive. The body cavity of specimens larger than 6 to 8 inches should be slit or preferably injected with undiluted formalin. Since live fish sometimes regurgitate food when put in formalin, those that are to be used for food habit studies should be suffocated in water, iced (for food habit studies where fish are not preserved but stomachs are removed and placed in formalin several hours after capture), or killed by piercing the brain. Alternately, an anesthetic like MS–222 can be used to render the fish unconscious before placing them in formalin without danger of regurgitation. Changes in length and weight following preservation generally continue for not more than thirty days (Sigler 1949). According to Parker (1963) changes in length and weight occurring during storage in formalin are relatively large and significant. Average initial weight gains up to 116 to 127 percent of original mean weight were observed for fish killed and stored in freshwater formalin. Weight subsequently fell to 105 to 111 percent of original live weight. The greatest relative gains and subsequent losses were associated with small-size fish. In salt water formalin weight initially fell to 87 to 101 percent but subsequently rose to 91 to 95 percent of live weight.

Stomachs and intestines for food habits analysis should be wrapped individually in cheese cloth and labeled as to species, collection number, and serial number. A soft lead pencil or India ink makes a durable mark. Each stomach analysis card should bear the above headings (unless the back of the scale envelope is used), and later the list of items in the stomach may be added (see chapter 12).

Intestines with a high water content, such as those of carp, require special attention. One way to remove water from stomach contents is to put them on an absorbent material (blotter paper for example) before measurement. Care should be used not to dehydrate specimens since this introduces an unpredictable error in volume determination.

How to Take Length and Weight Measurements

When measurements for weight or length are to be taken in the field, the use of an anesthetic greatly reduces both handling stress to the fish and handling difficulty for the researchers. An approved anesthetic such as MS–222 is recommended.

In comprehensive work the standard, fork, and total lengths are measured to the nearest millimeter. Standard length is the distance from the end of the snout to the hypural plate (the modified last vertebrae). Only "modern" fishes have a hypural plate. Fork length is the length from the end of the snout to the notch in the caudal fin. Total length is the length from the end of the snout to the end of the caudal fin when both lobes are brought together. All three lengths are often taken in a life history study where it is desirable to know the ratio between these three lengths or to develop a conversion factor from one length to the other. The conversion factors may, and often do, vary for different lengths.

The position of the hypural plate can be easily determined by bending the tail to one side and observing where a groove is formed. A long-bladed knife and a simple measuring board provide quick and accurate data; however, many workers prefer more complex boards (Woods 1968). In instances where the caudal fin is frayed, the standard length is often the only accurate measurement obtainable. Standard length measurements are not recommended for fishes which have vertebrae extending into the caudal fin (for example, sturgeon). Fork lengths are often used when defining legal lengths for commercial fishery operations since this measurement can be taken quickly. Certain fish, such as the bullhead catfishes which have truncate caudals, do not lend themselves to fork length measurements. The total length is the measurement most commonly used in establishing legal length limits for the creel. This is the measurement most easily understood by the general public.

Measurement of specific body parts may be necessary if fish are not intact or have been damaged (Anderson and Gutreuter 1983). Pectoral fin length, head length, the distance from the eye to the hypural bone, and others are possible. All should be standardized prior to a field investigation so that all investigators measure the same factor.

Accurate weights are more difficult to obtain under field conditions than lengths. Body surface and buccal cavity water introduce variations on individual specimens and between weight classes. Blotting specimens dry may reduce accuracy variation but tends to increase the standard deviation of weights (Parker 1963). Water accumulation on the scales may also introduce errors (Anderson and Gutreuter 1983).

Weights are recorded either in grams or kilograms. The precision of the scales should be stated. As a rule, the weights should be accurate to less than or equal to ± 0.01 the weight of the specimen.

Whatever techniques are utilized they need to be used consistently throughout the course of a project.

How to Sex Fish

The reproductive organs of fish are examined in order to obtain life history information by sex and to determine the age of maturity and time and age of spawning. Many species can be sexed by external characteristics, especially during the spawning season (Brauhn 1972; Moen 1959; Sigler 1948). The gonads are paired organs leading forward dorsally from the anal region. (The female yellow perch has only one ovary.) The sex of most mature fish is easily determined by internal inspection during the spawning season, but less so at other times of the year. Judgment in determining the sex of young fish can best be developed by starting with mature fish and working progressively toward younger and younger fish. Examination of gonads at 100× with a compound microscope is useful on small fish. Generally, the male gonads are finer in texture than those of the female. They tend to be white rather than yellow or orange in color, and frequently the male gonad is ribbon shaped in cross section, whereas the female gonad has a slightly oval cross section. Difficulty may be experienced in determining the sex of a particular age class of young fish, especially where some show marked sexual development and others none.

The gonads of some fish, such as the males of the family Ictaluridae, do not fit the above description. Perhaps this should serve as a warning that literature should be explored if sex differentials are to be an important consideration (and it should be in life history studies). The gonad development of the species being studied should be recorded in detail for each individual. This is probably best accomplished by appropriate coding of a reasonable number of developmental stages. Development of gonadal somatic index (GSI) data over time is a useful tool for determining spawning time (see chapter 14).

Literature Cited

Anderson, R. O., and S. J. Gutreuter. 1983. Lengths, Weight and Associated Structural Indices. Pp. 283–300 in L. A. Nielsen and D. L. Johnson, eds., *Fisheries Techniques*. Bethesda, Md.: American Fisheries Society.

Bayley, P. B., and R. F. Illyes. 1988. Measuring Fish and Recording Data in the Field Laboratory: A Microcomputer Application. *Fisheries* 13:15–18.

Brauhn, J. L. 1972. A Suggested Method for Sexing Bluegills. *Progressive Fish-Culturist* 34(1):17.

Deventer, Van J. S., and W. S. Platts. 1985. *A Computer Software System for Entering, Monitoring and Analyzing Fish Capture Data from Streams*. USDA Forest Service. Intermountain Research Station. Research Note INT-352. Ogden, Utah. 12 pp.

Hach, C. C. 1972. Understanding Turbidity Measurement. *Industrial Water Engineering* Feb/Mar 1972:5.

Layher, W. G., and O. E. Maughan. 1984. Comparison of Three Sampling Techniques for Estimating Fish Populations in Small Streams. *Progressive Fish-Culturist* 46(3):180–84.

Moen, T. 1959. Sexing of Channel Catfish. *Transactions of the American Fisheries Society* 88(2):149.

Parker, R. R. 1963. Effects of Formalin on Length and Weight of Fishes. *Journal of the Fisheries Research Board of Canada* 20(6):1441–55.

Platts, W. S., W. F. Megahan, and G. W. Minshall. 1983. *Methods for Evaluating Stream, Riparian, and Biotic Conditions*. Ogden, Utah: U.S. Department of Agriculture, U.S. Forest Service, Intermountain Forest and Range Experiment Station. General Technical Report INT–138. 70 pp.

Sigler, W. F. 1948. Determination of Sex in White Bass, *Lepibema chrysops* (Rafinesque), by External Characteristics. *Copeia* 1948(4):299–300.

———. 1949. *Life History of the White Bass*, Lepibema chrysops *(Rafinesque), of Spirit Lake, Iowa*. Agriculture Experiment Station, Iowa State College, Research Bulletin 366:201–44.

Taube, C. M. 1965. The Use of Paraformaldehyde as a Biological Preservative. *Progressive Fish-Culturist* 27(3):165–68.

Woods, C. S. 1968. An Improved Fish Measuring Board. *New Zealand Journal of Marine Freshwater Research, Fisheries Research Division* No. 125 2(4):678–83.

8. Toxicants and Anesthetics

The use of chemicals in fisheries work has increased steadily in the last fifty years. In that time, literally hundreds of chemicals have been utilized by fishery workers in attempts to find methods for eradication, removal, anesthetization, and disease control. As greater understanding was reached about the chemicals and the requirements of water quality and other treatment aspects of fisheries work, the number of chemicals utilized declined because they were not considered safe (for fish workers and the environment) or effective on the species for which they were used. The total number of chemicals both safe and effective and registered for use in various aspects of fisheries now is quite small. Efforts are under way at various federal and state agencies and private concerns to develop and register new toxicants, anesthetics, and chemotherapeutic agents for disease control. Schnick, Meyer, and Walsh (1986) present a summary of the status of fishery chemicals as of 1985.

Fish Control and Chemical Collection Methods

Cumming (1975) notes three reasons for the use of fish toxicants. By far the most prevalent reason is removal of an existing fish population and the subsequent reestablishment of one that will more closely meet fishing demands. The second reason for the use of fish toxicants is the removal of unwanted fishes to maintain monoculture or disease-free fish stocks. The third reason Cumming lists is the removal of contaminant species by fish farmers to reduce the conversion from fish food to fish flesh and clean out ponds for a new crop. Other reasons for the use of fish toxicants include the collection of fish from a particular aquatic ecosystem to study age and growth, species composition, or other management objectives. While most fish toxicants cause death of a large percentage of all or most species in treated areas, some toxicants are either selective for species or groups or can be applied at such rates that recovery of certain species or sizes of fish is possible.

Several chemicals that act either as an anesthetic or as a toxicant are used for fish collection. The best known of these is rotenone. Other chemicals employed for both collection or removal of fish include sodium cyanide, antimycin, and squoxin. As with other fish-control and collection techniques, toxicants have both advantages and disadvantages (biases) and must be carefully utilized in any given situation.

Toxicants have been used in various forms and for various reasons for hundreds of years; however, new and refined forms, many of which are species or group specific, have been developed in response to identified needs in research and management. Only rotenone and antimycin are registered as fish toxicants in the United States by the Environmental Protection Agency (EPA). Compounds used as fish-collecting aids are not regulated as pesticides, but other restrictions may apply. TFM and Bayer 73 are registered to control sea lampreys, but they are not discussed here because of their limited use in inland recreational fisheries work. Toxaphene, cresol, and sodium sulfite are not included in this text nor is the anesthetic methyl pentynol. These chemicals, because of registration constraints or lack of use, are not recommended for fishery applications.

In a fish eradication program the amount of chemical used is generally stated in ppm (parts per million), that is, one pound of chemical in a million pounds of water is 1 ppm. Volumes are usually calculated in acre-feet. One acre-foot is equivalent to one acre of water one foot deep, or 43,560 cubic feet, or 326,000 gallons, or 2,718,000 pounds (2.718 pounds of chemical equals 1.0 ppm) per acre-foot of water.

Rotenone

Rotenone is a chemical compound extracted from roots of several species of plants of the bean family (Leguminosae). In some areas it is called derris or cube root. It has been used for centuries by natives in South America to capture fish for food (Kinney 1965). Rotenone has been used in fish management in the United States since 1934. It is extremely toxic to most fishes, but is not particularly toxic to mammals. As dry rotenone is a respiratory and eye irritant to humans, a mask and goggles should be worn when there is chance of contact. Several rotenone formulations are registered for fishery use (Schnick, Meyer, and Walsh 1986; Lennon et al. 1970). Commercial rotenone formulations are available in liquid or powder form. The active ingredient varies from less than 1 to 20 percent, but the commonly used strength is 5 percent. Rotenone may be applied as a powder, a wettable powder, or a liquid containing from 2.5 to 5 percent rotenone.

The powder form (cube) loses its toxicity when exposed to air and is more difficult to apply. Wettable powders and liquid formulations are easier and safer to use. Liquid formulations can be stored in sealed containers for up to one year without loss of efficacy (Davies and Shelton 1983).

Rotenone is generally used to obtain a complete fish kill primarily because it is largely nonselective. It is also used as a spot toxicant to kill adult fish, fish eggs, or larvae. Rotenone may also be used as a selective fish toxicant if there is sufficient information on the sensitivity of the species in question (Rowe-Rowe 1971). According to Kinney (1965) threadfin shad and freshwater drum have been selectively killed by rotenone.

Gilderhus, Dawson, and Allen (1988), reporting on persistence of the Nox-fish formulation, note a half-life of 10.3 days in cold water (32°–41°F) and a half-life of 0.94 days in warm water (73°–81°F). Decomposition of rotenone followed a first-order decay curve.

In selective treatments to remove fish, fish managers may use as little as 0.10 ppm of 5 percent rotenone. Normal use ranges from 0.5 to 1.0 ppm, and hard-to-kill fish such as catfishes and carp may require as much as 2.0 to 4.0 ppm, especially if the water is rich in organic material (Kinney 1965). Marking and Bills (1976), reporting on laboratory tests of Noxfish (which contains 5 percent rotenone), noted toxicities to a wide variety of fish at concentrations ranging, in ninety-six-hour exposures, from 21.5 parts per billion (ppb) for Atlantic salmon to 497 ppb for goldfish. They report that the ninety-six-hour LC_{50} was less than 100 ppb for bowfins, six species of salmonids, northern pike, carp, longnose, and white suckers, smallmouth bass, yellow perch, and walleyes. The ninety-six-hour LC_{50} was greater than 100 ppb for goldfish, fat-head minnows, black bullheads, channel catfish, green sunfish, bluegills, and largemouth bass. Most of the sensitive species died in three-hour exposures to much lower concentrations than the resistant species.

Rotenone should be applied in a uniform and rapid manner throughout the treated area because fish may sense the chemical and avoid exposure. In small waters such as farm ponds, garden sprayers or gasoline powered pumps are desirable. Air-thrust boats are quite effective in shallow water; the toxicant can be dispersed through the propeller with a gasoline-powered pump.

Fish occasionally, but rarely, recover from rotenone toxicity. If it is desir-able to rescue fish, they should be dipnetted immediately as they appear at the surface and put in fresh, preferably running, water. Bouck and Ball (1965) report that a 5 to 10 ppm concentration of methylene blue can be used to revive stressed fish. However, methylene blue is considered a problem chemical by regulatory agencies and in any given situation may be subject to control by state, federal, or regional agencies. It should not be utilized until approval has been granted by appropriate authorities for a particular use or application. Toxic effects of rotenone can be eliminated almost immediately with potassium permanganate at 1 ppm for each 0.05 ppm of rotenone (Lawrence 1955). Potassium permanganate is also toxic to some fish, however, at concentrations of 3 to 4 ppm and is hazardous to apply. Marking et al. (1983), in testing rainbow smelt and common carp, report LC_{50}s to eggs for potassium permanganate of 0.074 mg/l (ppm) in ninety-six hours, and LC_{50}s to larvae of 0.26 mg/l in twenty-four hours, and 0.075 mg/l in ninety-six hours. For carp, the LC_{50} ninety-six-hour toxicity to eggs was 6.00 mg/l, and to larvae was 1.58 mg/l in twenty-four hours.

Lawrence (1955) found that at 81°F, potassium permanganate killed bluegills at 3 ppm, a large number of bass at 4 ppm, and fathead minnows at 5 ppm. At lower temperatures a higher amount of potassium permanganate was required. Various concentrations have been reported as effective, depending on environmental conditions and amount of rotenone used (Lennon et al. 1970). Although residual toxicity may be determined by placing boxes of live fish, preferably the same species which is to be stocked, at various depths in the water to determine possible mortality, directions or label instructions for time of restocking should be carefully read and followed.

Post (1958) stated the duration of toxicity in days (d) could be expressed as a function of temperature (t) in degrees Fahrenheit, where $d = 93 - 1.33t$ for temperatures between 45° and 60°F and $d = 38 - 0.43t$ for temperatures between 60° and 80°F.

A simple, fairly accurate chemical test exists for rotenone (Post 1955). Dawson et al. (1983) report on a laboratory method for measuring rotenone in water at piscicidal concentrations. The laboratory technique is accurate and reproducible but requires sophisticated equipment and trained technicians.

Detoxification may take longer in very soft water or in deeper, stratified bodies of water. Waters generally detoxify within a few days to a month from only natural chemical reactions. Factors favoring rapid detoxification are a low concentration of rotenone, high water temperature, high alkalinity, abundant light, and aeration (Kinney 1965). Detoxification by potassium permanganate is occasionally used in lakes or ponds, but is much more effective in streams where the toxicant should not proceed downstream beyond a certain point.

An additional consideration in the use of fish toxicants is the effect of the chemical on nontarget organisms. Houf and Campbell (1977) report that most benthic organisms appear to be unaffected by rotenone at concentrations applied for fish eradication. There are, however, reports of mortality among specific taxa exposed to low concentrations of rotenone. No immediate short-term effects from application of 2 ppm of rotenone were observed in experimental studies by Houf and Campbell. The major species of mayflies, dragonflies, damselflies, aquatic earthworms, snails, phantom midges, and true midges present before treatment were also present after treatment. Long-term effects on population densities could not be connected to treatment with rotenone. Burress (1982) reports that 2 or 5 ppb applications of rotenone caused a temporary reduction in both total numbers and diversity of benthic invertebrates and a total mortality of caged Asiatic clams. A partial mortality of a resident population of larval leopard frogs was also reported in the pond treated at higher concentration. Numbers of benthic organisms, based on number per square meter, were reduced 67 percent in the low-level application and 96 percent in the pond treated at the higher application. The diversity index declined sharply in both ponds between three and seven days after treatment. Approximately seventy days after treatment, total numbers of benthic organisms had more than doubled over those present in the low-number application, and more than tripled in the higher application rate pond. No significant deleterious effects from the treatments were observed on zooplankton populations.

Antimycin

Antimycin is an antibiotic produced in *Streptomyces* cultures. It has been used as a fish toxicant since 1964 (Lennon et al. 1970). Antimycin is an effective fish eradicant since it is highly toxic to fish at extremely low concentrations but only slightly toxic to mammals. It is considerably less hazardous to people than most other fish toxicants, and the degradation products of antimycin as verified by bioassay are nontoxic (Berger, Lennon, and Hogan 1969). Greselin, Herr, and Chappel (1967) feel that in view of antimycin's high specificity as a fish toxicant, its rapid breakdown, and lack of hazardous degradation products, it has a marked advantage over most other toxicants.

The reactions of fish to antimycin are slow and unspectacular. The first stages of distress are loss of orientation and progressively less response to stimuli. Response time may vary from a few to twenty-four hours (Gilderhus, Berger, and Lennon 1969). The effects of antimycin are irreversible at lethal concentrations. Its toxicity to fish is diminished by high alkalinity, high temperature, sunlight, and the metabolic activity of aquatic organisms (Davies and Shelton 1983). Antimycin detoxifies more rapidly at high pH, making it more useful in neutral or low pH water. It has been reported to have a half-life biological activity of five to eight days in soft, acid waters, but only a few hours at pH 8.5 and above (Marking and Dawson 1972). Antimycin can be detoxified with potassium permanganate similarly applied as with rotenone. It can be used more selectively than some other fish toxicants, and fish sensitivity to antimycin has been placed into three groups with high, moderate, and low sensitivity. Removal of scaled fish (except goldfish) from culture ponds of naked fish (e.g., catfish) can be effective using antimycin. Gilderhus, Berger, and Lennon indicate that 15 parts per billion (ppb) of antimycin will eliminate all cyprinids, catostomids, percids, and centrarchids and leave catfishes. Burress and Luhning (1969a, 1969b) report that antimycin can be used to control scaled fishes in a wide variety of habitat types and that selective control can be achieved by varying concentrations and selected treatment temperatures. Selective removal of sunfishes was accomplished by varied concentrations. Small fishes of a given species are more susceptible than large fish.

Use of low levels of antimycin does not affect even fingerling catfish, and temperature susceptibility varies greatly between 45° and 72°F; however, catfish can be controlled by higher levels of antimycin. At temperatures from 46° to 81°F, 8 to 22 ppb are required to kill channel catfish and 50 to 120 ppb to kill black bullheads.

Houf and Campbell (1977), in a study on the effects of antimycin on macrobenthos in ponds, report that at treatment concentrations of 20 and 40 ppb antimycin does not affect species diversity, emergence, seasonal dynamics, abundance, or relative numbers of taxa. In addition, they report that no dominant organisms which were present before treatment were eliminated by exposure to 40 ppb applications of antimycin. The species represented included mayflies, dragonflies, damselflies, phantom midges, true midges, snails, and aquatic earthworms. They additionally conclude that there is no consistent evidence of toxicant interference with insect emergence. Species diversity appeared unchanged as a result of pond treatment by toxicants at the specified concentrations. Jacobi and Degan (1977) report that in stream applications of antimycin varying from 17 to 44 ppm, populations of macroinvertebrates were drastically reduced two days after treatment, but all common taxa which had been identified prior to treatment were present in the stream one year later. One species of crayfish was unaffected by the treatment in the stream, and total benthic biomass one year following application of the toxicant approached or exceeded that before treatment.

Antimycin is currently registered for fisheries use in the United States and Canada (Schnick, Meyer, and Walsh 1986; Lennon et al. 1970) and is sold under the trade name Fintrol. It is presently available only as a concentrate (Schnick, Meyer, and Walsh). It was previously available in various formulations. Fintrol–5 and Fintrol–15 were formulations coated on sand grains that released the toxicant evenly in the first 5 and 15 feet of depth respectively. The liquid formulation was developed for use in flowing waters (Davies and Shelton 1983).

Sodium Cyanide

The value of sodium cyanide as a fish toxicant has been investigated by numerous workers (Wiley 1984; Doudoroff 1976; Lewis and Tarrant 1960; Bridges 1958). One of its most significant features is its ability to paralyze but not kill, if fish are removed promptly. The fact that sodium cyanide permits the removal of live fish suggests other possible uses: (1) collection of live fish, (2) harvest or transfer of hatchery fish, and (3) an aid in mark and recapture. Bridges found that 1 ppm of sodium cyanide is effective against fish even when temperatures are low (42°F) and pH values high (9.7) and concludes that sodium cyanide is inexpensive, easily applied, and has a short period of toxicity. Wiley lists the following advantages for collecting fish from streams with sodium cyanide: (1) it is relatively safe and easy to use if essential precautions are exercised, (2) a small amount can be used to sample several streams, (3) a detoxicant is not required at the end of the sample area, (4) it has a low degree of persistence in the environment, (5) there are apparently no toxic residues, (6) it is inexpensive, a 200-pound drum costing $160, and (7) it is effective in situations where electrofishing is not.

Hydrogen cyanide (HCN) is the principle form of cyanide toxic to fish. It affects fish more rapidly in warm water because the respiratory metabolic rate is higher. Wiley (1984) utilized Cyanobrik®, which is composed of 99 percent sodium cyanide and 1 percent inert ingredients. Cyanobrik® is readily soluble in water, forming free cyanide (CN-ion and molecular HCN). HCN is volatile, lighter than air, and diffuses rapidly into the atmosphere, consequently leaving no toxic residues in water. Fish affected by cyanide can be returned to clean water where they eliminate cyanide from the tissues (Wiley). Bridges (1958) found no noticeable effect on nontarget organisms (aquatic insects) in ponds; however, Tatum (1969) observed a 77 percent reduction in total benthos following application of sodium cyanide in streams.

A word of caution is in order regarding the uses of sodium cyanide. Cyanides are very deadly to humans. Wiley (1984) reports that hydrogen cyanide gas is rapidly absorbed in human lungs and death will result in twenty-five to thirty minutes if 135 to 270 ppm HCN vapor is inhaled. Inhalation of cyanide dusts is dangerous, as well, because the cyanide will dissolve on the moist mucous membranes of the lungs and be absorbed into the bloodstream. It is not currently registered for use in fisheries work in the United States (Schnick, Meyer, and Walsh 1986; Lennon et al. 1970). The Environmental Protection Agency does not regulate sodium cyanide as a pesticide when used as a fish-collecting aid; however, other federal, state, or local regulations may restrict its use because of its toxicity.

Squoxin

Squoxin is used as either a powder, liquid, or emulsion and is a selective toxicant to control squawfishes (Lennon et al. 1970). It is not currently registered for use, but efforts are being made to find support for registration (Schnick, Meyer, and Walsh 1986). Squoxin is extremely toxic to squawfish. It was developed and patented at the University of Idaho by Craig MacPhee as a result of research to identify selective toxicants. It is also toxic to other fish, particularly some salmonids, but there is a ten- to seventeen-fold margin between the minimum LC_{100} for two species of squawfish and maximum LC_0 for salmonids which are not tolerant. It does not repel squawfish (MacPhee and Ruelle 1968, 1969).

Squoxin, at concentrations lethal to squawfish, is reported to have little or no effect on aquatic invertebrates (Brusven and MacPhee 1974). Staley (1977) reports that squoxin was found to be much less toxic to aquatic invertebrates than it was to squawfish. The relationship between toxicity is evidently inversely proportional to adaptations by aquatic invertebrates to habitats having low levels of oxygen availability. The most sensitive invertebrate tested was blackfly larvae which are abundant in streams having high current velocity and high dissolved oxygen. These larvae exhibited an LC_{50} value of 60 ppb in forty-eight hours. Other aquatic invertebrate larvae which tolerate low oxygen conditions were resistant to treatments up to 10 ppm exhibiting a maximum response of 30 percent in ninety-six hours. Staley reports that the degradation of squoxin in surface waters was most rapid in water having a high pH and high alkalinity. Degradation also occurs in the presence of dissolved organic compounds of high molecular weight. He further states that because of its water solubility, low partition coefficient, rapid degradation, and the ability of a wide variety of organisms to excrete it, squoxin would not be biologically magnified to a significant degree in aquatic ecosystems.

Thanite

Thanite is an insecticide with low mammalian toxicity. Burress and Bass (1975) describe techniques for applying thanite solutions. The formulation generally used consists of thanite and kerosene emulsified in Atlox 1045A mixed in a ratio of 70:20:10 parts by volume. Other formulations use an 80:20 mixture of thanite and Atlox 1045A or another Atlox formulation.

Lewis (1968) was the first to use thanite for fish collection and reported excellent results in collecting largemouth bass in southern Illinois. Burress, Gilderhus, and Cumming (1976) report that fish exposed to effective concentrations of thanite tend to surface in distress and swim about in a disoriented manner. As sedation deepens, many fish move towards shore and some seek cover, while others float listlessly at the surface or settle to the bottom. Generally, small fish are affected first and die sooner than large ones. Low temperatures slow responses and delay the onset of mortality. Fish collected in early stages of sedation recover quickly after being placed in fresh water, but recovery times and mortality rates increase as exposures are lengthened. Burress, Gilderhus, and Cumming also indicate that thanite can be safely used to collect fish from selected areas of larger bodies of water without killing fish in untreated areas. Application levels of thanite include 0.8, 1.2, and 1.6 ppb. The 0.8 ppb was ineffective, but following a second application of 0.4 ppb, the collection of numerous sunfish and intermediate-size basses in one test pond was quickly facilitated. A third application of an additional 0.4 ppb was needed before adult sunfish and large-size bass were affected. In one test pond, two 1-ppb applications of thanite were made during a two-hour period. All fish were recovered alive, including largemouth bass, bluegill, and golden shiners. This pond was subsequently treated with rotenone and only four additional adult golden shiners were found, indicating that thanite can be effective in removing all fish alive in controlled pond situations. If live fish are to be maintained, adequate recovery facilities must be available. In at least one experimental situation, recovery facilities were insufficient and large numbers of fish died, probably due to oxygen deficiency resulting from overloading of the facilities.

Summerfelt and Lewis (1967) report that thanite repelled green sunfish at concentrations from 2 to 20 ppm and killed them at 0.5 ppm in six-hour exposures. Lewis (1968) reports that thanite selectively kills sunfish in the presence of catfish and minnows. Largemouth bass recovered if moved to fresh water before a lethal exposure had occurred.

Live fish bioassay tests indicate, in at least one experimental situation, that thanite had degraded to a nontoxic level by thirteen days after initial application. In an experimental situation, a 90 percent mortality of 1-cm long frog tadpoles was reported, but no mortality of other nontarget organisms was noted. Burress, Gilderhus, and Cumming (1976) conclude that thanite is an effective mechanism for collecting many sizes of several species of sport fish under a wide variety of environmental conditions. Bluegill, white crappie, small sunfish, and yellow perch were most sensitive to thanite. Less sensitive species include redear sunfish, warmouth, green sunfish, largemouth bass, lake chubsuckers, walleyes, and gizzard shad. Catfish were most resistant to thanite, although channel catfish were less resistant than brown or yellow bullheads. Yellow bullhead was the most resistant species tested. Northern pike collected in one test in an experimental situation were captured alive but none survived for twenty-four hours. The apparent conclusion from this is that the fish absorbed a lethal dose of chemical before they became sufficiently sedated to be vulnerable to netting. This information should be utilized when planning reclamation operations in areas of northern pike populations. Burress, Gilderhus, and Cumming also report that variations in pH, temperature, hardness, conductivity, and turbidity appear to have very little impact on thanite's efficacy. Treatment at low temperatures does, however, tend to reduce mortality. Viability of all species, other than northern pike, was excellent for those fish collected and placed in fresh and well-aerated water within two hours after treatment. Thanite appears to be particularly effective in collecting largemouth bass.

Anesthesial Methods

Many laboratory and field procedures require immobilizing fish for varying periods of time. Anesthetizing agents are therefore important in fish management and culture to produce a wide range of effects varying from mild sedation for routine handling operations to complete loss of consciousness or equilibrium for surgical or other procedures. Marking and Meyer (1985), based on information from 183 fishery workers at federal, state, and private organizations, report that literally millions of fish are anesthetized annually as an aid to spawning, transporting, tagging, or marking. The two most serious constraints on an anesthetic are its effectiveness and compliance with FDA registration. The FDA requires that any compound used in anesthetizing fish that may be used for human consumption, must either be excreted or metabolized before the fish are released or consumed. Otherwise, the residues must be proven to be safe. A wide variety of chemicals has been used to produce anesthesis in both coldwater and warmwater species. Due to the necessity for continuation of respiration through an aquatic medium, restraining devices and operating tables must incorporate provisions for almost constant flushing of the gills with well-oxygenated water and water-anesthetic combinations.

Four planes of anesthesis exist. The first is an escape or frenzied activity period as the fish reacts to the new environment and the irritation of the drug. In the second, as the drug takes effect, the fish slows down and loses equilibrium. The third plane has three parts: complete loss of balance, loss of response to tactile stimulation (surgical plane), and ceasing of opercular motion. The fourth plane is spasmodic gill flaring, cardiac arrest, and death (George Klontz, personal communication, 1978).

Many chemicals have been employed to anesthetize fish. The use of any anesthetic on a given fish requires determination of the concentration that will achieve the desired result. These concentrations are most generally arrived at by trial and error unless previous data are available. Changes in water quality, water temperature, size and species of fish, and other considerations may necessitate changes in procedures to facilitate a particular use.

Anesthetics used include carbon dioxide, electricity, diethyl ether, secobarbital sodium, amobarbial sodium, urethane, chloral hydrate, tertiary amyl alcohol, tribromoethanol, chlorobutanol, 2-phenoxyethanol, 4-styrylpyridine, methyl pentynol, quinaldine sulfate, tricaine methane sulfonate (MS–222), and benzocaine. Only MS–222, sodium bicarbonate, and carbonic acid are registered or approved for fishery use (Schnick, Meyer, and Walsh 1986). A project is under way at the La Crosse National Fishery Research Laboratory, Wisconsin, to more clearly identify the need for better anesthetics and to delineate the activity of known fish anesthetics. The laboratory then plans to determine which anesthetics have the best potential for registration and to initiate an effort to register them.

MS–222 (Tricaine Methane Sulfonate)

MS–222 is a white crystalline material which is freely soluble in water. It is probably the most popular anesthetic used in fisheries work. Induction time (surgical plane) is usually one to three minutes and most species can be maintained in that state for extended periods with no ill effects. Recovery time, even from extended periods of anesthesia, is generally three to fifteen minutes. Fish exposed repeatedly to MS–222 develop an increased tolerance to the drug that is manifested in increased induction time (Klontz 1964). MS–222 in

the Finquel formulation is approved for fisheries use. A twenty-one-day withdrawal period is required before food fish can be harvested (Schnick, Meyer,
and Walsh 1986).

MS–222 has been demonstrated to be toxic to some species of fish under
some temperatures, hardnesses, and size variations (Marking 1967). MS–222
has also been used to anesthetize fish for transportation but presents problems
if the level of anesthesis is too deep (Johnson 1972; McFarland 1960).

While MS–222 is probably the most popular and most widely used fish
anesthetic in North America today, two aspects deter from it being even more
widely used. The twenty-one-day withdrawal requirement before fish can be
released or consumed is a deterrent to the use of MS–222 for those operations which cannot retain large numbers of fish following treatment. FDA requirements, however, mandate this twenty-one-day waiting period, and until
sufficient research has been completed to change the requirements, this period
must be observed. The second aspect of MS–222 which detracts from its use
is cost. Reagent-grade MS–222 registered with the FDA is moderately expensive. While nonreagent-grade material is now available at a reduced cost, its
use is discouraged because of cost recovery allowances to the company which
produces the registered material.

Carbon Dioxide (CO_2)

Carbon dioxide (CO_2) is a colorless, odorless, noncombustible gas. It has
been used as a fish anesthetic since at least 1942 (Fish 1943). Induction time
is reported to be one to two minutes for adult salmon (Klontz 1964). Maintenance is good for short periods and recovery requires five to ten minutes.
A dosage of 200 ppm is reported for 45° to 55°F water temperature and can
be achieved and maintained by the successive addition of predissolved sodium
bicarbonate and dilute sulfuric acid (Klontz). Carbon dioxide can also be de-
livered into the water as a gas. While use of CO_2 has been limited, recent
reports suggest that it is very effective for anesthetizing fish. Britton (1983)
reports effective anesthesia of adult salmon by discharging carbon dioxide gas
through a carborundum stone and supplementing dissolved oxygen by aeration
(Marking and Meyer 1985). Carbon dioxide (carbonic acid) is approved for use
in fisheries work (Schnick, Meyer, and Walsh 1986). The limited amount of
information available on the use of carbon dioxide as a fish anesthetic makes it
difficult to assess its usefulness as a general anesthetic. One anticipated problem, however, even based on the limited data available, is its usefulness in
the field. The use of carbon dioxide either in the gaseous form or when it is

derived from a chemical reaction of sodium bicarbonate with acid in water necessitates the use of a considerable amount of ancillary equipment. These constraints may reduce the use of carbon dioxide as a fish anesthetic under field conditions. Yoshikawa, Ishido, and Ueno (1988) report the use of carbon dioxide to anesthetize carp for periods up to ten hours. Two concentrations were used, a high one (PCO_2 of 200–25 mm Hg) to induce anesthesia rapidly and a low one (PCO_2 100–25 mm Hg) to maintain anesthesia for long periods.

Sodium Bicarbonate

The use of sodium bicarbonate (baking soda) as a fish anesthetic has not been widely tested or utilized. Booke, Hollander, and Lutterbie (1978) report on the use of sodium bicarbonate as an inexpensive fish anesthetic for use in field studies. Sodium bicarbonate produces a known and controlled source of carbon dioxide for fish anesthesia. Sodium bicarbonate is a white powder that dissolves in water. It is currently registered and approved as a fish anesthetic in the United States (Schnick, Meyer, and Walsh 1986) but has not had wide use. Booke, Hollander, and Lutterbie used a household brand that was 99 percent pure. They report that for pHs between 6.5 and 7.5 and sodium bicarbonate amounts of 142 to 642 ppm, sodium bicarbonate effectively anesthetized rainbow trout, brook trout, and carp. The most effective combination was pH 6.5 and 642 ppm sodium bicarbonate. Within five minutes, 94 percent of rainbow trout and all brook trout were anesthetized. All fish anesthetized in this fashion recovered within ten minutes after removal to fresh water. Carp were not anesthetized within the five-minute requirement established for these tests, and 92 percent required from four to twelve minutes for anesthesia. All recovered, however, within fifteen minutes. Booke, Hollander, and Lutterbie (1978) also report that, at pH 7.0 and 7.5 and sodium bicarbonate dosages of 442 and 642 ppm, no plane two anesthetic effects were observed. The authors conclude that sodium bicarbonate can be used in the field as an anesthetic by fishery biologists and suggest the use of preweighed packets of this compound that can be placed in known volume containers. They indicate that sodium bicarbonate should be effective as an anesthetic in waters of pH 6.5 to 7.0.

Electricity

While electricity has been used primarily to collect fish from streams and lakes, it may also be used to narcotize them for surgery or other procedures.

Continuous flow direct current is safest for both fish and operator (Hartley 1967). Use of a rheostat in the circuit facilitates voltage selection and expedites the operation of the equipment. Kynard and Lonsdale (1975) report the use of uninterrupted 10-volt direct current to produce galvanonarcosis (see chapter 10).

Benzocaine (Ethyl-p-aminobenzoate)

Benzocaine is not water soluble and is usually applied with acetone as a carrier. Small fish are anesthetized with concentrations of 50 to 100 ppm, while large adult fish such as northern pike require 100 to 200 ppm. Temperature affects both sedation and recovery rates, but water hardness has little influence on benzocaine activity (Dawson and Gilderhus 1979).

Benzocaine is reported to be no more effective nor safer than MS–222. It does not depress the pH of poorly buffered waters, but MS–222 and quinaldine sulfate do (Dawson and Marking 1973). It is not currently registered for fisheries use in the United States, but has potential for registration (Schnick, Meyer, and Walsh 1986). Benzocaine has been selected as a priority chemical for registration as a fish anesthetic (Allen 1988). He reports a rapid residue elimination from fish muscle tissue when fish are held in flowing water.

Quinaldine Sulfate

Quinaldine is a colorless, oily liquid that is insoluble in water; however, quinaldine sulfate, a salt of quinaldine, is water soluble and much easier to use. The efficacy of the two compounds is essentially the same (Gilderhus et al. 1973a). It is not currently registered for use in fisheries in the United States, and no efforts are being made to register it (Schnick, Meyer, and Walsh 1986). It is related to a group of compounds that are carcinogenic.

Various dosage rates have been reported: from 0.01 to 0.03 ppm and 15 to 70 ppm have been used on fish including rainbow trout, lake trout, brown trout, brook trout, channel catfish, largemouth bass, and bluegill. Efficacy is influenced by acid pH and by temperature for some species (Locke 1969; Schoettger and Julin 1969; Klontz 1964).

Fish anesthetized with quinaldine behave differently than fish exposed to other anesthetics. Response to irritation by the drug is the first reaction, followed by a loss of equilibrium without a pronounced stage of sedation (Schoettger and Julin 1969).

Quinaldine Sulfate:MS–222 Mixtures

Both quinaldine sulfate and MS–222 are effective fish anesthetics when used separately. Gilderhus et al. (1973b) report on tests involving fifteen species of coldwater and warmwater fishes and the use of mixtures of these two drugs. Combinations of quinaldine sulfate:MS–222 in concentration ratios of from 10:20 to 5:20 to 10:40 were tested on salmonids. Warmwater species were tested in concentration ratios ranging from 5:15 to 10:40 to 20:50 to 20:75. Combination of the drugs produces anesthesis with the attributes of both individual drugs and induces anesthesis more effectively than quinaldine sulfate alone and more safely than MS–222 alone. Fish can be held safely for up to one hour, which greatly exceeds the safe holding time for MS–222. Lower concentrations of both drugs can be used in combination, resulting in lower chemical costs. This combination of chemicals is not currently registered for fisheries use in the United States, and efforts are not presently being made to register the combination (Schnick, Meyer, and Walsh 1986).

Literature Cited

Allen, J. L. 1988. Residues of Benzocaine in Rainbow Trout, Largemouth Bass, and Fish Meal. *Progressive Fish-Culturist* 50:59–60.

Berger, B. L., R. E. Lennon, and J. W. Hogan. 1969. *Laboratory Studies on Antimycin A as a Fish Toxicant, Investigations in Fish Control No. 26.* Washington, D.C.: U.S. Department of the Interior, U.S. Fish and Wildlife Service. 21 pp.

Booke, H. E., B. Hollander, and G. Lutterbie. 1978. Sodium Bicarbonate, an Inexpensive Fish Anesthetic for Field Use. *Progressive Fish-Culturist* 40(1):11–13.

Bouck, G. R., and R. C. Ball. 1965. The Use of Methylene Blue to Revive Warmwater Fish Poisoned by Rotenone. *Progressive Fish-Culturist* 27(3):161–62.

Bridges, W. R. 1958. *Sodium Cyanide as a Fish Poison.* Special Scientific Report, Fisheries No. 253. Washington, D.C.: U.S. Department of the Interior, U.S. Fish and Wildlife Service. 11 pp.

Britton, E. 1983. *Constant Carbon Dioxide (CO_2) and Oxygen (O_2) Aeration to Anesthetize Adult Salmon.* Vancouver, B.C.: Fisheries and Oceans Information Memorandum No. 49, February 1, 1983. 1 p.

Brusven, M. A., and C. MacPhee. 1974. An Evaluation of Squoxin on Insect Drift. *Transactions of the American Fisheries Society* 103(2):362–65.

Burress, R. M. 1982. *Effects of Synergized Rotenone on Non-Target Organisms in Ponds, Investigations in Fish Control No. 91.* Washington, D.C.: U.S. Department of the Interior, U.S. Fish and Wildlife Service. 7 pp.

Burress, R. M., and D. G. Bass. 1975. Thanite (Isobornyl Thiocyanoacetate) as an Aid for Live Collection of Fishes in Florida Ponds. *Proceedings of the Annual Conference of Southeastern Association of Game and Fish Commissioners* 28(1974):115–23.

Burress, R. M., and C. W. Luhning. 1969a. *Field Trials of Antimycin as a Selective Toxicant in Channel Catfish Ponds, Investigations in Fish Control No. 25.* Washington, D.C.: U.S. Department of the Interior, U.S. Fish and Wildlife Service. 12 pp.

———. 1969b. *Use of Antimycin for Selective Thinning of Sunfish Populations in Ponds, Investigations in Fish Control No. 28.* Washington, D.C.: U.S. Department of the Interior, U.S. Fish and Wildlife Service. 10 pp.

Burress, R. M., P. A. Gilderhus, and K. B. Cumming. 1976. *Field Trials of Isobornyl Thiocyanoacetate (Thanite) for Live Collection of Fishes, Investigations in Fish Control No. 71.* Washington, D.C.: U.S. Department of the Interior, U.S. Fish and Wildlife Service. 13 pp.

Cumming, K. B. 1975. History of Fish Toxicants in the United States. Pp. 5–21 in P. H. Eschmeyer, ed., *Rehabilitation of Fish Populations with Toxicants: A Symposium.* North Central Division, American Fisheries Society. Special Publication 4.

Davies, W. D., and W. L. Shelton. 1983. Sampling with Toxicants. Pp. 199–213 in L. A. Nielsen and D. L. Johnson, eds., *Fisheries Techniques.* Bethesda, Md.: American Fisheries Society.

Dawson, V. K., and P. A. Gilderhus. 1979. *Ethyl-p-aminobenzoate (Benzocaine): Efficacy as an Anesthetic for Five Species of Freshwater Fish. Investigations in Fish Control No. 87.* Washington, D.C.: U.S. Department of the Interior, U.S. Fish and Wildlife Service. 5 pp.

Dawson, V. K., and L. L. Marking. 1973. *Toxicity of Mixtures of Quinaldine Sulfate and MS–222 to Fish, Investigations in Fish Control No. 53.* Washington, D.C.: U.S. Department of the Interior, U.S. Fish and Wildlife Service. 11 pp.

Dawson, V. K., P. D. Harman, D. P. Schultz, and J. L. Allen. 1983. Rapid Method for Measuring Rotenone in Water at Piscicidal Concentrations. *Transactions of the American Fisheries Society* 112(5):725–27.

Doudoroff, P. 1976. Toxicity to Fish of Cyanide and Related Compounds, a Review. Duluth, Minn.: U.S. Environmental Protection Agency. Environmental Research Series, EPA–600/3–76–038.

Fish, F. F. 1943. The Anaesthesia of Fish by High Carbon Dioxide Concentrations. *Transactions of the American Fisheries Society* 72(1942):25–29.

Gilderhus, P. A., B. L. Berger, and R. E. Lennon. 1969. *Field Trials of Antimycin A as a Fish Toxicant, Investigations in Fish Control No. 27.* Washington, D.C.: U.S. Department of the Interior, U.S. Fish and Wildlife Service. 21 pp.

Gilderhus, P. A., B. L. Berger, J. B. Sills, and P. D. Harman. 1973a. *The Efficacy of Quinaldine Sulfate as an Anesthetic for Freshwater Fish, Investigations in Fish Control No. 49.* Washington, D.C.: U.S. Department of the Interior, U.S. Fish and Wildlife Service. 9 pp.

———. 1973b. *The Efficacy of Quinaldine Sulfate:MS–222 Mixtures for the Anesthetization of Freshwater Fish, Investigations in Fish Control No. 54.* Washington, D.C.: U.S. Department of the Interior, U.S. Fish and Wildlife Service. 9 pp.

Gilderhus, P. A., V. K. Dawson, and J. L. Allen. 1988. Deposition and Persistence of Rotenone in Shallow Ponds During Cold and Warm Seasons. U.S. Fish and Wildlife Service. *Investigations in Fish Control No. 95*. National Fisheries Research Center, La Crosse, Wisc. 7 pp.

Greselin, F., E. Herr, and C. Chappel. 1967. Toxicology Studies of Antimycin, a Fish Eradicant. *Transactions of the American Fisheries Society* 96(3):320–26.

Hartley, W. G. 1967. Electric Fishing Methods and Apparatus in the United Kingdom. Pp. 114–24 in R. Vibert, ed., *Fishing with Electricity—Its Applications to Biology and Management, Contributions to a Symposium, European Inland Fisheries Advisory Commission*. Rome: Food and Agriculture Organization of the United Nations.

Houf, L. J., and R. S. Campbell. 1977. *Effects of Antimycin A and Rotenone on Macrobenthos in Ponds, Investigations in Fish Control No. 80*. Washington, D.C.: U.S. Department of the Interior, U.S. Fish and Wildlife Service. 29 pp.

Jacobi, G. Z., and D. J. Degan. 1977. *Aquatic Macroinvertebrates in a Small Wisconsin Trout Stream Before, During, and 2 Years After Treatment with the Fish Toxicant Antimycin, Investigations in Fish Control No. 81*. Washington, D.C.: U.S. Department of the Interior, U.S. Fish and Wildlife Service. 24 pp.

Johnson, F. C. 1972. *Fish Transportation Improvement—Phase II*. Final Report prepared for State of Washington, Department of Fisheries, Olympia, Washington. 63 pp.

Kinney, E. C. 1965. *Rotenone in Fish Pond Management*. U.S. Bureau of Sport Fisheries and Wildlife, Leaflet FL–576. 7 pp.

Klontz, G. W. 1964. Anesthesia of Fishes. *Proceedings of the Symposium on Experimental Animal Anesthesiology, 14–16 December, 1964, Brooks Air Force Base, San Antonio, Texas*. 22 pp.

Kynard, B., and E. Lonsdale. 1975. Experimental Study of Galvanonarcosis for Rainbow Trout (*Salmo gairdneri*) Immobilization. *Journal of the Fisheries Research Board of Canada* 32(2):300–302.

Lawrence, J. M. 1955. Preliminary Results on the Use of Potassium Permanganate to Counteract the Effects of Rotenone on Fish. *Progressive Fish-Culturist* 18(1):15–21.

Lennon, R. E., J. B. Hunn, R. A. Schnick, and R. M. Burress. 1970. *Reclamation of Ponds, Lakes and Streams with Fish Toxicants: A Review*. FAO Fisheries Technical Paper 100. Rome: Food and Agricultural Organization.

Lewis, W. M. 1968. Isobornyl Thiocyanoacetate as a Fish Drugging Agent and Selective Toxin. *Progressive Fish-Culturist* 30(1):29–31.

Lewis, W. M., and R. M. Tarrant, Jr. 1960. Sodium Cyanide in Fish management and Culture. *Progressive Fish-Culturist* 22(4):177–80.

Locke, D. O. 1969. *Quinaldine as an Anesthetic for Brook Trout, Lake Trout, and Atlantic Salmon, Investigations in Fish Control No. 24*. Washington, D.C.: U.S. Department of the Interior, U.S. Fish and Wildlife Service. 5 pp.

McFarland, W. N. 1960. The Use of Anesthetics for the Handling and the Transportation of Fishes. *California Fish and Game* 46(4):407–31.

MacPhee, C., and R. Ruelle. 1968. Fish Culture by Squawfish Population Eradication. U.S. Patent Number 3,389,685. June 25. 5 pp.

———. 1969. A Chemical Selectively Lethal to Squawfish (*Ptychocheilus Oregonensis and P umpquae*). *Transactions of the American Fisheries Society* 98(4):676–84.

Marking, L. L. 1967. *Toxicity of MS-222 to Selected Fishes, Investigations in Fish Control No. 12*. Washington, D.C.: U.S. Department of the Interior, U.S. Fish and Wildlife Service. 10 pp.

Marking, L. L., and T. D. Bills. 1976. *Toxicity of Rotenone to Fish in Standardized Laboratory Tests, Investigations in Fish Control No. 72*. Washington, D.C.: U.S. Department of the Interior, U.S. Fish and Wildlife Service. 11 pp.

Marking, L. L., T. D. Bills, J. J. Rach, and S. J. Grabowski. 1983. Chemical Control of Fish and Fish Eggs in the Garrison Diversion Unit, North Dakota. *North American Journal of Fisheries Management* 3(4):410–18.

Marking, L. L., and V. K. Dawson. 1972. The Half-Life of Biological Activity of Antimycin Determined by Fish Bioassay. *Transactions of the American Fisheries Society* 101(1):100–105.

Marking, L. L., and F. P. Meyer. 1985. Are Better Anesthetics Needed in Fisheries? *Fisheries* 10(6):2–5.

Post, G. 1955. A Simple Chemical Test for Rotenone in Water. *Progressive Fish-Culturist* 17(4):190–91.

———. 1958. Time Versus Water Temperature in Rotenone Dissipation. Pp. 279–84 in *The 38th Annual Proceedings of the Western Association of Game and Fish Commissioners.*

Rowe-Rowe, D. T. 1971. Rotenone Tolerances of Some Freshwater Fishes of Natal. *Progressive Fish-Culturist* 33(4):206–9.

Schnick, R. A., F. P. Meyer, and D. F. Walsh. 1986. Status of Fishery Chemicals in 1985. *Progressive Fish-Culturist* 48(1):1–17.

Schoettger, R. A., and A. M. Julin. 1969. *Efficacy of Quinaldine as an Anesthetic for Seven Species of Fish, Investigations in Fish Control No. 22*. Washington, D.C.: U.S. Department of the Interior, U.S. Fish and Wildlife Service. 10 pp.

Staley, G. S. 1977. The Impact of Squoxin on Aquatic Invertebrates and an Assessment of its Fate in the Aquatic Environment. M.S. thesis. University of British Columbia, Vancouver. 93 pp.

Summerfelt, R. C., and W. M. Lewis. 1967. Repulsion of Green Sunfish by Certain Chemicals. *Journal of the Water Pollution Control Federation* 39(12):125–31.

Tatum, W. R. 1969. Field Observation and the Use of Sodium Cyanide in Streams. Pp. 361–63 in *Proceedings of the 22nd Annual Conference of the Southeastern Association of Game and Fish Commissioners*.

Wiley, R. W. 1984. A Review of Sodium Cyanide for Use in Sampling Stream Fishes. *North American Journal of Fisheries Management* 4(3):249–56.

Yoshikawa, H., Y. Ishida, and S. Veno. 1988. The Use of Sedating Action of CO_2 for Long-Term Anesthesia in Carp. *Nippon Suisan Gakkishi* 54(4):545–51.

9. Nets and Other Fishing Gear

Nets have been used to collect fish from marine and fresh water for hundreds of years. According to biblical records, Isaiah (approximately 700 B.C.) writes in 19:8, "The fishers also shall mourn, . . . and they that spread nets upon the waters shall languish." In approximately A.D. 30, Matthew 4:18 states, "And Jesus, walking by the sea of Galilee, saw two brethren, Simon called Peter, and Andrew his brother, casting a net into the sea: for they were fishers." John 21:6 reads, "And he said unto them, Cast the net on the right side of the ship, and ye shall find. They cast therefore, and now they were not able to draw it for the multitude of fishes." The Greek classic, Oppian (approximately A.D. 180), is said to have written about the use of nets. Butler (1930) notes, "Nets were of all sizes and shapes—casting nets, drag-nets, trawls, seines, ground-nets, ball-nets, and, as Oppian says, there are a thousand forms of nets with cunning entanglements." Brandt (1964a) writes, "compared with the age of fishing, the net is a young invention, although it may still be some thousands of years of age." Properly set and cared for, nets of various kinds are capable of capturing large numbers of fish with minimal effort.

Fishery research makes use of various types of nets to capture fish for a variety of reasons. Nets can and are used in situations where other collection gear (e.g., electrofishing—chapter 10, or toxicants—chapter 8) are inappropriate. Nets and associated traps offer certain advantages over other types of collection gear. Among these advantages are: personnel are not generally required to stay with the net or trap while it fishes; large numbers of nets or traps can be set and run on a rotating basis by the same crew; net size and mesh size can be varied to allow capture of a particular size or species of fish; and nets or traps can be fished in areas of known fish concentrations.

The principle disadvantage of net gear used in fishery research (e.g., gill nets) is that few fish are recovered alive. This drawback can be lessened by more frequent retrieval of the nets. Death occurs to a lesser extent in many of the types of traps used.

Types of Nets

Nets are made from either natural or synthetic fibers. Most now are made of synthetic fiber because of its increased resistance to rotting. Of the two primary synthetic fibers, nylon is more elastic than braided or twisted polyethylene.

There are two types of nets used for both commercial fishing and fishery research: passive (entrapment or entanglement) and active (haul). There are six basic kinds: gill, trap, trammel, seine, trawl, and cast. Each of these six types has several variations which are given specific names (Andreev 1966; Brandt 1964a, 1964b).

Passive Net Gear

Nets which are placed in one location and rely on the fish passing that particular location are considered passive (nonmoving). These include two basic types of capture mechanisms: entrapment or entanglement. Net types included in this group are gill, trammel, and trap nets.

Gill Nets

Gill nets are designed to catch fish by the opercles (figure 9.1) or other body projections as they swim into the net. Fish are trapped by the mesh when they make an effort to escape. Some fish may be caught by the teeth rather than being gilled. Gill nets consist of a body of fine thread webbing supported along the top by a float line and held down at the bottom by a lead line. Wooden, cork, plastic, or blown glass floats strung on the float line have been used to float gill nets in the past. Until recently, glass floats were especially popular with the Japanese fleets off the west coast of the United States. (Numerous floats have washed ashore on the California coast and are highly prized by beachcombers.) For many years the lead line was constructed of lead weights strung, crimped, or otherwise fastened onto the line to weight the net and to hold it straight. Because both float lines and lead lines tend to tangle with the meshes and catch on either the side of the boat or other obstructions, foam

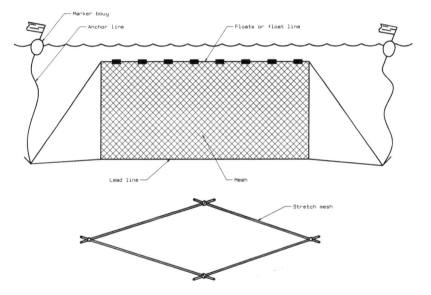

Figure 9.1. Gill net.

core float lines and lead core lead lines are becoming more popular in many areas (Hubert 1983).

Gill nets used in the North Atlantic may be as long as 4,571 m (15,000 feet) and as deep as 3.65 m (12 feet). In recent years, series of floating gill nets in the Pacific may be as long as thirty miles. Many gill nets used in fresh water are only 38 m (125 feet) long and 1.8 m (6 feet) deep. The mesh size of these nets is recorded as bar mesh (the distance between close knots) or stretch mesh (the distance formed by stretching the webbing between two opposing knots). Stretched mesh size is approximately twice that of bar mesh size. The mesh is a uniform size in commercial nets; they range from 6.35 cm (2.5 inches) stretched mesh for small freshwater fish to 41 cm (16 inches) for Pacific coast sharks. Experimental gill nets, used almost exclusively in fisheries research, may have five 7.6-meter (25-foot) blocks of webbing which grade from 3.8 to 12.7 cm (1.5 to 5 inches) stretched mesh. Regier and Robson (1966) suggest that for general sampling purposes it would be more efficient for the mesh sizes to increase in a geometric progression rather than the usual arithmetic progression. These nets, within limits, catch fish by species and size in relation to their relative abundance.

In the marine environment, gill nets are used extensively for salmon, shark, smelt, flying fish, and barracuda on the Pacific Coast, and pollock on the Atlantic Coast. This type of net is also used widely in the Great Lakes and many other freshwater lakes and impoundments (Gordon 1968). Gill nets may be either divers (the lead line is heavy enough to sink the net) or floaters (the cork line supports the top of the net at the surface of the water). Surface set gill nets may be either anchored or free floating. Gill nets are rarely set in waters where there is an appreciable current. An exception to this rule is the drift nets used for salmon in the Columbia River. In areas devoid of current and debris, they are one of the most commonly used nets in freshwater fisheries.

Gill nets may be hung in varying ratios. The hanging ratio (hanging basis) determines the shape of the net mesh when it is set. The hanging ratio is the ratio between the length of the float line and the length of the stretched mesh hanging from the float line. For example, if a net of 100 m stretched length were hung on 40 m of float line, the hanging ratio would be 40/100 or 0.40. Effectiveness of the mesh shape varies with the morphology of fish being sought (Welcomme 1975) and obviously with the size of fish.

The method of setting and retrieving a gill net varies depending on the area to be fished, time of year, number of personnel available, and the depth and location of the sampling site. Most commonly, gill nets are set off the bow of boats in either a floating or sinking (bottom-set) configuration. Depending on the length of the net to be set, the size of the boat from which it is set, and the experience of the personnel, the net can be previously hung with anchors, or anchors can be attached as the net is played out. Once the location of the first end buoy has been established, the net can be fed out over the bow as the boat is backed away. Care should be taken to align the net in a proper fashion depending on how it is to be fished. Nets set perpendicular to the shore will catch those species of fish which tend to cruise along the shore at a particular distance from it. Nets placed in deeper water can be set with a particular orientation if information is available concerning the movements of the target species. Nets set perpendicular to the wind in water less than 15 feet deep tend to roll up and tangle due to wave action (Skidmore 1970). Additionally, nets set perpendicular to the wind are more difficult to retrieve than those set parallel to it. Setting gill nets under ice can be accomplished with some ease by drilling a series of holes along the line on which the net is to be set and sequentially pushing the float line or a rope from one hole to the next. The traditional willow stick method used to pass a rope through one hole and up through a second has been replaced in many situations with a Murphy's stick which utilizes sections of small-diameter aluminum pipe or other light material hinged and equipped with a float. An attached rope can be pushed from one hole to another and pulled through the ice with a grappling hook. An ice-jigger (Hewson 1959) made of planking can also be used.

A bottom-set net will sample fish swimming or feeding near the bottom while a midwater depth set may be made either by suspending the net from drop lines attached to large buoys or held below the surface by lines attached to anchors. Gill nets can also be floated at the surface. Gill nets can be set with the long axis of the net perpendicular to the water's surface. This technique is utilized to determine vertical fish distribution (Vigg 1978). In this utilization it is generally necessary to attach rigid or semirigid lightweight bars (e.g., PVC pipe) to hold the net open. Vertical sets can be used to document seasonal distribution of fish at depths in relation to physical or chemical factors (e.g., thermocline). Depth distribution of fish in small lakes and a quickly constructed vertical gill net are discussed by Chadwick, Cook, and Winters 1987. Gill nets can also be used in a more active sense by setting them near areas of suspected fish concentrations and driving the fish into the net by using air screens, noise, light, electrical fields, or chemicals. A modification of the standard use of gill nets is to utilize it more or less as a seine. The gill net is deployed as usual from the bow of the boat but is used to encircle a group of fish. This technique is used by mullet anglers in northwest Florida who float quietly at night into areas of mullet feeding migrations. When they hear the slap on the water of the jumping fish they rapidly put one end of the net on shore and drive the boat in a large circle, beaching the other end of the net.

These nets are approximately 100 m (328 feet) long and 1.2 to 1.8 m (4 to 6 feet) deep. Once the net is set around the school of fish, they are driven into the net by banging on the side of the boat or slapping the surface of the water. In one early morning setting of a net of this type several hundred fish were caught in just a few moments, with the inadvertent aid of a dolphin in the general area. Every time the dolphin moved, more fish, in an attempt to escape, became entangled in the net.

When gill nets are retrieved they should be pulled in hand over hand and coiled like a rope into a tub or other container. To avoid entangling the net or overrunning it, it is generally best to retrieve the net from the downwind end when wind is an appreciable factor. Gill nets are useful in areas which are free of obstructions, snags, or floating debris, and where there is very little current. They are especially useful in sampling species that have daily migrations over substantial distances.

In most instances fish captured by gill nets will be killed either by the entanglement in the net or by the handling required to free them. Some species can be retrieved from gill nets alive if the nets are run frequently. Wyoming often uses short-duration sets to capture wild fish for spawning purposes. This method can be effective but is labor intensive. Some species such as gar appear to suffer little from the experience.

The obvious bias of a gill net is related to the mesh size. For any given mesh size, fish of an appropriate size for that mesh are entangled and held securely. Fish that are smaller than the mesh can swim through without becoming entangled, and fish that are much larger than the mesh will not be able to penetrate the net far enough to become entangled. Hubert (1983) indicates that two generalizations regarding size selectivity are (1) the optimum girth for capture is about 1.25 the stretched mesh diameter and (2) fish more than 20 percent longer or shorter than the optimum length are seldom caught. The catch rate of gill nets vary with species, location, and duration of the set. Once a given, but generally unknown, portion of the meshes have captured fish, catch rate will decrease notably. On the other hand, a few entangled fish seem to decoy others. Standardized samplings can be completed utilizing gill nets on a year-to-year basis or between water bodies. It is important, however, to control as many variables as possible, such as season, time, location, duration of the sets, and the construction of the nets. Hanging ratio can influence the selectivity and efficiency of the gill net as can the diameter and kind of the net twine, the color of the twine, and the flexibility of the mesh. Color of netting may also affect gill net catch (Tweddle and Bodington 1988). White gill nets caught 1.79 times as many fish as black nets during controlled experiments. Fishes dependent upon vision during movement (such as cyprinids) showed the highest white:black catch ratios. Other considerations in selecting a gill net for a particular species are the elasticity, strength, and visibility of the material, and the location where the net is to be fished. Monofilament line is the most efficient of all materials used in gill nets. The most effective use of the gill net is probably to set it overnight and empty it early in the morning after fish movement has ceased or decreased. Catches are generally recorded as set hours multiplied by the length of net.

Trammel Nets

Trammel nets are constructed by hanging three sets of net webbing to a single top and bottom line. The two outside webs (called webbing) are of larger mesh and thread size than the inner web. The fish are captured when they go through the outside (large-size web) on one side and then push the inner (smaller webbing) through the outside of the opposite side. The pocket that is formed is an effective trap and holds the fish (figure 9.2).

Trammel nets may be fished either by anchoring or drifting. When location is fixed, one end is placed near shore and the net is laid out so that it forms several spirals (tight circles) as it leads in the deep water. Fish can be frightened and driven into the net by such noises as researchers striking the bottom of the boat or the water.

Trammel nets are generally constructed of cotton or nylon webbing, but numerous designs have been employed, especially by commercial fishermen. Trammel nets are set essentially the same way as gill nets but are most effective when set around a large known grouping of fish. The fish are subsequently driven into the nets. In contrast to gill nets, trammel nets can and have been used successfully in large river habitats. Trammel nets are, however, infrequently used in fisheries stock assessment or for experimental work. Trammel nets are selective for fish species which have rough surfaces and protrusions such as catfish and temperate basses. Trammel nets generally do not damage captured fish as much as gill nets do but have similar sampling biases.

Trap Nets

Fish traps are made of netting and consist mainly of a lead or fence and a heart. The lead or fence directs the fish into the V-shaped throat (figure 9.3). The natural tendency of fish is to follow the webbing which leads into the crib. Fish traps vary considerably in design and size. The more commonly recog-

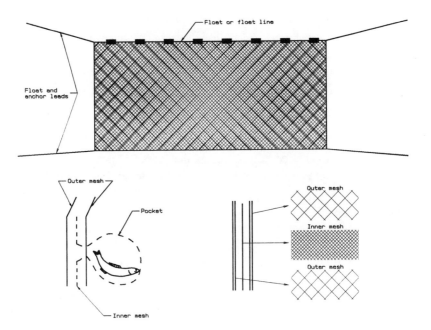

Figure 9.2. Trammel net.

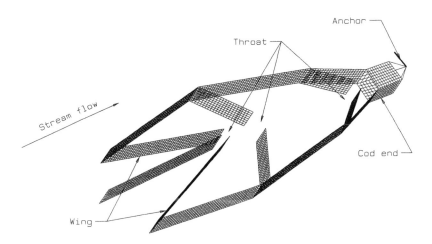

Figure 9.3.   Trap net.

nized types are Alaskan pound, Great Lakes, hoop, and fyke. These traps are set either on the bottom (submarine) or at the surface (floating). They may be set either in shallow or deep water. The two more common of the larger trap types are the Alaskan and the Great Lakes. Trap nets fall into the general broad category of entrapment (as opposed to entanglement) devices.

Alaskan Pound Trap Nets

Alaskan pound trap nets are constructed on piling which extends outward from shore. Pilings are connected by wooden stringers which are used primarily for hanging webbing leads which guide fish into the pot. In some cases these leads may be 300 meters (984 feet) or more long. These large traps have one or two holding areas on one side or two holding areas on each side. As in the case of all trap nets, effectiveness depends on the fish's basic instincts to follow leads and not to make sharp turns, but rather go in a more or less straight line.

Great Lakes Trap Nets

Great Lakes traps are constructed in all sizes, up to 18 meters (59 feet) in height and set in depths up to 61 meters (200 feet). Size designation normally consists of height in feet at the first throat or heart; this is also the height of the lead. The baling crib or pot on a 9-meter (30-foot) net (the size often used in Oahe Reservoir, South Dakota) is usually 2.4 or 3 meters (8 or 10 feet) deep. They can have either covered or uncovered hearts. Those at Oahe are covered.

Hoop Trap Nets

Hoop nets are used in rivers, reservoirs, and other waters where fish travel in a predictable direction. Hoop nets take their name from the rounded support structures which hold the body of the net. Hoops may be made of fiberglass, wood, or steel. It is intended that the fish work their way deep enough into the throat or funnels of the trap so that they are unable to find their way out. The throat should not be large enough to allow fish to pass back through. Most nets have no more than two or three throats. Small nets have only one. Hoop diameter varies from under 0.6 to 3.1 meters (2 to 10 feet) with from four to eight hoops in a net. Either cotton or nylon webbing is used around the hoops, the size ranging from less than 1.27 cm (0.5 inch) to over 7.5 cm (3 inches) bar mesh. In flowing water, hoop nets are generally set with the mouth opening downstream and the closed end of the net, called the cod end or the pot, attached to a firmly implanted stake at the upstream end. The cod end of the net is equipped with a drawstring to allow it to be opened so fish can be removed. In most instances hoop nets are fished baited, so there is a tendency for selection of species which are attracted to the bait. Other species seeking cover may also be attracted to hoop nets. Fish captured in hoop nets are generally not injured and can be utilized to gather study information and then released unharmed.

As with other net fishing gear, hoop nets have a bias related to size, place, and time. The bias is related to hoop diameter, mesh dimensions, and mouth sizes. Color and/or material of construction is less important. In general, larger diameter nets capture not only more fish but more species than do smaller nets.

A variation of the hoop net is the brook hoop net. This is a small net used to catch bait and other small fish. It is equipped with a semicircular mouth which leads into the funnel of the trap.

Fyke or Frame Trap Nets

The fyke net is a variation of the hoop net. It may be equipped with one wing or leader, but more generally with two wings or leads with float or lead lines. These leaders or wings form effective barriers that lead the fish into the net. The body of the fyke net is structurally a hoop net (figure 9.4).

The construction of fyke nets is essentially identical to hoop nets as far as the central net portion itself is concerned. Wings, generally set at a 45-degree angle to the axis of the hoop net, may be attached to the first hoop to expand the area over which the net is effective. Fyke nets are generally effective in shallow water. Ponds, lakes, and reservoirs can be fished with fyke nets, and they have been utilized in stream sampling in areas of moderate current velocity (Swales 1981). In areas of even moderate current it may be advisable to replace the round hoops on the first and perhaps second hoops with a rectangular or semicircular frame. This tends to keep the nets from rolling when set where the current is perpendicular to the long axis of the net.

Weirs

Weirs are guidance devices which divert fish across a stream section and into a trap. The weir structure or some form of it must be built across the entire stream width to be effective. Weir traps have been utilized in many areas in the Pacific Northwest and elsewhere to trap downstream anadromous salmonid smolts. Smolts migrating downstream tail first sense the change in velocity

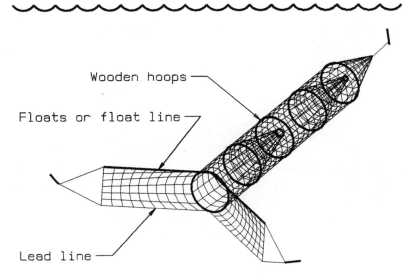

Wooden hoops

Floats or float line

Lead line

Figure 9.4.   Fyke net.

as the water passes through the weirs and tend to move along the weir to the mouth of the trap where the current again resembles the normal downstream flow and pass into the trap. The large traveling screens which have been installed in the last several years on dams in the Columbia River drainage serve the same function as weirs, guiding the fish to safe passage facilities within the dam.

Pot Gear

Pot gear is a generic term used to describe any number of structures which are generally dropped into place individually and are frequently baited. Pot gear is constructed of rigid materials, and most contain some sort of funnel device which allows entry but prevents escape. Multiple funnels increase the probability of the captured animal being retained. Crab pots, eel pots, minnow traps, and lobster pots are examples of pot traps.

Active Net Gear

Active net gear is utilized to collect fish from varied habitats. The major difference between active and passive fish collection gear is that active gear is moved by the operators with or without the assistance of mechanical devices. Several types of active net gear are currently utilized commercially and in various aspects of fisheries research. These include seines, trawl nets, cast nets, plankton nets, and lift nets.

Seines

A seine is a net of any size with a float line and a lead line. It is pulled through the water either by manpower or by some mechanical device. Larger ones routinely have bags or purses in the center, whereas smaller seines may be straight (no bag).

Beach or Haul Seines

The beach or haul seine is one of the oldest types of fishing gear and is in common use today (Gordon 1965). Beach seines are fished primarily in shallow water, both marine and fresh, on beaches which have a smooth, relatively unobstructed bottom. Since this gear is utilized on beaches or other land the outlay for boating equipment is relatively small, but this saving is partially off-set by the need for a larger crew. Haul seines range in length from 1.5-meter (5-foot) bait minnow seines to 524-meter (1,719-foot) or occasionally much longer nets used in the Great Lakes and elsewhere. The Iowa Department of Fish and Wildlife at one time fished seines that were 2 miles long (10,560 feet).

A beach seine is constructed of a body of webbing supported by a cork line and floats (figure 9.5). The lead line is made up of paired left-hand and right-hand lay (these terms refer to the direction of the twist) synthetic fiber rope. A large seine is made up of two wings, a bag section in the middle, brails (upright staffs attached to the end of the net by means of a bridle), and hauling lines. The mesh size of the wings may decrease from the outer end of the wing to the bag section, and the depth of the wings may increase over the same distance. The bag, which is about as long as it is wide, has smaller mesh size than the wings. The smaller mesh size of the bag prevents excessive escape or gilling of fish caught in the bag.

Brails may be constructed of hardwood or other lightweight, floating ma-terial and have a rope bridle attached to them to aid in pulling. Brails are generally leaded (weighted) on the bottom, especially on larger seines, so that they ride upright in the water. Leading is usually accomplished by fitting a heavy section of pipe over the lower one fifth of the braille. In the case of very large seines a haul or sea line and a braille can be attached to bridles at 61- to 122-meter (200- to 400-foot) intervals on each wing as well as the bridles at the end of the net. This facilitates landing the net. On small seines the haul line may be attached to the bridle only.

Beach seines are used in both lakes and streams, as well as in hatcheries. The use of a beach seine is most effective in shallow water with no obstruc-tions. If the lead line is not held in contact with the bottom, fish will escape underneath. Specific techniques for each situation must rely on the investiga-tor's experience since fish can escape from even a very small opening under the net. Carp are particularly adept at escaping under the lead line of a beach seine, and it is sometimes necessary to have personnel stand on the lead line inside the bag as it is pulled in or hold it down with a shovel or similar piece of equipment. Fish such as largemouth bass may escape by jumping over the float line.

Purse Seines

A purse seine is a large encircling net made of webbing supported by floats at the water surface and weighted by leads at the bottom (figure 9.6). A purse

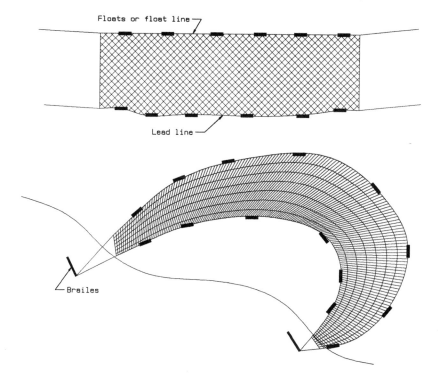

Figure 9.5. Beach seine.

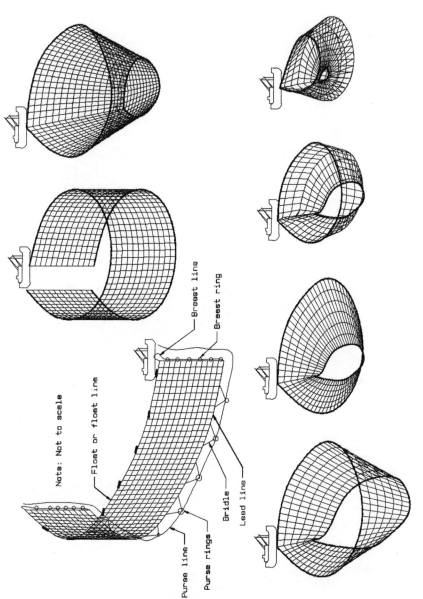

Figure 9.6. Purse seine.

line which runs through rings attached by rope bridles at varying intervals closes the bottom of the seine after it has been cast in a circle around a school of fish. After the seine is closed by the purse line, the lead line is then hoisted on the deck of the boat and all the webbing that can be moved is hauled on board. The fish are then brailed (removed) into the ship's hold or into live boxes in shallow water operations. Purse seining is used extensively in both the Atlantic and Pacific oceans for menhaden, mackerel, herring, sardine, tuna, salmon, and barracuda. They are used in fresh water more perhaps in research than commercially. The type and size of boat differs with the fishery; large seagoing vessels may range from 13.7 to 27.4 meters (45 to 90 feet) in length. Freshwater operations may utilize boats no more than 4.8 meters (16 feet) long or larger boats which are generally operated by commercial fishing crews. Purse seines lend themselves only to very large and unobstructed bodies of water.

Lampara Seines

A lampara seine is a large baglike net which consists of two wings of coarse mesh and a central bag of fine mesh. The lead line is much shorter than the cork line, forming a floor to the bag as the net is pulled in. The lampara seine is used off the coast of California in the sardine and mackerel industry to supply live bait to tuna boats and as minnow nets in the Great Lakes. When a school of fish is sighted, one end of the net, fastened to a buoy, is cast loose from the boat. The boat then circles around the school of fish paying out net. When the circle is complete the buoy is picked up and both ends of the net are pulled in, the shortened lead line forming the floor and enclosing the fish.

Trawl Nets

A trawl is a large bag-shaped net which is fished by pulling it through the water with a boat. It consists of a top and bottom seamed together on the outer edges to form a bag which has two wings attached and leading forward. Lines from the wings lead to the boat. The wings are pulled apart by means of otter boards (large weighted frames also called doors) which, if towed at the proper speed, hold the mouth of the bag open. The cod, or tail end of the net is tapered to a small size so that fish circle around in this area rather than escape by swimming back out of the mouth of the net. As made up, the net is basically two lines leading from a boat back to two otter boards attached to the wings which are in turn attached to the forward end of the bag. The bag consists of a forward belly section and an after cod end section (figure 9.7). A further refinement of trawls was developed in the 1950s and utilizes an electric field of direct current which guides (repels) the fish into the net with negative electrodes and restrains (attracts) them there by means of a positive electrode (Ellis and Pickering 1973).

In marine fisheries these nets are towed along the ocean floor in search of sole, cod, flounder, hake, and dogfish (Reeves and Sidonato 1972). These large marine trawls may be considerably more than 30 meters (98 feet) long (Bruce 1967). Large trawls such as this have some application in freshwater fisheries research. These nets have been used in various inland situations to sample a variety of species. Some small freshwater trawls may be only 3 or 4.5 meters (10 or 15 feet) long. In recent years midwater trawls have become increasingly popular in freshwater commercial fisheries and in fisheries investigations. The effectiveness of trawls is increased when used in conjunction with sonar (see below).

Cast Nets

In recent years the ancient art of catching fish with cast nets has become increasingly popular as a recreational pursuit, particularly in the southeastern United States (Floyd 1965). Cast net fishing has been practiced by commercial and sport anglers for centuries in many parts of the world. It was probably introduced to the New World by the first settlers during the sixteenth century. Sport anglers in northeastern Florida use them in the inland waterway to fish for mullet, which travel in large schools after dark. An experienced angler can capture large numbers of mullet from a single school with very little effort.

A cast net is a circular piece of netting with lead weights secured around the perimeter. The lead weights help form the pocket during retrieval. It has a rope rigged to the center for retrieving. The net can be cast over fish by anglers wading in shallow water or it may be cast from the shore, a dock, or a boat. Generally a high degree of patience and skill is required to learn to throw a cast net. Floyd (1968) states that the technique, though not complicated, does take practice and patience to master. Cast nets are constructed so that the circumference of the open end of the mesh cone is greater than the circumference of the lead line. As the net is retrieved the extra mesh forms pockets, entrapping the fish (Hayes 1983).

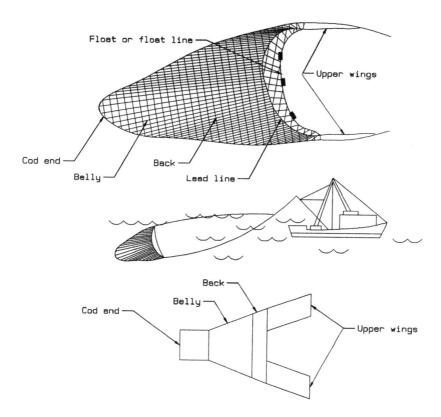

Figure 9.7. Trawl net.

Plankton Nets as Fish Samplers

Plankton nets have been used to catch larval fish, small adults, and eggs for many years. One of the early and productive uses of plankton nets was by merchant marine ships in the Atlantic. In this case the out-migration of larval European and American eels was discovered as a result of these tows. Today low- and high-speed plankton samplers such as the Miller and Gulf types are playing an ever-increasing role in the sampling of larval fishes. Efficiencies and other data have been collected for many net types (Regner 1981; Morioka 1979). Marcy and Dahlberg (1980) provide a classification of basic sampling problems, defining causes and important variables which influence ichthyoplankton sampling. Plankton nets equipped with coarse mesh are generally used for collecting smaller planktonic stages of fish.

A plankton net consists of a funnel-shaped body made of mesh which will rapidly filter water passing through the mouth and a holding device on the cod end of the net to retain samples too large to pass through the mesh. Plankton nets can be fished in almost any direction and can be utilized in either lakes or streams. Snyder (1983) provides a comprehensive summary of the problems associated with using plankton nets for surveying or monitoring fish eggs and larvae. Additionally he provides several sources for comparisons of plankton net gear and discussions of design and use.

Two broad categories of plankton nets can be described: low-speed and high-speed nets. Larger nets are generally utilized at lower speeds. Plankton nets with mouth diameters of 0.5 m (1.6 ft) or larger are generally towed at about 2 m (6.6 ft)/sec or less. High-speed nets, with reduced mouth openings, may be towed at speeds in excess of 2 m (6.6 ft)/sec.

Many variations for sampling both streams and lakes have been reported (Hettler 1979; Kovalev and Kurbatov 1979).

Other Net Gear

Other net gear includes lift nets with rectangular or circular frames which may be set below the water surface or on the bottom and lifted to capture fish as they pass over the net. Fish may be drawn to such nets using bait or light attraction at night. This technique is extremely effective in large hatchery ponds to capture small numbers of fish.

Other Data Collection Equipment

Bass and Hitt (1980) report that detonating cord has been successfully utilized to collect fish in warmwater streams in northwest Florida. Block nets were used to aid in recovering dead or stunned fish, and detonating cord was placed on the bottom parallel to the shoreline. In addition to the techniques described above for collecting and/or studying fish, three techniques which are currently being utilized are sonar, scuba, or snorkel gear and biotelemetry. Each of these techniques has definite applications in fisheries research. Each also has inherent disadvantages and biases. Video-recording techniques also have great potential for both surface and underwater data or event recording.

Sonar Gear

The word "sonar" is an acronym for the phrase "sound navigation and ranging." Sonar operates on the same principle as radar but transmits sound waves instead of radio waves. Sonar may be either active or passive. In an active system the sound is transmitted and the echo received. Distance is computed as one half the elapsed time multiplied by the speed of sound in water. A passive system is a listening device and only one direction can be determined (Dubach and Taber 1968).

The speed of sound in water is affected by temperature, salinity, and pressure. An increase in any of these results in an increase in sound velocity. Originally sonar was used for submarine detection and navigation but more recently has been used for fish finding. A depth-finding sonar is correctly called an echo sounder but is sometimes referred to as a fathometer, a registered trademark of one company producing echo sounders.

The level of sophistication of fish-finding gear has been greatly improved in recent years. A complete review of the theory and applications of sonar in fisheries research is beyond the scope of this text. Interested individuals are encouraged to read such review articles as chapter 12, "Hydroacoustics," by Thorne (1983) in the American Fishery Society's publication *Fisheries Techniques*.

Briefly, Thorne (1983) lists the following advantages of hydroacoustics over other assessment techniques: (1) independence from fishery catch statistics, (2) favorable time scale, (3) relatively low operational costs, (4) low variance, and (5) potential for absolute population estimation. He lists limitations of hydroacoustic assessment techniques as (1) poor species discrimination,

(2) little or no sampling capability near bottom and surface, (3) relatively high complexity, (4) high initial investment, (5) lack of biological samples, and (6) potential bias associated with target strength and calibration.

The use of hydroacoustic techniques for various aspects of fisheries studies will increase as the level of sophistication of the equipment and reduced operational complexity results. Fisheries managers responsible for fish stocks where hydroacoustics may be useful should keep in mind the potential uses of the various hydroacoustic equipment available for their particular fisheries stock.

Snorkel and Scuba Gear

The introduction of scuba in 1947 provided the American public with a new form of recreation and fishery biologists with another research tool. Over half of the state resource departments in the U.S. presently use scuba in one or more phases of their fishery program. According to Poole, Kuester, and Witt (1963) the various ways in which scuba is being used in fishery programs are as follows: (1) enumerating fish populations such as salmon and steelhead in resting pools and censusing fish in farm ponds, (2) evaluating toxicant programs by looking for live fish and counting dead ones following chemical treatment, (3) life history studies which include observation of behavior and habits of fish such as spawning, migrations, and reaction to pollutants, (4) evaluating habitat improvement structures such as brush shelters and reefs, and (5) collecting specimens.

The use of snorkel or scuba gear for direct underwater observation of fish habits and movement has gained widespread use and acceptance in the last several years. Direct observations of fish when using snorkel or scuba gear have several advantages. These are observation and enumeration of target species, collection of benthic samples and small fishes or larger more mobile forms, and determination of species microhabitat preferences. Additionally, direct underwater observations have the advantage in most cases of being nondestructive. An additional modification to the base observation technique uses a calibrated mask-bar on the face plate of the diving mask to facilitate nondestructive measurement of fish. Measurements of fish under field conditions were accurate to ±10 percent (Swenson, Gobin, and Simonson 1988). Fish microhabitat can be tagged and measured for such parameters as velocity, temperature, and depth. Fish can also be collected for food habits or age and growth studies. This can be done either with a small spear or with a stun gun. An effective stun gun can be made by utilizing a battery encased in waterproof acrylic material attached to a 1 meter rod, the far end of which holds a single lightweight blasting cap. Extending the meter rod toward the fish and detonating the blasting cap generally stuns the fish sufficiently that it may be collected by the diver. James et al. (1987) report on a diver-operated electrofishing device which can be effectively used to capture individual fish. A variation of these techniques, which utilizes only snorkel gear, has been effectively utilized in streams in Idaho for censusing fish populations and with an underwater stun gun for collecting fish in support of studies of microhabitat requirements of various salmonids. Griffith (1981) has utilized snorkeling to estimate age frequency distribution of stream-dwelling salmonids in small streams in Idaho. This technique allows precise determination of microhabitat conditions and in addition provides the potential for age and growth and/or food habits data from the collected specimens.

Both scuba and snorkeling gear have associated disadvantages. Snorkeling is generally limited to very small shallow areas in either streams or lakes where water clarity is high. Divers must wear wet or dry suits in cold streams if they are submerged more than a few minutes. Small fish are difficult to observe using either snorkel or scuba gear, and bottom-dwelling fishes may be difficult to see. Scuba eliminates the primary difficulty of snorkeling, that of restricted time under water and depth to which the investigator can easily descend. Turbidity limits the distance a diver can observe fish, and many fish are frightened by noises and bubbles associated with scuba gear. Scuba equipment is relatively expensive and heavy and should not be used by untrained personnel. Extended use of scuba gear requires either a certified air compressor or the availability of a commercial air station. Scuba diving is potentially dangerous and should not be attempted by those who have not been certified through a recognized scuba diving course, and never alone.

Helfman (1983) discusses many of the basic premises associated with underwater observation with either scuba or snorkel. Disadvantages and advantages of each are discussed.

Biotelemetry

Underwater biotelemetry involves attaching a sending device of one of two types to the organism being studied. Either ultrasonic or radio signals may be utilized for this purpose. Tags with varying life (based on battery size) can be utilized to study fish. In concert with mobile tracking stations and/or fixed base shore stations, fish movement habits can be determined rather precisely.

The advantages of biotelemetry techniques include (1) capability to monitor large numbers of fish simultaneously, (2) inclusion of special equipment on the sender which indicates either temperature and/or depth data, and (3) lack of a disturbance by humans during study of the animal under direct observation.

Disadvantages of biotelemetry include (1) high initial equipment costs, (2) a high level of sophistication in equipment operation, (3) many aquatic habitats unsuitable for telemetry studies because of background noise and/or naturally caused disturbances such as ripples and rapids, and (4) the potential for disruption of the fish's normal behavior pattern by attachment and/or insertion of the telemetry device.

Both radio and sonic tags have been utilized successfully in a wide variety of conditions. Studies on the Columbia River documenting movements of adult anadromous salmonids have been enhanced through the use of radio telemetry devices. The radio tags, which were surgically implanted or placed in the gut through the mouth, provided data on the movements of individual fish for periods up to six weeks. This information is useful in determining how these fish migrate through the large pool areas behind the dams on the Columbia River. Winter (1983) summarizes the features, advantages, and disadvantages of both ultrasonic and radiotelemetry systems.

Video Recorder Techniques

The rapid development of sophisticated video-recording devices and their universal availability should not be overlooked by fisheries workers as a technique for recording data and/or providing graphic visual presentation of ecosystems and/or organisms. Modern video recorders can be utilized in the field with built-in microphones to both film and narrate, providing a useful record of field conditions for later laboratory analysis. The audio portion of the film can be utilized to make notes without the hindrance of having an additional separate writing pad. Visual presentation of data which has been permanently recorded also allows other investigators to see essentially what the field investigator saw without relying on memory or recall.

While moderately expensive, video recorders provide a semipermanent record of field observations. Newer hand held and easily portable units have increased the adaptability of this mechanism for field studies. With suitable design these units can also be utilized under water. This use may, however, require additional lighting and certainly requires a watertight container for the camera.

Literature Cited

Andreev, N. N. 1966. *Handbook of Fishing Gear and Its Rigging*. (Translated from Russian.) Published for the U.S. Department of the Interior and the National Science Foundation, Washington, D.C., by the Israel Program for Scientific Translations. 454 pp.

Bass, D. G., Jr., and V. G. Hitt. 1980. Quantitative Sampling of Warmwater Stream Fish with Detonating Cord. *Proceedings of the 31st Annual Conference, Southeastern Association of Fish and Wildlife Agencies* 31:519–21.

Brandt, A. von. 1964a. *Fish Catching Methods of the World*. London and Tonbridge: Fishing News (Books) Limited, Whitefriars Press Limited. 191 pp.

———. 1964b. Modern Fishing Gear of the World 2. Arranged by the technical staffs of *Fishing News International* and *Fishing News* from papers and discussion at the Second FAO World Fishing Gear Congress, London, 1963. London: Fishing News (Books) Limited, Ludgate House. 603 pp.

Bruce, R. A. 1967. *North Atlantic Trawl Nets*. U.S. Bureau of Commercial Fisheries, Fishery Leaflet 600. 23 pp.

Butler, A. J. 1930. *Sport in Classic Times*. London: Ernest Benn Limited. 213 pp.

Chadwick, J. W., M. F. Cook, and D. S. Winters. 1987. Vertical Gill Net for Studying Depth Distribution of Fishes in Small Lakes. *North American Journal of Fisheries Management* 7:593–94.

Dubach, H. W., and R. W. Taber. 1968. *Questions About the Oceans*. Washington, D.C.: National Oceanographic Data Center, U.S. Naval Oceanographic Office. Publication G–13. 100 pp.

Ellis, J. E., and E. N. Pickering. 1973. The Catching Efficiencies of a 21.3-meter (Headrape) Standard Wing Trawl and a 21.3-meter Electrical Wing Trawl in the Saginaw Bay Area of Lake Huron. *Transactions of the American Fisheries Society* 102(1):116–20.

Floyd, H. M. 1965. Castnets Constructed of Machine-Made Netting. U.S. Bureau of Commercial Fisheries, Fishery Leaflet 579. 13 pp.

———. 1968. *How to Throw a Castnet*. U.S. Bureau of Commercial Fisheries, Fishery Leaflet 609. 12 pp.

Gordon, W. G. 1965. *Haul Seining in the Great Lakes*. U.S. Bureau of Commercial Fisheries, Fishery Leaflet 577. 15 pp.

———. 1968. *Great Lakes Gill Net*. U.S. Bureau of Commercial Fisheries, Fishery Leaflet 606. 8 pp.

Griffith, J. S. 1981. Estimation of the Age-Frequency Distribution of Stream-Dwelling Trout by Underwater Observation. *Progressive Fish-Culturist* 43(1):51–53.

Hayes, M. L. 1983. Active Fish Capture Methods. Pp. 123–46 in L. A. Nielsen and D. L. Johnson, eds., *Fisheries Techniques*. Bethesda, Md.: American Fisheries Society.

Helfman, G. S. 1983. Underwater Methods. Pp. 349–69 in L. A. Nielsen and D. L. Johnson, eds., *Fisheries Techniques*. Bethesda, Md.: American Fisheries Society.

Hettler, W. F. 1979. Modified Neuston Net for Collecting Live Larval and Juvenile Fish. *Progressive Fish-Culturist* 41(1):32–33.

Hewson, L. C. 1959. A Study of Six Winter Seasons of Commercial Fishing on Lake Winnipeg, 1950–1955. *Journal of the Fisheries Research Board of Canada* 16(1):131–45.

Hubert, W. A. 1983. Passive Capture Techniques. Pp. 95–123 in L. A. Nielsen and D. L. Johnson, eds., *Fisheries Techniques*. Bethesda, Md.: American Fisheries Society.

James, P. W., S. C. Leon, A. V. Zale, and O. E. Maughan. 1987. Diver-Operated Electrofishing Device. *North American Journal of Fisheries Management* 7:597–98.

Kovalev, A. V., and B. V. Kurbatov. 1979. A Modified Technique and Gear for Zoo- and Ichthyoplankton Sampling. *Biological Morya* (Kiev) 49:77–78.

Marcy, B. C., Jr., and M. D. Dahlberg. 1980. Sampling Problems Associated with Ichthyoplankton Field-Monitoring Studies with Emphasis on Entrainment. Pp. 233–52 in C. H. Horcutt and J. R. Stauffer, Jr., eds., *Biological Monitoring of Fish*. Lexington, Mass.: Lexington Books.

Morioka, Y. 1979. Filtration Efficiency of Plankton Nets with Particular Reference to the Norpoc Net and MTD Net. *Bulletin Japanese Sea Reg. Fish. Res. Laboratory* 30:123–30.

Poole, R. L., D. R. Kuester, and A. Witt, Jr. 1963. The Status of Spearfishing and the Use of SCUBA in Fish Management Programs in the Freshwaters of the United States. *Transactions of the American Fisheries Society* 92(1):30–33.

Reeves, J. E., and G. S. Sidonato. 1972. *Effects of Trawling in Discovery Bay, Washington*. Washington Department of Fisheries. Technical Report No. 8. 45 pp.

Regier, H. A., and D. S. Robson. 1966. Selectivity of Gill Nets, Especially to Lake Whitefish. *Journal of the Fisheries Research Board of Canada* 23(3):423–54.

Regner, S. 1981. The Catching Efficiency of Four Different Plankton Nets Relative to Ichthyoplankton Objects. Pp. 1–6 in *Notes. Inst. Oceanogr. Ribon.*, Split 44.

Skidmore, W. J. 1970. *Manual of Instructions for Lake Survey*. Minneapolis: Minnesota Department of Natural Resources, Division of Fish and Wildlife, Section of Fisheries. Special Publication No. 1.

Snyder, D. E. 1983. Fish Eggs and Larvae. Pp. 165–97 in L. A. Nielsen and D. L. Johnson, eds., *Fisheries Techniques*. Bethesda, Md.: American Fisheries Society.

Swales, S. 1981. A Lightweight, Portable Fish-Trap for Use in Small Lowland Rivers. *Fisheries Management* 12(3):83–88.

Swenson, W. A., W. P. Gobin, and T. D. Simonson. 1988. Calibrated Mask-Bar for Underwater Measurement of Fish. *North American Journal of Fisheries Management* 8:382–85.

Thorne, R. E. 1983. Hydroacoustics. Pp. 239–59 in L. A. Nielsen and D. L. Johnson, eds., *Fisheries Techniques*. Bethesda, Md.: American Fisheries Society.

Tweddle, D., and P. Bodington. 1988. A Comparison of the Effectiveness of Black and White Gill Nets in Lake Malawi, Africa. *Fisheries Research* 6:257–69.

Vigg, S. 1978. Vertical Distribution of Adult Fish in Pyramid Lake, Nevada. *Great Basin Naturalist* 38(4):417–28.

Welcomme, R. L., ed. 1975. *Symposium on the Methodology for the Survey, Monitoring, and Appraisal of Fishery Resources in Lakes and Large Rivers*. Rome: Houghton Agriculture Organization of the United Nations, European Inland Fisheries Advisory Commission. Technical Paper No. 23 (Supplement 1). 2 volumes.

Winter, J. D. 1983. Underwater Biotelemetry. Pp. 371–95 in L. A. Nielsen and D. L. Johnson, eds., *Fisheries Techniques*. Bethesda, Md.: American Fisheries Society.

10. Electricity in Fisheries

Ever since humans became hunters they have sought ways to rapidly and efficiently gather large quantities of edible meat. Equipment to collect fish from inland and marine waters has progressed through spears, nets, and toxicants, to the use of electricity in various forms. The effectiveness of electricity in collecting fish and other aquatic organisms is demonstrated by laws (current or recent) in some southern states that outlaw the "telephoning of catfish," a practice of using crank telephones to generate current in a watercourse, thereby attracting fish for easy collection. The use of electricity by fishery managers and biologists to attain both management and research objectives has evolved from original crude devices and utilization to fairly sophisticated equipment and techniques.

The use of electricity to gather or control aquatic organisms is at least 100 years old. The effects of electric current on the orientation and movement of fish was first described by Mach (1875), Hermann (1885), and Hermann and Matthias (1894). British patents for electric fishing equipment were granted in 1863 and 1895. The earliest reliable date of an electric screen (alternating current) used in the United States is 1917 (Vibert 1963). Pulsed electric current was first used in the late 1920s (Vibert 1967). Although electric fishing attracted some attention after World War I, most of the improvement in equipment and techniques has been achieved since World War II.

Electrical Theory

Definitions of Electrical Terms

Commercially, the two basic types of electricity are alternating (AC) and direct (DC) current (figure 10.1). Standard household service in the United

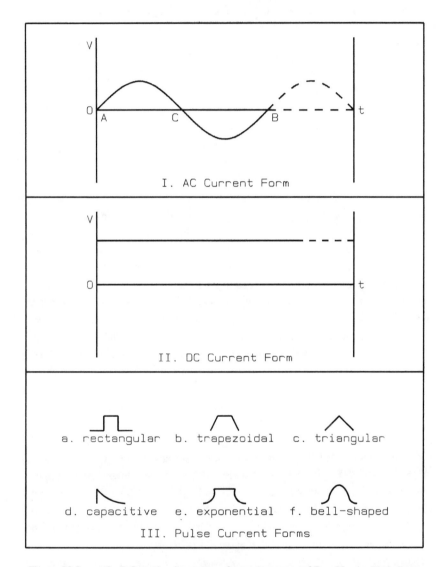

Figure 10.1. AC, DC, and pulse current forms (courtesy of Ron Harris, Utah State University).

States is 120-volt, 60-hertz (cycle) AC. These and other electrical terms are best described by the simple electric circuit shown in figure 10.2. Every circuit has a source of electrical energy called a generator. In DC the generator is sometimes a battery. A generator has two terminals, a positive (anode) and a negative (cathode). It is conventional to assume that electric current flows out of the positive terminal and into the load which is the high-resistance water (figure 10.2). The purpose of the generator is to increase the energy of the electric charges composing the current. Electrically, this is analogous to a pump increasing the potential energy of each cubic centimeter of fluid pumped. The unit of energy associated with a generator is a volt. One volt (V) of potential energy will drive one ampere (A) of electric current through one ohm (ω) of resistance. The resistance of the water is its tendency to resist the flow of electricity through it. All substances have resistance to the flow of electric current, some very low (e.g., copper) and some very high (e.g., glass insulators). For AC generators, the positive terminal alternates between the two terminals at a rate determined by the frequency (hertz). One complete period of reversal from positive to negative back to positive is called a hertz (cycle). Most commercial electricity is 60 hertz (per second), hence household current is called 60-hertz AC. In electrofishing equipment, the AC frequency varies from 60 to 450 cycles. The formula that relates current to voltage is Ohm's law: $V = IR$, where V equals volts applied across the resistance, I equals current (defined as the rate at which electric charge flows across a cross-sectional area), and R equals a proportionality constant between V and I (the total resistance of the medium through which current is flowing).

Definitions of terms used in electrofishing include: current (I), the movement of electric charge from one position to another (assumed to be from the positive terminal through the load and then to the negative); equipotential, an area (e.g., boat) or surface which is connected in such a fashion that the electrical potential of the entire surface is equal; narcosis (narcotized), a state of immobility resulting from slackened muscles; tetany (tetanus), a state of muscular rigidity; electrotetany, a muscular rigidity induced by an electric field; oscillotaxis, an artificial swimming motion induced by an alternating current; galvanotaxis, an artificial swimming induced by a new (e.g., pulsating DC) stimulus; electrotaxis, a fish swimming induced by any kind of electric current; galvanonarcosis, a state of immobility, induced by DC where fish are still and facing the anode; pulse, a short duration voltage between the generator terminals; pulse rate, the number of complete pulses per second; duty cycle, the proportion of time current flows in each second, essentially a measure of on-to-off time. Duty cycle is defined as $K_d = 1/Q$, which is the reciprocal of the pulse duty factor Q. $Q = T/t_{total}$, where t is pulse spacing and T is pulse

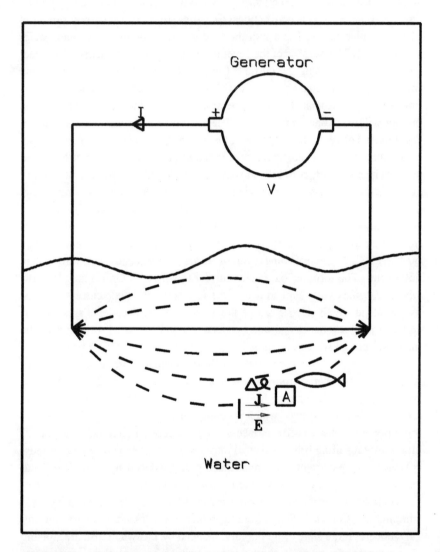

Figure 10.2.   Simple electrical circuit in water. A is 1 cm² cross-sectional area.

Table 10.1 Salt content designations of waters

Designation	Salt content-g/liter
Fresh water	up to 1
Brackish water	1–25
Water with marine salinity	25–50
Salt waters (higher than marine)	above 50

sequence duration. A watt (W) is a unit of power; 1 W equals 1 Joule/second (J/s; J = joule). A joule is a unit of energy. A 3.5 KW generator is capable of producing 3.5 kilowatts of power.

Current density and current are difficult to measure under most field operating conditions, while voltage is relatively simple to measure. The basic electrical parameter useful for measuring current flow is voltage drop. Since total voltage drop between two terminals is the same for all flow lines (figure 10.2), the voltage drop per unit of length is less on the longer lines. Thus, we define voltage gradient as the rate of change of voltage per unit length. The negative of voltage gradient is called the electric field E (V/cm), E being the electric field vector. In a medium such as water, which has three-dimensional volume, the resistance in a given direction is not necessarily equal. This causes the electric current to spread out into a nonuniform pattern. The conductive water represented in figure 10.2 results in a current field shaped like a football. The distribution of current in the water is described by current density, $J(A/cm^2)$, or current per unit area. In the simple circuit, the flow lines in the water represent the current flow. Current density is greater near the electrodes than far from them. The nature and distribution of J and E are critical to effective electrofishing. The two quantities are related by Ohm's law (at every point) by: $J = \sigma E$, where σ is conductivity. This relationship is important in electrofishing because while voltage can be controlled to some extent, conductivity generally cannot be controlled or affected.

Effect of Conductivity

Electrical conductivity of natural water is based on the amount of its several dissolved salts. Conductivity can be calculated mathematically when the kind and amount of dissolved salts are known. For fishery work, measurement with a conductivity meter is sufficient.

Sternin, Nikonorov, and Bumeister (1972) divided natural waters according to their content of dissolved salts into the groups listed in table 10.1.

The resistivity of water is governed by its temperature and the electrolytes (salts) dissolved in it. Resistivity and conductivity are related by the formula: $\sigma = 1/\rho$, where ρ is resistivity. In other words, conductivity is equal to the reciprocal of resistivity. Some high mountain lakes have a resistivity (due to very low levels of dissolved salts) of 10,000 ohm-cm; seawater has a resistivity of about 10 ohms-cm. When resistivity is high, it requires a high voltage to force an electric current through the water. Water with a large quantity of electrolytes (very low resistivity) also requires a considerable amount of voltage because the power is dissipated within the electrolytes. In seawater, which averages about 500 times the conductivity of most fresh water, electrofishing is restricted almost entirely to the use of pulsed current because the production of continuous-flow current requires an inordinately large power plant. A high voltage capability is important, but the current gradient (that is, the volts per centimeter or inch in the water, or amperes/cm^2) is the performance criterion for an electric shocking machine.

Waveforms and Pulses

Pulsing devices, which yield short powerful voltages repeatedly, are often used in electrofishing to attain large currents and voltages from comparatively low power supplies. Pulses of various shapes have been used successfully (figure 10.1). Pulses include rectangular, trapezoidal, triangular, bell-shaped, exponential, or capacitive, and those with exponential leading and/or trailing edges (Sternin, Nikonorov, and Bumeister 1972). Pulsed currents have the advantages of ease in storing and releasing. Pulses are much more powerful than interrupted current, given a common power source. Sharber and Carothers (1988) report significantly higher proportions of injury to rainbow trout using one-quarter sine waves than from either exponential or square wave pulses. Reynolds and Kolz (1988) offer an explanation of the injury mechanics and countermeasures to prevent injury.

Pulsed direct current has been utilized effectively over a wide range of operational conditions (Burnet 1959). When capacitor-discharged (pulsed) or interrupted DC is used, three factors are considered: (1) the pulse rate, (2) the shape of the pulse, and (3) the duty cycle (Rollefson 1958; Taylor, Cole, and Sigler 1957).

Applications of Electrofishing in Fisheries

Electrofishing is useful in many types of fishery investigations. In streams and lakes or ponds (e.g., in the littoral zone) electrofishing can be utilized to capture or direct movement of fish for a variety of reasons.

While electrofishing is an excellent qualitative tool, its use in quantitative studies must be preceded by a determination of the effect of electrofishing bias, including physiological changes of fish collected. The primary bias of electrofishing is related to its size selectivity (large fish of a given species are more affected than small ones) and species selectivity (e.g., escape capability, the ability of some species to more readily sense and thereby escape an electric field). Advantage may be gained for a given species by changing waveforms and current levels (particularly with pulsed DC) assuming adequate information or experience (Mahon 1980; Novotny and Priegel 1974; Sternin, Nikonorov, and Bumeister 1972).

In qualitative samples, it may not be important if fish are affected physiologically or when an unknown number escape capture. But in quantitative sampling both the numbers and species caught, as well as missed, are important. Physiological changes and responses are also important.

Qualitative Population Sampling

Almost any water body can be sampled with electrofishing to determine species present (Gerard et al. 1989). Sampling can be of short or extensive duration. If no information is available, a preliminary survey at low voltages can be followed by efforts with increasing power, until the investigators are satisfied that a representative sample of species has been collected. Studies initiated with low-voltage settings will allow collection of both species and size groups without the liability of fish deaths associated with initial sweeps at high voltages (provided that is a concern). If a data base is required for waters not previously electrofished, it is beneficial, when acceptable, to follow the electrofishing with toxicant treatment (e.g., rotenone) so that efficiency can be established for species and size groups.

Quantitative Population Sampling

Two aspects of quantitative sampling with electrofishing are of primary concern. Violations of the precepts of the sampling scheme or estimator (also a valid concern with other collection methods) may produce bias in the sample, for example, a presumption of equal catchability being necessary. Changes in the physiological status of the fish may affect subsequent tests or data collected. Physiological changes may also be related to invalidation of the assumptions of the estimators.

Discussion

Indices (Peterson, Schnabel, Jolly, Zippen, Leslie, DeLury) of various types and application are used widely (see chapter 3). Basic assumptions of the indices relevant to electrofishing are: (1) both marked and unmarked fish are equally available to gear, (2) chances of capture for both marked and unmarked fish are equal and random, and (3) fishing (capture or effect) does not change probability of being caught.

Physiological change (both of captured and missed fish) may be manifested in altered behavior, such as sensitivity to electric current or physiological inability to respond to current due to tetany or exhaustion.

High proportions of marked fish in second catches with two-hour intervals between fishings may be the result of marked fish being more susceptible to capture, or to unmarked fish being less catchable, or a combination of both factors (Cross and Stott 1975). Cross and Stott report that unmarked fish are less readily caught, resulting in a proportion of marked fish in second and subsequent fishings that is too high. The authors suggest a correction method for low depletion estimates. The correction is based on use of only the second and subsequent catches to provide a regression line. This is used on the first-catch data for obtaining a population estimate (extrapolated from the position of the first catch on the ordinate to where the abscissa is crossed). This technique may result in errors in either direction (over- or underestimates), however, and the errors may be of greater magnitude than the error of the initial estimator (Mahon 1980).

There is a tendency for a fish to flee when it first contacts a weak electric field (Vibert, Lamarque, and Cuinat 1960). This reaction may be related, in second and subsequent catch efforts, to a fish learning to avoid capture by responding quicker and fleeing more effectively (Cross and Stott 1975). During second or subsequent fishings it is also possible that fish become so affected by the electrical field (DC) that no response toward the anode is physically possible. Absence of this effect in fishing separated by more than twenty-four hours suggests that the behavior is not learned but physiological (Mahon 1980; Cross and Stott 1975).

Cross and Stott, reporting on replicate fishing in ponds with a DC pulse machine, note that catch data from two-hour interval fishings resulted in significantly higher proportions of marked fish than expected (based on seine hauls). If, as they point out, some fish are affected by a first fishing, all fish present in the population for the second fishing are not equally available. Proportions of marked and unmarked fish in second catches were not significantly different from expected when time intervals exceeded one day. Cross and Stott also note that other authors report decreased catchability in rainbow trout after a first fishing. While a decrease in efficiency of electrofishing between passes would be serious, a change (decrease) in availability of fish is more important when estimating populations with a depletion method. Cross and Stott suggest that lengthening the time interval between fishings may be inconvenient but completion of enough samplings to enable development of a reasonable graph without use of the first sample may be acceptable. As noted, others have had problems with this correction.

The implications of changed catchability, if manifested in the estimators, are changes in estimated numbers of fish in the total population. The Peterson index is used as an illustration: $\hat{N} = MC/R$, where $\hat{N}$ is the population estimate, M is the number of fish marked and released, C is the recapture sample size (both marked and unmarked), and R is the number of marked fish recaptured.

Reduced rates of recapture (R) result in a smaller denominator, thereby yielding a larger than actual estimate of $\hat{N}$. But if C is lowered for fish affected by the first pass, the numerator is too small, and the estimate is lower than actual.

Summary—Electrofishing Applications in Fisheries Research

If, as published data and experience indicate, use of electrofishing results in violations of the assumptions of the estimator, then electrofishing data will be biased. The bias problem centers on the assumption of equal catchability, both in initial and subsequent fishing efforts (Mahon 1980; Chmielewski et al. 1973). Size and species selectivity by electrofishing gear cause potential violations of the assumptions in first passes. Physiological changes, altered catchability, and altered availability cause violations of the assumptions in second and subsequent passes.

Single-pass (capture and mark) and second-pass (recapture) mark-recapture estimators are probably affected to the greatest extent and are most affected if the recapture pass is completed in less than twenty-four hours or perhaps less than one week. Catch depletion estimators may be less affected by electrofishing bias and effects. Recaptured fish are not used in estimates and therefore do not provide the bias associated with mark-recapture estimates. However, depletion sampling may still be affected by the reduced catchability or reduced availability of fish after second or subsequent passes (Mahon 1980; Chmielewski et al. 1973).

Electrofishing can be used effectively within the guidelines presented below.

1. *Qualitative Sampling—Species Diversity*
   Some sizes of most species of fish can be collected by electrofishing. It is essential that netters collect all fish, not just large ones.

2. *Population Age—Size Structure*
   Size bias in electrofishing will tend toward capture of greater numbers of large fish of a given species. Length frequency data will almost certainly favor larger size groups, allowing for misinterpretation of the relative abundance of smaller fish. The size at which selectivity becomes a factor is related to species, electrofishing conditions, water conductivity, etc. Above a certain size (variable by species and/or water body) capture efficiency should be approximately equal, allowing assessment of "stock size" fish (Reynolds 1983, 1979).

3. *Relative Population Abundance Estimates*
   Between species or between water bodies, estimates of relative abundance can be made using electrofishing, assuming relative catchability between species can be assessed. Larger sized fish will tend to be captured in greater relative numbers than actually exist, but above a given size for each species, catch per unit effort can be effectively used in comparisons.

4. *Population Dynamic Factors*
   Size selectivity bias with electrofishing gear makes an unbiased estimate of such factors as recruitment, reproduction, mortality, and growth rate quite difficult. Studies of population dynamics can be best accomplished with electricity in conjunction with other gear.

5. *Capture for Experimental Procedures*
   Often fish of various species are collected from the wild and transported to artificial areas for research. Electrofishing is often the most efficient method of collecting large numbers of fish, but the use of these fish in subsequent experiments must be approached with caution. Aside from the immediate and somewhat obvious potential effects such as tetany, ruptured blood vessels and damaged vertebra, subtle physiological changes, such as blood gas composition and muscle oxygen debt, may manifest themselves for periods from one to several weeks.

Electrofishing—Theoretical Considerations and Uses

Theory

Simply stated, the theoretical basis for electrofishing is that application of an electric current affects a percentage of the fish present in such a fashion that they can be collected. In an AC field, electrical stimulus immobilizes fish (electronarcosis or electrotetany). Fish may be immobilized at depths beyond which they can be recovered (netted) or even seen. In DC fields, fish near the anode may be drawn to it by galvanotaxis. Pulsed DC is more effective than continuous-flow DC because of the short recovery time between pulses. This sequentially draws the fish to the positive electrode by forced swimming.

The concept of an electrical field to collect fish incorporates the theory of current density at three levels: (1) electrical field perceived by fish (perception level), (2) a higher level of current density at which galvanotaxis (DC fields) or electrotetanus (AC fields) occurs (effective level), and (3) an even higher level of current density at which complete galvanonarcosis (DC fields) occurs, immobilizing the fish or drawing it to the anode, and lethal effects more often caused by AC may occur (lethal or danger level) (Novotny and Priegel 1974).

The most effective electrofishing (maximum number of fish recovered with minimum numbers of deaths or physiological damage) occurs when the electric field has a very small perception level zone, a large effective level zone, and a small or absent lethal level or zone. The most important factors in determining the current and voltage distribution in water are size, shape, and spacing of electrodes. Two simple shapes—cylinders and spheres—work well and encompass the majority of electrode shape characteristics (Novotny and Priegel 1974). How these systems are utilized and factors which modify or alter electrofishing success are discussed below. Effective electric field definition is used in electric screens to divert or attract fish to or from certain areas.

Uses

The following list of uses of electrofishing is not inclusive but indicates its versatility. Four major use areas exist:

1. Capture, which includes harvesting and censusing, rescuing fish from low or polluted waters for transplanting, catching spawners for artificial propagation, selective removal of certain species and/or size classes, sanitary removal of "sick" fish, and electrified tuna hooks and whaling harpoons.

2. Movement control, which includes controlling fish movements and activities by electric screens (e.g., protection of planted juveniles against predators etc., blocking entrances to turbines and pumps, directional fish fences for regulating migratory paths), using direct electric current to attract fish to suction pumps after capture (e.g., purse seines), and counting migrating fish.
3. Anesthesia, which includes narcosis for fish handling (e.g., transportation, tagging).
4. Other uses include electrocution of catches to improve quality of fish flesh. The electrocution of sardines in a net prevents struggling and therefore the loss of scales, which decreases market value. It is reported that the keeping quality of electrocuted fish is better, but they must be packed in ice at once, because after rigor mortis decomposition proceeds more rapidly than that of fish killed normally (Dethloff 1959). There is an interesting procedure based on the declining resistance of fish flesh after death to electric current. This phenomena can be used to devise instruments for the objective measurement of the freshness of fish in commercial or other processing operations (Sternin, Nikonorov, and Bumeister 1972).

In fisheries research the principal use of electrofishing is to capture fish for a defined purpose. As noted above, there are potential problems in utilizing electrofishing for various studies.

Three principal types of electrofishing gear are used to capture fish: boom-shockers, portable units, and shore-based units. Each type has advantages and disadvantages associated with its use.

Boom-Shockers

Electric shocking machines operated in deep water require a different physical setup than those used in shallow streams, lakes, or ponds. The unit most commonly used in water over three feet deep is known as a boom-shocker (figure 10.3). A boom-shocker is mounted on a heavy-gauge aluminum boat of appropriate size, generally 14 to 18 feet with a motor capable of maintaining both travel and trolling speeds. Both personnel and equipment are carried in the boat. This physical setup means that operators, generators, and all electric equipment are housed in a very small and somewhat unstable space. Collectively, this means that procedural discipline (relative to both safety and successful capture of fish) must be precise, with caution extreme and mental alertness acute.

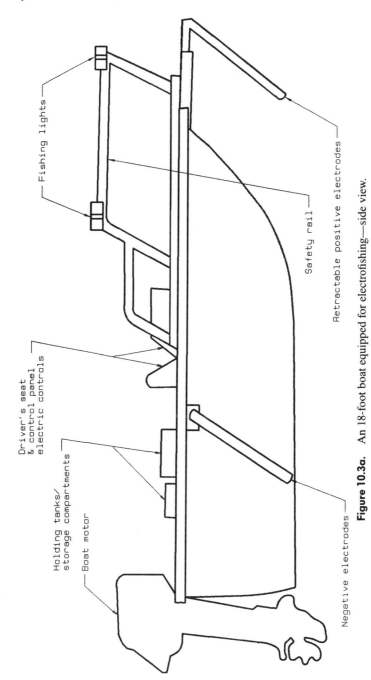

Fishing lights

Safety rail

Retractable positive electrodes

Driver's seat
& control panel
electric controls

Holding tanks/
storage compartments

Boat motor

Negative electrodes

Figure 10.3a. An 18-foot boat equipped for electrofishing—side view.

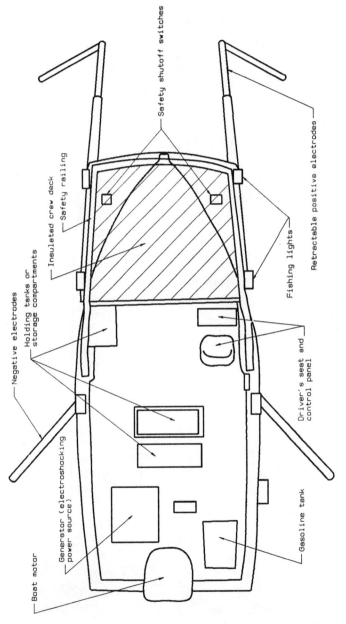

Figure 10.3b. An 18-foot boat equipped for electrofishing—top view.

Many boom-shocker generators have an output of 240 volts and 1500 to 5000 watts, with 60-hertz AC. Reynolds (1983) suggests that a three-phase, 230-volt generator with 3500-watt capacity gives the greatest flexibility for electrofishing; however, three-phase generators are more expensive and not essential to successful electrofishing. As few as two electrodes may be used: one over the bow and one near the stern. Generally, however, either four (figure 10.3) or six electrodes are employed or at least two anodes (positive) and one cathode (negative). The positive electrodes can be constructed of suitable conductive material and either be adjustable for depth or of fixed length and rigid. Heavy, one-piece rods can be used for the anodes and extended out over the bow of the boat. Alternatively, lengths of cable can be used. Heavy weights on the ends will tend to keep the cables straight. The cables can also be braced at intervals to prevent twisting. Care should be taken to prevent the anodes and cathodes from coming in contact with one another, resulting in an electrical short and a blown fuse. Stiff anodes tend to remain more vertical than do flexible cables, but they have disadvantages in shallow water or heavy plant growth unless they can be easily and safely raised and lowered from the bow of the boat. The negative electrode(s) is generally flexible cable or chain that will trail along the side or stern of the boat, clear of the motor propeller. The use of additional electrodes tends to increase the size of the field and decreases its intensity (voltage gradient), theoretically affecting more fish while reducing the hazard to both fish and operators (see below).

The capture efficiency of a boom-shocker, depending on the situation and operator experience, is fairly low, perhaps 5 to 25 percent. Its use as a quantitative tool should be carefully examined. It is an effective device for general collections when netting or other methods fail or are impractical (Smith, Franklin, and Kramer 1959) and a useful tool for fisheries research.

Fish react to the electric field of an AC boom-shocker by: (1) attempting to escape, (2) dashing about near the surface, (3) lying immobilized near or at the surface, (4) becoming tetanized and sinking to the bottom, or (5) drifting with the current. Fish that come to the surface must be quickly netted because they recover rapidly, and the boat is generally moving (Loeb 1955). Both the horizontal and vertical fields of a boom-shocker are relatively small. Water depths of more than 8 to 10 feet are considered excessive. This will vary with the type of bottom and the physical constraints of the water (conductivity). Performance can be modified by altering the physical configuration of the electrodes. Electrodes with corners (e.g., rectangular, triangular) cause areas of high current density in the electric field. These areas of high current density can harm fish. Circular electrodes eliminate most of this problem. Diameter of the circles (cylinders) can be increased to maximize effective range or decreased if voltage is insufficient with large diameter ones.

Boat-operated electrofishing requires specialized equipment and knowledgeable operators. The boat should be specifically designed for electrofishing or be modified permanently (equipotential established). Equipotential is accomplished by connecting all metal to the metal boat hull with more metal, thus eliminating the danger of electroshock to personnel. There should be two separate power units, one for electrofishing, and one for operating lights, aerators, and other equipment. The boat operator, preferably experienced, should have control of all electric functions from the driver's console (see below for additional safety considerations). There should be pressure-activated, positive-action, low-voltage switches controlled by the pilot and by at least one netter in the bow of the boat.

Portable and Shore-Based Units

Portable electrofishing units are useful in many situations where large boat-mounted or shore-based generators are inappropriate. They provide flexibility that larger units lack and can be used effectively in small, shallow areas.

Most shore-based electrofishing generators in the United States (both AC and DC) range in power from 0.4 to 5 KW (Patten and Gillaspie 1966). Good results have been obtained in Israel with a machine supplying up to 7.5 KW (Vibert 1967), and a 7.5 KW, 110-volt AC machine has been used successfully in Utah on an experimental basis.

Backpack and Tow-Along Units

Portable electrofishing units are of two types: backpack and tow-along. Both units are designed to be used in water less than 4 feet deep, with the operators either carrying all of the equipment or towing the power unit in a small boat.

Two types of backpack units have been used successfully. The first are small units that operate from a deep storage battery carried in a pack frame. They can be used for small streams or shore areas of lakes and ponds. These units are highly effective in remote areas, where weight is a factor and where only short-duration collections (i.e., for species diversity) are required. They are severely limited by the storage capacity of the battery (unless recharging is available) and by current output. They can be used effectively for species identification in stream surveys in areas where only limited data is required.

The second type of units are small AC generators, also used as backpack shockers. They have an advantage over battery units in that they will function as long as fuel is available. They are potentially dangerous because the electric generator is mounted on the back of one crew member, and they have power output limitations.

In both battery- and generator-powered units, the power source should be mounted on an insulated pack frame and weatherproofed. Both the person carrying the unit and the crew member(s) with electrodes should have pressure-activated, positive-action shut-off switches that will either shut off the generator or disengage the circuit in case of a fall or other accident and a tilt-switch with manual reset. For either system, selection capability for voltage output, frequency, and duty cycle are the minimal options required.

Towed units generally are in between boom-shockers and backpack units in size. Towed units incorporate the flexibility of a backpack unit with the electrical output capabilities of small boom-shockers. Typically, the unit consists of a generator and power control panel, both of which are carried in a small boat (preferably of nonconductive material such as fiberglass), and an array of electrodes. The unit is towed, pushed, or rowed by one crew member while others operate the electrodes and pick-up nets. Realistically, a minimum of five people are needed for this type of operation unless water depths and stream size are quite small.

Electrodes for all of these small systems can be relatively simple. Safety considerations should include fiberglass handles with metal hoops of appropriate size. For many situations, a ring electrode is ideal (Reynolds 1983). The attachment of the electrified hoop to the handle can be angled so that the electrode can be held parallel (see below).

Shore-Based Units

Shore-based units generally utilize large (i.e., 3.5 to 7.5 KW generators) power sources, since weight and size are not restrictive. They are designed for operations in which the power requirement (current output) exceeds what can be safely carried in a boom-shocker unit. Large, shore-based units provide more power than either portable units or boom-shockers, and they can be used (to a defined, but generally unknown limit) with multiple electrode arrays without overloading the generator. Functional water depths are generally limited to 3 or 4 feet, depending on physical operating conditions (e.g., stream substrate and velocity). In AC operations, both electrodes are hand held and operated in close proximity to one another (5 to 10 feet apart). In DC operations, both anode and cathode can be hand held, or the cathode can be a metal grid placed on the stream bottom, then the anode(s) moved around it or remote from it (Reynolds 1983). For practical as well as safety reasons, the generator should be as close to the cathode as possible. Often the cathode can be placed outside the area of fishing activity, reducing the hazard to both fish and operators. James Reynolds (personal communication, 1986) feels that shore-based electrofishing is the most dangerous of all types. Extreme caution is recommended when using these units.

Electrodes

In general for DC machines, a number of small anodes rather than a single large one is preferred. The anodes may be connected one after the other (electrically parallel) by a single wire. The operators have more mobility when using this arrangement and often the anodes can be electrified dipnets that function both as producers of current and as capture devices. This latter method was first used at Utah State University in the mid-1950s. When dipnets are electrified, fish should be held in them for only a short time (less than 1 minute). Many federal and state safety standards now prohibit the use of dipnets as electrodes. Flexible electrodes may be desirable under certain circumstances (Ellis 1971). This technique increases the area of electrical field, but also increases the danger to both fish and operators. Reynolds (1983) indicates that cylinder or ring electrodes most effectively minimize regions of high voltage and fish damage, being adjustable and capable of negotiating weeds and obstacles. In addition, these types of electrodes are easily assembled, and they minimize surface disturbance, thereby enhancing visibility.

A cylinder electrode is pipe shaped, usually about 1 m (3.3 feet) long. A ring electrode consists of about twelve "dropper" electrodes attached at equal intervals from a horizontal aluminum ring about 1 meter in diameter. Each dropper electrode is a 6-inch-long stainless steel tube attached to a length of insulated wire 12 to 18 inches long (Novotny and Priegel 1974). The number and/or size of the anodes can be increased until the generator is operating at full capacity. If a higher than needed voltage gradient exists, the anode size can be increased, resulting in a larger area of effective shocking. Generator capacity should not be exceeded, however. Smaller electrodes are required if the generator is at capacity.

The cathode can be quite large, that is, within reasonable limits; in any event it should be no smaller than the total area of the anodes. The resistance of the cathode can be minimized by increasing its surface, theoretically to infinity, without risk of overloading. Other things being equal, if anode size is increased, the amount of power needed to produce an identical voltage gradient increases. The cathode should be distributed over a wide ground surface and it should be in contact with the ground in a number of places (Novotny and Priegel 1971). If the cathode is being used only as a ground, it needs to be placed on the bottom of the stream or lake. When it is to be used as a ground and also as a fish barrier, it should be in contact with the bottom as well as being placed vertically in such a manner as to present an electric field against fish movement (Burnet 1967). From a practical standpoint, it is easiest and generally most effective to use two or more cathodes for this latter type of effort. A number of small cathodes commonly connected in electrical parallel may on occasion be better than a single large one (Cuinat 1967). In extremes of very high or very low water conductivity, the use of two negative electrodes approximately 5 feet apart may substantially increase the voltage gradient at the anode.

The cathode may consist of one to several pieces of grating or other metallic material. Researchers at Utah State University have had good success with chicken wire netting. It is inexpensive and can be stored compactly. The anode can be one or more fiberglass dipnets, each with a metal hoop, allowing fish to be picked up by the operator when they are drawn to it and reducing the number of people required for an operation.

In situations that require somewhat larger equipment, the generator and other equipment such as live boxes can be floated or carried in a small boat or raft (preferably of nonconductive material). The negative electrode can be a cable of appropriate size and length at the back of the boat, and two anodes can be operated forward of the boat. With boom-shockers, larger lengths of cable have been used as anodes in deep-water streams such as the Snake River, Idaho, to fish for sturgeon, but care should be taken to prevent the two cables from tangling. Tangling of the anode cables causes unpredictable changes in the electric field, but will not cause electric problems as will tangling the anode and cathode cables. To prevent tangling, place stiff braces such as PVC pipe at intervals between the two cables. Cuinat (1967) reports little practical difference between the relative conductivity of copper, iron, and steel when used as electrodes.

AC machines do not have distinguishable anodes and cathodes, since the polarity changes with each cycle. Such electrofishers often have the same number and size of electrodes connected to each pole, or at least they should present an equivalent total surface. Practical applications with AC indicate that good results can be obtained with electrodes of equal size.

On large, boat-mounted devices, electrodes may be constructed from a variety of materials and be of various sizes, depending on the anticipated use. Novotny and Priegel (1974) provide a guideline for selecting electrodes and voltages in water of varying conductivity (table 10.2). The data are based on a boat-mounted generator rated at 11.7 amperes using alternating current.

Table 10.2. Electrode and voltage selection in waters of various conductivity (from Novotny and Priegel 1974).

Range of Conductivity (micromhos/cm)	Voltage (V)	No. of Electrodes
10–50	460	6
50–70	390	6
70–100	320	6
100–200	230	6
200–400	160	6
400–1200	90	6
1200–2000	90	3

These values are for a specific electrofishing system and may require modification for use with other systems.

Using boom-shocker anodes made of two steel rods that project 3 to 6 feet under water may be effective in some situations, while long cables that extend 15 to 20 feet under water may be required in others. The boat can be used as the cathode thus providing ten times the size of the anodes. With a metal boat and separate cathodes, the boat is "live." The important safety aspects are related to having all metal surfaces in the boat at equipotential. The danger of electric shock comes from different potentials in the boat which personnel can touch, not from contact with the anodes (James Reynolds, personal communication, 1984).

Factors Governing Electrofishing Success

Physical Factors

The conductivity and temperature of water are directly related. As the temperature of the water increases, so does the conductivity, with both proceeding at equivalent rates (Sigler 1969). Bruschek (1967) found this to be true in Austrian streams except in the spring, when the conductivity of the water rose less rapidly than the temperature because of the small amounts of electrolytes in snow melt. The response of brook trout to electric current is low in cold water, but increases with temperature to 50°F. If the temperature continues to rise above that mark, the response decreases (Elston 1942). At 70°F, trout response to DC may range from poor to unsatisfactory (Webster et al. 1955). Vincent (1971) reports capture of salmonids at temperatures from 32° to 50°F and that galvanonarcosis increases while galvanotaxis decreases below 40°F.

Webster et al. report greater success with brown trout at 46°F than at 62°F when using either AC or DC.

Water temperatures can affect an electrofishing operation either positively or negatively. High water temperatures increase fish metabolic rates and their sensitivity to (perception of) electric fields. It also increases the conductivity of water. Low temperatures decrease flotation of stunned fish, reducing the likelihood of capture (Reynolds 1983).

Shoreline characteristics of either streams, lakes, or ponds can affect results. Developed shorelines increase fish vulnerability, and very steep shoreline slopes make electrofishing less effective because of limited accessible habitat for sampling (Reynolds 1983). Large bodies of water (either lotic or lentic environments) are harder to electrofish than small ones because of the lesser proportional area that can be sampled effectively. Highly conductive bottom materials may reduce electrofishing effectiveness by drawing off and "short-circuiting" the electrical field, resulting in a smaller than expected effective area. This problem can, to some extent, be reduced by keeping electrodes off of the bottom (Novotny and Priegel 1974).

Salt in some form can be added to water to increase conductivity. For most electrofishing operations, however, the amounts of salt required (and the subsequent change in water quality) make it cost prohibitive.

When DC electrodes are placed in water and a potential difference is applied to them, polarization phenomena and electrocorrosion occur at the interface between the electrode and the electrolyte (salt solution). These phenomena may create additional electrical resistance (load) on the electrofishing gear, which can affect its performance despite the conductivity. All electrode polarization factors in concert, however, have (relative to electrofishing success) limited effect on the electrode potentials of the anode and cathode. Factors that may be of concern are the roughness of the electrode surfaces and the material of which the electrodes are made. Chrome nickel stainless steels present the fewest problems with polarization phenomena. A positive benefit of electrode polarization is a more uniform current distribution over its surface, resulting in fewer variations in the field around the electrode. In DC, only the material of the anode is attacked as a result of electrocorrosion and the material of the cathode is not destroyed, but may actually be deposited upon. Electrode design, therefore, should take into account the following factors: (1) cathodes will not disintegrate with DC and therefore may be made of any metal or alloy, design considerations being the only criterion, (2) cathodes may be made of light, strong metals, or even of wood, plastics, or other materials and covered with thin, metal-plated sheets or a layer of metal, but may then only be used for DC applications, (3) metal-plated material cannot be used for anodes because the metal is not thick enough and will be destroyed (corroded) quickly. Stainless steel and aluminum alloys are the structural materials which combine (in fresh water) high resistance to electrocorrosion and sufficient mechanical strength (Sternin, Nikonorov, and Bumeister 1972).

Biological Factors

Conductivity of Fish

The conductivity of fish flesh as it relates to electrofishing is as important a consideration as water conductivity. Many earlier experimental studies of fish behavior in an electrical field proceeded on the hypothesis that a fish body was a homogeneous ellipsoid with a given electrical conductivity (Sternin, Nikonorov, and Bumeister 1972). In assessing the difference between fish species, however, it is more nearly correct to regard the fish as a body with a given electrical conductivity, enclosed in a thin envelope with another given, but different, electrical conductivity. Such an envelope simulates the higher electrical resistance of the skin and scales.

The defensive function of skin and scales is particularly clear in fresh water and drops abruptly when the electrical conductivity of the water increases. The protective nature of these layers, other conditions being equal, may account, in part, for the lower threshold values of field intensity (TVFI) of trout and pike compared with those of carp and tench. The protective role of the skin finds practical expression in the abrupt drop in threshold values of fish whose skin cover has been damaged, thus potentially assisting in electrofishing removal of injured fish.

Reactions of Fish to Electric Currents

The theoretical and historical assumption that the field of an electrofishing device is homogeneous has been discredited. Therefore, in the nonhomogeneous fields utilized in electrofishing operations, fish reactions differ from those in a theoretical field (Sternin, Nikonorov, and Bumeister 1972). Important considerations when operating an electrofishing device are: the vector of the initial swimming speed of the fish when entering the electric field and the direction of the fish's motion relative to the electric current field lines, taking into account as well the vectors of the motion of the electrodes (e.g., movement of the boat or operators).

Sternin, Nikonorov, and Bumeister (1972) propose a classification scheme for the reactions of fish to electric current (table 10.3) that can be used in training operators and in field applications.

Table 10.3. Possible scheme for classifying the reactions of fish to electric current (from Sternin, Nikonorov, and Bumeister 1972).

Motion intensity	Numerical designation	Fish orientation vs. electrode position	Numerical designation
Natural mobility	1	Lack of orientation	1
High mobility (first reaction, occasional tremors, dashes to the side, turning)	2	Fish body perpendicular to electric field line (galvanotaxis)	2
Low mobility (retarded swimming, tremors, disintegration of schools, partial immobility)	3	Position (turning) of the fish body parallel to streamlines (anodic electrotaxis, half-turn toward anode or cathode, longitudinal oscillotaxis)	3
Forced swimming (taxis, electrotropism, swimming similar to optomotor swimming, anodic electrotaxis)	4	with head toward anode with head toward cathode with head toward AC electrode	3 + a 3 + c 3 + e
Pseudo-forced swimming (periodically unbalanced swimming, e.g., on the side, on the back; convulsive muscle contractions; partial loss of equilibrium)	5	Directed motion (anodic galvanotaxis, cathodic galvanotaxis frightening effect) along field lines to anode along field lines from anode along field lines to cathode along field lines from cathode from AC electrode	4 4 + a 4 − a 4 + a 4 − c 4 − e
State of shock (full loss of equilibrium, loss of sensitivity, rigidity, narcosis, numbing, drowsiness, permanent convulsive state, complete immobilization, sinking to the bottom, tetanus, paralysis)	6	Circular motion (circling in place with or without bending of the body; periodic motion along some closed paths with or without escape from the field; "rotary" and "riding-school" oscillotaxis)	5
Irreversible immobility (death)	7	Bending of the fish body (symmetrical bending or half-turning) to anode from anode to cathode from cathode to AC electrode from AC electrode	6 6 + a 6 − a 6 + c 6 − c 6 + e 6 − c

Reactions to Direct Current

It is oversimplified but useful to describe three responses that fish exhibit to DC electric fields: (1) they may be repelled, (2) they may be led toward the positive pole or repelled from the negative pole, or (3) they may be narcotized and may or may not sink (Lewis and Charles 1957).

The reaction of a fish to continuous DC is a fluttering of the entire body when the fish is parallel to the direction of the current (figure 10.2). If it is transverse to the lines of current, it turns its head toward the anode (Halsband 1967). When parallel to the direction of current, the fish may also swim toward the anode (Haskell, MacDougal, and Geduldig 1954). This reaction is termed galvanotaxis. If a fish is transverse to the lines of electric force, it does not inevitably swim toward the anode; sometimes it will do so only when a new stimulus is applied, hence the value of pulsed DC. The term galvano-narcosis (electronarcosis) applies when a fish becomes incapable of movement (Halsband).

In a laboratory study by Haskell and Adelman (1955), rapid (180 per second) pulses of DC produced movement toward the electrode at about 20 percent lower voltage than did slow (1 per second) pulses. Taylor, Cole, and Sigler (1957) obtained the best results with a pulse rate of 96 per second and a duty cycle of 0.33. Very high pulse rates produced quicker anesthesia and less reliable movement toward the anode. In highly resistive waters, however, high pulse rates effectively and reliably produce movement toward the anode. Lower pulse rates of 20 to 50 per second are now commonly used and are particularly effective for large fishes (James Reynolds, personal communication, 1985).

According to Halsband (1967), the initial reaction of a fish to interrupted DC, with pulses of a square wave or in the shape of capacitor discharges or quarter-sine waves (figure 10.1), is spasmodic quivering of the body. Other observers believe that initial reactions of fish to above-threshold currents is extremely varied. The second reaction, according to Halsband, is the turning of the fish and its swimming toward the anode. This is only true, however, when the pulses have a rapid growth and a slow decay. When the pulse has a slow growth and a rapid decay, the fish swims toward the cathode. Other workers believe that a slow growth and rapid decay pulse is more effective in fresh water. The fish's body in a DC field is generally limp and never rigid.

This principle can be used in some flowing waters to stun fish with DC (or possibly AC) and allow them to drift to a block net for capture (Herbert et al. 1961).

Reactions to Alternating Current

In theory, fish lying parallel to the lines of force in an AC field should face the positive and negative electrodes as many times per second as the current alternates (cycles). Obviously this is a physical impossibility because of the time-response factor. In practice, AC repels fish from both electrodes and their response is erratic and more or less random. Fish affected by an AC field generally become rigid (tetany). In streams of moderate speed, fish can be captured downstream of the electrodes before they recover from the effect of the field. In turbid or swift streams, many fish will be lost when fishing with AC unless block nets are placed at the bottom of each section fished and the fish removed as they arrive.

Summary

DC capacitor-discharge electroshockers have the greatest neurophysiological effect on fish and are thus the most useful for most electrofishing operations, other conditions being equal. Next in effectiveness is continuous AC, and lastly continuous DC. Fish affected by DC become limp and may not always be recovered. DC capacitor-discharge units have the maximum initial physiological effect and the least residual effect on the nervous system of fish. In streams that are brushy and/or turbid, some investigators favor continuous AC, while others prefer capacitor-discharged DC because of its potential to draw fish from cover.

In a stream study in New York comparing AC and DC, AC was reported twice as effective (80 percent recovery) as irregular, intermittent DC (Webster et al. 1955). James Reynolds (personal communication, 1985) points out that much of the interpretation problem associated with voltage effectiveness between AC and DC is related to misinterpretation of voltage meter readings. Many volt meters accurately measure average RMS (root-mean-square) voltage, which is satisfactory for DC but underestimates the effective AC voltage. Therefore, if a machine is switched from DC to AC, and the same voltage setting is retained, peak voltage increases 2.8 times. Fish response may lead an operator to believe that AC is therefore better at raising fish than DC. This is not the case, because DC will fish as well as, if not better than, AC, if both are measured as peak voltages. It is important for operators to know if a volt meter is measuring RMS or peak voltage.

Effects of Electric Current on Fish

General Physiological Effects

It has frequently been stated that electrofishing is not harmful to fish health, reproduction, or growth. This statement carries the strong implication, however, that electrofishing machines are being used according to recommended standards by operators aware of their operational parameters (Sigler 1969). It can be easily demonstrated that fish can be killed with electricity in their natural environment, as well as under laboratory conditions (Godfrey 1957; Pratt 1955; Hauck 1949). Risks to fish vary with the type of current, AC cycles, time of exposure, intensity of the field, and perhaps most important of all, experience of the operators. Schreck et al. (1976) report that fish shocked in laboratory experiments showed significant increases in mean blood plasma levels three hours after treatment and that lactic acid levels in the blood doubled immediately after fish were shocked and remained high for one hour. Electroshocking did not significantly affect packed cell volumes, plasma proteins, calcium, magnesium, and androgen levels. None of the isoenzyme systems examined appeared to be influenced by electroshocking. Immediate deaths are probably due to direct trauma such as respiratory failure, hemorrhaging, and fractured vertebrae. Death occurring hours after shocking is most likely the result of the combined effects of trauma, paying for oxygen debt incurred, and the exhaustion phase of the general adaptation syndrome (Schreck et al.). They recommend caution concerning the assumptions associated with mark-recapture studies (e.g., equal vulnerability) for population estimates because shocked fish are not fully recovered for a substantial period of time (e.g., not the same day).

Noncaptured fish have a recovery period immediately following the action of the electric field. This recovery period has two phases: the immediate recovery, including resumption of respiration and locomotion, etc., and the later recovery of other vital functions that may have been disrupted by exposure (Sternin, Nikonorov, and Bumeister 1972).

Kynard and Lonsdale (1975) report recovery of rainbow trout in twelve hours, after six hours of exposure to 10 volts DC. McCrimmon and Bidgood (1965) report no fractured vertebrae in their tests made to determine the effect of electroshocking on percentage of fractured vertebrae in rainbow trout, but they caution that such damage and other adverse effects can occur.

The potential effects of electric fields on fish are shown in figure 10.4 (from Sternin, Nikonorov, and Bumeister 1972). All of these consequences should

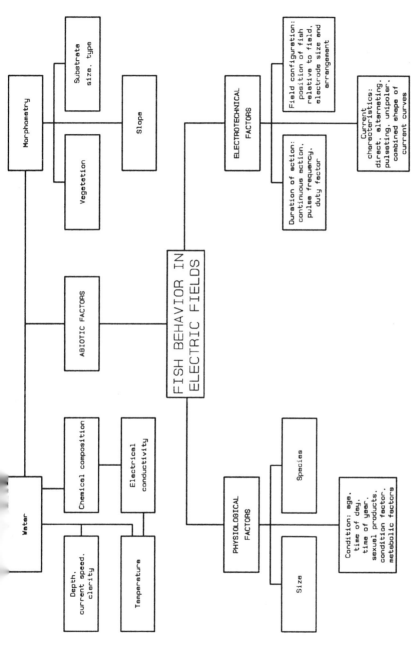

Figure 10.4. Factors affecting fish behavior in an electric field (modified from Sternin, Nikonorov, and Bumeister 1972).

be considered when planning an electrofishing operation in a particular area at a designated time of year with respect to the type of data to be collected.

Immediate recovery has been monitored by systematic checking of such variables as blood gases. In general, return to normal gas metabolism, frequency of breathing, and temperature of intestine (for comparable actions at a prescribed level) are 20 minutes for pulsating DC, 70 minutes for continuous-flow DC, and 120 minutes for AC (Sternin, Nikonorov, and Bumeister 1972). Time varies for required restoration of oxygen metabolism after exposure to different kinds of current and for potentially affecting data collected for a specific purpose (figure 10.5).

Effects of electric fields on fish that do not recover immediately is physiologically extremely complex and involved. The information below is not a complete and detailed coverage of the subject, but it includes some factors to be considered in using electricity in fishery management.

In addition to lethal effects, researchers have noted various functional disturbances, injuries, bruises, ruptured muscles, and abnormal composition of the blood. Fish generally recover from disturbances such as irregular gas exchange, reduced motor activity, upset feeding patterns, altered features of schooling behavior, changes in pigmentation, etc. Recorded reversion times range from minutes to days. The passage of current through blood at even considerable densities and exposures does not cause any substantial changes in composition. The red blood cell count, hemoglobin level, erythrocyte sedimentation reactions, leucocyte readings, and glycemia level remain close to normal (Sternin, Nikonorov, and Bumeister 1972).

Research was conducted on the growth and development of 25- to 30-cm common carp using pulsating DC and AC of industrial frequency, at intensities that momentarily immobilized the fish, (reaction 61, table 10.3) and lasted up to 60 seconds. The results identified no differences in lengths and mean weight increases between experimental and control fish over half a year. No difference was recorded for exposure of up to 30 minutes (Sternin, Nikonorov, and Bumeister 1972). Intensive shocking of bream and other species in the inshore lake waters during spawning did not reveal any effect on the course of the spawning or on the gonads. In investigations with spawning grass carp, there was no difference between the development of eggs and larvae of the experimental and control groups. Spawners exposed to electrical current, however, may lose eggs or milt if they are ripe. Juvenile salmon had a high mortality rate when exposed to an electric field intensity only slightly higher than threshold for 5 minutes. Pulse frequency rates also affect mortality. Survival tends to increase as pulse rates increase from 2 to 15 pulses (Hz) (Sternin, Nikonorov, and Bumeister).

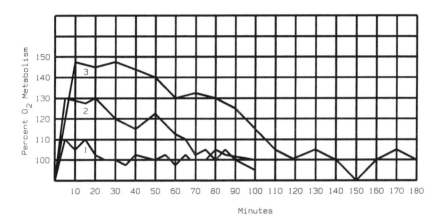

Figure 10.5. Time of restoration of oxygen metabolism in trout after 20-second exposures to different kinds of current (from Sternin, Nikonorov, and Bumeister 1972). 1 = pulsating, 2 = direct, 3 = alternating.

Effect of Electric Fields on Eggs, Larvae, and Food Base

The smaller the dimensions and the lower the level of organization of an organism, the less the danger of aftereffects following exposure to an electrical field. Nevertheless, the literature dealing with the direct effect of exposure on eggs, larvae, and invertebrates is of interest. When pike sperm were subjected to the action of AC and DC for 30 seconds, rudd eggs for 360 seconds, and fertilized and unfertilized pike eggs for 20 seconds, there were no tangible differences between experimental and control groups in either hatching or larvae survival. Lowered survival rate of eggs were much more noticeable if eggs were exposed to current several days just before hatching, rather than a few days after fertilization and then only following extremely high rates of exposure (Sternin, Nikonorov, and Bumeister 1972).

Samples of zooplankton and benthos taken in an area through which an (AC) electrified trawl had passed revealed that the numbers of live and damaged organisms (water fleas, rotifers, *Bosmina*, *Leptodora*) reflected no harm (Sternin, Nikonorov, and Bumeister 1972).

Generally, all types of current with a TVFI-inducing reaction 61 (see table 10.3) may be applied for an exposure of 2 to 4 seconds to fish and other aquatic organisms, without causing immediate or long-term effects. The only unresolved question concerns the possibility of fish deaths due to side effects (asphyxiation upon immersion in mud, predators, etc.) during recovery.

Species Differences in Electrical Fields

Variation in the reactions of different species of fish (but identical in size) to the effects of any electric current may be due to a number of causes such as behavior, body shape, and electrical resistance of the body. Behavioral actions involve various combinations for different species' manifestations of activity (e.g., the nature of the swimming motions, the terete shape of the pike's body, and its ability to produce strong spurts of speed) and its individual central and peripheral nervous systems (Sternin, Nikonorov, and Bumeister 1972). Where two or more species of importance occur together, it may be necessary to modify established techniques to safely collect both species.

Summary

There are several factors that influence the external manifestations of electrophysiological processes and determine the behavior of fish in an electrical field (figure 10.4, table 10.3). The diagram contains only those factors and their main interrelationships important under practical conditions. These factors can be divided into four groups: electrotechnical, physiological, physiochemical, and water medium. The electrotechnical factors take into account the kind and level of the stimulant. The physiological factors and the parameters of the water medium determine the character of the defensive reactions of the fish. The physiochemical factors are related to changes in the fish during and after exposure.

The reactions of fish to electric current have been classified by the different kinds of current, the symptoms as expressed by swimming motions of the fish, physiological and biological traits of vital activity, and the initial position of the fish in the field (table 10.3, figure 10.4).

To characterize the effects of DC and pulsating current, many researchers have proposed a classification consisting of three successively occurring main reactions of fish: excitation, electrotaxis, and electronarcosis.

Human Factors

As in numerous other fishery endeavors, electrofishing success is strongly influenced by the people operating the equipment and their knowledge of both the equipment and objectives. Even with functional equipment and ideal electrofishing conditions, working with inexperienced operators can be a frustrating process. However, experience in electrofishing is best gained by doing it, and while crews can be trained regarding fish species identification and behavior patterns, safety and procedural guidelines, and other factors, it is difficult to gain proficiency at electrofishing without practice. Human factors which influence the outcome of an electrofishing operation should not be relegated only to getting fish into the holding box. Rather all aspects of safety, fish health, statistical requirements for the data collected, and equipment use and care should be considered when a crew is operating electrofishing equipment.

Safety Considerations

Start-up and safety procedures for all motors (boat and generators) should be written and carried in a loose-leaf notebook. All crew members should be familiar with these procedures. When lengthy operations are anticipated, adequate rest periods should be built into the schedule to prevent excessive fatigue. This is particularly important when operating at night.

Crew members should wear appropriate insulated boots with nonskid soles. Especially when deep water may be encountered, all crew members should wear Coast Guard-approved inflatable or skier's type life vests. Generally, they should be worn at all times. The crew chief should have, within easy reach, controls for power consoles and boat operation controls. Crew members should be cautioned about reaching too far to capture an elusive fish.

Technique Consideration

In wading operations with AC, the electrodes should be kept off the bottom at a uniform distance from each other, and where depth permits, totally submerged. With DC, the negative may be installed on the bottom, or in some cases, in the water column, away from the operators. Variations of current type, voltage, etc., may be necessary when fishing new waters. Changes in the operating parameters of the equipment should be based on at least theoretical gains in performance and should be done in accordance with physical and biological considerations. All electrical settings and changes should be recorded. Deep holes of only a few yards across may be fished with limited efficiency by tossing an electrode into the area, allowing it to sink to near the bottom and then retrieving it slowly.

In boom-shocker operations, boat speed, observations of the crew, and maneuverability of the boat all affect success. Approaches to areas to be electrofished should be investigated prior to the initial pass. Hazards in the water should be noted and either marked or remembered by the operator. Boomshocker operations conducted at dusk or after dark are often more effective than daylight operations. In a series of collections, locations to be compared should be fished at the same time and in the same way, if possible.

Experience

Inexperienced crews tend to hurry electrofishing operations, particularly when lunker fish are turned. Slow, steady progress, in either boat or wading operations, with a predefined path of movement will produce both more fish and less crew fatigue. Trying to outrun fish simply does not work. An inexperienced crew can learn to fish successfully if the principles of electrofishing are understood and followed.

Effectiveness

Reynolds (1983) discusses the variables that determine electrofishing effectiveness and points out that electroshock effectiveness is directly related to electric current density. It is highest near the electrodes and decreases rapidly with linear distance from the electrode. Because a fish has resistance, a given current density at one end of the fish will result in a lowered density at the other, producing a voltage gradient within the fish. Current density, however, cannot be measured, nor can energy, which would be the best indicator of electrofishing effectiveness. The only electrical field parameter that can be measured is voltage gradient, which is largely controlled by voltage output and electrode size. Voltage gradient is only an indirect measure of electrofishing effectiveness because fish conductivity and water conductivity actually determine how much power (watts) is required, how much energy (watts/sec) fish are receiving, thus defining how effectively the gradient is operating (James Reynolds, personal communication, 1985).

Voltage gradients of 0.1 to 1.0 volts/cm are most effective for stunning fish and can be maintained in most fresh waters of normal conductivity (100–500 micromhos/cm) by adjusting circuit voltage to produce a current of 3 to 6 amperes. Reynolds (1983) points out that water becomes more conductive than the fish at high conductivity, and the current then tends to flow around the fish, resulting in little or no voltage effect. At low conductivities (less than 100 micromhos), the water is more resistive than the fish, but the electrical field is limited to the immediate area of the electrodes. A fish thus may not be stunned until it touches the electrodes, which may result in death. Maximum transfer of power from water to fish occurs when both have the same conductivity (rarely known) and results in the best electrofishing efficiency.

Fish may be theoretically viewed as an electrically homogeneous body (skin and scale variations included) of regular shape, in an electric field within an electrically homogeneous conducting medium. In fresh water, the current lines are parallel to the fish body if conductivity of fishes and water are equal; current lines are drawn into the fish when its conductivity is higher than the water and pushed away when lower. In sea water they are pushed away from the fish body because water conductivity is always greater (Sternin, Nikonorov, and Bumeister 1972).

Electrofishing efficiency (based on total numbers of individuals and species collected) varies widely with the type of unit used. Heidinger et al. (1983) compared three portable units and note significant differences among capture efficiencies. For long-term studies in which capture efficiency is important, changing types of electrofishing gear can affect catch results. All other factors being equal, electrofishing equipment will more effectively capture the larger fish of a given species. Hartley (1980) feels that the most significant factor affecting electrofishing effectiveness is user experience.

Safety Recommendations for Electrofishing

Utilization of no other fishery management technique or research tool can so quickly result in injury or, very rarely, death to investigators as electrofishing. For this reason, we provide the following safety recommendations for both wading and boom-shocker operations. The dominant factor is inarguably common sense.

Wading Operations

Because of the potential for individual action and separation from others in the crew, wading operations have great potential for accidents. Danger to personnel is minimal if recognized safety precautions are followed. The exception is a person with a cardiac condition. In the United States, there are no laws regulating the safe use of electrofishing machines. Most federal and state agencies have regulation and procedure manuals for electrofishing, but the burden of safety falls on the crew chief. The following procedures provide a basis for safe operation:

1. All personnel should understand and follow all manufacturers' recommendations for the equipment being used.
2. Operators should wear either rubber hip boots or chest waders depending on water depth. A good rule is to use chest waders if water is over knee deep. Boot sole types should provide traction for the substrate type anticipated. A quick method to increase traction of boots in streams is to glue kitchen scratch pads (nylon) on their heels and toes.
3. Operators should wear rubber gloves; heavy-duty high-voltage linesmen gloves can be used but are expensive and hard to manipulate. Any gloves preventing electrical shock are sufficient.
4. All crew personnel should be aware of the principles of electrofishing and understand the equipment.
5. Electric generators designed for commercial or domestic applications may have one side of the output grounded to the frame. This creates a hazard when the machine is used for electrofishing, since it can cause the supporting unit (earth in particular) to become "live" and it can damage the unit. This ground should be disconnected. In addition to the hazards involved in using a grounded machine, its performance may be erratic. The use of a commercial machine (available from a

number of manufacturers in the United States) specifically designed for electrofishing and incorporating necessary safety devices is best.

6. Handles of all electrodes and dip nets should be made of nonconductive material or be heavily insulated. Fiberglass handles with metal hoops have become popular for many electrofishing applications.

7. Positive-action, pressure-activated safety switches, which must be held down for the unit to operate, should be available to at least one, and preferably all, electrode operators. In addition, the electric line should have a plug that can be quickly disconnected, as safety switches occasionally fail.

8. All electric generators should have a fuse box or circuit breaker and a knife-blade (or other type) switch for fast shutoff.

9. Multiple grounding in DC machines at times produces unpredictable electric fields in the vicinity of the generator and in the area between the electrodes (anode and cathode). This should be kept in mind by operators, especially if observers or curious spectators are present.

10. Use an assigned buddy system.

11. One person should be in charge and his or her authority should not be questioned during an operation.

Boom-Shocker Operations

Some aspects of boat electrofishing are more dangerous than land-based ones. Falling overboard into an electric field may pose a difficult rescue operation (assuming the current shutoff does not function immediately). Footing is likely to be treacherous. Space to move is limited. Rough water or objects in the water are navigational hazards. Noise from the generator and boat motor are distracting and interfere with hearing; ear plugs are tempting, but they reduce communication unless they are part of a radio communication system. Limited visibility, particularly at night, is frustrating and reduces the effective field of rescue operations (Loeb 1957). The following safety considerations should be followed:

1. All personnel should understand and follow manufacturers' recommendations for the operation of the equipment.

2. Coast Guard-approved life jackets should be worn by all personnel at all times.

3. Coast Guard-approved fire extinguishers and first aid kits should be on all boats. At least one member of the crew (preferably more) should be trained in cardiopulmonary resuscitation (CPR) and first aid.

4. Low-cut, easily removed rubber footwear should be worn by all crew members. Hip boots and chest waders can be worn provided users have had accredited water safety survival training. The need for them is rare.

5. The light source for fishing and general observations should not be connected to the circuit that has the safety switches for the electrofishing gear on it. The light source should be totally independent of the shocking machine so that the shocker can be turned off without affecting the light.

6. There should be a guardrail around the boat, except the aft one fourth and across the stern. It should be high enough to strike most operators not lower than 12 inches above the knees. Most commercially available electrofishing boats in the United States provide this feature.

7. All operational features of the generator and electric control panels should be lighted, independent of the electroshocker circuit and marked with appropriately colored warning shields (e.g., red = danger, yellow = caution).

8. There should be warning devices or signs on or near the boat to alert observers and spectators or people in the water, or there should be a crew member on shore to warn people of the use of the shocker. One person in the crew should keep specific watch for swimmers. This is particularly important at night.

9. The bottom of the boat and/or the catwalks, particularly in the bow area, should be covered with nonskid and nonconductive material, such as a rubber mat. Some operators believe all shocker boats should have a high-capacity battery-operated bilge pump.

10. Operators should remain constantly alert and avoid excessive fatigue or drowsiness, even if this necessitates frequent breaks.

11. The boat should be equipped with positive-action, pressure-activated switches to disconnect the electrodes from the generator in the event of an accident. One or both bow netters should have these switches, and the pilot should have both a foot switch for use while standing and a switch on a mat on the seat for use while sitting.

12. One person should be in charge and his or her authority should not be questioned during an operation.

Movement Control Methods

Electricity is used to divert fish around or away from potentially hazardous situations such as turbines and irrigation ditches. An electric fish screen can be imagined as an electric wall of water. In practice, there are three types

of electric screens: (1) those intended to stop or turn back fish, (2) those designed to direct fish into safe areas (passageways, lifts, traps, etc.) (Maxfield,
Monan, and Garrett 1969; Maxfield, Liscom, and Lander 1959; McLain 1956;
McLain and Nielsen 1953), and (3) those designed to kill (Applegate, Smith,
and Neilsen 1952).

The theoretical basis for any successful use of fish screens of the first two
types is that the fish must be gradually introduced to the unpleasant situation
of an electric field and allowed to learn how to avoid it, before they will behave
as desired. It is important to avoid panicking the fish or destroying their ability
to swim (Hartley and Simpson 1967). Screens for upstream migrants are comparatively simple, since even if a fish is partially immobilized, it will drift back
downstream and out of the electric current. Screens designed to control downstream migrants are more complex. An example of these are electric screens
that are intended to prevent young salmonids (smolts) from entering turbines
or irrigation ditches located in the Columbia River drainage. The third type of
screen, designed to kill, is used to combat sea lampreys in streams tributary to
the Great Lakes.

Electricity as an Anesthetic

Electricity may be used to narcotize fish for such operations as tagging,
weighing, examining, or surgery. Hartley (1967) used continuous-flow DC because, although it is the least effective type of electricity for this operation, it
is the safest for both operator and fish. Fish are quickly paralyzed by DC (but
remain limp) and can be maintained in this condition (surgical plane of anesthesia) by half the initial voltage gradient. A rheostat in the circuit expedites
the operation and voltage selection. Fish recover even after several hours of
narcosis. From short-duration paralysis they recover almost instantly. Kynard
and Lonsdale (1975) report the use of uninterrupted 10-volt DC to produce
galvanonarcosis (fish roll over on one side, face the anode, and are incapable
of movement). Fish narcotized by this method for 1 or 2 hours recovered locomotion immediately. Fish narcotized for 4 or 6 hours required up to 12 hours
to recover. Gunstrom and Bethers (1985) report on the use of an electrified fish
basket for anesthetizing large chinook salmon. A 12-volt car battery was used
to provide current to a basket which contacted the electrodes when lifted from
the water. Voltage was regulated by a rheostat and a 250-ohm potentiometer.
No side effect was noted and fish tagged in this operation were subsequently
recovered from distances up to several hundred miles. Electricity is approved
as a fish anesthetic (see chapter 8).

Summary

Two types of current are used in electric fishing: alternating (AC) and direct (DC). DC is most effective and efficient when it is capacitor discharged. AC has a greater potential for harming fish and operators. AC either repels or teta-nizes fish; DC may narcotize fish or draw them to the positive (anode) pole. This latter characteristic is valuable when collecting fish in murky water or around inaccessible cover.

In electric fishing the modifying factors are: conductivity of the water, size and species of fish, topography and dimensions of the body of water, elec-trode configuration, the size and type of machine producing the current and the experience and efficiency of the operators. The conductivity of the water is governed by the amount of electrolytes (salts) it contains. The conductivity and temperature of water have an approximately straight line relationship; that is, as the temperature increases so does the conductivity at an equivalent rate. Big fish intercept more current than small fish; naked fish (e.g., catfish) are more affected than scaled fish, other factors being equal. A median to low pulse rate (30) is more desirable than a high one (180).

Both electrodes on AC electrofishing machines either stun or repel fish. The number (or total area) and size of the electrodes attached to the poles should be about the same. In the case of a DC machine (either a capacitor-discharged, interrupted-, or continuous-flow machine), the negative electrodes may differ from the positives in size and number. In all instances, however, the total area (size) of the negative(s) should equal or exceed that of the positive(s). In either AC or DC machines, it is generally better to have several small electrodes than one large one. This produces a larger electrical field and, by reducing the voltage gradient, one that is safer for both fish and operators.

Use of electrofishing in fisheries research should be reviewed carefully be-fore each use to ascertain the possible effect of electrofishing bias and potential invalidation of the estimator assumptions. Electrofishing performs well as a qualitative tool, but for quantitative uses, possible biases should be docu-mented.

Literature Cited

Applegate, V. C., B. R. Smith, and W. L. Neilsen. 1952. *Use of Electricity in the Con-trol of Sea Lampreys: Electromechanical Weirs and Traps and Electrical Barriers*. U.S. Fish and Wildlife Service Special Scientific Report, Fisheries No. 92. 52 pp.

Bruschek, E. 1967. Investigations of Conductivity for Electric Fishing in Austrian

Streams. Pp. 3–51 in R. Vibert, ed., *Fishing with Electricity—Its Applications to Biology and Management, Contributions to a Symposium, European Inland Fisheries Advisory Commission*. Rome: Food and Agriculture Organization of the United Nations.

Burnet, A. M. R. 1959. Electric Fishing with Pulsatory Direct Current. *New Zealand Journal of Science* 2(1):45–56.

————. 1967. *Electric Fishing Equipment Design Notes*. Fisheries Techniques Report No. 19. Wellington: New Zealand Marine Department. 48 pp.

Chmielewski, A., R. Cuinat, W. Dembinski, and P. Lamarque. 1973. Investigation of a Method for Comparing the Efficiency of Electrical Fishing Machines. *Polish Archives of Hydrobiology* 20:319–40.

Cross, D. G., and B. Stott. 1975. The Effect of Electric Fishing on the Subsequent Capture of Fish. *Journal of Fish Biology* 7(3):349–57.

Cuinat, R. 1967. Contribution to the Study of Physical Parameters in Electrical Fishing in Rivers with Direct Current. Pp. 131–73 in R. Vibert, ed., *Fishing with Electricity—Its Applications to Biology and Management, Contributions to a Symposium, European Inland Fisheries Advisory Commission*. Rome: Food and Agriculture Organization of the United Nations.

Dethloff, J. 1959. Electro-Fishing. Pp. 583–85 in H. Kristjonsson, ed., *Modern Fishing Gear of the World*. London: Fishing News (Books) Limited.

Ellis, J. E. 1971. Flexible Electrodes for Fish Shockers. *Progressive Fish-Culturist* 33(4):205.

Elston, P. F. 1942. Effects of Temperature on Activity of *Salvelinus fontinalis*. *Journal of the Fisheries Research Board of Canada* 5(5):461–70.

Gerard, L. B., L. E. Karnman, A. Surmount, and B. Mitchell. 1989. Longitudinal Differences in Electrofishing Catch Rates and Angler Catches in Cave Run Lake, Kentucky. *North American Journal of Fisheries Management* 9:226–30.

Godfrey, H. 1957. Mortalities Among Developing Trout and Salmon Ova Following Shock by Direct Current Electrical Fishing Gear. *Journal of the Fisheries Research Board of Canada* 14(2):153–64.

Gunstrom, G. K., and M. Bethers. 1985. Electrical Anesthesia for Handling Large Salmonids. *Progressive Fish-Culturist* 47(1):67–69.

Halsband, E. 1967. Basic Principles of Electric Fishing. Pp. 57–64 in R. Vibert, ed., *Fishing with Electricity—Its Applications to Biology and Management, Contributions to a Symposium, European Inland Fisheries Advisory Commission*. Rome: Food and Agriculture Organization of the United Nations.

Hartley, W. G. 1967. Electric Fishing Methods and Apparatus in the United Kingdom. Pp. 114–24 in R. Vibert, ed., *Fishing with Electricity—Its Applications to Biology and Management, Contributions to a Symposium, European Inland Fisheries Advisory Commission*. Rome: Food and Agriculture Organization of the United Nations.

————. 1980. The Use of Electrical Fishing for Estimating Stocks of Freshwater Fish. Pp. 91–95 in T. Boehiel and R. L. Welcomme, eds., *Guidelines for Sampling Fish in Inland Waters*. EIFAC Technical Report No. 33. Rome: European Inland Fisheries

Advisory Council, Food and Agriculture Organization of the United Nations.

Hartley, W. G., and D. Simpson. 1967. Electric Fishing Screens in the United Kingdom. Pp. 183–97 in R. Vibert, ed., *Fishing with Electricity—Its Applications to Biology and Management, Contributions to a Symposium, European Inland Fisheries Advisory Commission*. Rome: Food and Agriculture Organization of the United Nations.

Haskell, D. C., and W. F. Adelman, Jr. 1955. Effects of Rapid Direct Current Pulsations on Fish. *New York Fish and Game Journal* 2(1):95–105.

Haskell, D. C., J. MacDougal, and D. Geduldig. 1954. Reactions and Motion of Fish in a Direct Current Electric Field. *New York Fish and Game Journal* 1(1):47–64.

Hauck, F. R. 1949. Some Harmful Effects of the Electric Shocker on Large Rainbow Trout. *Transactions of the American Fisheries Society* 77(1947):61–64.

Heidinger, R. C., D. R. Helms, T. I. Hiebert, and P. H. Howe. 1983. Operation Comparison of Three Electrofishing Systems. *North American Journal of Fisheries Management* 3(3):254–57.

Herbert, D. M., J. S. Alabaster, M. C. Dart, and R. Lloyd. 1961. The Effect of China-Clay Wastes on Trout Streams. *International Journal of Air and Water Pollution* 5(1):56–74.

Hermann, L. 1885. Eine wirkung galvanischer strome auf organismen. *Pflugers Arch. ges. Physiol.* 37:457–60.

Hermann, L., and F. Matthias. 1894. Der galvanotropismus der von *Rana temporia* und der fische. *Pflugers Arch. ges. Physiol.* 57:391–405.

Kynard, B., and E. Lonsdale. 1975. Experimental Study of Galvanonarcosis for Rainbow Trout (*Salmo gairdneri*) Immobilization. *Journal of the Fisheries Research Board of Canada* 32(2):300–302.

Lewis, W. M., and E. Charles. 1957. Flotation of Fishes Following Stunning by Electrical Shock. *Transactions of the Illinois State Academy of Science* 50:38–40.

Loeb, H. A. 1955. An Electrical Surface Device for Carp Control and Fish Collection in Lakes. *New York Fish and Game Journal* 2(2):220–31.

———. 1957. Night Collection of Fish with Electricity. *New York Fish and Game Journal* 4(1):109–18.

McCrimmon, H. R., and B. Bidgood. 1965. Abnormal Vertebrae in the Rainbow Trout with Particular Reference to Electroshocking. *Transactions of the American Fisheries Society* 94(1):84–88.

McLain, A. L. 1956. The Control of the Upstream Movement of Fish with Pulsated Direct Current. *Transactions of the American Fisheries Society* 86(1):269–84.

McLain, A. L., and W. L. Nielsen. 1953. *Directing the Movement of Fish with Electricity*. U.S. Fish and Wildlife Service Special Scientific Report, Fisheries No. 93. 24 pp.

Mach, E. 1875. *Grundlinien der lehre von den bewegungsempfindungen*. Leipzig, Germany.

Mahon, R. 1980. Accuracy of Catch-Effort Methods for Estimating Fish Density and Biomass in Streams. *Environmental Biology of Fishes* 5(4):343–60.

Maxfield, G. H., K. L. Liscom, and R. H. Lander. 1959. Leading Adult Squawfish (*Ptychocheilus oregonensis*) within an Electric Field. U.S. Fish and Wildlife Service Special Scientific Report, Fisheries No. 298. 15 pp.

Maxfield, G. H., G. E. Monan, and H. L. Garrett. 1969. *Electrical Installation for Control of the Northern Squawfish*. U.S. Fish and Wildlife Service Special Scientific Report, Fisheries No. 583. 14 pp.

Novotny, D. W., and F. R. Priegel. 1971. *A Guideline for Portable Direct Current Electrofishing Systems*. Madison: Wisconsin Department of Natural Resources. Technical Bulletin 51. 22 pp.

―――. 1974. *Electrofishing Boats: Improved Designs and Operational Guidelines to Increase the Effectiveness of Boom Shockers*. Madison: Wisconsin Department of Natural Resources. Technical Bulletin 73. 49 pp.

Patten, B. G., and C. C. Gillaspie. 1966. *The Bureau of Commercial Fisheries Type IV Electrofishing Shocker—Its Characteristics and Operations*. U.S. Fish and Wildlife Service Special Scientific Report, Fisheries No. 529. 15 pp.

Pratt, V. S. 1955. Fish Mortality Caused by Electrical Shockers. *Transactions of the American Fisheries Society* 84(1954):93–96.

Reynolds, J. B. 1979. Electrofishing Efficiency and its Influence on Stock Assessment Strategy. Paper presented at an Electrofishing Workshop, Region 6, USFWS, March 9–10, 1978, St. Paul, Minnesota. 18 pp.

―――. 1983. Electrofishing. Pp. 147–64 in L. A. Nielsen and D. L. Johnson, eds., *Fisheries Techniques*. Bethesda, Md.: American Fisheries Society.

Reynolds, J. B., and A. L. Kolz. 1988. Electrofishing Injury to Large Rainbow Trout. *North American Journal of Fisheries Management* 8:516–18.

Rollefson, M. D. 1958. The Development and Evaluation of Interrupted Direct Current Electrofishing Equipment. *Colorado Cooperative Fishery Research Unit Quarterly Report* 4:38–40.

Schreck, C. B., R. A. Whaley, M. L. Bass, O. E. Maughan, and M. Solazzi. 1976. Physiological Responses of Rainbow Trout (*Salmo gairdneri*) to Electroshock. *Journal of the Fisheries Research Board of Canada* 33(1):76–84.

Sharber, N. G., and S. W. Carothers. 1988. Influence of Electrofishing Pulse Shape on Spinal Injuries in Adult Rainbow Trout. *North American Journal of Fisheries Management* 8:117–22.

Sigler, W. F. 1969. Electricity in Fishery Research and Management. Logan: Agricultural Experiment Station, Utah State University, *Utah Science* 30(3):72–79.

Smith, L. L., Jr., D. R. Franklin, and R. H. Kramer. 1959. Electrofishing for Small Fish in Lakes. *Transactions of the American Fisheries Society* 88(2):141–46.

Sternin, V. G., I. V. Nikonorov, and Yu. K. Bumeister. 1972. *Electrical Fishing Theory and Practice*. Moscow: Pishchevaya Promyshlennost'. Translated from Russian by E. Vilim., Israel Program for Scientific Translations, Jerusalem, 1976. Jerusalem: Keterpress Enterprises. 316 pp.

Taylor, G. N., L. S. Cole, and W. F. Sigler. 1957. Galvanotoxic Response of Fish to Pulsating Direct Current. *Journal of Wildlife Management* 21(2):201–13.

Vibert, R. 1963. Neurophysiology of Electric Fishing. *Transactions of the American Fisheries Society* 92(3):265–75.

———. 1967. General Report of the Working Party on the Applications of Electricity to Inland Fishery Biology and Management. Pp. 3–51 in R. Vibert, ed., *Fishing with Electricity—Its Applications to Biology and Management, Contributions to a Symposium, European Inland Fisheries Advisory Commission*. Rome: Food and Agriculture Organization of the United Nations.

Vibert, R., P. Lamarque, and R. Cuinat. 1960. Tests et indices d'efficacité des appareits de peche electrique. *Annuls Stn. Cnet. Hydrobiol. appl. Biarritz* 8(1):53–89.

Vincent, R. 1971. River Electrofishing and Fish Population Estimates. *Progressive Fish-Culturist* 33(3):163–69.

Webster, D. A., J. L. Forney, R. H. Gibbs, Jr., J. H. Severns, and W. F. Van Woert. 1955. A Comparison of Alternating and Direct Current in Fishery Work. *New York Fish and Game Journal* 2(1):106–13.

11. Age Determination, Rate of Growth, and Length-Weight Relationships

The ability to accurately determine the age of fish from their bony structures is one of the most important aspects of fishery science. Ageing fish provides basic knowledge regarding age composition and longevity of a population that helps managers manipulate stocks through fishing regulations and/or stocking programs. Ageing also provides information on how fast fish grow in a particular environment and is a reflection of the condition of the habitat.

Interpretation of zonations of skeletal parts of fish vary, and validation is the subject of research and some dispute. The preferred skeletal structure used for age determination may vary both among species and workers on the same species (Brothers 1983; Prince and Pulos 1983).

Ageing of fish is accomplished using a variety of bony structures, including otoliths, opercular bones, vertebral centra, fin-rays, branchiostegal rays, scales, and cleithra. However, determining the age of fish from bony parts is not easy. It takes months or even years of experience, a broad knowledge in fishery biology, and detailed information on the species in question. Ageing fish today is an art assisted by science. Proficiency therefore cannot be achieved without a considerable amount of experience and objective analysis. For example, the assumption that because a species from one area has been aged reliably by a particular method, that the same species may therefore be aged elsewhere by the same method is not necessarily valid.

Some early investigators maintained that there was no relationship between the concentric lines on scales and age, but Agassiz (1834) believed that the concentric lines reflected the edges of the lamellae and increased in number with growth of the scale. According to Van Oosten (1929), Hintze in 1888 contributed the first bit of experimental evidence toward the determination of age of fish by scales. In 1898, Hoffbauer published a paper in which he set

forth the true character of the annulus (Van Oosten). Hoffbauer very carefully
described the finer structures of carp scales and the correct method of age determination. These fish had been reared in commercial ponds. In later years,
Hoffbauer supplied further evidence to support his hypothesis. Walter in 1901,
in critically reviewing Hoffbauer's work, discovered the fundamental principle
underlying the method of calculating the length of a fish for each year of life
by the proportionate width of the band in its scales (Van Oosten). His method
was later refined and revised by Dahl (1907) and Lee (1912).

In 1929 Van Oosten published his classical paper on the life history of lake
herring, with a critique of the scale method. This work using fish scales became the basis for ageing. It established by inference, and citations of the work
of many others, the principles used in ageing. The works of Petersen (1894),
Johnston (1905), Lea (1910), Jordan and Evermann (1911), Gilbert (1913), Van
Oosten (1923, 1929), Creaser (1926), Hile (1936, 1941), and Chugnova (1963)
gave fishery biologists a well-founded confidence and a much-needed impetus
in fish life history studies. According to Sych (1974), Johnston (1905 cited by
Sych) established the basic hypothesis for ageing salmon and sea trouts, and
justified it empirically. In the United States, salmon age determination was
started by McMurrich (1912).

Age and growth studies were first used in fishery management about the
turn of the century. In 1894, Petersen proposed a method for determining the
age of fish by using length-frequency curves. In 1898, Hoffbauer briefly discussed the determination of the age of carp from scales and is credited with the
first use of this ageing technique. This determination was followed by finding
that the rate of scale and fish growth are closely related, and by development
of tools and techniques to utilize this technology.

Dominant age groups were studied by Hjort (1914) and Lea (1929). They
also followed year classes by using scale anomalies that could be identified in
successive years. Van Oosten (1929) used lake herring scales and Hile (1936)
cisco scales to obtain life history data.

The first biologists who studied fish scales were concerned primarily with
development of the scales, their structure and chemical composition, and
sometimes with the relation of the scales to taxonomy. This interest paved the
way for an appreciation of the relief structure of the scales upon which the scale
ageing method is based. After the invention of the microscope, fish scales became the object of intense interest. Hooke (1667) wrote a brief description of
the microscopic appearance of fish scales. Leeuwenhoek (1686) is generally
given credit for presenting the first detailed description of a fish scale. He concluded that a carp scale which he was studying was from a forty-year-old fish.
Judging from the size of the fish, it is likely that he was regarding circuli as
annuli.

Due to the inherent problems of ageing with scales, this method is rapidly losing favor to other bony structures and its validity is being seriously challenged. Scales are not generally useful where fish live more than six years. According to Eric Prince (personal communication, 1986), if a structure does not give an adequate picture for all size classes, it is the wrong structure.

PART ONE—THEORY AND METHOD

The Need to Validate

Validation is a determination of the accuracy (nearness to the true population value) of an ageing method. Precision is a measure of technique repeatability or consistency. Both are necessary in ageing, but validation is more important. Beamish and McFarlane (1983) report that validation of age determinations (a significant problem in routine work) has been and continues to be neglected by fisheries researchers. They determined this after they had reviewed 500 fisheries papers that utilized age estimates derived from numerous techniques. They feel that all ages for each species must be validated. Their general findings indicate that age-determination methods probably provide accurate estimates of age over the range of more rapid growth. When growth is reduced because of sexual maturity, food limitations, or environmental or other effects, a change in annuli appearance may occur, necessitating a change in the method of age determination. Validation of the technique is the single most important aspect of ageing.

Beamish and McFarlane (1983) report that the consequences of using ageing techniques which have not been validated for all ages can include nonrandom errors biased toward younger ages, resulting in an accumulation of ages in the vicinity of the age at which a particular technique breaks down. Mortality and growth estimates can be overestimated and the importance of strong year classes can be masked. The necessity of validation for both a particular technique and on a particular stock is hard to overstate.

Methods of Ageing

Fish may be aged and the technique validated in three ways, each with its benefits and limitations. First, direct observation of individual fish of a known age allows for information collection over a period of time regarding growth and age at sexual maturity and at death. This method is very exact for individual fish but requires not only large amounts of holding space but also years to accumulate data. Additionally, fish held in artificial environments may not grow or behave as wild fish do. This practice can be extended to wild fish if they are captured, marked individually or by year class, released, and recaptured.

The second method of ageing, interpretation of plots of length-frequency histograms (now considerably enhanced by computer use), involves plotting lengths of fish in suitable groupings. This technique generally has limited usefulness, but there are situations where it may be adequate. Application of this technique to a particular species may or may not be appropriate (Perry and Tranquilli 1984; Cadwallader 1978; Pollard 1971; McDowall 1968). Length is plotted on the abscissa (X or horizontal axis) and number of fish on the ordinate (Y or vertical axis). The frequency distribution of the number of fish in a particular length group is then used to assign peaks to the numbers; each peak represents an age class of fish. Its principal difficulty, which usually restricts its widespread use, is that older age fish tend to be grouped together, reducing the number of peaks that can be distinguished and thereby reducing the value of the information.

The third method involves use of bony parts which have discernible marks. The assumption is made that each mark (annulus) represents a year of growth. A further assumption is that the marks bear a determinable or at least consistent relationship to fish size, generally length (Casselman 1983). Recently, daily growth rings (circuli) have been used to support annuli as representations of yearly growth marks (Campana 1983b; Taubert and Tranquilli 1982).

Ageing Theory

Background Information

Age and rate of growth data are perhaps the most significant ingredients in a study of individual fish. These data can help characterize not only the age composition and growth rate of a population, but can also indicate environmental changes. Records of a fish population should include information as to age-length composition, length-weight relationships, longevity, and growth rate, including maximum, minimum, and yearly variations. It should also include relationship of rate of body growth to rate of bony part growth, as well as condition factor, and age and size at sexual maturity and senility. Once the growth relationship between body length and bony part is defined, the lengths of the fish at the end of each preceding year, as well as its yearly rate of growth, can be back-calculated. Ability to assess the age of fish makes it possible to establish maximum rate of growth, longevity, years of reproduction, and age in relation to weight and length. When these data are accurate within known limits, predictions can be made as to what age or size of fish should be taken (harvested) to provide a desired yield (Royce 1984) or meet other management objectives. Age and growth studies enable biologists to set fishing regulations in regard to time of season, minimum size and number of fish in the creel, as well as to monitor changes in the population with some scientific precision. Age and growth studies help forecast probable fishing success and assist regulation of the harvest such that desirable creel returns are achieved. Fish populations are also studied in relation to year classes (the year hatched) that can be followed through a period of years with accurate age and growth data.

One area of concern in age and growth work is undefined or ambiguous terminology. Casselman (1983) points out that such terms as slow-growth zones, fast-growth zones, winter zones, and summer zones are ambiguous or communicate little useful information. Additionally, terms such as "light and dark" or "black and white" are ambiguous when the method of illumination is unspecified.

The term annuli, based on the Latin derivation, means concentric rings with no reference to yearly occurrence. For age determination, a technically more correct term might be annual mark or year mark (Wilson et al. 1983), but we use annuli. Other terms that should be defined and used consistently include: pseudoannuli or false annuli—similar to annuli, but associated with discontinuous or incomplete checks and zones; opaque—a zone that inhibits the passage of light; translucent—a zone that allows the passage of light; circulus —the concentric bony ridge on bony parts; and check—an abrupt discontinuity in a zone or band. Focus or core should be used in reference to the center of an ageing structure; in otoliths, primordium is the preferred term.

Fish rarely grow at a steady rate throughout the year. Their growth rate is determined primarily by available food and ambient temperatures. Casselman (1974) found that 80 percent of the annual growth of pike occurred during 22 percent of the calendar year. White bass in Spirit Lake, Iowa, completed most of their growth in six weeks, when young yellow perch provided an abundant food source (Sigler 1949).

The sex of a fish cannot be determined from its scales. However, some fish can be identified to species rather accurately (Mosher 1969). In addition, bony structures sometimes indicate the occurrence of special life events. Hatchery fish, particularly trout, may produce a mark when they are removed from the hatchery and released into the wild or when they are moved from a small to a large rearing pond. Anadromous species may produce a check mark on the scales when they smolt and begin their migration to the sea. Fish may produce so-called false annuli because of such phenomena as spawning, shortage of food, high water temperatures, handling, tagging, onset of maturity, and adverse environmental factors which cause them to temporarily stop growing (Campana 1983a; Smith 1972). Lahontan cutthroat trout raised at the Lahontan National Fish Hatchery, Gardnerville, Nevada, sometimes show a discernible check when they are stressed by handling or an increase in temperature (Sigler et al. 1983).

Time of annulus formation depends upon the environment, species, and age of fish. It occurs earlier in young, sexually immature fish than in spawning adults (Crawford, Coleman, and Porak 1989). Sexual maturity is generally associated with a delay in the time of annulus formation, presumably because of the demand for calcium in the reproductive process.

Assumptions and Problems in Ageing

Essentially, the soundness of methods (based on annular ridges in bony parts) for determining the age of a fish and for back-calculating the annual increments of growth depends upon the validity of three assumptions:

1. The annual increase in length of the bony part (otolith, scale, etc.) maintains proportionately a constant or at least an understandable ratio with the annual increase in body length throughout the life of the fish.
2. Annuli are formed yearly and at the same time of the year or at some other determinable time.
3. Skeletal structures used maintain their integrity and retain their identity throughout the life of the fish.

Much of the disagreement in reading scales (and to some extent other bony parts) is due to one or more of the following items: (1) the formation of accessory or secondary rings which are difficult to distinguish from true annuli, such as occurs in southern waters or thermally disturbed waters (Taubert and Tranquilli 1982), (2) the indistinctness of certain annuli, (3) the crowded condition of annuli in old fish or small, slow-growing fish, (4) late formation of annuli in fish collected early in the year, (5) failure to lay down annuli (as found in Clear Lake, Iowa, yellow bass [Buchholz and Carlander 1963]), (6) failure to recognize regenerated scales which at times may appear similar to nonregenerated scales (not a problem with other bony parts), and (7) the erosion or resorption of portions of the bony part in older fish, common in salmon at breeding.

It is generally recognized that annuli are not as well defined in artificially reared fish as they are in wild fish. This is attributed to the fact that hatchery fish are fed every day at a uniform rate and that water temperature generally does not vary nearly as much as it does in the wild. There are other possible sources of error in ageing artificially reared fish. For example, rainbow trout in the Utah Division of Wildlife Resources production hatchery near Glenwood produced a mark on the scales when they were changed from a small to a large rearing pond.

One method of directly establishing the validity of the annulus as a year ring is to mark, release, and recapture, over a period of years, a number of known-age wild fish. These can be recognized by a number of marking methods including staining (Siefert 1965), tagging, fin clipping, or others. According to Van Oosten (1929), this technique was first successfully tested by Johnston in 1905 and 1907 on Atlantic salmon. The technique offers the researcher nearly irrefutable evidence that an annulus is, or is not, laid down each year. A limited number of marked fish collected from the population each year, over a period of years, provides additional proof (McConnell 1952). Except under unusual circumstance, only young-of-the-year fish should be considered known-age fish; and even then, the population should have been under observation from near hatching until the first capture.

If an annulus is laid down each year, it is possible, by collecting at regular intervals and bracketing the probable time of annulus formation, to determine at what time of year annulus formation occurs. These data can also be used to determine the rate of growth within the year. Van Oosten (1923, 1929) concludes that since the body and scale growth of whitefish are closely correlated, any factor that retards the growth rate of the body may (will) have a primary influence in the formation of annuli on scales. This holds true for other skeletal structures as well.

Techniques and Procedures

The age and rate of growth of fish are studied by using bony structures. Only a very small fraction of most fish populations is used in age and growth studies. Therefore, the fraction should accurately reflect population characteristics, necessitating carefully planned and executed collections. Resolution of this requirement is best assured by recording several or many entire catches by nonselective gear by lengths, preferably in centimeters or millimeters. A number of fish in each length group is then used for age and growth studies. In this way the approximate age composition of the entire population can be estimated. The mortality factor may be computed from the number of fish disappearing from each successively older age class of the population (assumes equal year classes).

As far as possible, collections of fish for age and growth studies should be made at random or by predesigned statistically based sampling patterns. In addition, the bias attributable to the type of gear used should be determined or estimated. This can best be evaluated, generally subjectively, by plotting a number of length groups against each type of gear (see chapter 9).

Recording Age

The age of a fish is recorded as the number of annuli appearing on bony structures. Ages have generally been assigned Roman numerals. Under the roman numeral system, young of the year, with no annulus, constitute the age 0 group; those with one annulus are recorded as the age I group, etc. To avoid large roman numerals, arabic numerals may be used for ages, and year classes may be recorded by calendar year (e.g., year class 1986).

Sample Size Considerations

The size of each age and growth sample must be determined by availability, economics, logistic limitations, the required degree of accuracy, and variability within the population. This latter item is often quite difficult to determine. Consequently, a large field sample is often desirable. In the final analysis, criteria for an adequate sample are whether the sample is large enough to correctly reflect the variation within the population, whether it is statistically valid, and whether it can be collected with available resources.

Sources of Error in Ageing

Theoretically, the ageing technique is based on an accumulation of calcified material that increases in size with age and continually lays down growth rings. Under certain conditions the mineralization process of scales can be reversed and some annuli lost. Simkiss (1974) found that there is absorption in salmon and trout scales when the fish stop feeding in the deeper ocean waters, and this process continues until feeding resumes when the fish return to the ocean after spawning. Of greater importance is the fact that under certain conditions, or perhaps more often, lack of growth, scale resorption occurs in many fish other than anadromous salmon and trout. The implications of scale resorption or no growth are considerable when scales are used for determining age. Since one or more annuli are reabsorbed, the result is assignment of too low an age.

Linfield (1974) found when stunting was particularly severe in roach, scale erosion often obliterated a full season's growth on the scales but had relatively little effect on the opercula. It has been suggested that scales may be resorbed to provide calcium during periods of deficiency such as during maturation. This in turn explains the formation of spawning checks on the scales of certain fish.

False checks, which may be mistaken for annuli, are probably more common in stunted fish populations than in others. This adds to the already difficult job of ageing. The annual growth increments of fish from severely stunted populations can be so small for one or more years that the annuli become almost superimposed. In these circumstances, erosion of the scale may add to the confusion. This same problem may also occur with older fish. Cui-ui in Pyramid Lake, Nevada, grow at a modest rate for six years, but from that time on, the scales are virtually unreadable, in part because of erosion and slow growth (Sigler, Vigg, and Bres 1985).

The first and possibly second annulus may be obliterated on the operculum of older fish by basil thickening of the bone. This is particularly difficult to detect unless the opercula of young, known-age fish are available for comparison (McConnell 1952).

One problem in ageing certain fish is establishing the position of the first annulus. This not only varies between year classes, but within a year class between early and late hatched fish. When breeding occurs late in the year and the fish do not hatch until mid or late summer, no annulus may be formed the first year. This error is particularly likely to occur if the early growth of the second year is slow. In this event, fast-growing, early hatched fish from the following year will show the same age as fish hatched late the previous year. Although this constitutes an error in ageing, from a practical management standpoint the effects are probably nil.

It has generally been held that the position of each circulus, once it is laid down on the scale, is fixed. This may not always be true. The scale focus, for example, appears to vary in size over time. If the position of each new circulus changes with time, it can have a significant effect on any method of estimating growth in the younger years of a fish's life. A change in the relative position of the circulus-focus would obviously change the estimated length at that age (Bilton 1974).

Annulus Determination Criteria

One criteria for determining a true annulus is that it is consistent throughout the bony structures of any one fish. Age determination should be made at least twice, preferably by independent readers with no previous knowledge of population length structure. The second reading should be done without reference to the first. Many biologists strongly believe that bony parts which cannot be read with confidence should be discarded. Others believe this procedure introduces a bias and recommend that the best age, determined by subjective judgment, be assessed, particularly those in advanced age groups. Known-age fish and dominant-year classes can provide insight into proper interpretations of readings but do not answer the above question.

One method used to validate annulus formation is the use of the chemical oxytetracycline hydrochloride. Fish are injected with tetracycline, and if necessary, tagged so they can be individually recognized when recaptured. The date these fish were tagged is noted and the fish are released into their original habitat. This method requires additional time and effort to capture, tag, inject, release, and recapture sufficient numbers to support a valid study. Because tetracycline remains detectable for only two to four years (longer in some situations), studies must be of relatively short duration. Tetracycline is absorbed into bony structures in a few weeks. Growth that occurs on bony parts at that time appears as a narrow ring marking the deposited zone. Tetracycline is readily absorbed and deposited where active calcification is taking place. Therefore, the number of zones outside the tetracycline mark can be determined. It fluoresces yellow in ultraviolet light where it has been deposited and is easily detected by trained individuals. Injection with tetracycline offers one direct method of determining the time of annulus formation.

Structures Used in Ageing

Use of Otoliths

Collection of otoliths require that the fish be sacrificed. This may be a deterrent when working with valuable or endangered species. Otoliths are composed mainly of needle-shaped crystals of calcium carbonate radiating outward in three dimensions from a primordium and passing through a network of organic material. Otoliths grow as additional material is deposited on the outer surface in the form of new crystals. The new material is deposited in two forms in alternating patterns, thereby forming concentric patterns radiating out from the primordium. Otoliths vary considerably in size (relative to fish size and species) and shape (relative to species) (Williams and Bedford 1974).

Ageing with Otoliths

Ageing with otoliths requires somewhat more preparation than other methods. Techniques, such as burning (Christensen 1964), can also be varied (appendix B presents removal and preparation procedures). As with other bony part ageing techniques, a recognizable pattern of growth rings must be present. Additionally, a time-growth relationship between the otolith pattern and temporal events must be discernible (Williams and Bedford 1974). Any recognizable event (daily, monthly) can be used (Miller and Storck 1982). Otolith rings of some species are impossible to read without preparation. Bouain and Siau (1988) report on a staining technique for otoliths which allows reading of otoliths not readable fresh or burned.

Some species of fish may have large otoliths which can be aged with the naked eye (e.g., grunts). Ones with smaller otoliths (e.g., blue marlin) require the use of a low-power microscope. Species which have relatively thin and translucent otoliths can be aged using the whole otolith. Sectioning is required on species with thick or optically dense structures.

Two lighting methods are used to view either whole or sectioned otoliths. Light may be directed at the surface (reflected) to be examined from above or through the otolith (transmitted). Viewing may be improved by immersion of either the whole otolith or a prepared section in an aqueous medium (water or oil) using a dark background and lighting from above. With transmitted lighting the whole otolith or a section can be placed between two glass slides and lighting provided from underneath (Williams and Bedford 1974). The type of ring counted is dictated by individual preference. In many species the width of the translucent zone is regular and relatively narrow while the opaque zone is of decreasing width and more easily delineated (Williams and Bedford).

Many studies report the use of daily growth rings on otoliths. This has proven useful in establishing spawning dates and early life history data of young fishes (Geffen 1983).

Taubert and Tranquilli (1982) determined that the numbers of daily rings between the annulus-like bands in sagittal sections of largemouth bass otoliths approximated the number of potential growing days per year. Growth rings on otoliths of age three and older fish could not be counted because of the asymmetrical form and the crowding of daily growth rings. Otolith annuli were all formed during the same season; back-calculated lengths compared well with lengths from a mark-recapture study, and the number of otolith-annuli agreed with known ages of fish. This method has also been used with many other species (Taubert and Coble 1977). Pollard (1971) found otoliths could not be used to age a species of landlocked *Galaxias* but had some success with length-frequency analysis. McDowall (1968) found that neither otoliths nor length-frequency analysis was applicable on a species of *Galaxias* with an extended breeding season.

Validation

Taubert and Tranquilli (1982), reporting on annulus formation in otoliths of largemouth bass, were able to validate annuli by four methods: (1) the number of daily rings between successive annuli was similar to the potential numbers of growing days in each of the three years of life, (2) most annuli were formed between the last of April and the first part of July, (3) back-calculated lengths of ages one through four largemouth bass from otoliths were very similar to those determined from a mark-recapture study, and (4) the number of annulus-like marks in known-age largemouth bass were counted. This last approach is particularly appropriate since it is the only conclusive direct evidence.

Kohler (1964), consistent with bony structure validity premises (that is, the need to determine the time between the formation of zones), states the three methods of validating otoliths for age determination are: (1) annual change in the type of edge material found in the cross-section of the otolith (marginal increment analyses), (2) the consistency of age data showing strong and weak year classes in a population, and (3) the consistency of yearly production of annuli in the otoliths of fish in definable length groups as found by the Petersen method. Only the first method is a direct way of validating the accuracy of the ageing structure used.

Use of Other Osseous Parts

Many other bony structures of fish may be used for ageing. These include: operculum, cleithrum (pectoral girdle bone), maxillary bone, vertebra, hypural plate, scute, fin-ray, teeth, fins, and branchiostegal rays. The most compelling reason for using structures other than scales is that scales are not always an accurate ageing technique. Another obvious reason for using parts other than scales for ageing is that some fish have no scales. Sturgeons, for example, have scutes, and the North American freshwater catfishes are naked. Another reason for using certain bony parts is that some do not require sacrifice of the fish. Two examples where scales are unsatisfactory are the irregularly scaled common carp (sometimes called leather or mirror carp), which inhabits many waters of the Midwest and West (Sigler 1958), and cui-ui older than six years from Pyramid Lake, Nevada (Sigler, Vigg, and Bres 1985).

Fin-Rays

Fin-rays have been used to obtain age estimates for blue suckers (Rupprecht and John 1980), walleye, pollock, Pacific cod, and albacore (Beamish 1981), brown trout (Shirvell 1981), Atlantic skipjack (Antoine, Mendoza, and Coyré 1983), sailfish (Hedgepeth and Jolley 1983), and other species.

The use of fin-rays for ageing entails the removal of one or more fin-rays. Beamish (1981) notes their use does not require sacrifice of fish, and annuli are more prominent than in scales for many species. Shirvell (1981) states that fin-rays are formed earlier in life than scales, thus providing a more accurate record of early age. Fin-rays can be prepared for viewing by air drying and mounting in a firm base with epoxy resin or other suitable material, then sectioning. Larger fin-rays do not require mounting for sectioning. Thin sections (0.5 mm) are cut from the basal end of the fin-ray and placed in glycerol or other medium for viewing under a microscope. Determination of growth zones and subsequent calculations are similar to those for other structures.

Cleithra

Cleithra bones (flat bones of the pectoral girdle) have not achieved the popularity of other bony part ageing methods. Cleithra have been used to age pike (Casselman 1974), muskellunge (Harrison and Hadley 1979), Atlantic cod (Scott 1977), and have been proposed and demonstrated for other esocids (Casselman and Harvey 1975).

Advantages of ageing with cleithra include: (1) ease of removal of cleithra in the field with minimal equipment, (2) larger size of cleithra in comparison with other bones relative to fish size, (3) naked eye visibility of annuli in many species, (4) lack of special preparation requirements for growth analysis measurements (Harrison and Hadley 1979). A disadvantage of using cleithra for age determination is the necessity of sacrificing the fish.

Cleithra can be removed in the field and either cleaned and stored in 65 percent glycerol at 2°C or stored in sealed jars of water. Cleaned cleithra are air dried, labeled with India ink or other marker, and placed in separate envelopes (Harrison and Hadley 1979; Casselman 1974). Harrison and Hadley report that the use of cleithra is equivalent to the scale method (for muskellunge and potentially other species) for young fish but is superior for older fish or in situations where scales are difficult to read.

Use of Scales

Scales have been the preferred structure for age and growth studies since the discovery of the procedure about 1900. A large portion of this favored status may have been due to the ease of collection, despite inaccuracies in ageing with scales. Scales from many species have been used to establish the age of fish populations from a wide variety of habitats. The validity of the scale method, under certain circumstances, has been questioned for many years, but by 1980, serious challenges began to arise. At present, other structures, such as otoliths, vertebrae, and fin-rays, are frequently being examined instead of scales.

PART TWO—EQUIPMENT

General Requirements

Equipment required to age fish ranges from small, relatively inexpensive binoculars or 35-mm projectors to sophisticated semiautomatic computer-controlled machines. Light sources can vary from sunlight (in the case of large opercles) to high-quality microprojectors. A commonly used machine is a microprojector with several lenses designed after a model built by Van Oosten, Deason, and Jobes (1934). The type of lighting used for illumination may be either indirect or transmitted. When material is to be aged only (no back-growth calculations), or when it is only a preliminary investigation, a magnifying glass or a low-power binocular microscope may be adequate. When measurements between annuli are to be made to calculate earlier growth, the image of the structure is magnified and projected onto a surface on which measurements can be taken.

Use of Impressions

Impressions (acetate replicas) of scales and some other bony parts can be made using a variety of materials. This technique has the advantage of allowing the use of a set of ageing material by more than one investigator, of preserving the original material, and of more clearly showing the essential ageing features.

In age and growth rate studies there has been a trend during recent years toward the use of plastic impressions of fish scales instead of mounted scales. There are two general methods of making fish scale impressions. One method employs a pneumatic press with sufficient heat to cause the plastic to flow; the second method involves a pressure roller press.

Projection and Marking Techniques

Images of impressions or of bony parts may be projected onto sheets of 1-mm grid graph paper. Each structure is then oriented so that the longest axis lays along the lines of the grid and the center of the focus at the edge of the sheet. The outer edges of the images of each circulus from the focus to the edge of the structure can then be marked on the graph paper, as can any checks (Bilton 1974). Projections can also be made onto computer graphics pads and read from these devices.

Computer Enhancement Devices

Two types of computer-assisted equipment (reading and processing) are available. Programs for analyzing age and growth data (Duncan 1980; Hesse 1977) are widely available at universities, state and federal agencies, and private companies. Given the proper data they will produce age composition, rate of growth, body-bony part relationship, and length-weight relationship, all by sex, age class, year class, and locality.

Mason (1974) describes a computer-controlled optical scanner made from a microscope, an image dissector that senses transmitted light, an interface to the computer, and a teletypewriter. This apparatus is used to make counts and measurements of circuli in part of the ocean growth zone of scale impressions of sockeye and chinook salmon. In this study, using scale impressions from eighty fish, Mason found a mild tendency for the human count to be slightly higher (more circuli counted) and to measure greater distances than the machine recorded for sockeye. Human counts were slightly less than the machine for chinook. Operator time for processing one scale averaged less than four minutes.

Image analysis systems using television scanners have also been used to determine the age of fish by measuring the number of annual marks intercepted on a single line scan. Necessary contrasts between annual marks and background is achieved by a variety of illumination methods. The advantages and disadvantages as discussed by Fawell (1974) include introducing objectivity and reducing the tedious process of locating annuli. This enables less experienced staff to process routine work. A personal computer, a commercially available digitizing board, and a video camera attached to a microscope were combined by McGowan, Prince, and Lee (1987) to analyze zonations in skeletal structures. This system, in addition to the noted equipment, requires two circuit boards for camera interface, digitizing ability, and enhanced video display. The authors report that inexperienced readers (on dorsal spines) did as well as a more experienced reader, with no decrease in precision of counts. Total processing time was less with the computer system, and if data entry with the conventional microscope method is included, the computer-based method is fifty times faster. Other advantages of this system include the ability to save images on floppy disks, digitization of the entire skeletal part image, and enhancement of the image prior to reading.

Computer programs for age and growth rate studies have generally required highly structured data input and access to mainframe computers (Frei 1982). Frei developed a microcomputer software package which reduces both the tedium and error potential of scale reading. The program, designed for use with smelt scales, is potentially adaptable to other species. Computer-based bony-part reading devices are now commonly available from commercial suppliers.

PART THREE—RELATED INFORMATION

Calculation of Body-Bony Part Relationships

Fish length-scale length data were first used by Lea (1911) to calculate fish length at time of annulus formation. Lee (1912), however, determined that it was not all that simple. "Lee's phenomenon," still not completely understood, involves the tendency of growth rates back-calculated from scales of larger and older fish to be progressively lower (McHugh 1970). Potentially, lengths back-calculated from other bony structures could present similar problems.

Calculating Yearly Growth

The calculated average growth by years is prepared in final form as in table 11.1. The average increment of growth for each year of life is calculated from the weighted averages of all fish in that group. For example, for age 1 fish this is 72×225 plus 133×219 etc. divided by 676. The increments of growth are calculated by taking the difference between the weighed averages of

Table 11.1. Summary of the mean calculated fork lengths (FL) and increments of growth for Lahontan cutthroat trout collected from Pyramid Lake, Nevada, from November 1975 through November 1976 (Sigler et al. 1983).

Age Group	Number of fish	Calculated FL (mm) at end of each year of life						
		1	2	3	4	5	6	7
1	72	225						
2	133	219	294					
3	216	216	293	365				
4	121	217	290	362	429			
5	87	215	287	358	429	494		
6	41	213	286	360	440	506	574	
7	6	212	286	362	433	508	565	629
Grand average		217	291	362	431	499	573	629
Increments of growth		217	75	72	70	66	66	64
Number of fish		676	604	471	255	134	47	6

two consecutive age groups. The same fish must be used in each calculation. In table 11.1, the length at the end of the second year of life is the weighted average of the 604 fish in column 2 minus the weighted average of these same fish in column 1 (72 fish are dropped).

Length Conversion Factors

Conversion factors, from one length to another (e.g., total to fork) are useful when working with large numbers of fish and converting one set to another (table 11.2). Confusion about and misuse of the terms total length and fork length require that researchers define these terms as they use them. Maximum total length and maximum standard length, a less convenient measurement, are the terms of choice in the United States (Anderson and Gutreuter 1983). The same fish from both groups must be used to determine a conversion factor. The data used for conversion from one length to another should be analyzed to determine that there is no change in conversion ratio with growth (size). When there is a change in ratios between lengths, it is necessary to determine a series of factors, or a formula, to convert from one length to another (Carlander and Smith 1945).

Table 11.2. Factors for converting total length (TL) to fork length (FL) and standard length (SL) to fork length (FL) for cutthroat trout from Pyramid Lake, Nevada (Sigler et al. 1983).

TL = 1.07 FL	(189–490 mm)
TL = 1.05 FL	(500–590 mm)
TL = 1.03 FL	(> 590 mm)
SL = .888 FL	(189–300 mm)
SL = .893 FL	(301–500 mm)
SL = .895 FL	(> 501 mm)
FL = .935 TL	(202–524 mm)
FL = .953 TL	(525–620 mm)
FL = .970 TL	(> 608 mm)
FL = 1.13 SL	(168–266 mm)
FL = 1.12 SL	(268–447 mm)
FL = 1.12 SL	(> 447 mm)

Length-Weight Relationships

Theory

Length and weight data provide statistical foundation for fisheries research and management (Anderson and Gutreuter 1983). The length-weight relationship in a population of fish can generally be described by the formula $W = aL^b$, where W = weight, L = length, a and b are constants (Sigler 1949).

The relationship between growth in length and growth in weight is important in fisheries biology (Royce 1984). It is at times necessary to determine (or estimate) weight of a fish when only length data are available. In the length-weight relationship formula, both a and b have been shown to vary seasonally for several species (Raitt 1968; Bagenal 1957). Both values should therefore be calculated for a particular population. If the calculated exponent b is equal to 3.0, the fish are growing without change in shape or specific gravity (isometrically) (Willis 1989). An exponent value of 3.0 is rare; values generally fall between 2.0 to 3.5 (Anderson and Gutreuter 1983).

Units of Measurement

Measurements may be in either metric or English units when calculating length-weight factors. In practice, the logarithmic form (Log W = log a +

b log L) rather than arithmetic values is generally used. When the standard to total length conversion factor is available, the length-weight graph can be so constructed that both standard length in millimeters and total length in inches (upper and lower abscissa) can be read. The weights are then given in both metric and English units (on right and left ordinates).

Condition Factors

The weight of a fish increases roughly as the cube of its length. The condition factor (K) is a measure of plumpness or robustness (Helm 1964). It is calculated from the formula: $K = (W \times 10^5)/L^b$, where W = weight in grams and L = standard length in millimeters.

Weight may also be in ounces and the total or fork length in inches (Anderson and Gutreuter 1983; Neuhold 1955). The K factor may also be calculated from graphs or a table of reciprocals. The K factor and weight are generally studied in relation to length, age, and sex (Sigler 1951). Inconsistency in K factors may be due (especially in salmonids) to fish growing alternately in weight and length (George Klontz, personal communication, 1980). Bolger and Connolly (1989) warn that both the form of the condition index and properties of the data can dictate the pattern of condition observed. They suggest selection of any index only after a detailed examination of both the underlying assumptions of the index and the properties of the data set.

Relative Weight Factor

In addition, there is the traditional power function $W = aL^b$, used to relate length and weight in fishes, and condition factors of the form $K = (W/L^3)x$ where x is an arbitrary scaling factor. Wege and Anderson (1978) present the concept of relative weight (Wr) which is calculated as $Wr = (W/W_s) \times 100$, where W is the weight of an individual and W_s is a length-specific standard weight. Calculation of W_s values are based on the formula $W_s = a^1 L^{b^1}$, where a^1 and b^1 theoretically account for shapes characteristic of a species. Theoretically a mean Wr of 100 for a broad range of size groups may reflect existing physiological and/or ecological optimal conditions for a population. Values of Wr notably below 100 indicate food (prey) and/or feeding-associated problems. Values notably above 100 may indicate best use of available prey. Values of Ws have been developed for only a few species (Anderson and Gutreuter 1983).

Literature Cited

Agassiz, L. 1834. Recherches sur les poissons fossiles. 1833–1834. 2 livraison, t. I Neuchatel.

Anderson, R. O., and S. J. Gutreuter. 1983. Length, Weight and Associated Structural Indices. Pp. 283–300 in L. A. Nielsen and D. L. Johnson, eds., *Fisheries Techniques*. Bethesda, Md.: American Fisheries Society.

Antoine, M. L., J. Mendoza, and P. M. Coyré. 1983. Progress of Age and Growth Assessment of Atlantic Skipjack Tuna *Euthynnus pelamis,* from Dorsal Fin Spines. Pp. 91–98 in E. D. Prince and L. M. Pulos, eds., *Proceedings of the International Workshop on Age Determination of Oceanic Pelagic Fishes: Tunas, Billfishes, and Sharks.* U.S. Department of Commerce, National Oceanic and Atmospheric Administration, National Marine Fisheries Service, Southeast Fisheries Center, Miami Laboratory. NOAA NMFS Technical Report No. 8.

Bagenal, T. B. 1957. The Breeding and Fecundity of the Long Rough Dab *Hippoglossoides platessoides* (Fabr.) and the Associated Cycle in Condition. *Journal of Marine Biological Association of the United Kingdom* 36(2):339–73.

Beamish, R. J. 1981. Use of Fin-Ray Sections to Age Walleye, Pollock, Pacific Cod and Albacore, and the Importance of this Method. *Transactions of the American Fisheries Society* 110(2):287–99.

Beamish, R. J., and G. A. McFarlane. 1983. The Forgotten Requirements for Age Validation in Fisheries Biology. *Transactions of the American Fisheries Society* 112(6):735–43.

Bilton, H. 1974. Effects of Starvation and Feeding on Circulus Formation on Scales of Young Sockeye Salmon of Four Racial Origins and of One Race of Young Kokanee, Coho, and Chinook Salmon. Pp. 40–62 in T. B. Bagenal, ed., *The Ageing of Fish, Proceedings of an International Symposium, European Inland Fisheries Advisory Commission of FAO.* Old Woking, Surrey, England: Unwin Brothers Limited, Gresham Press.

Bolger, T., and P. L. Connolly. 1989. The Selection of Suitable Indices for the Measurement and Analysis of Fish Condition. *Journal of Fisheries Biology* 34:171–82.

Bouain, A., and Y. Siau. 1988. A New Technique for Staining Fish Otoliths for Age Determination. *Journal of Fish Biology* 32:977–78.

Brothers, E. B. 1983. Summary of Round Table Discussion on Age Validation. Pp. 35–44 in E. D. Prince and L. M. Pulos, eds., *Proceedings of the International Workshop on Age Determination of Oceanic Pelagic Fishes: Tunas, Billfishes, and Sharks.* U.S. Department of Commerce, National Oceanic and Atmospheric Administration, National Marine Fisheries Service, Southeast Fisheries Center, Miami Laboratory. NOAA NMFS Technical Report No. 8.

Buchholz, M. M., and K. D. Carlander. 1963. Failure of Yellow Bass, *Roccus mississippiensis,* to Form Annuli. *Transactions of the American Fisheries Society* 92(4): 384–89.

Cadwallader, P. L. 1978. *Age, Growth, and Condition of the Common River Galaxias,*

Galaxias vulgaris *Stokell, in the Glentui River, Canterbury, New Zealand.* Fisheries Research Bulletin No. 17. Wellington: Fisheries Research Division, New Zealand Ministry of Agriculture and Fisheries. 35 pp.

Campana, S. E. 1983a. Calcium Deposition and Otolith Check Formation During Periods of Stress in Coho Salmon. *Comparative Biochemistry and Physiology, A Comparative Physiology* 75(2):215–20.

————. 1983b. Feeding Periodicity and the Production of Daily Growth Increments in Otoliths of Steelhead Trout (*Salmo gairdneri*) and Starry Flounder (*Platichthys stellatus*). *Canadian Journal of Zoology* 6(7):1591–97.

Carlander, K. D., and L. L. Smith, Jr. 1945. Some Factors to Consider in the Choice Between Standard, Fork or Total Lengths in Fishery Investigations. *Copeia* 1945(1):7–12.

Casselman, J. M. 1974. Analysis of Hard Tissue of Pike *Esox lucius* L. with Special Reference to Age and Growth. Pp. 13–27 in T. B. Bagenal, ed., *The Ageing of Fish, Proceedings of an International Symposium, European Inland Fisheries Advisory Commission of FAO.* Old Woking, Surrey, England: Unwin Brothers Limited, Gresham Press.

————. 1983. Age and Growth Assessment of Fish from Their Calcified Structures— Techniques and Tools. Pp. 1–18 in E. D. Prince and L. M. Pulos, eds., *Proceedings of the International Workshop on Age Determination of Oceanic Pelagic Fishes: Tunas, Billfishes, and Sharks.* U.S. Department of Commerce, National Oceanic and Atmospheric Administration, National Marine Fisheries Service, Southeast Fisheries Center, Miami Laboratory. NOAA NMFS Technical Report No. 8.

Casselman, J. M., and H. H. Harvey. 1975. Selective Fish Mortality Resulting from Low Winter Oxygen. *Verhandlungen der Internationalen Vereinigung für theoretische und angewandte Limnologie* 19:2418–29.

Christensen, J. M. 1964. Burning of Otoliths, a Technique for Age Determination of Soles and Other fish (Osteichthyes). *Journal of the Permanent International Council for the Exploration of the Sea* 29(1):73–81.

Chugunova, N. I. 1963. *Age and Growth Studies in Fish.* Translated from Russian. Jerusalem: Israel Program for Scientific Translations. 132 pp.

Crawford, S., W. S. Coleman, and W. F. Porak. 1989. Time of Annulus Formation in Otoliths of Florida Largemouth Bass. *North American Journal of Fisheries Management* 9:231–33.

Creaser, C. W. 1926. *The Structure and Growth of the Scales of Fishes in Relation to the Interpretation of their Life History, with Special Reference to the Sunfish,* Eupomotis gibbosus. Ann Arbor: Museum of Zoology, University of Michigan. Miscellaneous Publication No. 17. 82 pp.

Dahl, K. 1907. *The Scales of the Herring as a Means of Determining Age, Growth, and Migration.* Report on Norwegian Fishery and Marine Investigations, Volume II, Part II, Number 6, Bergen. 36 pp.

Duncan, K. W. 1980. On the Back-Calculation of Fish Lengths; Modification and Extension of the Fraser-Lee Equation. *Journal of Fish Biology* 1980(16):725–30.

Fawell, J. K. 1974. The Use of Image Analysis in the Ageing of Fish. Pp. 103–7 in

T. B. Bagenal, ed., *The Ageing of Fish, Proceedings of an International Symposium, European Inland Fisheries Advisory Commission of FAO*. Old Woking, Surrey, England: Unwin Brothers Limited, Gresham Press.

Frei, R. V. 1982. Measurement of Fish Scales and Back-Calculation of Body Lengths Using a Digitizing Pad and Microcomputer. *Fisheries* 7(6):5–8.

Geffen, A. J. 1983. The Deposition of Otolith Rings in Atlantic Salmon *Salmo salar* L., Embryos. *Journal of Fish Biology* 23:467–74.

Gilbert, C. H. 1913. Age at Maturity of the Pacific Coast Salmon of the Genus *Oncorhynchus*. *Bulletin of Fisheries, Washington* 32:3–22.

Harrison, E. J., and W. F. Hadley. 1979. Biology of Muskellunge (*Esox masquinongy*) in the Upper Niagara River. *Transactions of the American Fisheries Society* 108(5):444–51.

Hedgepeth, M. Y., and J. W. Jolley. 1983. Age and Growth of Sailfish *Istiophorus platypterus* Using Cross Sections from the Fourth Dorsal Fin Spine. Pp. 123–30 in E. D. Prince and L. M. Pulos, eds., *Proceedings of the International Workshop on Age Determination of Oceanic Pelagic Fishes: Tunas, Billfishes, and Sharks*. U.S. Department of Commerce, National Oceanic and Atmospheric Administration, National Marine Fisheries Service, Southeast Fisheries Center, Marine Laboratory. NOAA NMFS Technical Report No. 8.

Helm, W. T. 1964. Yellow Bass in Wisconsin. *Transactions of the Wisconsin Academy of Science, Arts, and Letters* 53:109–25.

Hesse, L. 1977. A Computer Program for the Computation of Fishery Statistics on Samples with Aged and Non-Aged Subsamples. *Fisheries* 2(3):28.

Hile, R. 1936. Age and Growth of the Cisco *Leucichthys artedi* (Le Sueur) in the Lakes of the Northeastern Highlands, Wisconsin. *Fishery Bulletin of the U.S. Bureau of Fisheries* 48(19):211–317.

———. 1941. Age and Growth of the Rock Bass, *Ambloplites rupestris* (Rafinesque), in Nebish Lake, Wisconsin. *Transactions of the Wisconsin Academy of Science, Arts, and Letters* 33:189–337.

Hjort, J. 1914. Fluctuation in the Great Fisheries of Northern Europe Viewed in Light of Biological Research. *Conseil Permanent International pour l'Exploration de la Mer. Rapp. Proc.—Verb.* 20:228 pp.

Hoffbauer, C. 1898. *Die Altersbestimmung des Karpfen an seiner Schuppe. Allg. Fisch. Zeit., Jg.* 23:341–43.

Hooke, R. 1667. *Micrographia: Or, Some Physiological Descriptions of Minute Bodies Made by Magnifying Glasses, with Observations and Inquiries Thereupon*. London. 246 pp.

Johnston, H. W. 1905. The Scales of Tay Salmon as Indicative of Age, Growth, and Spawning Habit. *Rep. Fishery Board, Scotland* 23:63–79.

Jordan, D. S., and B. W. Evermann. 1911. *A Review of the Salmonoid Fishes of the Great Lakes, with Notes on the Whitefishes of Other Regions*. Bulletin of the U.S. Bureau of Fisheries, Volume XXIX, 1909 (1911), VII Pls. 41 pp.

Kohler, A. C. 1964. Variations in the Growth of Atlantic Cod. *Journal of the Fisheries Research Board of Canada* 21(1):57–100.

Lea, E. 1910. On the Methods Used in the Herring Investigations. Copenhagen: Conseil Permanent International pour l'Exploration de la Mer. *Publ. de Circonstance* (53):7–17.

————. 1911. A Study in the Growth of Herrings. Copenhagen: Conseil Permanent International pour l'Exploration de la Mer. *Publ. de Circonstance* (61):35–37.

————. 1929. Investigations on the Races of Food Fishes. III. The Herring's Scale as a Certificate of Origin: Its Applicability to Race Investigations. Copenhagen: Conseil Permanent International pour l'Exploration de la Mer. *Rapp. Proc.—Verb.* 54(3):21 pp.

Lee, R. M. 1912. An Investigation into the Methods of Growth Determination in Fishes. Copenhagen: Conseil Permanent International pour l'Exploration de la Mer. *Publ. de Circonstance* (63):35 pp.

Leeuwenhoek, A. V. 1686. An Abstract of a Letter . . . concerning the . . . Scales of Eels. Pp. 883–95 in *Philosophical Transactions, Royal Society of London*, Volume XV, 1685 (1686), London and Oxford.

Linfield, R. S. J. 1974. The Errors Likely in Ageing Roach *Rutilus rutilus* (L.), with Special Reference to Stunted Populations. Pp. 167–72 in T. B. Bagenal, ed., *The Ageing of Fish, Proceedings of an International Symposium, European Inland Fisheries Advisory Commission of FAO*. Old Woking, Surrey, England: Unwin Brothers Limited, Gresham Press.

McConnell, W. J. 1952. The Opercular Bone as an Indicator of Age and Growth of the Carp, *Cyprinus carpio* Linnaeus. *Transactions of the American Fisheries Society* 81(1951):138–49.

McDowall, R. M. 1968. Galaxias maculatus *(Jenyns), the New Zealand Whitebait.* Fisheries Research Bulletin, New Zealand Marine Department, No. 2. 84 pp.

McGowan, M. F., E. D. Prince, and D. W. Lee. 1987. An Inexpensive Microcomputer-Based System for Making Rapid and Precise Counts and Measurements of Zonations in Video Displayed Skeletal Structures of Fish. Pp. 385–95 in R. C. Summerfelt and G. E. Hall, eds., *Age and Growth of Fish*. Ames: Iowa State University Press.

McHugh, J. L. 1970. Trends in Fishery Research. Pp. 25–56 in N. G. Benson, ed., *A Century of Fisheries in North America*. Washington, D.C.: American Fisheries Society. Special Publication 7.

McMurrich, J. P. 1912. On the Life Cycles of the Pacific Coast Salmon Belonging to the Genus *Oncorhynchus*, as Revealed by Their Scale and Otolith Markings. *Transactions of the Royal Society of Canada* 3, Ser. 6:9–28.

Mason, J. E. 1974. A Semi-Automatic Machine for Counting and Measuring Circuli on Fish Scales. Pp. 87–102 in T. B. Bagenal, ed., *The Ageing of Fish, Proceedings of an International Symposium, European Inland Fisheries Advisory Commission of FAO*. Old Woking, Surrey, England: Unwin Brothers Limited, Gresham Press.

Miller, S. J., and T. Storck. 1982. Daily Growth Rings in Otoliths of Young-of-the-Year Largemouth Bass. *Transactions of the American Fisheries Society* 111(4):527–30.

Mosher, K. H. 1969. *Identification of Pacific Salmon and Steelhead Trout by Scale Characteristics*. U.S. Fish and Wildlife Service, Bureau of Commercial Fisheries Circular 317. 17 pp.

Neuhold, J. M. 1955. Age and Growth of the Utah Chub *Gila atraria* (Girard), in Pan-guitch Lake and Navajo Lake, Utah, from Scales and Opercular Bones. *Transactions of the American Fisheries Society* 85(1957):217–33.

Perry, L. G., and J. A. Tranquilli. 1984. Age and Growth of Largemouth Bass in a Thermally Altered Reservoir, as Determined from Otoliths. *North American Journal of Fisheries Management* 4(2B):321–30.

Petersen, C. G. J. 1894. On the Biology of Our Flatfishes and on the Decrease of Our Flatfish Fisheries, Appendix V. On the Labelling of Living Plaice. *Report of the Danish Biological Station* 4:140–43.

Pollard, D. A. 1971. The Biology of a Landlocked Form of the Normally Catadromous Salmoniform Fish *Galaxias maculatus* (Jenyns). 1. Life Cycle and Origin. *Australian Journal of Marine and Freshwater Research* 22:91–123.

Prince, E. D., and L. M. Pulos, eds. 1983. *Proceedings of the International Workshop on Age Determination of Oceanic Pelagic Fishes: Tunas, Billfishes, and Sharks.* U.S. Department of Commerce, National Oceanic and Atmospheric Administration, National Marine Fisheries Service, Southeast Fisheries Center, Miami Laboratory. NOAA NMFS Technical Report No. 8.

Raitt, D. F. S. 1968. The Population Dynamics of the Norway Pout in the North Sea. *Marine Research* 1968(5):1–24.

Royce, W. F. 1984. *Introduction to the Practice of Fishery Science.* Orlando, Fla.: Academic Press, Inc. 428 pp.

Rupprecht, R. J., and L. A. John. 1980. Biological Notes on Blue Suckers in the Mississippi River. *Transactions of the American Fisheries Society* 109(3):323–26.

Scott, J. S. 1977. Back-Calculated Fish Lengths and Hg and Zn Levels from Recent and 100-year-old Cleithrum Bones from Atlantic Cod (*Gadus morhua*). *Journal of the Fisheries Research Board of Canada* 34(1):147–50.

Shirvell, C. S. 1981. Validity of Fin-Ray Ageing for Brown Trout. *Journal of Fish Biology* 18(4):377–83.

Siefert, R. E. 1965. Early Scale Development in the White Crappie. *Transactions of the American Fisheries Society* 94(2):182.

Sigler, W. F. 1949. *Life History of the White Bass* Lepibema chrysops *(Rafinesque), of Spirit Lake, Iowa.* Iowa Agricultural Experiment Station Bulletin 366:203–24.

———. 1951. *The Life History and Management of the Mountain Whitefish* Prosopium williamsoni *(Girard) in Logan River, Utah.* Utah State Agricultural Experiment Station Bulletin 347. 36 pp.

———. 1958. *The Ecology and Use of Carp in Utah.* Utah State Agricultural Experiment Station Bulletin 405. 63 pp.

Sigler, W. F., W. T. Helm, P. A. Kucera, S. Vigg, and G. W. Workman. 1983. Life History of the Lahontan Cutthroat Trout, *Salmo clarki henshawi*, in Pyramid Lake, Nevada. *Great Basin Naturalist* 43(1):1–29.

Sigler, W. F., S. Vigg, and M. Bres. 1985. Life History of the Cui-ui *Chasmistes cujus* Cope, in Pyramid Lake, Nevada: A Review. *Great Basin Naturalist* 45(4):571–603.

Simkiss, K. 1974. Calcium Metabolism of Fish in Relation to Ageing. Pp. 1–12 in

T. B. Bagenal, ed., *The Ageing of Fish, Proceedings of an International Symposium, European Inland Fisheries Advisory Commission of FAO*. Old Woking, Surrey, England: Unwin Brothers Limited, Gresham Press.

Smith, D. B. 1972. Age and Growth of the Cisco in Oneida Lake, New York. *New York Fish and Game Journal* 19(1):83–91.

Sych, R. 1974. The Sources of Error in Ageing Fish and Considerations of the Proofs of Reliability. Pp. 78–86 in T. B. Bagenal, ed., *The Ageing of Fish, Proceedings of an International Symposium, European Inland Fisheries Advisory Commission of FAO*. Old Woking, Surrey, England: Unwin Brothers Limited, Gresham Press.

Taubert, B. D., and D. W. Coble. 1977. Daily Rings in Otoliths of Three Species of *Lepomis* and *Tilapia mossambica*. *Journal of the Fisheries Research Board of Canada* 34(3):332–40.

Taubert, B. D., and J. A. Tranquilli. 1982. Verification of the Formation of Annuli in Otoliths of Largemouth Bass. *Transactions of the American Fisheries Society* 111(4):531–34.

Van Oosten, J. 1923. The Whitefishes (*Coregonus clupeaformis*), a Study of the Scales of Whitefishes of Known Ages. *Zoologica* II(7):380–412.

———. 1929. *Life History of the Lake Herring*, Leucichthys artedi *LeSueur, of Lake Huron as Revealed by Its Scales, with a Critique of the Scale Method*. Bulletin of the U.S. Bureau of Fisheries 44(1928):265–428.

Van Oosten, J., H. J. Deason, and F. W. Jobes. 1934. A Microprojection Machine Designed for the Study of Fish Scales. *Journal du Conseil Permanent International pour l' Exploration de la Mer* 9(2):241–48.

Wege, G. J. and R. O. Anderson. 1978. Relative Weights (Wr): A New Index of Condition for Largemouth Bass. Pages 79–91 in G. D. Novinger and J. G. Dillard, eds., *New Approaches to the Management of Small Impoundments*. North Central Division, American Fisheries Society, Special Publication 5.

Williams, T., and B. C. Bedford. 1974. The Use of Otoliths for Age Determination. Pp. 114–23 in T. B. Bagenal, ed., *The Ageing of Fish, Proceedings of an International Symposium, European Inland Fisheries Advisory Commission of FAO*. Old Woking, Surrey, England: Unwin Brothers Limited, Gresham Press.

Willis, D. W. 1989. Proposed Standard Length-Weight Equation for Northern Pike. *North American Journal of Fisheries Management*. 9:203–8.

Wilson, C. A., E. B. Brothers, J. M. Casselman, C. L. Smith, A. Wild. 1983. Glossary. P. 207 in E. D. Prince and L. M. Pulos, eds., *Proceedings of the International Workshop on Age Determination of Oceanic Pelagic Fishes: Tunas, Billfishes, and Sharks*. U.S. Department of Commerce, National Oceanic and Atmospheric Administration, National Marine Fisheries Service, Southeast Fisheries Center, Miami Laboratory. NOAA NMFS Technical Report No. 8.

12. Food Habits

Anglers are interested in what fish are eating so they can use this information to catch them. A casual observer may delight in the antics of fish leaping for food at dusk. The biologist is interested in the welfare of fish and the management implications of food, its presence and availability to the species. Whatever the basis for the interest in food habits, it is apparent that we cannot study the life history of a fish and ignore what it eats or how and when it feeds.

Theory and Application

The primary reason for studying food and feeding habits of a fish population (e.g., largemouth bass in a particular reservoir) is to determine the impact of that group on its environment (Hiatt 1947) as well as their relationship to other species. Biologists and anglers are also concerned with the relationship between what is available and what is being eaten. Strictly speaking, food habit studies should be divided into food habits (diet) and feeding habits (mechanisms), the latter representing the manner of taking food. In literature, these two terms are frequently confused or ignored. We use "food habits" to mean, specifically, the diet.

Contemporary food habits studies have been numerous in fisheries literature since 1975. Most recent studies present no strictly new information but rather geographic variation in the diet for a species. Larkin (1979) quoted J. C. Stevenson, editor of the *Journal of the Fisheries Research Board of Canada*, as saying, "I sometimes think we should have a form paper titled, 'the food of the blank in blank lake,' and then authors would only have to fill in the numbers of fish sampled and the percentage of each kind of food, and we would be spared the agonies of editing." New food habits or feeding habits studies should be conducted to (1) provide data for solution of a management problem, and (2) present genuinely unique data or data on a unique species not presently in the literature. An example is a study to document feeding habits of one game species in relation to another game species to ascertain their relationship. Determination of whether a species is food limited or habitat limited also has management implications (see chapter 3).

Techniques

Analysis of the removed digestive tract is the most commonly used and generally the best method of studying fish food habits. There are several reasons for using digestive tracts for food habits studies. An adequate sample generally represents such a small fraction of the population that no harm is done by limited collections. There are exceptions. Large numbers of fish can be taken quickly and easily, and samples can be preserved for an indefinite period (Moen 1953, 1955) allowing subsequent analysis or reexamination. Small fish (and, rarely, large ones) are often preserved intact. Care should be taken to prevent fish which are dropped alive into preservative from disgorging the stomach contents. Generally, fish should be suffocated in deoxygenated water, placed in ice water, or put in a freezer for a few minutes before they are placed in a preservative.

Valid results can best be obtained by capturing enough fish to determine the population size-frequency distribution, the distribution throughout the habitat, and the amount and quality of recent feeding. After these data have been established, a subsample of the collected fish can be retained and the balance of the catch released (Momot 1965). Sample size considerations are briefly discussed later in this chapter.

Direct observation of feeding fish is difficult or, at times, impossible. Yet certain studies demand that few or no fish be killed, notably experiments using a limited number of animals or wild populations of trophy or otherwise individually valuable specimens (Kendle and Morris 1965; Stains 1959). Under favorable conditions wild fish can be observed feeding by using scuba or snorkel gear (see chapter 9). Feeding can also be observed in some experiments. For example, known amounts of food may be introduced into small aquaria. Direct observation or use of time-phase photography or video tape may help the researcher learn the manner of feeding and degree of selectivity as well as the amount eaten.

Several methods of removing food items from live fish have been used successfully (Van Den Avyle and Roussel 1980). Stomach pumps work on fish which are amenable to such handling. Baker and Fraser (1976) report on a method for pumping gut contents from small fish. They successfully removed the entire contents of the alimentary tract of some species of killifish. Emetics, such as a weak solution of arsenious hydrochloric acid, can cause regurgitation. Some form of gastric lavage has also been used by various authors (Light, Adler, and Arnold 1983).

Relationships

A food habits study should tell not only what the fish eats, but also the relationship to what is available. A fish's food preference as well as its activity may be seasonal (Swift 1964). The knowledge of what a fish has eaten means much more when the animal's degree of selectivity is established. Food selectivity is determined by comparing the kinds of food and amounts eaten to what items are available and their abundance (Ivlev 1961; Allen 1942; Leonard 1942; Hess and Swartz 1941).

The basic form of the electivity index (Ivlev 1961) is $E = (R_i - P_i)/(R_i + P_i)$, where R_i is equal to the proportion of food (i) in the fish's ration, and P_i to the proportion of food in the environment. E values range from -1 to $+1$, and when $E = 0$ there is no selection. The positive values of E mean a preference for selection for food type. Negative values mean an avoidance or selection against a food (Durbin 1979). Electivity indices are of considerable value relative to the rate of prey selection and its influence on fish nutrition (Strauss 1979, 1982). Many patterns of selectivity have been found in fish diets that are a function of prey size and shape, time taken by fish to capture and eat a prey organism, prey color, and combinations of these and other parameters (Pyke 1979; Kislalioglu and Gibson 1976a, 1976b; Moore and Moore 1976).

Durbin (1979) provides a review of food selection characteristics by plankton-feeding fishes and points out that with the advent of the modern teleostean fishes, a trend toward feeding on small prey, especially plankton, developed. She notes that the size of prey relative to that of predator gradually diminished. For typical macrophagists, a ratio of prey size:predator size ranges from 1:2 to 1:20. In microphagists, this ratio ranges from 1:20 to 1:200. Filter feeders, which are the most specialized of the microphagists and eat the smallest prey, have a prey:predator size ratio range from 1:150 to 1:20,000. Food habits studies and documentation of available prey to predator biomass (Jenkins 1979) may in some cases assist fishery managers in planning prey species stocking or prey/predator species combinations.

Food items may vary in abundance and availability according to seasons. Ideally, these data should be in absolute numbers. Frequently only relative figures are available. On a relative frequency basis, it is possible to compare foods such as true bugs, which are taken infrequently by most fishes, to certain other insects (e.g., midge larvae), which are eaten by many species of fish. Relative frequencies also facilitate comparison between groups of fish such as suckers and catfishes which are omnivorous and species such as adult northern pike which feed only on vertebrates.

A feeding fish may adversely affect the sport fishery by competing with or eating scarce game fish, or it may improve the prey availability for game fish by destroying their predators or competitors. Nongame fish such as suckers and minnows may compete throughout their life with young game fish if food is limiting. A fifteen-pound carp is a formidable competitor for a bass weighing one-half ounce.

A Hypothetical Example

A comparison of a hypothetical food habits study of northern pike and carp demonstrates the varied effects each has on food available (table 12.1). The northern pike ate 20 percent invertebrates (this was food of very young pike) and 80 percent fish. Neither walleye nor largemouth bass, the other important game fish in the area, were fed upon by northern pike, but most other fish were taken in higher numbers than reflected by relative abundance. For example, 19 percent of the northern pike diet was yellow perch, but the habitat supported only 11 percent. Carp ate 92 percent invertebrates, 2 percent fish, and 6 percent plants (not recorded as part of the biomass). The difference in the use of the food resources and their effect on the ecosystem of these two fish is notable.

A large fish or a small pugnacious one may neither prey on nor compete with other fish but still prevent them from feeding. At times the mere presence of certain fish causes other fish to move out of the area. Cutthroat trout were observed to move out of a bay on Strawberry Reservoir in central Utah when large schools of carp moved in (W. F. Sigler, personal observation).

Presentation of Data

Fisheries literature is replete with food habit studies of fish and food habit study techniques dating back to 1883 (Wydoski and Bennett 1981; Hyslop

Table 12.1. A hypothetical example of food eaten and percent of occurrence in the environment of a population from Blue Lake, Kansas, June 11, 1981. (Percentage based on live weight of prey at capture.)

Available Food Items*	1	2	3	4	5	6	7	8	9	10	11	12	13	14	15
					Stomach Contents in Percent										
Northern pike	20	—	19	14	19	12	—	3	—	4	9	—	—	—	—
Carp	92	—	—	—	—	—	2	—	—	—	—	—	—	—	6
Dace	82	—	—	—	—	—	—	—	—	—	—	—	—	—	18
Bluntnose minnow	70	—	—	—	—	—	—	—	—	—	—	—	—	—	30
Common shiner	88	—	—	—	—	—	—	—	—	—	—	—	—	—	12
White sucker	89	—	—	—	2	—	—	2	—	—	—	—	—	—	7
Bigmouth buffalo	92	—	—	—	—	—	—	—	—	—	—	—	—	—	8
White bass	62	2	19	8	—	—	—	2	—	—	—	—	1	—	6
Largemouth bass	30	5	16	12	4	4	—	1	—	2	19	—	1	—	6
Sunfish sp.	84	—	—	1	2	—	—	1	—	5	—	—	1	—	6
Yellow perch	87	—	—	1	6	—	—	—	—	2	—	—	—	—	4
Walleye	21	5	13	—	16	4	2	9	—	14	5	6	—	—	5
Freshwater drum	88	—	—	—	5	—	—	3	—	3	—	—	—	—	1

* Food items found in the environment. The percent composition of available food items is in parenthesis.

1 = Invertebrates (21)	6 = Bigmouth buffalo (7)	11 = Freshwater drum (3)
2 = Carp (17)	7 = White bass (6)	12 = Largemouth bass (2)
3 = Yellow perch (11)	8 = Bluntnose minnow (6)	13 = Dace (2)
4 = Sunfish sp. (9)	9 = Northern pike (4)	14 = Walleye (1)
5 = White sucker (8)	10 = Common shiner (3)	15 = Plants

1980; Keast 1979; Windell and Bowen 1978; Pyke, Pulliam, and Charnov 1977; Werner 1974; Werner and Hall 1974; Goodson 1965; Forbes 1883). A good overall review of the various mechanisms of feeding by fish is provided in the Sport Fishing Institute book, *Predator-Prey Systems in Fisheries Management*, edited by H. Clepper (1979). Chapter 14 of this text discusses feeding mechanisms.

Three basic methods for presenting data on food are occurrence (appearance), volume, and number. All methods of food habits research presented in the literature use one or more of these three categories or some variation thereof. For example, the weight method and the volume method are essentially the same since the specific gravity of most food can be determined within reasonable limits.

The point method, as originally described by Swynnerton and Worthington (1940), uses a system in which the food items in each stomach are listed on a frequency basis. The importance method, essentially a subjective treatment of the volumetric method, or the numerical method, is determined by numbers, size, and nutritive value assigned to various food items. The importance method has the advantages of being rapid and of allowing the investigator to list large numbers of items within an individual fish. Numbers can become so large, however, that nonsubjective judgment (often mere estimates) is either impossible or impracticable (e.g., in food habits studies of carp in North America or sabalo in Argentina) as documented by Sigler (1958) and the senior author's personal observations. The importance method has the disadvantage of being highly subjective (every method does to some degree) and of being equated to the highly artificial scale devised by the investigator.

Hynes (1950) suggests the dominance method which specifies dominant food. It is actually a simplification of the occurrence method. This technique has the advantage of tending to show food preference and the disadvantage at times of being highly subjective. Hynes's so-called fullness method estimates the fullness of stomachs. This value may be worthwhile when dealing with piscivorous or at least carnivorous fish (Bennett and Gibbons 1972), but it leaves the investigator with the very real problem of determining the potential total volume of highly elastic fish stomachs. At times an abbreviated method of any analysis is necessary (Borgeson 1963).

Volumetric displacement of prey items, measured by water displacement, is simple and efficient when using a partially filled graduated cylinder. Food items are added one at a time and the change in volume recorded either for entire samples or for individual prey items by species or other breakdown. This procedure is followed until the entire contents of the stomach are measured. The simple way to attain the most accurate measurements is to use a cylinder with a volume approximately 10 percent larger than necessary to hold the entire stomach contents. This technique has the inherent advantage over individual measurement of having errors of measurement compensatory rather than additive. That is, the total error is no more than the largest single error. This method presents some problem with very small items because individual displacements may be difficult to read. This problem may be avoided by presorting samples into some identifiable group such as food items by species, a technique which is perhaps impractical with zooplankton.

An intensive study of fish food habits may, on occasion, be so time consuming that it displaces other desirable studies. When a study is not cost efficient, a rapid descriptive method such as that presented by Borgeson (1963) may be in order. This method utilizes large jars, prefilled with formalin, for each sample period. The number of jars is determined by the number of fork length intervals into which the fish collected are to be divided. This requires some previous knowledge of the specimens to be collected. Stomach contents are then emptied into the appropriate labeled jar (by length group) during each collection period. Empty stomachs are not considered in this method. In later laboratory analyses, volumes are determined for each taxonomic category based on preliminary laboratory examination. Borgeson removed the less numerous organisms such as fish and large insects and counted them independently before their volumes were determined. Smaller organisms were suspended and a sample of known volume taken for segregation into taxonomic categories. The volume of each category was then measured. Subsamples were analyzed to determine sampling accuracy and provide a basis for an estimate to establish sample size. This method eliminates handling of individual stomachs or contents in the field. While it does not allow measurement of the frequency of occurrence of food items in the combined stomach contents analyses, it does provide volumetric and numerical analyses, which may be sufficient depending on study objectives.

Any shortcut taken for food habits analysis must, by definition, omit something. The most obvious and time-saving shortcut examines a composite sample (Borgeson 1963) of fish, that is, the stomach contents of all fish are put into a common container. These contents are analyzed as one, or, more often, only subsamples are analyzed. By using several containers, fish may be divided by size, sex, time, etc. Another field shortcut identifies items based only on occurrence. If the forage item under consideration is fish, then one fish of any kind constitutes an occurrence, and regardless of how many more fish appear (in one stomach), the occurrence is one.

In numerical analyses, individual items can be either counted or estimated based on individual fish stomach contents or on composite samples which have been subsampled. Complete enumeration of even subsamples can be tedious and time consuming. Before attempting to enumerate all stomach contents, the investigator should decide whether the data at that level of accuracy is sufficiently valuable to justify the time or whether a less time-consuming method should be used. All too often complex data analyses are planned but not executed. Biologists should be realistic about what will be accomplished. If detailed and complex analyses are required to fulfill study objectives, computer programs can be utilized. Human preparation of raw data is still required.

In all food habits analyses, the number of empty stomachs should be listed. If the number of empty stomachs is not recorded, data will be biased in the final analysis, indicating that more fish are feeding than is actually the case.

Often the food habits picture is more understandable when percentages of the totals, rather than actual numbers, are used. A statement should give totals on which percentages of occurrence, volume, and number are based. This enables another investigator to check, compare, and judge the scope of the study. Frequently, at least two methods of presenting a food habits study are employed, but rarely is it necessary to use more. When food items are complete and intact, presentation by either volume or number is often satisfactory. However, this rarely occurs. When food items have been partially digested, a determination of the volume as it occurs in the stomach may result in a lower determination of food intake than is actually the case. It may be necessary to identify food items and then determine volumes of whole organisms from separate collections.

In presentations of food habits data, the food of carnivorous fish are usually reported by both occurrence and volume: the stomach and upper intestinal contents of herbivorous and/or invertebrate-feeding fish by both occurrence and estimated volume, or rarely, estimated number. The problem generally determines the method. Presentation by occurrences only rarely gives the best evidence. However, extensive on-the-spot field data may be obtained by this method, and sometimes this is all the information that can or will be collected. Each method has its strong and weak points.

A food habits study may be presented in two or more ways. When this is done, data often appear to conflict. The judgment of the researcher, sometimes highly subjective, must resolve these differences and define the actual relationship between fish and prey.

No amount of statistical treatment, regardless of its quality, relieves the researcher of the obligation of interpreting data in a food habits study. Not only do investigators have this obligation but should have the ability to better interpret the data than anyone else. Investigators should discuss data as presented, and incorporate experience, based on overall knowledge of the problem, into the presentation. To facilitate both presentation and understanding by the readers, comprehensive food habits studies may be presented in tabular, graphic, or thesis form (tables 12.2 and 12.3). Tabular data, while conveying information and meaning in an acceptable fashion, takes more time to read and interpret than various illustrative techniques. The use of simple pie charts (figure 12.1) with species or other categories may be delineated and explained in either the text or figure heading. Bar graphs may be used to explain or demonstrate variations in feeding activity, oftentimes more easily interpreted than straight tabular data. The use of three-dimensional plots allows inclusion of a third parameter and clarifies the relationship that the data demonstrates.

For fish feeding largely on invertebrates, the usual techniques sometimes need modification. A common method is to first measure the entire contents of the digestive tract, then, after mixing thoroughly, extract a subsample. The animals are counted by species and totals calculated by number and volume (Tom Moen, personal communication, 1984; Borgeson 1963). Occurrence can also be determined from this information (Bennett and Gibbons 1972; Minckley et al. 1970).

Table 12.2. Stomach analysis data for twenty-five largemouth bass from Blue Lake, Kansas, collected August 16, 1979.*

Specimen Number	Item	Number of Animals	Volume (ml.)
1	Algae	—	Tr
2	Bullfrog	1	16
	Undetermined animal	10	5
3	Bullfrog	1	16
4	Leopard frog	1	10
	Bullfrog	1	18
	Undetermined animal	10	10
5	Leopard frog	1	9
6	Leopard frog	1	11
7	Leopard frog	1	8
	Undetermined animal	20	20
8	Leopard frog	1	8
9	Leopard frog	1	7
10	Carp	5	8
	Undetermined fish	8	10
	Leopard frog	1	20
11	Algae	—	3
	Carp	15	9
	Undetermined fish	10	15
	Leopard frog	2	27
	Undetermined animal	20	10
12	Carp	10	8
	Black crappie	5	2
13	Black buffalo	2	5
	Black crappie	3	2
14	Black buffalo	4	9
	Black crappie	10	5
15	Black buffalo	4	9
	Black crappie	10	7
16	Algae	—	16
	Black buffalo	8	16
	Black crappie	4	2
	Undetermined animal	20	15
17	Inorganic material	—	3
	Shortnose gar	4	4
	Black buffalo	7	20
	Black crappie	3	2
18	*Chironomus*	60	10
	Undetermined insect	100	20
	Black buffalo	3	3
	Black crappie	4	1

Table 12.2. *(Continued)*

Specimen Number	Item	Number of Animals	Volume (ml.)
19	Undetermined insect	50	20
	Black buffalo	2	2
	Black crappie	8	4
20	*Chironomus*	60	10
	Undetermined insect	25	10
	Black buffalo	5	11
	Black crappie	7	5
21	Lesser duckweed	—	7
	Undetermined insect	125	25
	Black buffalo	3	7
	Black crappie	6	3
	Largemouth bass	2	5
	Undetermined animal	20	15
22	Inorganic material	—	5
	Algae	—	16
	Shortnose gar	3	3
	Black buffalo	2	3
	Black crappie	5	2
	Largemouth bass	1	1
23	*Chironomus*	139	30
	Black buffalo	3	6
	Undetermined forage fish	1	2
	White bass	2	2
	Largemouth bass	2	9
24	Notonectidae	75	15
	Black buffalo	4	8
	Undetermined forage fish	2	4
	White bass	2	3
25	Notonectidae	65	10
	Tanytarsus	1	Tr
	Shortnose gar	3	3
	Black buffalo	3	6
	Undetermined forage fish	2	4
	Northern pike	1	20

Total possible number of occurrences 25
Total number of animal items 1,000
Total volume, plant and animal .... 675 mls
*Field data is not published.
Tr = trace, less than 1 percent.

Adequacy may be defined by use of a statistical measure or when consecutive counts of species from subsamples become consistent or respectable. Although there is great variability between species and with varied food habits, an estimate (e.g., $\bar{y}$), whose standard error does not exceed 10 percent, $\bar{y}$ would probably be a useful reference point on which to base further sampling

Table 12.3. Food of twenty-five largemouth bass from Blue Lake, Kansas, collected August 16, 1979. Total lengths in inches: maximum, 16.5; minimum, 4.3; average, 12.1; volume of food, 675 cubic centimeters; number of animals, 1,000. Based on percentages of occurrence, number, and volume. Thirty-four fish were taken, nine stomachs were empty.

	Occurrences		Animals[a]		Volume	
	No.	Percent	No.	Percent	No.	Percent
Animal	24[b]	96	1,000[b]	100	675[b]	93
Undetermined	6	24	100	10	75	11
Determined	24	96	900	90	550	82
Frog	9	36	12	1	150	22
Bullfrog	3	12	3	Tr	50	7
Leopard frog	8	32	9	1	100	15
Fish	16	64	188	19	250	37
Undetermined	2	8	18	2	25	4
Determined	16	64	170	17	225	33
Game fish	2	8	75	7	75	11
Northern pike	3	12	1	Tr	20	3
White bass	11	44	4	Tr	5	1
Largemouth bass	16	64	5	Tr	15	2
Black crappie	3	12	65	7	35	5
Forage fish	16	64	95	10	150	22
Shortnose gar	3	12	10	1	10	1
Carp	3	12	30	3	26	4
Black buffalo	13	52	50	5	105	16
Insect	7	28	700	70	150	22
Undetermined	4	16	300	30	75	11
Determined	5	20	400	40	75	11
Chironomidae	4	16	260	26	50	7
Chironomus	3	12	259	26	50	7
Tanytarsus	1	4	1	Tr	Tr	0
Notonectidae	2	8	140	14	25	4
Plant	4	16	Tr	Tr	42	6
Lesser duckweed	1	4	Tr	Tr	7	1
Algae	2	8	Tr	Tr	35	5
Inorganic material	Tr	Tr	Tr	Tr	8	1

[a] Plants cannot be handled under this category.
[b] Columns 1, 3, and 5 should not appear in published tables.
Tr = trace, less than 1 percent.

requirements. Information is then used to estimate total number and/or total volume of each item in the digestive tract. Plants do not lend themselves to numerical counts; however, they may be recorded as occurrences or estimated volume by species. Plants may also be recorded by weight.

Nutrient value (determined calorically or at times by nutrient analysis), in concert with volumetric studies, may be determined. This determination must be made carefully to allow for that portion of the prey item which is of no value. Total volume determinations can be misleading when percent of diges-

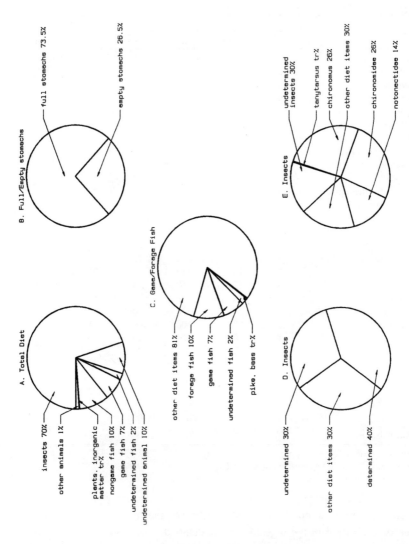

Figure 12.1. Graphic representations of the numerical data from table 12.3 depicting the relationships of food items.

tion is unknown and cannot be determined, or when differential digestion has quickly removed soft-bodied organisms. This factor can sometimes be evaluated by examining nondigestible parts such as the chitinous head capsules of soft-bodied insects. However, this may lead to overestimation of the amount of food in the gut, unless the live weight of the organism can be determined based on the size of the head capsule.

To summarize, comparison of food items by numbers is reliable to whatever extent the size of the items being eaten are constant in size. Food item data by volume is accurate when there has been no digestion or when the percent can be determined. Food habits recorded by occurrence are quickest and easiest to accomplish, but they may be of the least value. However, the occurrence method can give more extensive data and probably requires the least complex field procedures. When plant material, undefinable organic and inorganic material, and large numbers of small invertebrates are eaten, the volumetric method allows the best determination of food consumed for a reasonable time expenditure. Hyslop (1980) provides a review of methods for stomach contents analysis and the application of each technique. Bowen (1983) presents information on techniques for completing quantitative diet descriptions.

Example of a Hypothetical Food Habits Study

In this hypothetical case the contents of twenty-five largemouth bass stomachs are analyzed. Table 12.2 lists the individual stomach contents by number and by volume. Occurrence can be determined from these data. Table 12.3 presents the material as it would be published, excluding columns 1, 3, and 5, which are included here for clarity.

Within limits, items in a food habits table should be arranged in phylogenetic order. However, it is frequently desirable to use artificial categories, such as game fish, which cut across taxonomic lines. The headings "determined" and "undetermined" are used to demonstrate the extent of item identification in the table. For example, some material may be recognizable as fish but not which species of fish. Traces are arbitrarily set up by the investigator, generally less than 0.1 or 1.0 ml. They are recorded as Tr, trace.

Calculations involving numbers and volume are relatively simple. The method of determining occurrence is slightly more complex. Column 2 of table 12.3 is calculated as follows: there are 24 occurrences of animal food out of a possible 25 stomachs. The percent of occurrence is therefore 96 (line 1, column 2). Likewise, 6 occurrences of undetermined animal food becomes 24 percent.

The same procedure is used for calculating percent of animal items eaten. There is a total of 1,000; the total percent of all undetermined animal items is 100, or 10 percent. The volume of each item is listed in column 5 and its percent of the total follows in column 6.

The data in table 12.3 are presented progressively from major divisions to the most minute item identifiable. For example: Animal and Plant, then under the Animal heading the major divisions are Frog, Fish, and Insect. Fish are listed by species and are arbitrarily divided into Game and Forage fish. By definition, a fish that is eaten is a forage species. Separation of data by game and forage (nongame) species, however, provides additional information which is potentially useful to managers. Fish within each of these two categories are listed phylogenetically.

Frequently, it is desirable to know how heavily or recently a population of fish has fed. An indication of this can be gained by recording the number of empty stomachs and on occasion how nearly full each stomach is and how far digestion has progressed (Kimball 1972; Bennett 1962; Allen 1942).

Data in one table may be from one day's collection, or it may vary in time, place, and size or age of fish. The degree of detail for final recordings is established by amount of data, use to which the information will be put, and the media of publication. Some common food habits comparisons of one species are between bodies of water, age, or size group and time of year. Table 12.4 (after Sigler 1958) lists food taken by adult carp during April for two consecutive years.

The food habits example (table 12.2) lists a small number of fish so that the presentation can be studied without undue repetition. Rarely will a sample containing as few fish as twenty-five be used to determine food habits. Sample size considerations are discussed below. Data in table 12.2 were selected in part to show how wide the discrepancies can appear to be between presentation methods. In this hypothetical study the occurrence method is nearly meaningless. It does little more than tell that the diet was almost entirely vertebrate animal. But numerical data are refined enough to be meaningful. This population of largemouth bass fed mainly on fish; of these, more were nongame than game fish. In the choice of what procedure to use to discover the food preferences of fish, more refinement and better agreement exists between number of animals fed upon and corresponding volume. Less agreement exists between either of these methods when compared to the number of occurrences. Data may be presented in graphic rather than tabular form. The two types of graphs that are easily prepared and read are pie graphs and bar graphs. Data can be presented in graphic form to emphasize a point or for demonstration and verbal presentation. Relationships such as the percentage of game fish versus non-

Table 12.4. Food of adult carp (700 mm or greater total length) from Bear River Refuge during April 1954 and 1955, expressed as percentages of total volume of stomach contents and as percentages of frequencies of occurrence.

Collection number		S54–1		S54–2		S55–5		S55–6	
Date of collection (April)		1954		1954		1955		1955	
Time of collection (24-hour clock)		1000		1130		1230		0920	
Number of stomachs taken		20		21		28		19	
Number of stomachs containing food		19		21		26		7	
Percent of stomachs containing food		95		100		93		37	
Total volume of stomach contents (cc)		516.7		592.0		699.6		14.8	
	Vol.	Occ.	Vol.	Occ.	Vol.	Occ.	Vol.	Occ.
	Percent		Percent		Percent		Percent	
Animal	87	100	87	100	89	100	75	100
Insecta	86	100	87	100	86	100	75	100
Odonata	—	—	—	—	—	—	Tr	14
Hemiptera	Tr	5	Tr	10	—	—	—	—
Coleoptera	—	—	—	—	—	—	—	—
Diptera	86	100	87	100	86	100	75	100
(larvae)	66	100	63	100	63	100	70	100
(pupae)	20	100	24	100	23	100	5	57
Unidentified	Tr	10	—	—	—	—	—	—
Crustacea	1	100	Tr	90	2	88	1	43
Cladocera	Tr	10	—	—	—	—	—	—
Copepoda	—	—	Tr	5	—	—	—	—
Ostracada	1	100	Tr	90	2	88	1	43
Amphipoda	Tr	5	—	—	—	—	—	—
Hydracarina	—	—	—	—	—	—	Tr	14
Plant	13	100	13	100	11	100	23	86
Debris	13	100	13	100	11	100	22	86
Green fragments	—	—	—	—	Tr	4	—	—
Seeds of aquatic plants	Tr	21	Tr	70	Tr	11	1	43
Algae (filamentous)	—	—	Tr	5	—	—	—	—

Tr = trace, less than 1 percent.

game fish eaten or the percentage of game fish eaten as a portion of the entire diet can be depicted to demonstrate a point (figure 12.1).

Sample Size Consideration

Sample size considerations for food habits studies and other data collections must be a part of the preliminary study design for any project. While statistical design is outside of the scope of this text, some guidelines are given below. For more detail the reader is referred to any standard statistical methods textbook or one or more of these texts: Cochran 1977; Ott 1977; Lehmann 1975; Mendenhall, Ott, and Scheaffer 1971; Sokal and Rohlf 1969; and Steel and Torrie 1960.

Determining the number of observations to be taken is an important decision. (Field time and laboratory preparation cost time and money.) Too few samples will result in inadequate information and less valuable data; too many observations may not be cost effective. To estimate the approximate number of observations (samples) required for a stated degree of significance, it is necessary to put bounds on the error of estimation (e.g., equal to 2 standard deviations of the estimators, for instance y) and solve the resulting formula. An estimate of the population variance (s^2) is required but may be unavailable. It is possible to use the sample variance (s^2) in some instances. Prior data or similar data can help in the decision-making process when determining the number of observations (samples) required. If no data are available, it may be necessary to conduct a small-scale preliminary study to assess variability and establish a base for the full-scale investigation. The need for accepted statistical methods for planning research studies cannot be overemphasized, and the assistance of a statistician in the planning stages is recommended.

Literature Cited

Allen, K. R. 1942. Comparisons of Bottom Faunas as Sources of Available Fish Food. *Transactions of the American Fisheries Society* 71(1941):275–83.

Baker, A. M., and D. F. Fraser. 1976. A Method for Securing the Contents of Small, Live Fish. *Transactions of the American Fisheries Society*105(4):520–23.

Bennett, D. H., and J. W. Gibbons. 1972. Food of Largemouth Bass (*Micropterus salmoides*) from a South Carolina Reservoir Receiving Heated Effluent. *Transactions of the American Fisheries Society* 101(4):650–54.

Bennett, G. W. 1962. *Management of Artificial Lakes and Ponds*. New York: Reinhold Publishing Corporation. 283 pp.

Bolger, T., and P. L. Connolly. 1989. The Selection of Suitable Indices for the Measurement and Analysis of Fish Condition. *Journal of Fisheries Biology* 34(1989):171–82.

Borgeson, D. P. 1963. A Rapid Method for Food-Habit Studies. *Transactions of the American Fisheries Society* 92(4):434–35.

Bouain, A., and Y. Siau. 1988. A New Technique for Staining Fish Otoliths for Age Determination. *Journal of Fish Biology* 32(1988):977–78.

Bowen, S. H. 1983. Quantitative Description of the Diet. Pp. 325–36 in L. A. Nielsen and D. L. Johnson, eds., *Fisheries Techniques*. Bethesda, Md.: American Fisheries Society.

Clepper, H., ed. 1979. *Predator-Prey Systems in Fisheries Management*. Washington, D.C.: Sport Fishing Institute. 504 pp.

Cochran, W. G. 1977. *Sampling Techniques*. Third Edition. New York: John Wiley and Sons. 428 pp.

Crawford, S., W. S. Coleman, and W. F. Porak. 1989. Time of Annulus Formation in Otoliths of Florida Largemouth Bass. *North American Journal of Fisheries Management* 9(2):231–33.

Durbin, A. G. 1979. Food Selection by Plankton-Feeding Fishes. Pp. 203–18 in H. Clepper, ed., *Predator-Prey Systems in Fisheries Management*. Washington, D.C.: Sport Fishing Institute.

Forbes, S. A. 1883. The Food of the Smaller Freshwater Fishes. *Bulletin of Illinois Natural History Survey* 1:61–86.

Goodson, L. F., Jr. 1965. Diets of Four Warmwater Game Fishes in a Fluctuating, Steep-Sided California Reservoir. *California Fish and Game* 51(4):259–69.

Hess, A. D., and A. Swartz. 1941. The Forage Ratio and Its Use in Determining the Food Grade of Streams. *Transactions of the Fifth North American Wildlife Transaction Conference* 5(1940):162–64.

Hiatt, R. W. 1947. Food-Chains and the Food Cycle in Hawaiian Fish Ponds. Part I. The Food and Feeding Habits of Mullet, *Mugil cephalus,* Milkfish, *Chanos chanos,* and the Ten-Pounder, *Elops machinata. Transactions of the American Fisheries Society* 74(1944):250–61.

Hynes, H. B. N. 1950. The Food of Fresh-Water Sticklebacks (*Gasterosteus aculeatus* and *Pygosteus pungitius*), with a Review of Methods Used in Studies of the Food of Fishes. *Journal of Animal Ecology* 19(1):36–58.

Hyslop, E. J. 1980. Stomach Analysis—A Review of Methods and Their Application. *Journal of Fish Biology* 17(4):411–29.

Ivlev, V. S. 1961. *Experimental Ecology of the Feeding of Fishes*. Translated from Russian by Douglas Seatt. New Haven, Conn.: Yale University Press. 302 pp.

Jenkins, R. M. 1979. Predator-Prey Relations in Reservoirs. Pp. 123–34 in H. Clepper, ed., *Predator-Prey Systems in Fisheries Management*. Washington, D.C.: Sport Fishing Institute.

Keast, A. 1979. Pattern of Predation in Generalist Feeders. Pp. 269–80 in H. Clepper, ed., *Predator-Prey Systems in Fisheries Management*. Washington, D.C.: Sport Fishing Institute.

Kendle, E. R., and L. A. Morris. 1965. A Device for Holding Objects in the Stomach of Fish. *Transactions of the American Fisheries Society* 94(2):193.

Kimball, D. C. 1972. Quantitative and Temporal Aspects of the Feeding of Brown Trout and Mountain Whitefish in a Natural Lotic System. Ph.D. dissertation, Utah State University, Logan. 160 pp.

Kislalioglu, M., and R. N. Gibson. 1976a. Prey Handling Time and Its Importance in Food Selection by the 15-Spined Stickleback, *Spinachia spinachia* (L.). *Journal of Experimental Marine Biology and Ecology* 25(3):151–58.

———. 1976b. Some Factors Governing Prey Selection by the 15-Spined Stickleback, *Spinachia spinachia* (L.). *Journal of Experimental Marine Biology and Ecology* 25(3):159–69.

Larkin, P. A. 1979. Predator-Prey Relations in Fishes: An Overview of the Theory.

Pp. 13–20 in H. Clepper, ed., *Predator-Prey Systems in Fisheries Management*. Washington, D.C.: Sport Fishing Institute.

Lehmann, E. L. 1975. *Nonparametrics: Statistical Methods Based on Ranks*. San Francisco: Holden-Day, Inc. 457 pp.

Leonard, J. W. 1942. Some Observations on the Winter Feeding Habits of Brook Trout Fingerlings in Relation to Natural Food Organisms Present. *Transactions of the American Fisheries Society* 71(1941):219–27.

Light, R. M., P. H. Adler, and D. E. Arnold. 1983. Evaluation of Gastric Lavage for Stomach Analysis. *North American Journal of Fisheries Management* 3(1):81–85.

Mendenhall, W., L. Ott, and R. L. Scheaffer. 1971. *Elementary Survey Sampling*. Belmont, Calif.: Duxbury Press. 247 pp.

Minckley, W. L., J. E. Johnson, J. N. Reine, and S. E. Willoughby. 1970. Food of Buffalo Fishes, Genus *Ictiobus* in Central Arizona Reservoirs. *Transactions of the American Fisheries Society* 99(2):333–42.

Moen, T. 1953. Food Habits of the Carp in Northwest Iowa Lakes. *Iowa Academy of Science Proceedings* 60:665–86.

———. 1955. Food of the Freshwater Drum, *Aplodinotus grunniens* Rafinesque, in Four Dickinson County, Iowa, Lakes. *Iowa Academy of Science Proceedings* 62:589–98.

Momot, W. T. 1965. Food Habits of the Brook Trout in West Lost Lake. *Transactions of the American Fisheries Society* 94(2):188–91.

Moore, J. W., and J. A. Moore. 1976. The Basis of Food Selection in Flounders, *Platichthys flesus* (L.), in the Severn Estuary. *Journal of Fish Biology* 1976(9):139–56.

Ott, L. 1977. An Introduction to Statistical Methods and Data Analysis. North Scituate, Mass.: Duxbury Press. 730 pp.

Pyke, G. H. 1979. Optimal Foraging in Fish. Pp. 199–202 in H. Clepper, ed., *Predator-Prey Systems in Fisheries Management*. Washington, D.C.: Sport Fishing Institute.

Pyke, G. H., H. R. Pulliam, and E. L. Charnov. 1977. Optimal Foraging Theory: A Selective Review of Theory and Tests. *Quarterly Review of Biology* 52(2):137–54.

Sigler, W. F. 1958. *The Ecology and Use of Carp in Utah*. Utah State Agricultural Experiment Station Bulletin 405, Utah State University, Logan. 63 pp.

Sokal, R. R., and F. J. Rohlf. 1969. *Biometry. The Principles and Practices of Statistics in Biological Research*. San Francisco: W. H. Freeman. 776 pp.

Stains, H. J. 1959. Use of the Calcaneum in Studies of Taxonomy and Food Habits. *Journal of Mammology* 40(3):392–401.

Steel, R. G. D., and J. H. Torrie. 1960. *Principles and Procedures of Statistics with Special Reference to Biological Sciences*. New York: McGraw-Hill. 481 pp.

Strauss, R. E. 1979. Reliability Estimates for Ivlev's Electivity Index, the Forage Ratio and a Proposed Linear Index of Food Selection. *Transactions of the American Fisheries Society* 108(4):344–52.

———. 1982. Influence of Replicated Subsamples and Subsample Heterogeneity on the Linear Index of Food Selection. *Transactions of the American Fisheries Society* 111(4):517–22.

Swift, D. R. 1964. Activity Cycles in the Brown Trout, *Salmo trutta* L. II. Fish Artificially Fed. *Journal of the Fisheries Research Board of Canada* 21(1):133–38.

Swynnerton, G. H., and E. B. Worthington. 1940. Note on the Food of Fish in Haweswater (Westmorland). *Journal of Animal Ecology* 9:183–87.

Van Den Avyle, M. J., and J. E. Roussel. 1980. Evaluation of a Simple Method for Removing Food Items from Live Black Bass. *Progressive Fish-Culturist* 42(4): 222–23.

Werner, E. E. 1974. The Fish Size, Prey Size, Handling Time Relation in Several Sunfishes and Some Implications. *Journal of the Fisheries Research Board of Canada* 31(9):1531–36.

Werner, E. E., and D. J. Hall. 1974. Optimal Foraging and the Size Selection of Prey by the Bluegill Sunfish (*Lepomis macrochirus*). *Ecology* 55(5):1042–52.

Willis, D. W. 1989. Proposed Standard Length-Weight Equation for Northern Pike. *North American Journal of Fisheries Management* 9:203–8.

Windell, J. T., and S. H. Bowen. 1978. Methods for Study of Fish Diets Based on Analysis of Stomach Contents. Pp. 219–26 in T. Bagenal, ed., *Methods for the Assessment of Fish Production in Fresh Waters*. Third Edition. Oxford: Blackwell Scientific Publications.

Wydoski, R. S., and D. H. Bennett. 1981. Forage Species in Lakes and Reservoirs of the Western United States. *Transactions of the American Fisheries Society* 110(6):764–71.

13. Capture (Creel) Survey Methods

Both large and small businesses keep accurate records of their transactions. Such records are used to improve operations in terms of profit and cost. Keeping track of changes in use, production, and loss of items is important in any endeavor. Similarly, fishery biologists, resource managers, and economists require records that can be used to measure fisheries resources for better management. Freshwater resources are the basis for one of the largest businesses in the United States, and their managers need accurate information on recreational values, numbers of fish caught, and the amount of time expended fishing. Benefits or profit derived from lakes and streams include the number of fish caught, but must also include recreational benefits associated with catch-and-release or other nonconsumptive uses or values (Anderson 1975). Costs associated with that profit would include the amount of time spent fishing during the fishing trip (e.g., fishing effort). A creel census—complete enumeration of the fishing population—is rarely done. A creel survey, based on a portion of the fishing population, defined in its most simple terms, is a technique to define, with known limits of precision and accuracy, the number of fish which have been creeled, the effort expended (to derive catch per unit effort), and value derived.

An estimate of harvest for a fishery is determined based on two data sets: (1) $F = h\overline{X}$, where F = effort, $\overline{X}$ = the average number of anglers fishing (based on count data) during the period (or stratum), and h = number of possible hours of fishing in the period (or stratum), and (2) an estimate of $\bar{r}$ such as $\bar{r} = 1/n \sum c_i/t_i$, where $\bar{r}$ = period (or stratum) rate of success, c_i = the number of fish caught by the ith individual angler interviewed, and t_i = the number of hours fished by the ith individual angler. Harvest (H) then is defined as rate of success times effort or $H = \bar{r}F$.

Commercial Harvest Data

In most commercial fisheries, state and federal agencies collect information on total catch and value by species, the yield (marketable poundage), and value of processed products, the employment of workers, craft, and gear in the capture of fishery products, and other related information (Lyles 1968). More detailed information is published monthly for some of the major fisheries. For example, statistics describing the commercial fisheries for Gulf of Mexico shrimp are routinely collected and published in tables entitled "Gulf Coast Shrimp Catch by Area, Depth, Variety, and Size." These include information on the number of trawler fishing trips, an estimate of the total amount of fishing time, and the dockside value of total landings. Many states, such as California, have legal requirements for enumeration of catch based on receipts collected by the dealers (Butler and Borgeson 1965).

Scope and Value of Freshwater Catch Data

Collecting freshwater recreational fishery statistics is, unfortunately, more difficult than collecting commercial fisheries data. Easy angler access to and from thousands of lakes and streams makes it nearly impossible to enumerate the total catch and fishing effort, even within small areas. The resource manager is immediately confronted with the problem of selecting the lakes or streams of sufficient importance to necessitate the collection of valid data (Carlander, DiCostanzo, and Jessen 1958). Selections of suitable study areas are usually made on the basis of degree of use, the need for information for management of the fish stocks, the desire to define economic conditions, and the potential for enhancement of management practices.

Creel survey techniques have been used for many years. They provide information on the numbers and species of fish caught and the effort expended catching them. A complete census of anglers on a lake or stream is generally economically or physically unfeasible because of the number of field personnel required. Collections of creel data are therefore designed as creel sample surveys rather than a true census (Malvestuto 1983; Katherein 1953). One way of explaining a creel survey is to consider the total number of anglers on a given body of water on a given day as beans in a jar. A complete census is a count of every bean in the jar. In a sample survey, a fraction of the beans in the jar is counted and that number multiplied by the reciprocal of the fraction sampled. For example, if one fourth of the beans is sampled, the number of beans in that sample is multiplied by four.

Sample surveys entail observations of a portion of the fishing effort and harvest during selected time periods (Malvestuto, Davies, and Shelton 1978). These observations are then expanded to an estimate for the entire time. These expansions can provide good approximations of the actual population values (Moyle and Franklin 1957).

Besides computing estimates of total harvest and total fishing effort, the researcher wants to know how reliable these estimates are. One measure of reliability is the variance which should be calculated for the effort (F), rate of success (R), and harvest (H) estimates.

In creel survey work the terms accuracy and precision are often incorrectly used interchangeably. Precision is a measure of the repeatability of an estimator; in other words, if the precision is high, the values determined are spread closely around the expected value of the parameter being determined. Accuracy is a measure of the closeness of an estimate to the true population parameter. It is possible to have high precision but low accuracy. Inaccuracy may be due to chance variation and/or bias. Bias may be due to faulty sampling design. The concept of accuracy and precision in estimation techniques can be visualized as a set of four targets (figure 13.1) in which the bull's-eye is the actual and true population parameter being measured. Bias in a statistical sense is the difference between the true value of a population parameter and the expected value of an estimator of the given parameter. Ideally in estimation statistics, the bias is either zero or very small and both precision and accuracy are high.

Because precision is so important to creel sample surveys, any mechanism to increase it is valuable. Malvestuto, Davies, and Shelton (1979) report on a technique for predicting the precision of creel survey estimates of fishery effort, using climatic variables. Their regression equation explains 83 percent of the variation in the precision of monthly creel survey estimates of fishing effort. These types of predictive models can be used to reduce costs and improve techniques.

Sample Survey Design

The desired information, the duration of the survey, and the precision and accuracy required are the important factors in the design of a creel sample survey. Most efforts seek at least (1) an estimate of fishing effort and its variance,

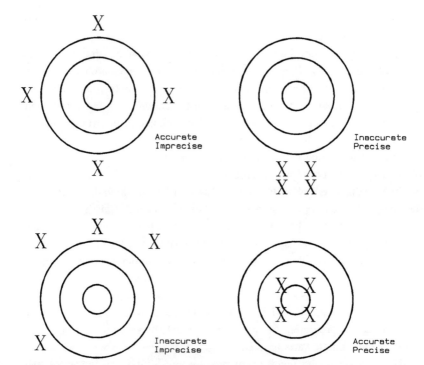

Figure 13.1. Representation of the theory of precision and accuracy.

(2) an estimate of harvest and its variance, and (3) species composition by number and weight (or length) and percent of the total harvest. Length may be preferred because it is quicker, and weight can be determined by length-weight tables.

The duration of the survey depends on the length of the fishing season and the portion of the season from which the information is required. For short intense seasons of one to two weeks (e.g., Bonneville cisco fishing in Bear Lake, Utah-Idaho), it may be desirable to sample every day. For some fisheries such as large impoundments, it is effective to use personnel at the principal landing points on the reservoir to obtain catch per unit effort (CPUE) data. Locations with restricted landing areas can, in most cases, be adequately covered by relatively few personnel. For some trout fisheries it may be necessary to collect data only during the first week or two of the season, or during the first two weeks and on subsequent weekends or holidays. In such cases the estimates will be valid only for that portion sampled and cannot be extrapolated for the entire season.

The precision of an estimate can generally be increased by increasing the proportion of the population sampled. In general, the greater the proportion of the true population counted, the smaller the error of the estimate. However, beyond a certain point any sample size increase may not greatly enhance the accuracy of the estimate. The cost of a survey increases with an increase in the fraction of the population sampled. Enhancing precision of a given survey often equates with increasing the cost, and there is a point at which an expected increase in precision does not warrant the attendant expenditure.

Estimates of fishing effort and harvest can be affected by unpredictable factors such as weather (Malvestuto, Davies, and Shelton 1979) and fishing success. Estimates are also influenced by the day of the week (e.g., weekend or weekday), holidays, and time of year. These phenomena are predictable. Higher numbers of anglers are associated with holidays, weekends, and opening days of fishing seasons. The number of anglers generally decreases as the fishing season progresses. A sample survey should consider the reasons for variations in angler numbers, otherwise the estimate of fishing effort will be biased and imprecise. One means of allowing for variations in angler numbers is by stratifying the sample. This technique is discussed in the following section.

Many devices are available to reduce effort associated with collection of field data. Zuboy et al. (1973) report on an automated card punch system which can be used in the field to collect creel survey data. Field-capable electronic data entry devices are available which can be programmed for creel survey data and transferred directly to a computer. These save time and reduce mechanical error.

Angler Counts

Bias and inaccuracies in creel survey information can be reduced if an accurate definition of angling time is used. Definitions may range from on the time with a line in the water to all activities during the period spent at the fishing location. Failure to use the same definition for angler counts and creel rate estimates can result in biased harvest estimates (Phippen and Bergerson 1987). Two basic types of counts are: (1) instantaneous, where all anglers are counted at once (or nearly so), and (2) progressive, where anglers are counted over a period of time. Neuhold and Lu (1957) report that progressive counts taken over a one-hour period were similar to counts taken from a vantage point, and Malvestuto (1983) found that progressive counts taken over a four-hour period were similar to counts taken over a one-hour sampling period. Instantaneous counts require several observation points or one or more airplanes so an area can be surveyed almost at once (figure 13.2). Field studies (Malvestuto) show that short counting periods provide better data, and ideally one would take short counts within a sampling period and average them to estimate the true instantaneous count. When an instantaneous count is required on a large lake, and planes are unavailable, it may be necessary to subdivide or stratify the lake into sampling units and have different people count the number of anglers within each unit. Depending on the objectives of the survey, it may not be necessary to count all individuals on the lake, but only those within the sampling unit randomly selected for that day's count. Starting time(s) also should be randomly selected. In a progressive count the sampler moves at a fixed rate of speed on foot, by car, or by plane (figure 13.3). Progressive counts will be biased if (1) starting points and starting times are not random, and (2) the time required for a complete count is not constant. Starting points and times not selected randomly inject a real but undeferred bias into counts. If time required for counts is not a constant, a time variable will be present in the varied count data.

It is assumed that anglers are randomly distributed around the lake, although it is understood they may not be. For example, anglers may concentrate in a given area during a given period. Repeated random sampling helps overcome lack of random distribution in time and space.

One sampling period for the survey may be inadequate. A more representative sample can be obtained by dividing the fishing day into several equal

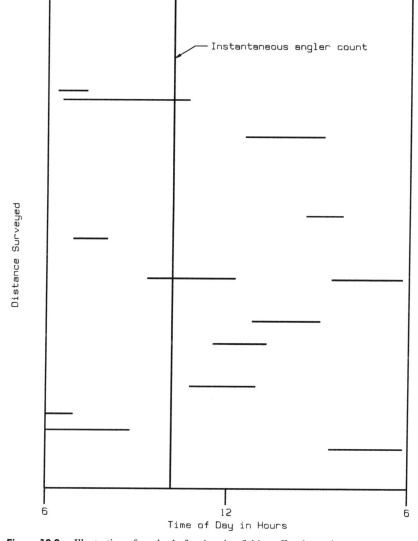

Figure 13.2. Illustration of method of estimating fishing effort by an instantaneous count. The horizontal lines represent the duration of a fishing trip, while the vertical line represents the angler count. The vertical axis of the graph represents the shoreline of the lake or stream.

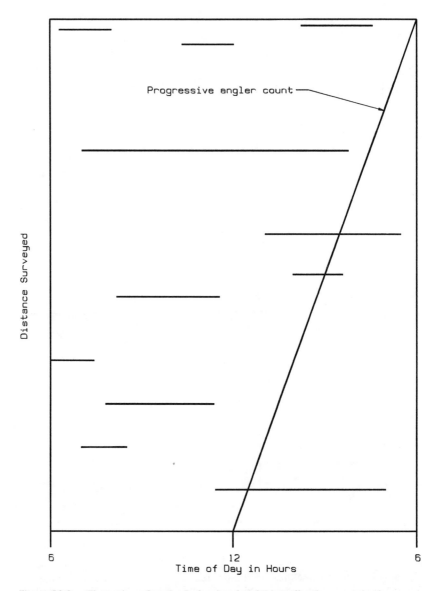

Figure 13.3. Illustration of method of estimating fishing effort by a progressive count. This count took six hours to complete.

periods. Four periods are used conventionally, but any number may be used. The starting time for each period should be selected by using a table of random numbers or similar procedure (sampling with replacement). Length of periods is constant.

The anglers counted may or may not be contacted. Adequate data can be obtained on the hours fished and the species, size, and number of fish in the creel by subsampling the fishing population. This can be done when they are fishing or at check points as they leave. Statistically, these latter data need to be handled separately from the angler count.

Fishing Effort (F)

Neuhold and Lu (1957) present a hypothetical ten-day fishing season in which there is a total fishing effort of 944 angler hours (figure 13.4). They also calculate estimates of fishing effort for various sampling designs. One creel survey is designed to sample once a day for five days. Results of that sampling design estimate 1,440 angler hours with a 95 percent confidence interval of ±6,838 hours. A second survey is designed to sample once a day for ten days. This provides an estimated 920 angler hours with a 95 percent confidence interval of ±552 hours. It is evident that the first creel survey design does not provide an acceptable (accurate) estimate (although not necessarily biased) of the actual fishing effort, but the second creel survey design provides a close approximation to the real value. In the second survey, however, the confidence interval is still very large. Thus this data provides a fairly accurate, but not very precise estimate. Neuhold and Lu show that increasing the number of counts made per day reduces the length of the confidence interval on the estimate of fishing effort. By increasing the number of counts to ten per day (e.g., a total of 100 counts), they were able to increase precision to ±124 for an estimate of 940 angler hours. If one were to repeatedly conduct the sampling design, in 95 percent of the samples the interval calculated would include the true number of angler hours (figure 13.5).

The object of a creel survey is to obtain reasonably precise estimates of fishing effort at minimum cost. This can best be achieved by stratifying the sample, thus reducing the variances of the individual sample estimates. Consider the hypothetical ten-day fishery: stratification suggests a subdivision of the periods into groups that have similar amounts of fishing pressure (known or anticipated). Stratification should be decided upon before sampling begins, not after. For most fisheries, there is limited information from previous seasons which can be used as a guide for stratification (Robson 1960).

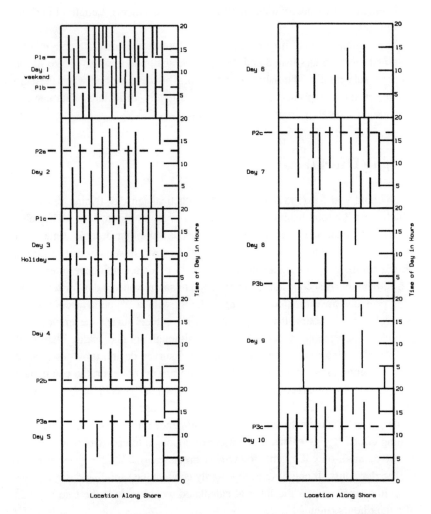

Figure 13.4. A hypothetical ten-day fishing season. Each day is represented by twenty hours. Each vertical line represents an angler, his or her location, and the time he or she fished. For illustration purposes, the dotted horizontal lines represent randomly selected samples within periods (P) 1, 2, and 3. Tables 13.1 and 13.2 reflect this data which is used in the harvest calculation.

For example, in many fisheries, the opening day and the first three weekends (Group 1) may be grouped together and all weekdays grouped together (Group 2), while all weekends after the third weekend may be grouped together (Group 3). Normally, within limits, the amount of fishing pressure is predictable on a daily basis. The least number of anglers are active on weekdays, more on weekends, and most will try the season's opening or special holidays. On this basis, it is possible and desirable to stratify (group) the sample prior to census initiation.

Fishing effort is estimated from angler count data. Count data are converted to angler hours of effort (or other appropriate estimators) by multiplying the mean number of anglers counted in each stratum by the number of hours in the sampling period (Neuhold and Lu 1957):

(1) $\quad F_i = h_i \overline{X}_i$

where F_i = fishing effort in hours for the ith stratum, h_i = number of possible fishing hours for the stratum, and $\overline{X}_i$ = mean number of anglers per count for the stratum.

In addition, the variance of the counts of anglers for each stratum or time period group is calculated in the following manner:

(2) $\quad \text{VAR}(X_h) = \dfrac{\sum X^2 - \dfrac{(\sum X)^2}{n}}{n-1}$

where $\text{VAR}(X_h)$ is the variance for the hth group and n is the number of observations in the group. In order to determine the confidence interval for the total fishing effort ($F_T = \sum F_i$, assuming all groups or stratum are sampled) it is necessary to determine the variance and standard error of F_T as follows:

(3) $\quad \text{VAR}(F_i) = h_i{}^2 \text{VAR}(\overline{X}_i)$

(4) $\quad \text{VAR}(\overline{X}_i) = \dfrac{\text{VAR}(X_h)}{n}$

and

(5) $\quad \text{VAR}(F_T) = \text{VAR } F_1 + \text{VAR } F_2 + \cdots + \text{VAR } F_k$

where k is the number of groups in the stratification (strata), and $\text{VAR}(F_i)$ is the variance of the ith group, assuming that the F_is are all independent and all covariance terms are zero based on random sampling. $\text{VAR}(F_T)$ is the variance of total fishing effort and the standard error of the total fishing effort,

(6) $\quad \text{SE}(F_T) = \sqrt{\text{VAR}(F_T)}$

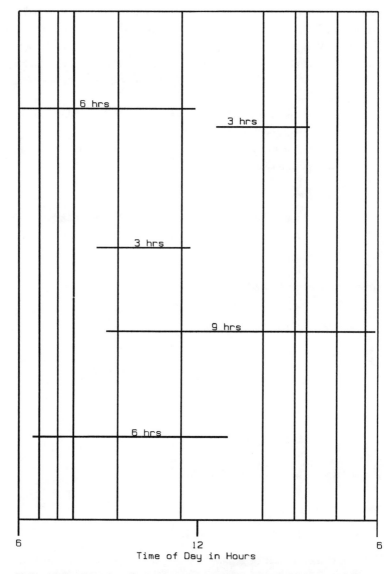

Figure 13.5. Illustration of method of estimating fishing effort for a hypothetical one-day fishery by an instantaneous count. The horizontal lines represent the length of the fishing trip for each of the five anglers, and the vertical lines represent the counts.

Table 13.1 Data and calculations for simplified fishery presented in figure 13.5.

Count Data	Calculations
X_i	
2	$s^2 = \frac{58 - \frac{(22)^2}{10}}{9} = \frac{58 - 48.4}{9} = 1.067$
2	$\mathrm{Var}(\overline{X}) = \frac{s^2}{m} = \frac{1.067}{10} = 0.1067$
2	
4	$\mathrm{Var}(\hat{F}) = h^2\, V(\overline{X}) = 144(.1067) = 15.36$
4	$\mathrm{SE}(\hat{F}) = 3.92$
2	95% C.I. for F is $\hat{F} \pm t_{1-a/2,v}\, \mathrm{SE}(F)$
2	$= 26.4 \pm 2.262(3.92) = 24.6 \pm 8.87$
2	$= 17.53$ to 35.27
1	
1	
$\mathrm{E}\, X_i = 22$	
$\overline{X} = 2.2$	

Using $\mathrm{SE}(F_T)$, it is possible to calculate the confidence interval (C.I.) for any level of confidence,

(7) $100(1 - \alpha)\%\ \mathrm{C.I.} = F_T \pm t_{(1- -,v)}\mathrm{SE}(F_T)$

where α is the significance level and V is the degrees of freedom, which has a general form of $V = n_1 + n_2 + \ldots + n_k - k$ (assuming equal variances) and a specific form for the data in table 13.4 of $V = (4 + 3 + 3) - 3 = 7$.

A simplified fishery (figure 13.5) is hypothesized as having five anglers fishing a total of twenty-seven hours in one day. Ten counts are assumed to be conducted during the one-day fishery, with a total of twenty-two anglers counted (table 13.1). The mean number of anglers per count is 2.2.

This is an average of 2.2 anglers fishing for the twelve-hour fishing day. Therefore, $F = h\overline{X} = 12 \times 2.2 = 26.4$ angler hours. This estimate is extremely close (accurate) to the actual number of hours expended by the five anglers. The 95% C.I. for F is 26.4 ± 8.87.

Rate of Success ($\bar{r}$)

In conjunction with estimating fishing effort, an estimate of the rate of success is made. The basic information required to make this estimate is obtained by interviewing anglers. The interviews provide information on the rate of success of each angler and, if desired, the species composition and size of their catches. These data are then used in conjunction with total effort data to calculate total harvest. The interviewer collects from each angler the time spent fishing (t_i) and the number (and sometimes size) of fish of each species caught (c_i).

It is important to record the above information for each angler separately so standard errors can be calculated. Care must be taken in collecting accurate information. It is preferable to count the fish in each angler's creel rather than accept verbal data. It is generally more desirable to ask anglers at what time they started fishing (assuming they are still fishing) rather than asking how long they have been fishing. All segments of the fishery should be interviewed. This means that sampling should be approximately proportional to the fishing effort. If this objective is not achieved, estimates of the rate of fishing success may be biased. A presurvey may be necessary to define areas and times of effort. One formula for calculating mean rate of success is:

$$(8) \quad \bar{r} = \frac{\sum r_i}{n} = \frac{1}{n} \frac{\sum c_i}{t_i}$$

where $\bar{r}$ = rate of success for a strata or period, r_i = the rate of success for the ith individual angler, and n = the number of individual anglers surveyed. Other estimates of $\bar{r}$ may be more appropriate for some objectives. The variance of the rate of success for each strata or period is calculated from

$$(9) \quad VAR\ (\bar{r}) = \frac{\sum r_i^2 - \frac{(\sum r_i)^2}{n}}{n(n-1)}$$

Harvest (H)

Harvest is estimated by multiplying the rate of success ($\bar{r}$) for the period or strata by the fishing effort (F from equation 1) in angler hours for the period:

$$(10) \quad H = \bar{r} \times F_i$$

where H = number of fish harvested, $\bar{r}$ = rate of success for the strata or period, and F_i = fishing effort in hours for the stratum. If $\bar{r}$ and F_i are independently subject to sampling error (assuming no correlation between the two variables) then the variance of the product $\bar{r} \times F_i$ is as follows:

$$(11) \quad VAR\ (H) = \bar{r}^2[VAR\ F_i] + (F_i)^2[VAR\ \bar{r}_i]$$

Table 13.2. Stratification of fishing season into periods and allocation of sampling (see figure 13.4) for ten-day hypothetical model (after Neuhold and Lu 1957).

Period	Days in Period (Strata)	Number of Counts	Sample Probability and Percent of Total Counts	Number of Possible Fishing Hours
1	1 and 3	4	0.4/40	40
2	2, 4, and 7	3	0.3/30	60
3	5, 6, 8, 9, and 10	3	0.3/30	100

A Hypothetical Ten-Day Season

Angler Counts

Assuming data were available on the distribution of fishing effort from models similar to that of Neuhold and Lu (1957), the population could be stratified into three Groups. For the hypothetical ten-day fishery, a total of ten counts might logically be considered adequate to provide a satisfactory estimate of fishing effort. Counts would be allocated among strata (periods) with 40 percent (sampling probability of 0.4) assigned the period with the higher fishing pressure (Period 1), 30 percent (sampling probability 0.3) to the intermediate period (Period 2), and 30 percent (sampling probability 0.3) to the period (Period 3) with the least fishing pressure (table 13.2). Days to count should be randomly selected if coverage is incomplete. Count data is shown in table 13.3.

Each sampling day consists of an instantaneous sample. The number of samples within each period (strata or Group) is allocated, if possible, equally between days. The starting point for each sample is selected from a table or computer-generated set of two-digit random numbers 00 to 19 representing the twenty fishing hours (available daily), sampling without replacement (figure 13.4).

Effort Estimates and Determination of Precision

In the example of the ten-day hypothetical fishery, days 1 and 3 (Period 1) have the greatest fishing pressure, days 2, 4, and 7 (Period 2) are intermediate, and the remaining days (Period 3) have less fishing pressure. Thus, by dividing the ten-day fishery into three separate periods, separate estimates of F can be calculated for each period.

Table 13.3. Period numbers, number of anglers counted per sample for each period, total anglers counted per period, and the average number of anglers per period (data from figure 13.4).

Period	Number of Anglers per Count	Total Number of Anglers Counted	Average Number per Period ($\overline{X}$)
1	16, 13, 12, 10	51	12.75
2	5, 7, 7	19	6.33
3	5, 5, 7	17	5.67

Since effort is based on count data, using equation (1), data in tables 13.2 and 13.3 allows interpretation of information from figure 13.4, resulting in:

Period	No. of Possible Fishing Hours (h_i)	Mean No. of Anglers/Count ($\overline{x}_i$)	Fishing Effort in Hours (F_i)
1	40	12.75	510
2	60	6.33	380
3	100	5.67	567
	Total angler hours (F_T)		1457

Confidence Intervals

Using the above data and information in tables 13.3 and 13.4, the confidence interval can be calculated for individual strata as well as total fishing effort. This provides an estimate of how much reliability can be placed in the estimate(s). As an example, the 95 percent confidence interval for Period 1 is calculated in a step-by-step process as follows (from table 13.3, Period 1):

$$EX_{1i}^2 = (16)^2 + (13)^2 + (12)^2 + (10)^2 = 669, \quad EX_{1i} = (51), \text{ and } n_1 = 4.$$

Using equation (2):

$$VAR(X_1) = 669 - \frac{\frac{(51)^2}{4}}{4 - 1} = 6.25$$

Using equation (4):

$$VAR(\overline{X}_1) = \frac{6.25}{4} = 1.56$$

Using equation (3):

$$VAR(F_1) = 40^2(1.56) = 2496$$

Table 13.4. Count of anglers by period, sample size, average number of anglers, and variances for each period.

Period	Total Number of Anglers Counted	Number of Counts	Mean Number of Anglers per Count $\overline{X}$	VAR (X_n)	VAR $(\overline{X}_n)$	VAR (F_1)
1	51	4	12.75	6.25	1.56	2496
2	19	3	6.33	1.33	0.44	1584
3	17	3	5.67	1.33	0.44	4400

and similarly for F_2, F_3 (summarized in table 13.4).
Thus, using equation (5):

$$\text{VAR}(F_T) = 2496 + 1584 + 4400 = 8480$$

and, using equation (6):

$$\text{SE}(F_T) = \sqrt{8480} = 92.09$$

and, using equation (7) we get the 95% C.I. for $F_T = 1357 \pm 2.365(92.09) = 1357 \pm 217.79$ or 1139.2 to 1574.8.

The 95 percent confidence intervals for each of the strata are obtained as follows:

$$\text{VAR}(F_1) = 40^2(1.56) = 2496$$

$$\text{VAR}(F_2) = 60^2(0.44) = 1584$$

$$\text{VAR}(F_3) = 100^2(0.44) = 4400$$

and

$$\text{SE}(F_1) = \sqrt{2496} = 49.96$$

$$\text{SE}(F_2) = \sqrt{1584} = 39.80$$

$$\text{SE}(F_3) = \sqrt{4400} = 66.33$$

95% C.I. $(F_1) = 510 \pm 3.182(49.96) = 510 \pm 159.0$ or 351.0 to 669.0
95% C.I. $(F_2) = 380 \pm 4.303(39.80) = 380 \pm 171.26$ or 208.74 to 551.26
95% C.I. $(F_3) = 567 \pm 4.303(66.33) = 567 \pm 285.4$ or 281.6 to 852.4.

The t-values are obtained from a two-tailed cumulative t-distribution table. As the degrees of freedom increase, the t-value decreases. The t-value, needed for the confidence interval for F_T, at the 95 percent level for 7 degrees of freedom (e.g., n–k = degrees of freedom) = 2.365. The t-test assumes equal variance quantities, which in the example cannot be justified. In this example, variances are not homogeneous (equal), so pooling of the degrees of freedom cannot be justified. We, therefore, use a conservative number (smallest sample size) of 2 degrees of freedom. The confidence interval for the estimated fishing effort of 1357 hours is ±217.8 hours with 2 degrees of freedom. For the individual strata estimates, the degrees of freedom are respectively 3, 2, and 2 for strata (Periods) 1, 2, and 3. To increase precision, more samples are needed from each group (Cochran 1977). This, in turn, will reduce the t-value. With other data, with wide variation in sample size, we recommend using formulas presented by Snedecor (1956). In actual practice, large numbers of samples are usually taken for each group. Individual fisheries managers may reduce confidence intervals to less than 95 percent in particular management situations without reducing data usefulness.

Rate of Success ($\bar{r}$)

Tables 13.5, 13.6, and 13.7 present raw data for angler effort (t_i), number of fish caught (c_i), and individual success rate (r_i) for each of the three groups in the hypothetical fishery. Angler interviews for the above data must be obtained from anglers fishing during that period (strata). Interview data need not be completed concurrent with count data, however. Interviews of thirty individuals is an arbitrary selection. Number of anglers interviewed should be predetermined to insure it is a representative sample. From such data the rate of success can be calculated, using equation (8), as:

$$\bar{r} \text{ for Period } 1 = \frac{1}{30}(16.734) = 0.558$$

and similarly for Periods 2 and 3. The variance of the rate of success for Period 1, equation (9), is:

$$\text{VAR}(\bar{r}_1) = \frac{17.688 - \frac{(16.734)^2}{30}}{30(29)} = 0.0096$$

$$\text{SE}(\bar{r}_1) = \sqrt{0.0096} = 0.098$$

Values for Periods 2 and 3 are calculated in a similar manner. Calculations for the confidence intervals for the rate of success ($\bar{r}$) are:

$$\bar{r}_i \pm t_{(1-\alpha/2, v)}\text{SE}(\bar{r}_i)$$

for Period 1 we obtain $0.558 \pm (2.045)(0.098)$ or $.558 \pm .200$ or 0.358 to 0.758.

Table 13.5. Raw data for Period 1 angler effort (t_i), number of fish caught (c_i), and individual success rates c_i/t_i.

Anglers Interviewed	Number of Hours Fished t_i	Number of Fish Caught c_i	Success Rates r_i c_i/t_i
1	7.5	4	0.533
2	12	2	0.167
3	1	1	1.000
4	4	1	0.250
5	6	2	0.333
6	9	2	0.222
7	8	3	0.375
8	12	6	0.500
9	4	12	3.000
10	9	4	0.444
11	4	1	0.250
12	9	2	0.222
13	7.5	3	0.400
14	7.5	4	0.533
15	8.5	5	0.588
16	12	6	0.500
17	7	7	1.000
18	9	8	0.889
19	6	2	0.333
20	6	1	0.167
21	6	3	0.500
22	5	0	0.000
23	9	7	0.778
24	9	6	0.667
25	5	5	1.000
26	7	4	0.571
27	7	3	0.429
28	6	2	0.333
29	6	0	0.000
30	12	9	0.750
TOTAL			16.734
MEAN			0.558

Table 13.6. Raw data for Period 2 angler effort (t_i), number of fish caught (c_i), and individual success rates c_i/t_i.

Anglers Interviewed	Number of Hours Fished t_i	Number of Fish Caught c_i	Success Rates r_i c_i/t_i
1	3	2	0.667
2	6	1	0.167
3	0.5	1	2.000
4	2	1	0.500
5	6	2	0.333
6	4	2	0.500
7	4	1	0.250
8	6	2	0.333
9	5	4	0.800
10	9	4	0.444
11	4	1	0.250
12	9	2	0.222
13	7	3	0.429
14	7	3	0.429
15	8.5	1	0.118
16	12	6	0.500
17	7	6	0.857
18	9	4	0.444
19	6	2	0.333
20	6	2	0.333
21	6	1	0.167
22	2	3	1.500
23	4	0	0.000
24	4	1	0.250
25	1	0	0.000
26	7	3	0.429
27	7	2	0.286
28	2	1	0.500
29	2	1	0.500
30	2	0	0.000
TOTAL			13.541
MEAN			0.451

Table 13.7. Raw data for Period 3 angler effort (t_i), number of fish caught (c_i), and individual success rates c_i/t_i.

Anglers Interviewed	Number of Hours Fished t_i	Number of Fish Caught c_i	Success Rates r_i c_i/t_i
1	1	0	0.000
2	3	1	0.333
3	3	1	0.333
4	1	1	1.000
5	0.5	1	2.000
6	12	7	0.583
7	2	0	0.000
8	8	4	0.500
9	3	1	0.333
10	4	1	0.250
11	9	4	0.444
12	9	4	0.444
13	1	0	0.000
14	12	6	0.500
15	7	6	0.857
16	9	4	0.444
17	1	0	0.000
18	1	1	1.000
19	1	0	0.000
20	1	3	3.000
21	2	1	0.500
22	9	1	0.111
23	0.5	1	2.000
24	7	3	0.429
25	7	4	0.571
26	1	2	2.000
27	1	0	0.000
28	1	1	1.000
29	1	0	0.000
30	4	1	0.250
TOTAL			18.882
MEAN			0.629

Calculation of Harvest (H)

An estimate of the individual Period harvest is calculated by multiplying the rate of success by the fishing effort in angler hours from equation (10):

$$H_1 = \bar{r}_1 \times F_1$$

$$H_1 = 0.558 \times 510 = 284.6 \text{ for } F_1$$

where H = number of fish harvested, $\bar{r}_1$ = rate of success for the group, and F_1 = fishing effort in hours for the period. If $\bar{r}_1$ and F_1 are independently subject to sampling error (assuming no correlation between the two variables) then the variance is calculated from equation (11):

$$VAR(H_1) = 0.558^2[2496] + (510)^2[.0096]$$

$$= 777.16 + 2496.96 = 3274.12$$

$$H_2 = (0.451)(380) = 171.4$$

and

$$VAR(H_2) = (0.451)^2(1584) + (380)^2(0.0057) = 1145.27$$

$$H_3 = (0.629)(567) = 356.6$$

and

$$VAR(H_3) = (0.629)^2(4400) + (567)^2(0.0178) = 7463.32$$

For total harvest

$$H_T = H_1 + H_2 + H_3 = 284.6 + 171.4 + 356.6 = 812.6$$

$$VAR(H_T) = VAR(H_1) + VAR(H_2) + VAR(H_3),$$

assuming the H_1s are independent

$$= 3274.12 + 1145.27 + 7463.2 = 11882.71$$

$$SE(H_T) = \sqrt{11882.71} = 109.01$$

95% C.I. for the total harvest H_T is $812.6 \pm (469.1) =$

343.5 to 1281.7.

Using the data from tables 13.5, 13.6, and 13.7 as examples we obtain the results presented in table 13.8 for Periods 1, 2, and 3. The correlation between h_i and r_i was calculated and values of -0.279 for Period 1, -0.202

Table 13.8. Summary of count, effort, CPUE, and harvest data for a ten-day hypothetical fishery. Key values within sections are italicized. Values for harvest calculation are italicized and emphasized.

Variable	Period 1	Period 2	Period 3
Count Data			
No. of Counts	4	3	3
No. of Possible Fishing Hrs (h)	*40*	*60*	*100*
Sampling Probability	0.4	0.3	0.3
Total No. of Anglers Counted	51	19	17
No. of Anglers per Count	16,13,12,10	5,7,7	5,5,7
Avg. No. of Anglers Counted ($\overline{X}$)	*12.75*	*6.33*	*5.67*
Effort Data			
Estimated Effort (F) $F = h\overline{X}$	*510*	*380*	*567*
VAR (F)	2496	1584	4400
CPUE Data			
$\bar{r}$	*0.558*	*0.451*	*0.629*
Er_i^2	17.688	11.098	27.369
VAR ($\bar{r}$)	0.0096	0.0057	0.0178
95% C.I. for $\bar{r}$	0.358 to 0.758	0.296 to 0.606	0.356 to 0.902
Harvest Data			
Harvest (H)	*284.6*	*171.4*	*356.6*
VAR (H)	3274.12	1145.27	7463.32
95% C.I. for (H)	102.5 to 466.7	25.8 to 317.0	0 to 728.3

for Period 2, and -0.225 for Period 3 were obtained. These values are not significant with alpha $= 0.05$, so our assumption that there is no correlation between them has not been violated.

Summary

The data presented above is for a simple creel survey to calculate effort and harvest. If harvest by species, by location, by boat versus shore anglers, or other variations are desired, separate calculations must be accomplished. Creel survey data can be collected for a specific species, incremental length data, or other variations. Age and growth data, involving the collection of lengths, weights, and bony parts may also be collected in the process of a creel survey. Calculation of economic value may also be a desirable part of a creel survey but also requires time and effort. Malvestuto (1983) cautions that creel surveys may intrude on angler privacy and enjoyment of recreational time. Creel surveys which require lengthy conversations with anglers or intrusions upon their time should be carefully considered prior to initiation. Efforts to involve anglers in the survey results, e.g., providing them with preliminary data or a summary of the purposes of the survey, may alleviate some bad public relations potential (Malvestuto). It is best to conduct such surveys as economic indicators in a separate survey of anglers or to ask the specific questions of a different group of anglers.

Literature Cited

Anderson, R. O. 1975. Optimum Sustainable Yield in Inland Recreational Fisheries Management. Pp. 29–38 in P. M. Roedel, ed., *Optimum Sustainable Yield as a Concept in Fisheries Management, Proceedings of a Symposium at the 104th Annual Meeting of the American Fisheries Society, Sept. 9, 1974, Honolulu, HI.* Washington, D.C.: American Fisheries Society. Special Publication 9.

Butler, R. L., and D. P. Borgeson. 1965. California "Catchable" Trout Fisheries. *California Fish and Game Fisheries Bulletin* 127:47 pp.

Carlander, K. D., C. J. DiCostanzo, and R. J. Jessen. 1958. Sampling Problems in Creel Census. *Progressive Fish-Culturist* 20(2):73–81.

Cochran, W. G. 1977. *Sampling Techniques.* Third Edition. New York: John Wiley and Sons. 428 pp.

Katherein, J. A. 1953. An Intensive Creel Census on Clearwater Lake, Missouri, During Its First Four Years of Impoundment, 1949–1952. *Transactions of the North American Wildlife Conference* 18:282–95.

Lyles, C. H. 1968. *Fishery Statistics of the United States, 1966.* U.S. Fish and Wildlife Service Statistical Digest 60. Washington, D.C.: U.S. Department of the Interior, U.S. Fish and Wildlife Service, Bureau of Commercial Fisheries. 679 pp.

Malvestuto, S. P., 1983. Sampling the Recreational Fishery. Pp. 397–419 in L. A. Nielsen and D. L. Johnson, eds., *Fisheries Techniques.* Bethesda, Md.: American Fisheries Society.

Malvestuto, S. P., W. D. Davies, and W. L. Shelton. 1978. An Evaluation of the Roving Creel Survey with Nonuniform Probability Sampling. *Transactions of the American Fisheries Society* 107(2):255–62.

——. 1979. Predicting the Precision of Creel Survey Estimates of Fishing Effort by Use of Climatic Variables. *Transactions of the American Fisheries Society* 108(1): 43–45.

Moyle, J. B., and D. R. Franklin. 1957. Quantitative Creel Census on 12 Minnesota Lakes. *Transactions of the American Fisheries Society* 85(1955):28–38.

Neuhold, J. M., and K. H. Lu. 1957. *Creel Census Method.* Salt Lake City: Utah State Department of Fish and Game. Publication No. 8. 36 pp.

Phippen, K. W., and E. P. Bergerson. 1987. Angling Definitions and Their Effect on the Accuracy of Count-Interview Creel Survey Harvest Estimate. *North American Journal of Fisheries Management* 7:488–92.

Robson, D. S. 1960. An Unbiased Sampling and Estimation Procedure for Creel Censuses of Fishermen. *Biometrics* 16(2):261–77.

Snedecor, G. W. 1956. *Statistical Methods Applied to Experiments in Agriculture and Biology*. Fifth Edition. Ames: Iowa State College Press. 534 pp.

Zuboy, J., R. T. Lackey, N. Prosser, and R. Corning. 1973. Computerized Creel Census System for Use in Fisheries Management. Pp. 570–74 in *Proceedings of the 27th Annual Conference of Southeastern Association of Game and Fish Commission*.

14. Ecology of Fishes

Most unabridged dictionaries define ecology as "the branch of biology that studies the relationships between organisms and their total environment, to include both animate and inanimate aspects." All ecological aspects of fishes in recreational fisheries have several things in common. Among them are existence in an aquatic medium, the need for adequate and suitable food, escape mechanism from predators and abiotic factors, areas suitable for reproduction, and protection for at least a portion of the annual progeny.

The ecological topics presented in this chapter indicate both the diversity and the complexity of freshwater fishes and their ecology. Any one aspect of fish ecology studied in isolation can be an absorbing topic. All aspects of ecology for a particular fish, studied in either a natural environment or an experimental setting, are complex, intriguing, and indicative of the diverse nature of freshwater fishes.

Distribution of Fishes and Habitat Types

Fishes occur in almost all types of aquatic habitats and may be ecologically grouped on this basis. They may be, for example, benthic, pelagic, planktonic, limnetic, or littoral. In streams they may additionally be classified as fast-water, slow-water, riffle, or pool dwellers, headwater, tributary, mainstream, valley-bottom, large-river, or small-river species. Of those factors that most often influence the distribution of fishes (temperature, dissolved oxygen, current, light, predators, and food), temperature is probably the single most limiting one. Some species such as the common carp can survive and prosper in a wide range of temperatures, but others such as the icefish will die if the temperature change is in excess of a few degrees centigrade (Rudd 1965). Species which can survive in a widc range of a particular variable are described as eury and those which have a relatively finely defined range for a particular characteristic are defined as steno. Fish that survive in a wide range of temperatures are therefore defined as eurythermal and those that have a rather narrowly defined temperature tolerance range are stenothermal.

Various species of fish prosper in large impoundments or natural lakes but do very poorly when put in small ponds or streams. Others do much better in higher altitude alpine or near-alpine lakes and streams or headwaters than they do in the more slowly moving, more heavily bottom-silted valley streams. Many species require relatively large lakes in order to complete their life cycle and will not reproduce if certain habitat requirements are unavailable. A good example of a species that is restricted by its habitat is the sockeye salmon. The landlocked form, the kokanee, has been transplanted into numerous inland waters and populations have become established. However the kokanee's life cycle requires a stream (or rarely a spring-fed lakeshore) in which it can spawn. Arctic grayling, which at one time were widespread in western North America, have been planted into many lakes and some streams. In only a few instances have these populations survived or succeeded in any measurable fashion. This stenothermal fish has rather narrowly defined habitat requirements. Where these needs were not met, the fish did not survive. Conversely, the common carp, which was transplanted into the United States in the late 1870s, has spread throughout the lower altitude waters of the contiguous forty-eight states and Canada. The carp obviously has a very broad range of acceptable water quality, temperature, and other habitat requirements. Carp live in a wide variety of habitats ranging from low-altitude, large rivers to rather cold oligotrophic mountain lakes above 5,900 feet.

An important ecological consideration is the species composition of a habitat being considered for new species. In the second half of the 1800s and early 1900s innumerable fishes were transplanted, particularly in the western United States, from the eastern United States into waters previously inhabited only by native species. These transplants have proven to be a mixed blessing; some species provide sport fishing, while others have ranged from a nuisance to a disaster. Nonnative fishes stocked over existing populations have overrun native species and in some cases extirpated them. Much time and effort has been spent in recent years by state and federal resource management agencies trying to identify habitat requirements of selected species. There are now publications dealing with instream flow and habitat requirements of several species of fish.

Movement Patterns

Fish movement or migration patterns can be divided into four broad categories: daily, feeding, reproduction, and avoidance. Few fishes live in the same place throughout their lives, although some may move no farther than from deep water to inshore or from a pool to a riffle area and back. Others move many thousands of miles. A majority of fishes start their spawning migrations at a definite stage of maturity and after a change in hormonal activity. Initiation of migration is generally tied to photoperiod or temperature changes, or both.

Truly migratory fishes that remain within fresh water during their migrations are termed potamodromous and those that remain in the marine environment during their migrations are termed oceanodromous. The most remarkable migration of an oceanodromous group may be that of the tunas. They spend their entire lives in the ocean and cover great distances. Bluefin tuna of the Atlantic migrate between Florida and Norway and between Norway and Spain (Bond 1979). Anadromous species migrate between fresh and salt water and return to fresh to spawn.

The most significant hazards of freshwater migrations include a change from an established habitat to an unknown one. This increases exposure to predators, changing water quality, and man-made obstructions. In addition, migrations over long distances require vast amounts of energy. It must be assumed, however, that the disadvantages are outweighed by the advantages and that from an evolutionary and a species survival standpoint the migrations are beneficial. Fish that change from salt to fresh water or vice versa make physiological adjustments. Sexual maturity is attained during long-range spawning migrations. This often results in deterioration of the other body tissues and functions since the majority of food ingested is diverted to the gonads.

Daily Migrations

Many species of fish, such as white bass in Spirit Lake, Iowa, and tui chub in Pyramid Lake, Nevada, have diel migrations either vertically or horizontally (Sigler 1949; Sigler and Sigler 1987). Generally, these fish are moving in response to either changes in photointensity or are following migrating prey. Some fish move into shallow water to feed at twilight then move back to the more protective deep water during daylight.

Feeding Migrations

Passive migrations to feeding grounds may begin in some fish as early as the egg or larval stages, when both the fish and eggs are true plankters. Active migrations may be a few yards or hundreds of miles. After reaching a specific size, some species of anadromous salmonids smolt, then migrate downstream from the spawning area to the ocean. These fish spend from one to four years in the marine environment, utilizing the vast food resources of the ocean to grow to maturity. They then return to the spawning grounds to continue their life cycle. Although some feeding migrations are daily, fish may also move because of the lack of food, either on a seasonal or a one-time basis.

Reproduction Migrations

Many freshwater and marine fishes as well as anadromous and catadromous species have distinctive migration patterns for reproduction. Among closely related forms of the same species (e.g., sockeye salmon and kokanee) the migratory form is considerably more abundant than the nonmigratory form (Nikolsky 1963).

Large-scale migrations that take place one or more times during the life of an individual can be grouped into several broad categories delineating the type and direction of the migration. The broad category of diadromous fishes (Bond 1979) can be subdivided into: (1) anadromous species that spend most of their lives in the sea and migrate to fresh water to spawn, such as the chinook salmon, (2) catadromous species that spend most of their lives in fresh water and migrate to the sea to breed, such as the American eel, and (3) amphidromous species (e.g., some herring species) that migrate from fresh water to sea or sea to fresh water at regular or definable stages, migrations unrelated to breeding.

The best known and perhaps best documented long-distance anadromous migrations include members of the genera *Oncorhynchus* and *Salmo*. These species often migrate hundreds of miles up freshwater streams to spawn. Pacific salmon die after spawning but Atlantic salmon and steelhead trout are potentially repeat spawners. Species of *Salmo* are genetically able to spawn more than once, but many West Coast stocks fail because of the arduous upstream journey in part through numerous hydroelectric plants and other man-made obstructions. This often effectively eliminates repeat spawning. Migration of other species such as the coastal cutthroat trout may include travel very close to shore or lengthy migrations along the coast to feeding grounds well off shore.

Bregazzi and Kennedy (1980) note that although many recaptures of pike were made in approximately the same area of first capture, a number of long-term recaptures indicated there was a definite spawning migration. This conclusion was partially supported by the high catches of mature pike made in spawning areas during the spawning season as well as evidence that the pike return to the same area of the lake each year to spawn. Outside the breeding season little evidence exists for particular trends in movement. The pike seemed prone to wander, and sampling did not lead to repeated recaptures.

Northern pike in Spirit Lake, Iowa, show a definite spawning migration. In Lake Oake on the Missouri River, they travel upstream maximum distances of 150 miles. Movement of 1 mile per day is not uncommon for those fish that traveled more than a total of 5 miles. Few fish continued to go further away from a tagging site with the passage of time (Moen and Henegar 1971).

Avoidance and Other Migrations

Large-scale out-migrations may occur in areas of violent water agitation such as shallow areas during a storm, in reservoirs where the water level is dropping rapidly, or where pollution or temperature levels adversely affect the species.

Another avoidance migration occurs in small lakes and reservoirs when oxygen is depleted in the hypolimnion and thermocline, leaving, in some cases, only a few feet of habitable water in the epilimnion. This occurs in a number of small impoundments in southern Iowa (Tom Moen, personal communication 1985). Point sources of pollution in streams, especially during low flows, often cause oxygen depletion, leading to fish out-migration or, in some cases, death. There are late fall to early winter migrations of fishes from widely dispersed populations of lakes, reservoirs, and streams into limited areas of deep water. These fishes generally are not avoiding cold water, but are congregating in dense, tightly packed masses. Common carp observed in Lake Okoboji, Iowa, in the 1940s under these conditions were easily captured by commercial seiners until they became alert and active after being disturbed repeatedly.

Many species of fish actively seek optimum temperatures and oxygen levels in early summer. Fish are either attracted to or repelled by heated effluents, depending on the time of year, species of fish, and the ambient temperatures.

Reproduction

Reproducing fish use a variety of mechanisms and adaptations. Fecundity, the ability to produce offspring, is highly varied. Individual fecundity is increased by fractional spawning, that is, when only part of the eggs are laid at one time. Fractional and prolonged spawning are mainly characteristics of tropical and subtropical species. In temperate latitudes only insignificant numbers of fish are partial spawners, and in the Arctic there is no partial spawning (Nikolsky 1963). The number of partial spawners in the tropics may be explained by the lack of any clear seasonal variation in the supply of food or other environmental conditions prerequisite to larval survival. This enables larvae to survive in an acceptable environment over a considerable part of the year. This rationale can be extended to North American species that live in habitats that have uniform water temperatures and food supplies year around, and where they spawn over a longer period than they could in a more restrictive environment. Examples are the pupfishes in the western deserts of the United States that live in near uniform thermal environments (Sigler and Sigler 1987).

Changes in fecundity may be produced by a decrease of food supply. Fast-growing individuals of a species usually have a higher fecundity than slow-growing ones of the same size. An increase, or decrease, in the fecundity of individuals within a population appears to be an adaptive response to environmental factors. Some East Coast marine species, when heavily cropped, may demonstrate stimulated growth and the onset of sexual maturity, such that individuals mature and spawn one, two, or even three years earlier than normal (W. B. Scott, personal communication 1986). Fish in a depauperate environment may be more prolific than those in a well-populated body of water.

Fecundity also varies with the amount of protection provided embryos and larvae. Fishes that defend or hide their eggs generally have low fecundity. The fecundity of marine fishes is usually somewhat higher than that of freshwater or diadromous species.

Some members of the salmon family provide no parental care following egg deposition and fertilization. Other members, particularly the trouts, protect the developing embryos by digging a nest in the gravel substrate, then fertilizing and covering the deposited eggs. Embryos hatch within the gravel substrate and fry emerge into the water column. Most North American catfishes construct fairly elaborate nests which are guarded by one or both parents. This guardianship is extended to parental care of the newly emerged fry. In most cases the number of eggs released per spawning increases with age to a certain point and then decreases as the fish approaches senility; medium-aged females produce the largest numbers and generally the most viable eggs.

The age at which a fish becomes sexually mature varies according to species, ultimate adult size, and food supply. Age is often a dominant factor over size: sunfishes (*Lepomis* spp.) will spawn at a length of no more than three inches after reaching an age of two or three years, although the usual size at sexual maturity is five to six inches. In general, fish living at higher latitudes mature later in life and later in the season than do ones from lower latitudes. The same is true for altitude. Certain fish, such as some cyprinodontids, mature at less than a year, but other species, including the white sturgeon, may not mature until they are fifteen or twenty years old. Within a species, variation by latitude may change the onset of maturation by one or more years.

Some fish spawn several times a year. Others may spawn once a year and still others may spawn only every other year or only once in a lifetime. Spawning ideally takes place when predators are relatively inactive or absent. Certain river-dwelling fishes spawn during rising water, when, because of greater turbidity, the eggs are less conspicuous. The California grunion spawns on the beach on the spring tide in damp sand, out of the water and away from aquatic predators.

The first females to reach a spawning ground are generally the medium-aged ones. This provides greater assurance that eggs from the most vigorous females in the population will receive the highest percent of fertilization. This works to the advantage of the species.

Sperm motility may last from ten seconds to twenty-four hours. Sperm becomes mobile on entering the water and must locate an egg and fertilize it (penetrate it through the microphyle) while motility persists. Sperm of fish that spawn in fast-running water retain their motility for only a few seconds; that of species released in slow-running water are motile longer. For fish spawning in stagnant or still water, the sperm retains the longest motility.

Reproduction among fishes may be triggered by an increasing photoperiod and warming temperatures in the spring or by shortened photoperiods and decreasing temperatures in the fall. Pond fish spawning may be initiated by an inflow of fresh water. These environmental factors trigger responses in the endocrine system that result in maturation of the sex products and initiate spawning.

Fishes that characteristically spawn at night generally do so in water that is shallower than that sought by fish spawning in the daytime. Night spawning provides a degree of protection against predators that hunt visually.

Fish reproduction can be divided into three broad categories with regard to embryo development: oviparous, viviparous, and ovoviviparous. Oviparous embryos are those which are hatched externally. Viviparous embryos are those which are hatched internally and produce free-swimming young. The intermediate term ovoviviparous indicates a condition in which embryos receive internal nourishment but are extruded as free-swimming young. The latter two categories are sometimes combined.

Three other delineations of reproduction are appropriate. They are dioecious, hermaphroditic, and parthenogenetic. Dioecious reproduction is by far the most prevalent. Here eggs and sperm are produced by separate individuals. Hermaphrodites have both sexes in one individual and may utilize self-fertilization. In parthenogenesis the development of young occurs without fertilization of the egg. The sperm serves no function in the hereditary characteristics of the species but is required only to initiate egg development. In most of these cases the resultant young are female.

Sexual Dimorphism

During the reproductive cycle, external sexual dimorphism may range from the obvious (modification of the anal or pelvic fins or color changes) to the difficult or impossible to discern. It is apparent throughout the life cycle of some species (e.g., mosquitofish and many other live-bearers), but less apparent in some species (e.g., minnows and suckers) where changes may be limited to breeding tubercles in males, which are present only just preceding and during the spawning season.

Males of some species of salmonids change color and the jaws become deformed at the onset of sexual maturity. Kokanee salmon males, for example, become a bright red on the sides and back and the snout becomes hooked. The female is less brightly colored.

Males are generally more colorful than females during the breeding season. They are also generally smaller except when the male guards the nest and/ or young; then the reverse is true. For example, the largemouth bass male is larger than the female, and the female of large northern pike are much larger than the males. This may be viewed as an adaptive mechanism: if the eggs are not to be guarded, then there should be many more of them.

Monogamy and Polygamy

Both monogamy and polygamy occur among fishes, but monogamy is rare. Because males usually remain on the spawning grounds longer than females, they spawn readily with several females. A female may also spawn with more than one male either concurrently or separately. Sex ratios in a given population vary considerably from species to species but generally are close to 1:1.

Gonadal Somatic Index

The relative maturity of a fish that spawns only once a year can be determined by comparing the ratio of the weight of the female gonads to total body weight. The maximum relative weight of the gonads (gonadal somatic index, GSI) for once-a-year spawners is greatest just prior to spawning and least immediately following spawning (Danilenko 1983; Milton and Arthington 1983). By observing the increasing GSI, the probable time of spawning can be determined.

Dominant-Year Class Formation

A particular aspect of fish reproduction of interest to fishery managers is the formation of dominant-year classes, that is, one that dominates all other year classes for the species. The characteristics of a population within a species are often affected by dominant-year classes. The presence of one or more abundant year classes may alter the population structure for several years. Various factors produce dominant-year classes and the factors generally operate at a very early life stage.

The age composition of a fish stock, relative strength of different age groups, maximum life-span, fecundity, and certain mortality factors are species characteristics. When a given species (e.g., many of the small cyprinids) characteristically exists as a population consisting of only a few age groups with a short life-span, the fish can be assumed to be adapted to living under conditions of high and variable mortality. Such fish must mature early and spawn annually in order to assure an adequate replacement of the stock, and dominant-year classes are rare. Rather, each age class prevails for a short period, in some cases for less than a year. Other species, including sturgeon, large sharks, and large catfishes tend to mature late and form populations in which the age groups (e.g., 1969 year class living until 1989) span one to several decades. The number of age classes is large, and the recruitment each year is normally a small percentage of the population. These populations, with their many age groups require a relatively stable food supply and tolerate only slight annual fluctuations in the mortality rate of mature individuals. If a substantial part of the population dies from any cause, replacement is slow (Nikolsky 1963). If a dominant-year class is produced in these species in this situation, it may influence the population for several years. Species that produce a dominant-year class can be exemplified by the Spirit Lake, Iowa, white bass, which may have as few as five age groups in fast-growing populations, but rarely more than eight or nine (Sigler 1949). Fluctuations in annual recruitment and the resultant production of strong or weak year classes have many causes. There may be several strong year classes of a certain species without a dominant-year class, as has occurred in some large reservoirs during filling. Some of these are: unusual predation on fry or young, epizootics, ecological conditions at spawning or hatching time, strength of the breeding stock, and living near the periphery of the range (Spirit Lake, Iowa, white bass).

Among many groups of fishes, including yellow perch and sunfishes, large individuals readily feed on smaller ones of their own species when other food is depleted. In this way the species maintains itself in the face of adversity; however, this process may prevent the production of a dominant-year class.

An important factor in the age composition of any stock is the rate of fishing. If the older, larger individuals are fished intensively, the average age of the breeding stock is generally reduced; this can result in either a rejuvenation of the breeding population or a depression of the biotic potential. When the fishery reduces the population to a point where the food supply of the remaining stock is improved, this generally produces accelerated growth and earlier maturity. This can potentially lead to production of a dominant-year class.

Egg Size and Physiology

The size of fish eggs varies considerably between species. Egg diameters may range from a fraction of a millimeter in some clupeoids to as much as 80 mm in certain sharks. As a general rule, the larger the eggs the fewer the number produced per female. In addition, many larger eggs have a protective hornlike membrane that ensures a higher rate of survival. The larvae from large eggs have a lower rate of mortality than do those from small eggs. This has been demonstrated within species by determining experimentally the survival rate of fry and larvae from eggs of varying size and under varying incubation conditions (Neitzel and Becher 1985; Reiser and White 1981, 1983). Fishes such as centrarchids that spawn on a rising temperature in spring have small eggs that hatch in a relatively short time, whereas some salmonids that spawn during falling temperatures deposit large eggs, with much yolk, to support a prolonged incubation period.

The two primary factors in egg hatching are time and temperature. The higher the temperature the shorter the hatching time. A formula with limited utility is temperature units (degree-days) above freezing (32°F) times number of days to hatching. Results are often too variable to be of much value, except perhaps in hatcheries with a constant temperature. Each species has both an optimum and a tolerance limit for egg hatching. The photoperiod is also an important factor in some species. Fishes that spawn in areas of low food supply produce embryos with large yolks lasting up to three weeks. Embryos that develop in areas with a low oxygen supply have considerably more respiratory pigments in the eggs than do eggs that normally hatch in an area of high oxygen. Weak pigmentation may be an adaptation associated with greater transparency which make the eggs less noticeable to predators (Nikolsky 1963). Both yolk size and pigmentation as well as other adaptations are useful later in allowing larvae to seek more suitable environment for development than that in which they were hatched.

Feeding

Fish spend a large portion of their time capturing food to survive, grow, and reproduce. Food requirements of a species vary with size, age, habitat, time of year, and stage of sexual maturity. Fish can be classified broadly as omnivores, carnivores, and herbivores. Although many species can be placed primarily in one of these three categories, they are insufficiently descriptive for the large variety of ways and methodologies in which fishes feed. A more precise classification of fish feeding habits would include the categories of predator, grazer, filter, sucker, scraper, and parasite. Additional classifications would include those fishes that feed at the surface, those that gather feed off the bottom, and those that feed in the water column. Many species would fall into more than one category. Additional classifications include: euryphagic, feeding on a variety of foods; stenophagic, feeding on only a few types of food; or monophagic, feeding on only a single type of food. To a large extent, most fish eat what is available. When a food source has been stable over a long period of time, a species may adapt to feeding on that food only, whereas a variable food supply necessitates adjusting to a greater variety of foods (see chapters 12 and 15).

Modes of Feeding

Ringler (1979) reports that prey selection by fishes is governed in part by ability to detect and locate prey. Once located, the prey is captured, manipulated, and in some cases, sorted prior to being ingested.

We define six feeding types: predatory, grazing, filtering, sucking, scraping, and parasitic. Each will be discussed and an example species provided.

Predatory Feeders—Northern Pike

Scott and Crossman (1973) report that after the yolk is absorbed, young pike feed heavily on large zooplankton and some immature aquatic insects for approximately seven to ten days. After that time, small fish enter the diet and by the time the young reach two inches, fish assume predominance in the diet. Adult northern pike can be classified as opportunistic carnivores in that they eat virtually any living vertebrate available to them within the size range they can ingest. Optimum food size for northern pike has been calculated at between one third and one half the size of the pike. Over the year the food of adults exceeds 90 percent fish, but adults do at times feed heavily on frogs and crayfish. Other vertebrates such as mice, muskrats, and ducklings may enter the diet. It takes five to six pounds of food for each pound increase in body weight of northern pike. Food selection by species is not apparent in the direct relation between size of food item and size of northern pike and pike is apparently not so pronounced as in the case of muskellunge.

Bregazzi and Kennedy (1980) report that pike in a eutrophic reservoir feed most actively in summer and autumn with less intensive feeding during the spawning season (spring) and in winter. Sixty-one percent of the diet of pike over 150 mm (6 inches) fork length was roach, 34 percent perch, 4 percent eels, and only 1 percent invertebrates. Pike less than 150 mm fork length were piscivorous but ate only roach. The smallest pike which had eaten roach had a fork length of 91 mm (3.5 inches) and weighed 5.3 grams (0.2 ounces). The size selection of prey species indicates that there was no marked consistent tendency for larger pike to select larger prey; however, the populations of both cyprinids and percids during the study were stunted, and few large prey fish were present.

Mann (1982) reports that northern pike, age one year and older, were predominantly piscivorous; less than 1 percent by weight of their prey were invertebrate animals. Variations in the composition of pike diets resulted from changes in the relative influences of prey availability, food selection, and the seasonal abundance of prey. Young pike ate cyprinids and migrating Atlantic salmon smolts. Large pike ate cyprinids, brown trout, and small pike. Cannibalism on pike six months to two years old accounted for most of the population's natural mortality. Mann suggests that due to competition and/or predation in game fisheries, removal of coarse fish and large pike may not always result in increased numbers of salmonids. The diet of northern pike in Spirit Lake, Iowa, is almost entirely fish (W. F. Sigler, personal observation).

Grimm (1981) reports that intraspecific predation plays a major role in the regulation of numbers of pike <1.6 inches fork length.

Grazing Feeders—Common Carp/Least Chub

Carp are considered to be omnivorous (Scott and Crossman 1973; Sigler 1958), consuming a variety of plant and animal tissues. The molarlike surfaces of the pharyngeal teeth greatly facilitate grinding of plants and invertebrates. When feeding, carp will suck up a mouthful of bottom ooze and detritus, expel it into the water, and select food items from the material. Many species of aquatic insects, crustaceans, annelids, and mollusks are prominent among the animals eaten, but chironomid larvae are preferred. Plants include many kinds of weed and tree seeds, wild rice, aquatic plants, and algae. Carp, in addition, will feed directly at the surface on floating animal organisms or algae. Common carp rarely feed on fish (Sigler).

Least chub, both in aquaria and natural environments, have been observed to grasp a piece of algae, then thrash and twist for ten to fifteen seconds until a clump is pulled loose. It is then eaten and another piece selected. These 1.5-to-2-inch-long fish must be considered active grazers and have evidently developed this rather specialized feeding technique to utilize an available food source.

Filter Feeders—Gizzard Shad

Broadly defined, all plankton-eating fishes can be classified as particulate feeders or filter feeders. Particulate feeders capture prey individually while filter feeders use their gill rakers as a sieve to strain plankton from the water. A fish may employ both particulate and filter-feeding mechanisms. Species which utilize both types evidently alter their behavior according to the available plankton (Durbin 1979). This is an adaptive advantage. Larval fish and most filter feeders are obligate planktivores. Presumption of gill raker feeding mechanisms are based, to some extent, on studies of gill rakers and stomach contents of various species. This includes such fish as the gizzard shad (Durbin). Among the largest of all fishes (e.g., whale shark, basking shark, and manta rays) filter feeding has obviously been successful from a size standpoint. Filter feeders do not pursue and capture prey items individually, but rather hold the mouth open with the gill rakers flared and feed by swimming. Water entering the mouth is strained through the sievelike gill rakers before exiting through the branchial arches. When the fish is not feeding, the gill rakers lie flat within the mouth cavity and do not filter water.

Analysis of swimming speeds and respiratory rates indicate that rapid acceleration and deceleration (e.g., prey pursuit) is more costly of energy than maintaining a steady cruising speed. The implication for filter feeders which maintain a steady speed while feeding is that they are more efficient than particulate feeders (Durbin 1979).

Sound data on filter feeding is generally lacking in regard to mechanisms, efficiencies, and selection. Becker (1983) reports that the earliest food of gizzard shad is probably protozoans. At a size of 20 mm (0.8 inch) shad feed almost entirely on small zooplankton. At 30 mm (1.2 inches) there is an increase in phytoplankton. Bodola (1966) reports that gizzard shad are filter feeders and their food varies depending on location and prey availability. For example, shad in open water feed mostly on free-floating phytoplankton. Gizzard shad also evidently pick up bottom debris and sand when food is plentiful. This suggests that sand is used to grind food items.

Sucking Feeders—White Sucker

Larval white suckers (0.5 to 1.0 inch) have an oblique mouth and feed near the surface on protozoans, diatoms, small crustaceans, and bloodworms. When the mouth migrates to the ventral position, the fish feed on or near the bottom. Both adult and juvenile white suckers feed throughout the day but are more active at night. Adults generally move into shallow water to feed after dark. They are largely omnivores. Food items include fish and fish eggs, mud, plants, mollusks, insects, diatoms, desmids, rotifers, crustaceans, and protozoans (Becker 1983). Despite reports to the contrary, Schneberger (1972), after examining several hundred white sucker stomachs, found only occasional fish eggs and concluded that it does not make a special effort to seek out fish eggs but inadvertently ingests them with other food.

There is a shift in the type of invertebrate food consumed with increasing size as well as with season. Cladocerans may constitute 60 to 90 percent of the food in summer. In production ponds where chironomid larvae are present, white suckers do well. Where filamentous algae cover the bottom, sucker production may be zero (Becker 1983; Scott and Crossman 1973).

Scraping Feeders—Mountain Sucker/Chiselmouth

An unusual feeding modification is found to a varying extent among some of the suckers and the cyprinid chiselmouth. Under most circumstances mountain suckers feed on algae and other attached material. Food is scraped from stones by use of the cartilage-sheathed lower jaw. They have been observed pulling themselves along while feeding with the expanded, suction cup-like mouth and scraping food from both the top and bottom of stones, even feeding upside down on various structures (Minckley 1973).

Feeding of adult chiselmouths is very specialized and consists of scraping its chisel-like lower jaw along rocks or other bottom objects for distances of 0.8 to 1.0 inch. This behavior consists of quick dives to algae-covered objects. They consume large quantities of filamentous green algae and diatoms, but the filamentous algae is presumably not digested (Scott and Crossman 1973).

Parasitic Feeders—Sea Lamprey

The ammocoetes of sea lamprey are sedentary filter feeders whose summer diet consists primarily of plant and animal material. Such items as filamentous green algae, detritus, diatoms, desmids, and protozoans have been identified in the diet (Scott and Crossman 1973). Following the ammocoete period when transformation occurs and the oral hood changes into a sucking disc, sea lampreys begin to feed parasitically as soon as prey can be found. Little growth occurs during winter, and although lampreys may be attached to hosts during this period, they may not be feeding. Attachment does not positively indicate feeding, for they have been observed attached to inanimate objects such as boats (Scott and Crossman).

The adults live as external parasites of fishes in fresh water and of fish and other aquatic vertebrates in marine environments. Attachment to a host is by use of the suctorial disc and is usually low on the body. Teeth on the tongue are used to rasp a hole in the skin and may at times penetrate to the body wall allowing the lamprey to feed on eggs or gut contents of the host. Generally, they feed on body fluids and blood, using the glandular secretion lamphredin to slow coagulation and aid in muscle tissue breakdown at the point of ingestion. A lamprey may stay on a particular host for less than 30 to over 200 hours. As many as four lampreys may be attached to one host. Species of economic importance which are attacked include lake trout, lake whitefish, chubs, white suckers, rainbow trout, channel catfish, and many others (Scott and Crossman 1973).

Sea lamprey is not generally considered a sport fish in North America. In

Europe it is prized as food and is caught in winter and grilled, fried, canned, and variously prepared. Its adverse effects on fish important in recreational fisheries have been well documented in the Great Lakes. Here its once tremendous population contributed to the severe decline of several species of commercial importance.

Relation to Growth and Reproduction

All fish must feed to provide energy for metabolism and growth. In most cases, fish feed on a daily basis. Many species important to recreational fisheries feed in a manner conducive to catching them on artificial lures which mimic natural foods. Mouth parts and mouth location are indicators of the manner of feeding. Small fish eat more per day per unit of body weight than do large individuals (Bond 1979). The amount of food eaten is related to the amount of tissue being created; larger fish require less food for tissue development and utilize the majority of energy intake for maintenance metabolism. Some adjustment for nutritive value also occurs, and a lesser amount of high-nutrition foods is required. As temperatures rise, the metabolic rate increases, and oxygen demand increases. The oxygen saturation level in water also decreases as temperatures rise, which more rapidly increases the oxygen demand, and, potentially, the level of stress. Active fishes need more oxygen than inactive ones to maintain acceptable body tissue oxygen levels. Other factors affecting metabolism include the species of fish, their size and condition, and the amount of carbon dioxide in the water. Fishes respond to stress by increasing their rate of respiration. Rainbow trout, for example, have a normal breathing rate of about 80/min, but when exercised it increases to 100/min (Bond).

Individuals of a given species have a genetic potential for growth that is particular to that species (Bond 1979). This potential may be modified by environmental factors. Temperature and available food are two factors that may modify growth, either increasing or reducing the final adult size. Abundance of food in a warm environment may allow a particular individual or population to achieve greater size than in cold waters or in an area of scarce food. Within a species, cool temperatures (northern latitudes) generally result in fish that grow slower, are somewhat smaller, and live longer than their southern counterparts.

To reproduce, fish must obtain sufficient nutrient input to allow development and maturation of the gonads. As maturation approaches in many species, a large percentage of the diet is incorporated into the sex products, often at the expense of maintenance of other tissues. The GSI is a useful measure of the status of sexual maturity. It can be monitored on a periodic basis to indicate time of sexual maturation and spawning.

Locomotion

Varying degrees of movement are necessary for fish to feed, migrate, and escape predators or adverse environmental conditions. The necessity for a particular fish to move is related not only to its habits but to its habitat. Some species may move only a very short distance (less than 100 yards) in their entire lives. Others range over hundreds or thousands of miles. Movement may be either slow and somewhat leisurely as in feeding bullhead catfishes or very rapid as in prey capture or avoidance of predators by cutthroat trout. The mechanisms of movement are also highly varied.

Travel or locomotion may be defined as passive or active. Passive travel includes drifting with the currents in oceans, lakes, or streams, and generally applies to eggs, larvae, or young. Active travel may be either upstream or downstream or from one location to another. A third method of travel is movement by external forces. There are documented accounts of fishes being picked up by strong wind currents in water spouts and later deposited elsewhere in rains (Dees 1967). Some fish-eating birds transport fish and fish eggs from one water body to another. Humans are the most active transporters of fish.

Locomotion and speed are related to body form. The swifter fish are essentially cylindrical or fusiform shaped, but other, more laterally or dorsally compressed fish, prevail in quiet or deep water. Modifications to survive in extremely swift current are particularly notable in the fishes of the Colorado River basin. Such species as the humpback chub and the bonytail demonstrate extreme modification that allow them to remain on the bottom and not be swept away or to fight the current.

Mechanisms of Locomotion

The caudal fin is of primary importance for sustained swimming speed for most species and for all fishes where high- or burst-speed activity is important. Other fins are used for propulsion to a lesser extent. The pelvics are used by most species to assist in rapid starts. Fins other than the caudal are for somewhat specialized movements such as maintaining depth and position. Median fins are used as keels in maintaining an upright position but also for maneuvering. Pelvic and pectoral fins may serve as keels but generally function in maneuvers such as climbing and diving, banking, turning, and stopping. In deep-bodied fishes, such as the sunfishes (*Lepomis* spp.), the pectoral fins are used in an upward thrust for stopping.

The movement of a fish's body can be characterized as a wave motion which starts near the head and continues through the tail. Tail beat frequency or the rate of the wave form traveling over the length of the body varies with speed as well as size and species (Lagler et al. 1977). They indicate that fish species variation exists in the outward swimming movement associated with muscle action. This lends itself to a simplified movement classification scheme for fishes based on three categories: anguilliform or eel-like; ostraciform or trunkfishlike; and carangiform or jacklike. The anguilliform type of locomotion is generally serpentine in nature resembling a crawling snake or swimming eel. In eels this swimming motion is brought about by sequential and alternate contractions of the muscles on either side of the body. Ostraciform locomotion is a wigwag motion especially notable in the sculling action of the tail. This motion is achieved by simple alternate contraction of all the muscle segments on one side of the body and then the other, causing the short tail to swing back and forth like a paddle. The carangiform locomotion, which is by far the most common, involves a fish driving itself forward by side-to-side sweeps of the tail. This motion is brought about by alternate contractions of myotomes of first one side of the body and then the other starting at the head and traveling backward.

Two types of muscles are present in almost all species of fish. The red muscles, highly obvious on salmonids, appear down the lateral extension of the body and comprise from 1 to 20 percent of the muscle tissue, depending on habitat. This muscle is used for sustained or low-speed swimming activity and functions aerobically. White muscle, which comprises a large percentage of the body of most species of fish, is utilized for high-speed bursts and acceleration swimming. White muscle generally functions anaerobically. Variations between the extent of the highly vascularized red muscle and the white muscle give a clue to the fish's characteristic movements.

Swimming Speeds

Speed used by various fishes may be grouped into three categories. Routine activity or cruising (sustained) speed is that at which the fish moves from one place to another. Maximum or prolonged sustainable speed is the speed a fish can maintain for lengthy intervals. Top speed or burst (sprint) speed can be maintained only for short durations and generally occurs when a fish is avoiding a predator or is actively pursuing prey. It may also be used when a fish is startled.

One of the primary considerations of swimming speed for a fish is the history of velocities to which it has been acclimated. That is, a fish that has been reared in velocities of 3 to 4 feet per second will be better able to cope with velocities in that range than a fish of the same species and size which has been reared in velocities of 0.5 to 1 feet per second.

Diana (1980) reports movements of northern pike monitored for five to fifty-one days by surgically implanted ultrasonic transmitters. The pike were inactive summer and winter during 80 percent of the 889 five-day unit intervals monitored. No regular change in diel activity was noted, except that pike were much more active at night. Swimming velocities calculated from gross displacements were a maximum of 42 cm/sec (0.91 body lengths/second, average 23.1 cm/sec 0.45 body lengths/sec).

Webb (1975) reports that sustained speed can be maintained for 200 minutes or longer and is used in activities such as routine cruising for forage, station holding, and territorial behavior. Prolonged speed can be maintained for periods from 15 seconds to 200 minutes and is strongly related to physiological criteria for individual species (an average capability is taken to be 100 minutes for these speeds). Burst speed can be maintained for approximately 15 seconds. Speeds are commonly expressed in body lengths per second. A rule of thumb, which must be interpreted with some caution, is ten body lengths per second for maximum sprint performance (Webb 1975; Haley 1966). Fatigue times for two salmonids demonstrate that, within the range of sustained activity, these fishes are capable of maintaining speeds of two to three body lengths per second for in excess of 90 minutes, whereas burst speeds of nine body lengths per second can be maintained for 6 to 10 seconds (figure 14.1). Salmonid swimming ability, as with most species, is related to body length (table 14.1). Fishes must achieve certain minimal velocities to pass migration barriers (table 14.2).

Locomotion Forms Other than Swimming

People typically think that fishes move by swimming. However, many species also burrow, walk, skip, crawl, soar, fly, or propel themselves by jets. Lampreys may at times attach themselves to hosts and not feed. Rather, the host is used to move them from one place to another. Inanimate objects may also be used in this fashion.

Some species of fish crawl along the bottom or on land. Species using

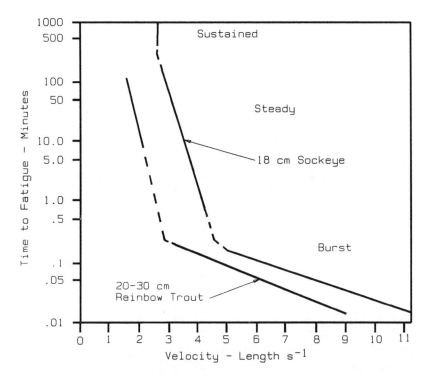

Figure 14.1.   Fatigue time for two species of salmonids.

Table 14.1. Swimming abilities of average-size adult salmonids (Reiser and Bjornn 1979; Bell 1986).

Species	Crusing Speed (200 minutes)	Sustained Speed (100 min. avg.) feet per second	Darting Speed (15 seconds)
Brown trout	0–2.2	2.2–6.2	6.2–12.7
Common carp	0–1.2	1.2–4.0	4.0–8.5
Chinook	0–3.4	3.4–10.8	10.8–22.4
Coho	0–3.4	3.4–10.6	10.6–21.5
Grayling	0–2.6	2.6–7.0	7.0–14.5
Lamprey	0–1.0	1.0–3.0	3.0–6.5
Shad	0–2.5	2.5–7.3	7.3–15.3
Sockeye	0–3.2	3.2–10.2	10.2–20.6
Steelhead	0–2.0	2.0–13.7	13.7–26.5
Sucker	0–1.5	1.5–5.4	5.4–10.5
Trout	0–2.0	2.0–6.4	6.4–13.5
Whitefish	0–1.6	1.6–4.5	4.5–9.2

Table 14.2. Depth and velocity criteria past which adult salmonids will migrate (Reiser and Bjornn 1979).

Species	Minimum Depth (inches)	Maximum Velocity (feet per second)
Steelhead trout	6.0	8.0
Large trout	6.0	8.0
Trout	4.7	4.0

varied forms of movement generally have moderate to extreme adaptations of either the pectoral fins or the pectorals and the caudal fin. One of the most widely known species that travels on land is the walking catfish which is present in warm water in several southeastern states and possibly in Nevada. It has distressed fisheries biologists by "walking" out of ponds from which the biologists have attempted to eradicate it with toxicants and traveling to a more suitable habitat.

Some fishes travel through the air from short to moderately long distances. Members of the salmon family are well known for their leaping characteristics when hooked as well as during migration, particularly spawning migrations. Leaps during spawning migrations are associated with the necessity to ascend high falls or other obstacles. Flying fish have been observed to travel distances of a quarter of a mile at a speed of 18 mph alongside ships. When they begin to lose altitude they rapidly beat their tails in the peak of waves and again achieve a gliding position. In almost all cases where adaptations for alternate travel mechanisms have developed, moderate to extreme adaptations of the body form and/or fins have occurred.

Age and Growth

Data on the age of a fish stock and its rate of growth are used to assess the condition of that stock with respect to reproduction, age and sexual maturity, longevity, growth rate, and optimum size for capture. Chapter 11 discusses the necessity of age and growth data, as well as philosophies and techniques for its application. Chapter 15 includes a discussion of age and growth information in the context of life history.

Interspecific and Intraspecific Relations

Competition among or between species can be divided, for discussion purposes, into three categories: resource, niche, and habitat partitioning. Competition for food and other resources both within and between species may play a central role in patterning of these relationships. Each species has habitat and reproductive requirements. These include adequate suitable food, shelter, and an acceptable level of oxygen. Niche partitioning may be interrelated to qualitative patterns in food size differences between species and size class differences in food use, as well as mixed competition/predation interactions in fishes (Sale 1979; Moermond 1979; Werner 1979).

Matheson and Brooks (1983) document habitat segregation for populations of mottled sculpin and Potomac sculpin in Macon Creek, Virginia. Habitat partitioning was most obvious in terms of current velocity and substrate type. Two groups were defined: male and immature Potomac sculpin preferred slow current and silty substrates over beds of aquatic vascular plants, while female and immature mottled sculpin preferred faster current and larger substrate particles or gravel beds. Male mottled sculpin and female Potomac sculpin were somewhat intermediate between these two groups in habitat preference. The possibility of interactive segregation between these two species exists. Despite lack of agreement among evolutionary biologists as to the causative factors, closely related organisms in sympatry often partition available resources. Further, interactive segregation or the magnification of interspecific ecological differences in areas of sympatry has been demonstrated in some organisms.

One of the major regulators of population size in fishes is compensatory mortality in juvenile stages. In salmonids this mortality is known to be density dependent, although disagreement exists on the importance of interspecific competition at the fry stage. The extent of inter- and intra-specific competition with older classes leading to density-dependent mortality has not been quantified but has been limited to estimates of predation by these factors on fry. Kennedy and Strange (1980) report that survival of trout fry is reduced by almost half when salmon parr are resident in the stream. They report that the results found in their stream work reflect changing patterns of competition for available stream resources following two introductions of salmon. Niche segregation and partial habitat preference in each species are suggested by these findings, in that both streams were only carrying about two thirds of their salmonid crop capacity prior to the introduction of salmon. The question then becomes whether displacement results from competition or whether competition does not occur because displacement has occurred. The extent of niche overlap in each age class of species which can be quantified from depth, flow, and feeding preferences should be the subject of continuing investigation.

Three species of sculpins (reticulate, torrent, and Paiute) overlapped and were strongly related to substrate characteristics in a study by Finger (1982). Finger reports that the reticulate sculpin occurs throughout the river system on all substrates, the torrent sculpin is found only where rock is present, and the Paiute sculpin is restricted to riffles that contain loose, cobble-sized rocks with many interstitial spaces. Local use of habitat by each species is strongly related to the presence or absence of other sculpin species. Reticulate sculpin use both pools and riffles where it exists alone, and is found in highest density near cover where it coexists with the riffle-inhabiting torrent sculpin. Reticulate sculpin occurs primarily in pools and in lower density than when alone. Paiute sculpin and torrent sculpin segregate within riffles. Finger further reports that the interactive mechanisms in this study were not thoroughly investigated, but predation, interference, and exploitation competition apparently complement each other in maintaining the spatial segregation of these three species. In this instance the niche interrelationships are of central importance to an understanding of the distribution and subsequently the abundance of the species involved. Both community structure over a short period of time and the long-term evolutionary pathways developed by coexisting organisms are strongly influenced by species interactions.

Competition for food between two resident sucker populations and introduced rainbow trout during the summer of 1977 in Payne Lake, Alberta, was reported by Barton and Bidgood (1980). Cladocerans, mostly *Daphnia,* were the major food for all three species, particularly in July and August, being 15.9 percent of the total food volume present in rainbow trout diet, 33.7 percent of white sucker diet, and 74.2 percent of longnose sucker diet for the four-month study period. Chironomid larvae were also important in the diet of the species in 1977, contributing, by volume, 18.3 percent for rainbow trout, 21 percent for white sucker, and 4.7 percent for longnose sucker. Certain items eaten by rainbow trout (Hymenoptera, 17.3 percent; Coleoptera, 6.2 percent; Chironomidae pupae, 11.9 percent) were scarce or absent in sucker diets. When these foods were unavailable for rainbow trout there was direct competition between trout and suckers for *Daphnia* and chironomid larvae. Feeding selectivity for *Daphnia* by all three species was apparent since copepods, also common in the lake, were virtually absent in the diets.

Magnan and Fitzgerald (1982) report the spatial distribution, food habits, and growth of an allopatric brook trout population compared with a trout population coexisting with creek chub. Sympatric trout differed in spatial distribution and food habits from allopatric trout suggesting a niche shift of the trout when they live with creek chub. Also, although there is a certain overlap in diet and spatial distribution, sympatric populations of the two species differed on these resource axes. However, growth of sympatric trout is not clearly related to the presence or absence of the creek chub, suggesting that factors other than interspecific competition may affect growth in the seven study lakes.

Paine, Dodson, and Power (1982) report that resource partitioning among four species of darters (Percidae: *Etheostoma*) in an Ontario stream was investigated by determining diet and relative abundance in two habitats. The four species partitioned both food and habitat resources. Rainbow darter and fantail darter dominated the riffles, the former taking prey from rock surfaces, the latter taking prey from between and beneath rocks. Least darter and johnny darter dominated the weed beds, the former feeding on prey on and around plants, the latter feeding on benthic prey. Diets were closely related to morphology, but habitat use was not. Identifying the difference of habitat versus food partitioning is difficult because microhabitat and foraging habitat may be nearly identical.

Gibson (1981) presents data on behavioral interactions between juvenile coho salmon, Atlantic salmon, brook trout, and steelhead trout in an artificial stream. His studies indicate that the more aggressive steelhead will displace any of the other three species from preferred locations, based on dominance by size. Dominant species demonstrated the best growth in all experiments. This work can be interpreted as a caution to introduction of nonnative species on existing populations of fish with sport or commercial value.

Associations

The species of fish and the types of habitat determine which fishes live together compatibly. This assumes there has been no undesirable stocking and no natural disasters. High, cold, clear, infertile bodies of water may have only one to three species, such as cutthroat trout, grayling, and brook trout. Further down the drainage where the flow is much greater, the water warm, at times turbid, and rich in nutrients, there may be twenty or more species including four or five sunfishes, two to four catfishes, several minnows and suckers, and sometimes walleye and northern pike.

Black bullhead and one or more species of sunfish often live together in warm, turbid, sometimes intermittent streams that will support no other fish. Sculpins are said to be good indicators of trout streams; at least they are often found together. Largemouth bass and bluegills are stocked together in ponds. They also live in close proximity in the wild, always to the benefit of the bass.

Perhaps the best example of habitat dictating the species present is the case of a stream being dammed, thus drastically altering the environment. Consider, for example, a thirty-mile section of a medium-sized, cool, turbid, in places fast-flowing mountain river that is impounded. The new habitat is a deep, cold, stratified reservoir, with a clear, cold stream for some miles below the dam. The original habitat supported native minnows and suckers, adapted to the fast current, the turbidity, and the water level fluctuations. There were also small numbers of common carp and green sunfish. The trouts were cutthroat and rainbow. There was one catfish (the channel cat) and mottled sculpin. After impoundment, some of the native minnows and suckers found the area totally inhospitable. The overriding negative factor was the lack of spawning ground. Other species of these two families, from upstream impoundments and better adapted to the changed conditions, took over. Brown and lake trout were the dominant salmonids. There were limited numbers of cutthroat and rainbow trout, primarily inshore and near or in the feeder streams, and a modest population of kokanee salmon. (Stocks of all species in the reservoir had either been present upstream or were stocked.) Channel catfish remained in small numbers. There were isolated populations of smallmouth bass, but no other centrarchids. Cutthroat trout and mottled sculpin were the only fishes in the stream below the dam. The water was too cold for reproduction of the native minnows and suckers.

It is sometimes difficult to determine what species have evolved and lived together over a long time, since few waters have escaped stocking. Some of the stocked species appear to fit into the ecological pattern, but many are disruptive. What may appear to be ecologically compatible species may be the result of one species keeping the numbers of another more prolific one in check by predation. Or the various species may have slightly different food or space requirements and not be competitive. Tolerance of another species or just another fish varies widely in the fish world.

Body Forms

In a very general sense, all fishes are similar. Most have gills for extracting oxygen from an aquatic medium, fins, and scales. In general, the body characteristics of head, trunk, and tail, as well as fins, can be readily recognized. However, the differences among species are almost as numerous as the numbers of species themselves.

Fins on most fishes are conspicuous features. The fins of modern fishes are supported by skeletal material and are composed of two types—paired and unpaired. Unpaired fins include the dorsal, caudal, and the anal fin; paired fins, the pectorals and pelvics.

One distinguishing characteristic is body form, which can be used to determine, to a certain extent, the fish's way of life. Fishes that are relatively fast swimming are streamlined and may be somewhat laterally compressed (e.g., trouts and black basses). Fishes that are capable of quick bursts of speed, but which do not sustain constant rapid motion, are generally laterally compressed (e.g., sunfishes). Fishes spending a large portion of their time on the bottom are generally flattened dorsoventrally (e.g., freshwater sculpins).

Modifications to facilitate both habitat and niche exploitation are numerous. The slender caudal peduncle and the large dorsal hump of the Colorado River drainage humpback chub and the bonytail are indications of modifications facilitating survival in extremely swift water. The flattened dorsoventral shape of ictalurids and the presence of barbels indicate both a bottom-dwelling tendency and the use of taste-smell organs for food location. Methods of reproduction also reflect the habitat in which a particular species survives. Many trouts, chars, or salmons typically prepare a nest which protects the eggs and emerging young from high-velocity currents, preventing the eggs and/or fry from being swept into less suitable rearing areas. In lower velocity streams and where predators are present, catfishes make elaborate nests and/or provide parental guardianship of both eggs and fry. Other species of fish such as the common carp insure survival by extremely high fecundity.

Observations of body form, fin shape, and size provide useful initial information on habitat, feeding, and swimming characteristics. More detailed observation of reproductive mechanisms, amount of red and white muscle, and final adult size can result in basic data on aspects of a species' way of life.

Relation to Humans

The relationship of humans to fish is multi-faceted. Fishes provide sport for anglers, food for millions of people, and byproducts which are feed for domestic animals. Fishes are kept in aquaria for study by ichthyologists and hobbyists. They are used to research new methods of disease control and to test water pollution or toxicant levels in water supplies. The diversity of fish life itself is an interesting study. Because no two species are alike (no two individuals are exactly alike), the amount of diversity and information available is enormous. Bond (1979) reports that the first known fishlike vertebrates occurred in the fossil record of the early Cambrian Period over 500 million years ago. All major groups of living jawed fishes were in existence by the middle of the Devonian, some 400 million years ago. Fishes can be studied in relation to what they do, where they are, what they eat, what they are eaten by, how they reproduce, their size, or how long they live. In all of these categories the diversity is tremendous. For instance, in reproduction fishes may produce only a very few eggs or more than a million. Some fishes, such as guppies and mosquitofish, produce young alive. Parents may provide no care and simply broadcast eggs and sperm or they may provide parental care for the eggs and for the young for several weeks. All of these aspects make interesting areas of study.

As humans continue to modify the environment in which they live, there must be a continued awareness of and concern for the existence of fishes as coinhabitants of this planet. This awareness must recognize alterations and consider alternatives which will lessen impact to fishes important to humanity. This should include not only species which are important for sport or commercial use, but those which have or can make important natural history contributions to knowledge of this vast group of organisms with which we have coevolved.

Literature Cited

Barton, B. A., and B. F. Bidgood. 1980. *Competitive Feeding Habits of Rainbow Trout, White Sucker and Longnose Sucker in Payne Lake, Alberta.* Fisheries Research Report, Fish and Wildlife Division, No. 16. 28 pp.

Becker, G. C. 1983. *Fishes of Wisconsin*. Madison: University of Wisconsin Press. 1052 pp.

Bell, M. C. 1986. *Fisheries Handbook of Engineering Requirements and Biological Criteria*. Portland, Oreg.: Fish Passage and Evaluation Program, Corps of Engineers, North Pacific Division. 290 pp.

Bodola, A. 1966. *Life History of the Gizzard Shad*, Dorosoma cepedianum *(LeSueur), in Western Lake Erie*. U.S. Fish and Wildlife Service Fisheries Bulletin 65(2):391–425.

Bond, C. E. 1979. *Biology of Fishes*. Philadelphia, London, Toronto: W. B. Saunders Company. 514 pp.

Bregazzi, P. R., and C. R. Kennedy. 1980. The Biology of Pike *Esox lucius* L., in a Southern Eutrophic Lake. *Journal of Fish Biology* 17(1):91–112.

Danilenko, T. P. 1983. The Reproductive Cycle of the Pike *Esox lucius* L. in the Kanev Reservoir. *Hydrobiological Journal* 18(4)(1982):21–27.

Dees, L. T. 1967. *Rains of Fishes*. Leaflet Number 513. Washington, D.C.: U.S. Department of the Interior, U.S. Fish and Wildlife Service. 5 pp.

Diana, J. S. 1980. Diel Activity Pattern and Swimming Speeds of Northern Pike *(Esox lucius)* in Lac Ste. Anne, Alberta. *Canadian Journal of Fisheries and Aquatic Sciences* 17(9)1454–58.

Durbin, A. G. 1979. Food Selection by Plankton Feeding Fishes. Pp. 203–18 in H. Clepper, ed., *Predator-Prey Systems in Fisheries Management*. Washington, D.C.: Sport Fishing Institute.

Finger, T. R. 1982. Interactive Segregation among Three Species of Sculpins *(Cottus)*. *Copeia* 1982(3):680–94.

Gibson, R. J. 1981. *Behavioural Interaction Between Coho Salmon* (Oncorhynchus kisutch), *Atlantic Salmon* (Salmo salar), *Brook Trout* (Salvelinus fontinalis), *and Steelhead Trout* (Salmo gairdneri) *at the Juvenile Fluviatile Stages*. Canadian Technical Report of Fisheries and Aquatic Sciences 1029. St. Johns, Newfoundland: Research and Resource Services, Department of Fisheries and Oceans. 116 pp.

Grimm, M. P. 1981. Intraspecific Predation as a Principal Factor Controlling the Biomass of Northern Pike *(Esox lucius* L.). *Fisheries Management* 12(2):77–79.

Haley, R. 1966. Maximum Swimming Speed of Fish. Pp. 150–51 in A. Calhoun, ed., *Inland Fisheries Management*. Sacramento: California Department of Fish and Game.

Kennedy, G. J. A., and C. D. Strange. 1980. Population Changes after Two Years of Salmon *(Salmo salar* L.) Stocking in Upland Trout *(Salmo trutta* L.) Streams. *Journal of Fish Biology* 17(5):577–86.

Lagler, K. F., J. E. Bardach, R. R. Miller, and D. R. M. Passino. 1977. *Ichthyology*. Second Edition. New York: John Wiley and Sons. 506 pp.

Magnan, P., and G. J. Fitzgerald. 1982. Resource Partitioning between Brook Trout *(Salvelinus fontinalis* Mitchill) and Creek Chub *(Semotilus atromaculatus* Mitchill) in Selected Oligotrophic Lakes of Southern Quebec. *Canadian Journal of Zoology* 60(7):1612–17.

Mann, R. H. K. 1982. The Annual Food Consumption and Prey Preferences of Pike (*Esox lucius*) in the River Frome, Dorset. *Journal of Animal Ecology* 51(1):81–95.

Matheson, R. E., Jr., and G. R. Brooks, Jr. 1983. Habitate Segregation between *Cottus bairdi* and *Cottus girardi:* An Example of Complex Inter- and Intraspecific Resource Petitioning. *American Midland Naturalist* 110(1):165–76.

Milton, D. A., and A. H. Arthington. 1983. Reproduction and Growth of *Craterocephalus majoriae* and *C. scercusmascarum* (Pices: Atherinidae) in South-Eastern Queensland, Australia. *Freshwater Biology* 13(6):589–97.

Minckley, W. L. 1973. *Fishes of Arizona*. Phoenix: Arizona Game and Fish Department. 293 pp.

Moen, T., and D. Henegar. 1971. Movement and Recovery of Tagged Northern Pike in Lake Oake, North and South Dakota, 1964–68. Pp. 85–93 in G. E. Hall, ed., *Reservoir Fisheries and Limnology*. Washington, D.C.: American Fisheries Society. Special Publication 8.

Moermond, T. C. 1979. Resource Partitioning: A Dynamic Competitive Balance. Pp. 303–10 in H. Clepper, ed., *Predator-Prey Systems in Fisheries Management*. Washington, D.C.: Sport Fishing Institute.

Neitzel, D. A., and C. D. Becher. 1985. Tolerance of Eggs, Embryos, and Alevins of Chinook Salmon to Temperature Changes and Reduced Humidity in Dewatered Redds. *Transactions of the American Fisheries Society* 114(2):267–73.

Nikolsky, G. V. 1963. *The Ecology of Fishes*. Translated from Russian by L. Birkett. London and New York: Academic Press. 352 pp.

Paine, M. D., J. J. Dodson, and G. Power. 1982. Habitat and Food Resource Partitioning among Four Species of Darters (Percidae: Etheostoma) in a Southern Ontario Stream. *Canadian Journal of Zoology* 60(7):1635–41.

Reiser, D. W., and T. C. Bjornn. 1979. Habitat Requirements of Anadromous Salmonids. Number 1 in a series by W. R. Meehan, ed., *Influence of Forest and Rangeland Management on Anadromous Fish Habitat in the Western United States and Canada*. Portland, Oreg.: U.S. Department of Agriculture, Pacific Northwest Forest and Range Experiment Station, General Technical Report PNW–96. 54 pp.

Reiser, D. W., and R. G. White. 1981. Incubation of Steelhead Trout and Spring Chinook Salmon Eggs in a Moist Environment. *Progressive Fish-Culturist* 43(3): 131–34.

———. 1983. Effects of Complete Redd Dewatering on Salmonid Egg Hatching Success and Development of Juveniles. *Transactions of the American Fisheries Society* 112(4):532–40.

Ringler, N. H. 1979. Prey Selection by Benthic Feeders. Pp. 219–30 in H. Clepper, ed., *Predator-Prey Systems in Fisheries Management*. Washington, D.C.: Sport Fishing Institute.

Rudd, J. T. 1965. The Ice Fish. *Scientific American* 213(5):108–14.

Sale, P. F. 1979. Habitat Partitioning and Competition in Fish Communities. Pp. 323–32 in H. Clepper, ed., *Predator-Prey Systems in Fisheries Management*. Washington, D.C.: Sport Fishing Institute.

Schneberger, E. 1972. *The White Sucker, Its Life History, Ecology and Management.* Wisconsin Department of Natural Resources, Publication No. 245–72. 18 pp.

Scott, W. B., and E. J. Crossman. 1973. *Freshwater Fishes of Canada.* Ottawa: Fisheries Research Board of Canada. 966 pp.

Sigler, W. F. 1949. Life History of the White Bass, *Lepibema chrysops* (Rafinesque), of Spirit Lake, Iowa. *Iowa Agricultural Experiment Station Bulletin* 366:203–24.

———. 1958. The Ecology and Use of Carp in Utah. *Utah Agricultural Experiment Station Bulletin* 405:63 pp.

Sigler, W. F., and R. R. Miller, 1963. *Fishes of Utah.* Salt Lake City: Utah State Department of Fish and Game. 203 pp.

Sigler, W. F., and J. W. Sigler. 1987. *Fishes of the Great Basin.* Reno: University of Nevada Press.

Webb, P. W. 1975. *Hydrodynamics and Energetics of Fish Propulsion.* Bulletin of Fisheries Research Board of Canada, No. 190.

Werner, E. E. 1979. Niche Partitioning by Food Size in Fish Communities. Pp. 311–22 in H. Clepper, ed., *Predator-Prey Systems in Fisheries Management.* Washington, D.C.: Sport Fishing Institute.

15. The Investigative Steps and Writing of a Fish Life History

A fish life history is written on information from literature, experience, research, and general knowledge. It may be brief or extensive depending on the amount of material available and its intended use. Fishery biologists rely on life history information to aid in making management decisions.

Data collected or collated during a life history study or writing serves both a scientific and a practical value. Information obtained in a scientific and systematic fashion is valuable not only for subsequent study and management of that species, but also aids in making inferences about other phylogenetically or spatially related species. Additionally, fundamental biological principles in studies of evolution, phylogeny, ontogeny, or ecology can be derived from or supported by scientifically supported data.

Many or few subheadings may be used in constructing a life history. Here we suggest nine: importance/status; range and distribution; taxonomy-morphology and genetics; age and growth; morbidity and mortality; food and feeding habits; reproduction; habitat, ecology, and behavior; and management.

Valid scientific names and accepted common names should be used. The accepted nomenclature for North American fishes is the current list of the American Fisheries Society (Robins et al. 1980). In considering any general variability in the taxonomy, the author should discuss subspecific divisions such as races, forms, hybrids, and such genetic data as chromosome number and protein specificity. Creation of an artificial key may be desirable in the case of rare or questionable species to define and delineate key characters. For most species, all the information noted here may not be available, or in some cases, of interest. Generally, however, as much information as possible should be included in a life history.

Importance/Status

The importance or status of a species of fish may be evaluated economically and ecologically. A species may be important as a large-scale production game fish (e.g., bluegill sunfish, black bullhead) or as a trophy fish (e.g., muskellunge, steelhead trout). Certain game fish lend themselves to specialized and restrictive fishing (e.g., trout in fly fishing only streams). Many nongame fish are also important as human food, as well as forage for larger fish. Fish often are listed as nongame if they do not readily take a hook, if they are considered to not have sporting characteristics, or if they lack appeal to local anglers, bigmouth buffalo for example. Several species of highly piscivorous fish are important to biologists because they are used as a management tool in reducing numbers of undesirable fish (e.g., northern pike versus suckers). A number of species, such as Pacific salmon, are taken both for sport and commercially.

Some species may have a negative impact on the environment and also may be economically unimportant. The common carp is, for example, a generally negative ecological factor in many areas of North America, but in some areas it has economic importance. It cruises far and wide in search of food and in the process becomes a formidable competitor for small game fish that feed on aquatic insects. Carp degrade the environment by increasing turbidity, thereby reducing the depth of photosynthesis and subsequently primary production. However, in some areas they are eagerly sought as game and food fish and are therefore important. Some nongame fish, such as the Utah sucker, feed throughout their lives on the same food as used by young game fish.

Fish that neither have measurable economic worth nor exert obvious effects on the environment may nevertheless be of high ecological importance (Pister 1976). These are the rare, sometimes indigenous, and often unique species that form an integral part of the vast natural history complex (Cairns 1975). For instance, they may be links in the phylogenetic sequence, or they may have developed in response to an unusual environment, such as the humpback chub.

Under the Endangered Species Act, the U.S. Fish and Wildlife Service uses three categories to express the degree of danger confronting fish species. They are special concern, threatened, and endangered. Threats to the welfare or existence of a species are generally listed under one or more of five headings: present or threatened destruction of habitat, overutilization, disease, hybridization, or competition with exotic or transplanted species, and restricted natural range (Williams 1981). Any legally defined status under federal or state law should be included and discussed (see chapter 6).

Range and Distribution

The area inhabited by a species of fish may be described on a local, national, and/or worldwide basis. Both the historical and present range should be indicated. When the present range differs from the historical, the probable reasons should be given for the extension (e.g., transplanting) or the contraction (e.g., destruction of habitat by pollution or apparent inability of the species to adapt to a changing world). The range of a species is most realistically described by stream drainages rather than political subdivisions. If the relative or absolute abundance within the range is known, it should be given. The geological era or period in which the fish first appeared may be noted.

Taxonomy-Morphology and Genetics

In a life history text, a fish is generally described by stating its taxonomic characteristics in narrative form. In addition, there is a "picture in words" of the fish as it is in life. The general appearance, and particularly the color and markings (not found in most taxonomic keys), are emphasized even though several factors affect the appearance of fish. Many fish are more colorful during the breeding season (e.g., rainbow trout, Pacific salmon), and numerous fish produce breeding tubercles at this time (e.g., minnows and suckers).

The body form of many fish changes from the larval to juvenile to adult stage (Nikolsky 1963). The external morphological characteristics and the changes noted should be those of egg, embryo, larvae, subadult, and adult. These changes are governed by age, species, and size (e.g., smolting and the accompanying color change of anadromous fish). The sex of some fish is most evident during the breeding season when color, body form, and malformations vary between sexes (e.g., color in sunfishes, deeper body in female trouts, hooked jaw in some male salmonids).

Frequently, chemical and physical factors in an environment cause changes in appearance (e.g., water clarity affects pigment coloration—melanophores expand in clear water). Occasionally the changes are dramatic. The quantitative data should indicate individual and geographic variations as well as morphological variations of any distinguishable subpopulations (Rosa 1962). Genetic data such as protein specificity and chromosome count (karyotyping) when properly collected and preserved is useful in distinguishing both among species and between races within species. Genetic information can be included under the headings of description or reproduction as well.

Age and Growth

The age composition of a single species is defined as the proportion of fish in each age group. This age breakdown extends from the numerous young to the few old fish. The term age and growth means age composition and rate of growth. The former is the actual age of each individual fish at capture. The latter is a composite of the size of each fish in relation to age at time of capture plus the back-calculated growth for earlier years of life. For purposes of example, the age composition of a sample is shown in table 15.1. This is based on the actual age of each fish at capture plus its size at the end of each earlier year of life (see chapter 11).

Within limits, age and growth studies reflect the effects of ecological factors such as abundance and quality of food, spawning status, physical and chemical habitat characteristics, and presence and abundance of competitors. The age at which fish spawn, the number of times they spawn, and when they reach senility are stated. Periods of growth, both within a year and within a lifetime, are revealed by repeated sampling at different times of the year. Age and growth data, along with other information, are used in fisheries management to establish levels of harvest and general welfare of the population.

It is generally necessary to use several types of gear if all sizes of fish are to be collected in the proper proportion (see chapters 7, 8, 9, and 10). The number of places and types of gear used in a body of water where collections should be made is determined in part by the mobility of different size (age) groups. It is often necessary to collect during both day and night. One key to success is to collect and measure (or more often estimate rather than actually measure) the lengths of large numbers of fish. The handling of large numbers of fish makes sample reliability more probable, since the length-frequency groups can better be related to age groups. Collection gear and place will affect many aspects of a life history.

Buck and Cross (1952) define overpopulation as a stunted condition of various game and panfishes caused by reduction of growth to a point where overlapping size ranges of different age groups introduce excessive interclass competition. Bennett (1962) points out the purely arbitrary nature of defining stunting but emphasizes that extremes of below average growth reflect this condition. Stunting, in most cases, is the result of extreme competition for a limited amount of food, resulting in reduced growth rates.

Age composition of a stock may be studied in relation to a population or a subpopulation, a catch, or in regard to such ecological variants as depth of water, distance from shore, species density, time of day, or season (Vigg

Table 15.1. Example of age composition of a fish sample.

Age group	0	1	2	3	4
Numbers	10,000	100	60	40	30
Estimated mortality (%)	—	99	40	33	25

1981). The sex ratio of the population may be studied in relation to size and age of fish, season of the year, and fish proximity to the spawning grounds.

The length-weight ratio of each population by age, time of year, and habitat conditions may be determined. Condition factor, which may change with age, is a reflection of the robustness of individual fish or of a group of fish and may be calculated from weight-length data with the formula $K = W/L^3$ (see chapter 11). Longevity involves the average life expectancy, the maximum age attained by fish, and the variation in that maximum within each population by sex and in relation to growth rate (Rosa 1962).

Morbidity and Mortality

Only a relatively small percentage of a year class/cohort survives the first year. Mortality is generally highest the first few days or weeks. Theoretically, the rate of mortality (or total mortality) by age group and sex may be determined from a reliable sample. While this is true in theory, determination of the mortality factors of the 0 age group (young) is a complex and time-consuming process (Kramer 1969). That is, the sample must have the same proportion in each age (and sex) group as exists in the wild. However, in practice, this is rarely achieved. Estimates can be made only if the sample is unbiased. Assuming the sample is representative of the entire population (generally not true), then both the mortality rate, by age group, and the longevity may be estimated. When this is true, the percentage of mortality for each group can be determined (Everhart and Youngs 1981). Consider, for example, the data presented in table 15.1.

Survival from age 0 (young of the year) to the 1-year group is 1 percent. The same procedure may be followed in determining differential sex mortality.

Mortality tables are determined using correctly aged and adequately sampled fish. Determining the correct age of fish may be difficult, but collecting a reliable age composition sample is extremely difficult.

Mortality is related to those fish that are not available for harvest. Haskell (1965) suggests that much of the time we may be "looking in the wrong direction" in both research and management. Efforts have been concentrated on population studies, creel surveys, and in related areas, all of which have yielded much information. We continue to measure and remeasure these indices. Haskell believes that the big unknown in fishery management does not center on the fish that survive but those that disappear. He says we should delve deeply into the causes of fish mortality from embryonic to senile stages. Efforts or studies that resulted in a reduction of mortality at any age would have obvious benefits. What has been done to prolong the life of the human population can be cited as an example of what could be done in fisheries. The percentage of elderly people has increased enormously in the last two or three decades. Quite obviously this was not accomplished by selective breeding nor by a study of those who survived to old age. Rather, the efforts that increased longevity dealt with environmental and physiological factors and control of diseases of younger age groups that are known to reduce the number of people in the older age groups.

According to Haskell (1965), present-day fishery research follows the general guidelines set up by Drs. Moore and Embody, which were established for the specific purpose of cataloging the limnological and fishery components of a body of water. These methods are not appropriate for the task of finding the causes of mortality in fish. Recent research on adult salmon and steelhead losses in the Columbia River typifies efforts to reduce mortalities through research into causes of that mortality. Only after causes of mortality are known, can management techniques be developed and survival rates improved.

Parasites and disease can be discussed under a separate heading or as part of a broader topic. Parasites and diseases should be discussed in relation to organism type, mode of infection (vectors), stages of parasites that infect the fish, and intensity of individual and population infection. Other relevant factors include the degree of population infection and its effects on physiology and behavior. The food value of diseased individuals, effects on population density, and its ability to recover should be considered. Apparent injuries and abnormalities should be noted and described in relation to their nature and cause. It is also necessary to discuss the fishes' ability to regenerate and the general effect of the causative agent on physiology and ultimate survival (Rosa 1962).

Food and Feeding Habits

The terms food habits (diet) and feeding habits (mechanisms) refer to the items and amounts of food taken by a species and its manner (timing, duration, etc.) of taking the food. In fisheries literature, this distinction is not always clear.

In a food habits study, dietary items are recorded by number, volume, or frequency of occurrence, generally in relation to what is available; that is, the degree of preference shown by the fish. Selectivity indices can be useful in expressing a fish species' preference for selected food items (see chapters 12 and 14).

Feeding should be discussed in relation to time of day, place, general area, method of food capture, how foods are selected, frequency of feeding, abstention from feeding, and variations in feeding habits. The same discussion must consider food availabilities, season of the year, age, sex, and physiological condition of the fish. The types of foods that are eaten should be noted in relation to their relative importance in the diet as this affects and is affected by nutritive value, volume, times of feeding, and intervals between feedings (McMullin 1979; Koster 1955; Simpson 1949).

Reproduction

Any study of fish reproduction must include the manner of spawning or fertilization of the female or her gametes, the number and type of eggs or young produced, the age composition of the spawning population, general spawning habitat, the type of redd or nest, if used, and the manner of caring for eggs and young. The ways in which fish spawn vary so much that they almost defy description; however, individual requirements are specific and demanding. Adverse physiological or ecological factors may inhibit, delay, or prevent spawning. After the eggs are laid, even minute ecological changes may destroy eggs or larvae. A comprehensive study recognizes every stage in spawning, migration, and maturity in relation to the environment.

A complete study of reproduction may include a substantial number of factors under such categories as sexuality, maturity, mating, fertilization, gonads, and spawning (Rosa 1962). Detailed information on the genetic makeup of a species may be included. In unusual cases, fish may be hermaphroditic, heterosexual, or intersexual. Further, they may display sexual dimorphism. Under a discussion of maturity, the age at which the fish first matures (by sex, subpopulations, and size) should be determined. Mating habits of fish may be monogamous, polygamous, or more frequently promiscuous. Fertilization may be internal or external. All of the appropriate factors should be discussed.

Under the general heading of spawning, the following items should be included: age at maturity; the number of spawnings per year and in a lifetime; the spawning season, its beginning, peak, and end; the time of day; ages and sizes of fish participating; the age-time sequence of spawning of individuals in a population; ratio and distribution of sexes on spawning grounds; nature of mating acts; and variations in mating behavior. Factors that may influence or induce spawning such as water temperature, runoff, photoperiod, lunar or tidal cycles, size and age of fish, and latitude and altitude may be noted. The relation of time of breeding to that of related and/or associated fishes, location and type of favored spawning grounds, variations in timing and probable cause, and variations in acceptable spawning grounds are also relevant. A description of the spawn (defined as laid eggs either fertilized or unfertilized) should include size, shape, color, opacity, texture and type of membrane, degree of buoyancy, and adhesiveness (Rosa 1962).

The annual rates of reproduction versus mortality help forecast potential survival and, therefore, the yield of a population. Density-dependent factors such as cannibalism, food supply, and predation affect reproduction and survival, as do density-independent physical factors such as water movement, temperature, storms, direction and strength of the wind, and brood strength (Reiser and White 1981a, 1981b; Reiser and Bjornn 1979).

In a study of female gonads, the relation of gonad size and egg number to body length and weight as well as coefficients of fecundity (specific and relative fecundity—based on number of eggs/individual and number of eggs/unit-weight respectively) should be determined (Nikolsky 1963). The gonadal somatic index, or gonosomatic index, (GSI)—ratio of gonadal weight to total body weight—helps determine the beginning and peak of spawning and may provide an insight into the physiological effects of spawning (Nikolsky). The number of eggs or broods produced by a female during a year and a lifetime, as well as variations in fecundity in relation to size, is important. The number of spawn or young produced and the nature of the environment may be correlated (Reiser and White 1981a, 1981b).

Habitat, Ecology, and Behavior

The chemical, physical, and biological characteristics of a body of water where a fish lives define its environment. Water chemistry largely determines productivity (e.g., low levels of nutrients or high acidity). Topography, nature, and temperature of a body of water dictates species of fish and productivity, (e.g., shallow eutrophic lakes versus deep oligotrophic lakes). Environment may be judged acceptable from a species perpetuation standpoint if fish are able to grow to maturity and reproduce. Describing a theoretically ideal habitat and a very poor habitat can generate better understanding of a species' ecological limitations. Fish such as walleye may seek waters in which they grow rapidly but which are so warm they cannot or do not spawn (Prentice and Clark 1978).

In each stage of life, that is, embryo, fry, juvenile, and adult, fish have differing requirements (Starrett and Fritz 1965). Schools of young fish often seek a different type of habitat than do adult fish (Reiser and Bjornn 1979; Joseph et al. 1977). Physical and chemical variables in the habitat are tolerated or have been adapted to by fishes. Tolerances may vary by development stage or by time of year. Each variable should be discussed as it affects the species and individuals.

The hardiness (adaptability) of individuals of a species is determined by their limits of tolerance to such factors as changes in either environment or feeding grounds, or to handling either in the field or in an artificial environment. Hardiness ratings change with species, age, size, and physiological condition.

Competitors, predators, and associates should be discussed in relation to a fish species and its abundance and reactions, all in relation to age, size, and sex. How each of these three groups of fish affect the welfare of the population should be considered.

Fish migrations and local movements should be described in relation to the extent of travel and its function, direction, time and season; changes in patterns; age and physiological condition of the fish; and temperature and other environmental factors.

Management

Fishery management practices vary with consumer demand, fish availability and productivity, and general agency management philosophy (Bennett 1962). Management generally has as its primary goal a maximum sustainable yield and an equitable distribution of the take (Larkin 1980). Anderson (1975) and Voitland and Duttweiler (1984) present arguments for including other aspects of recreational fisheries in management goals besides numbers of fish creeled. If management goals involve large numbers of small, fast-growing, warmwater fishes, regulations may be very liberal regarding gear, minimum size limit, and creel. The production and harvest of trophy fish demand different standards. Valuable food or sport fish not recognized as such by the public may necessitate an angler education program. Fish that are vulnerable to fishing only a few days or weeks of the year have to be harvested when available. Examples of this type of fish include: Bonneville cisco in Bear Lake, Utah-Idaho, which are harvested by dipnet during a two-week spawning run starting in mid-January; and steelhead trout in the Columbia River, which are harvested in the upper reaches of the Snake, Clearwater, and Salmon rivers during the final stages of their spawning runs. The points that give a species prestige with the public vary widely among geographic areas, individual anglers, and other less easily defined factors. A fishery manager quickly learns and accepts prevailing opinions regarding high-status fish. They may then try to modify these opinions to fit the available fishery or manipulate the fishery to fit the opinions. A discussion of existing management practices versus previous or planned changes may also be appropriate. Concern for other species of importance should be incorporated into management plans for specific species because a change in the ecosystem (e.g., feeding rate or place, numbers of adults) may affect other important species.

The efficiency of a fishery may be adversely affected by reducing the number of units open to fishing, limiting the catch either by day, possession, or season, and restricting the type of gear. Population protection involves such procedures as closing areas during the spawning season, limiting size and efficiency of gear, or rarely, restricting the sex of the fish taken during a period of time or for an entire open season (see chapter 3). For example, the state of Idaho has, in recent years, allowed a catch-and-release fishery on steelhead trout in the Clearwater River above Lewiston. This management technique allows anglers to enjoy all aspects of fishing for this trophy fish except the actual keeping of the fish. At the same time, management has conducted an education program that helps anglers understand the need to preserve the wild stock and is providing information and education so anglers can distinguish between wild and hatchery-reared steelhead. A program encouraging the voluntary release of all wild steelhead has been instigated.

It should be remembered that management objectives for a particular fishery, unless there is a valid reason to impose restrictions, should tend toward providing maximum opportunities to catch fish for the highest possible numbers of the fishing public. Endangered species or other species that require temporary or permanent protection are obviously in a special category. Management must be tied to species-specific cases. Even good "trout" management can encounter difficulties between species such as cutthroat trout and brown trout.

The physical environment can be modified by regulation of water flow (volume), control of water level (wetted perimeter), prevention of soil erosion, construction of fishways or screens, improvement of spawning grounds and by habitat improvement that may include building artificial reefs, and controlling domestic and industrial pollution (see chapter 3). In small farm ponds, aquatic vegetation may be reduced. Fish foods in the form of invertebrates or pellets are provided in artificial situations. Control of parasites and diseases is occasionally possible. Population manipulation by such practices as total erradication using toxicants, or rarely, spot poisoning of nongame fish, is being used less often than formerly, but may be a viable management option in some situations.

Examples

Rainbow Trout *Oncorhynchus mykiss* (Richardson)*

Importance/Status. The rainbow trout is the most important trout in North America, if its contribution to the fishery is considered as the main criteria. This species is continuously stocked in substantial numbers in the United States and Canada. It fights well, leaping repeatedly when hooked. Whether eaten smoked, fresh, or canned, it is highly palatable. Total catch and catch rate are generally very high.

Rainbow is the easiest and most economical of all trout to raise and is stocked extensively over a wide range of waters from farm ponds to large rivers. Some stocked strains are domesticated, but in the eyes of hatchery workers and some anglers, this is not important. Commercial trout farmers in North America raise and sell more rainbow trout than any other coldwater species. In south-central Idaho, the Thousand Springs area alone produces millions of pounds of rainbow trout each year for commercial markets.

A sea-run form of rainbow, the steelhead, adds an important dimension to the species in the Pacific Northwest and other locations. It grows faster and is larger than most inland rainbow. It is eagerly sought by anglers, and a catch of one fish per day satisfies many. Kamloops, another form of rainbow, grows best in large lakes that contain an abundance of forage fish, and is also eagerly sought by anglers.

Range and Distribution. The original range of the rainbow trout is the Pacific Coast of North America, mainly west of the Rocky Mountains in the north and the Sierra Nevada in the south. It extends from Rio del Presidio, Durango, Mexico, to the Kuskokwim River, Alaska. Stocking throughout North America has greatly increased its range. It has also been introduced into New Zealand, Australia, Tasmania, South America, Africa, Japan, southern Asia, Europe, and Hawaii (Lee et al. 1980).

In Canada it is present in British Columbia and from the Avalon Peninsula of Newfoundland, across the southern portions of the provinces from Nova Scotia to Ontario, north through central Manitoba and central Saskatchewan, to northern Alberta and the Yukon Territory (Scott and Crossman 1973).

*Adapted from Sigler and Sigler 1987.

Steelhead, the anadromous form of rainbow trout, originally was native to the Snake River, Idaho, and its tributaries as far upstream as Shoshone Falls. Dams have now reduced this range to below Hell's Canyon and to the drainages of the Salmon and Clearwater rivers, Idaho. The Kamloops has been introduced from British Columbia into Pend Oreille Lake, Idaho (Simpson and Wallace 1978).

Behnke (1981) points out that several desiccated basins north of Lahontan and west of Alvord basins in Oregon, all have the interior form of rainbow trout (redband trout) as their native trout. The redband trout is the interior form of rainbow trout which is not presently recognized taxonomically but considered a part of *Oncorhynchus mykiss*.

Taxonomy-Morphology and Genetics. The body is elongate, moderately compressed, and rather deep. The rainbow has cycloid scales which number 120 to 160 in the lateral series. The head is short, the snout is rounded, eyes are moderate, and the mouth is terminal. There are small sharp teeth on the jaws and tongue, but they are poorly developed in the vomer and are absent from the basibranchial plate (the base of the tongue) between the lower ends of the gill arches. The dorsal and anal fin-rays both number eleven and the caudal fin is slightly forked (Robert Behnke, personal communication, 1983; Simpson and Wallace 1978).

The color in rainbow trout is variable and depends on habitat, size, and sexual condition. Lake residents tend to be silvery, but stream residents and spawners have darker and more intense colors.

An adult rainbow is normally bluish to olive green on the back; the sides are lighter and silvery with a reddish horizontal band; the belly may either be white or silvery. There are generally irregular black spots on the back, side, and head. The dorsal, adipose, and caudal fins are also spotted. Although there are no nuptial tubercles during the breeding season, minor changes in head and mouth shape occur among spawning males.

Young trout are silver to white on the sides, blue to green on the dorsal surface, and white on the belly. There are generally five to ten irregular marks on the dorsal fin and five to ten oval parr marks on the sides and straddling the lateral line. Steelhead and Kamloops are generally more silvery than other forms of rainbow.

Some stocked rainbow trout in the Great Basin have a trace of a cutthroat slash along the crease of the lower jaw. This presumably indicates some cutthroat ancestry.

Age and Growth. A size of 2 to 4 pounds is average for adult nonmigratory rainbow trout, excluding Kamloops, that are considered large at 6 to 8 pounds.

Simpson and Wallace (1978) report a Kamloops weighing 37 pounds from Pend Oreille Lake in 1947; Idaho steelhead trout range from 4 to 20 pounds. Steelhead weighing up to 28 pounds have been taken from the Columbia River (Don Chapman, personal communication, 1983). The all-tackle hook-and-line record (probably a steelhead) weighing 42 pounds, 2 ounces, was from Belle Island, Alaska (Kutz 1982). Kamloops, when introduced from Pend Oreille Lake into other areas in Idaho, show no better growth than other forms of rainbow trout (Simpson and Wallace). This response is at times true of other strains of rainbow trout when introduced outside their natural habitat. This may in some cases be due to differences in available forage.

Rainbow trout markedly larger than 2 to 4 pounds in size are often piscivorous. However, there are some notable exceptions to this rule. Kamloops introduced into some fishless lakes which contained vast numbers of *Gammarus* and other large crustaceans grew to 14 pounds in as few as three years. According to Scott and Crossman (1973) growth rate in these lakes often decreases as the trout population increases. However, they state that other lakes are able to maintain populations of fish to 4 or 5 pounds on invertebrates alone. The invertebrate population in Paul Lake, British Columbia, was adequate to produce large Kamloops before the introduction of the redside shiner. The shiner competed with the trout for food to the detriment of the Kamloops. By feeding on the shiners, some trout were larger after the shiner was introduced, the tradeoff being a few large trout for a larger population of moderate-sized ones (Johannes and Larkin 1961).

As soon as a rainbow trout fry absorbs its yolk sack it emerges from the gravel. At this time it is from 0.375 to 0.625 inches long. By the end of the first summer it may be 4 inches long and weigh 0.4 ounces.

Rainbow trout from high mountain lakes may live only four to five years. Simpson and Wallace (1978) believe the rainbow trout life-span is fairly short. Moyle (1976) states the oldest known rainbow, age eleven years, was from Eagle Lake, California, an alkaline former arm of ancient Lake Lahontan. Steelhead, Moyle believes, occasionally reach nine years of age, but the maximum age for most rainbow is seven years. In a Logan River, Utah, study only about 3 percent of the stocked rainbow lived through the first winter. Ones stocked in lakes have a higher overwintering survival rate than stream-stocked rainbow. Life expectancy may be as low as three or four years in stream and lake populations of rainbow, but for steelhead and Great Lakes populations it would appear to be six to eight years (Scott and Crossman 1973).

Morbidity and Mortality. Fishing is by far the number one mortality factor for rainbow trout, since it is easily caught and avidly sought. Most domestic strains of rainbow trout are relatively short lived in the wild. The eggs (embryos) of rainbow trout that spawn in the spring in high-flow turbulent streams face both stream bottom scouring and siltation. Both the numbers and health of emerging fry are affected. Fry are pushed downstream into undesirable habitat during high flows. According to Wydoski and Whitney (1979) although 95 percent of wild rainbow trout eggs may be fertilized, only 65 to 85 percent survive the embryonic stage. But according to Don Chapman (personal communication, 1983), the average embryonic stage survival may be as low as 30 percent.

Temperatures of 60°F are ideal for rapid growth of rainbow trout (Leitritz and Lewis 1980). Female rainbow are most productive when water temperatures do not exceed 56°F (or preferably 54°F) for six months before spawning. Temperatures of 42°F or lower also adversely affect egg development (Leitritz and Lewis). Water temperatures in the high seventies, except under otherwise ideal conditions, may cause stress which predisposes disease, or, in some cases, death. According to Leitritz and Lewis, yearlings and adults can withstand temperatures up to 78°F but only for a short time. The upper lethal temperature for fingerling Kamloops was 75.2°F when they had been acclimated at 51.8°F (Black 1953). Scott and Crossman (1973) state rainbow trout are most successful in habitats with temperatures of 70°F or slightly lower, but will survive higher temperatures if there is cooler, well-oxygenated water into which they can retreat. Moyle (1976) notes rainbow trout will survive temperatures as high as 82°F if they have been acclimated to the high temperature and oxygen is at saturation. The rigors of spawning induce stress that not infrequently results in up to 100 percent postspawning mortality (Wydoski and Whitney 1979; Simpson and Wallace 1978). This applies to long-distance migrating fish. Idaho steelhead populations which migrate in excess of 700 miles and through several dams to reach the spawning grounds, probably have few repeat spawners. On shorter coastal rivers, repeat spawners may constitute 5 to 20 percent of steelhead runs, and in some cases, repeat spawners may equal up to 38 percent of the run in Gualala River, California (Robert Behnke, personal communication, 1983).

Mortality is highest in stocked rainbow when they are planted in relatively small numbers in a stream that contains a wild trout population. The planted fish are evidently unable to break into the established hierarchies. Diseases carried by the planted fish may also decimate them without seriously affecting the wild stocks. When the stocked trout are put there in large numbers, the effect of sheer numbers appears to disrupt the established hierarchies of the wild fish, making them more vulnerable to angling and dislocation. This factor does not operate in lake stocking (Moyle 1976).

Rainbow trout are subject to predation by fish, diving birds, and mammals. Logan River, Utah, has produced several prize-winning brown trout of 14 to

23 pounds. The associates of these large, fast-growing brown trout are a few mottled sculpin, moderate numbers of mountain whitefish, and large numbers of stocked rainbow trout.

Changes in water quality may adversely affect rainbow trout populations. Quick changes in pH may have particularly drastic effects. Rainbow do well in waters of pH from 7 to 8 but can survive in waters ranging from 5.8 to 9.6 pH. The Eagle Lake, California, population has adapted to the highly alkaline water of a pH from 8.4 to 9.6.

Food and Feeding Habits. Young rainbow trout feed on small benthic invertebrates, primarily insects and crustaceans. More than any other trout, rainbow tend to feed on algae and, to a lesser extent, on vascular plants. This may in part be incidental and the nourishment slight. The rainbow continues a primarily invertebrate diet until it reaches a size of one to two pounds; then there is a tendency to become piscivorous. Although rainbow trout primarily feed on drift organisms, they also rise to the surface and feed. This is a fact exploited by anglers fishing with flies.

Stream-dwelling rainbow tend to feed heavily on abundant drift organisms in the summer, but still actively feed on bottom invertebrates. The rate of feeding and available food are considerably reduced in winter, primarily due to an almost complete lack of drift organisms, and perhaps more importantly, to the fact that cold water has reduced the rainbow's metabolic rate.

Moyle (1976) believes rainbow trout in lakes have a greater propensity for becoming piscivorous than do stream-dwelling rainbow, although he states that fish do not normally become an important element in the diet until trout are 12 to 14 inches long. In some high-altitude, low-productivity mountain lakes, rainbow may be forced to feed heavily on terrestrial insects. In general, they feed on various invertebrates, including zooplankton, crustaceans, such as *Gammarus;* at older ages they may continue to feed on these organisms or become piscivorous.

Reproduction. Nonmigratory wild rainbow trout normally spawn in the spring; however, strains have been developed that spawn every month of the year. In Washington state there is a winter and a summer spawning run of steelhead, although some probably migrate upstream in every month of the year (Wydoski and Whitney 1979). Both winter and summer steelhead runs spawn in the spring.

Rainbow trout are stream spawners and, unlike the chars (*Salvelinus*), are rarely able to spawn in lakes. There are, however, instances where rainbow populations have spawned in lakes, generally on gravel bars formed near the outflow. Some of these populations are rainbow-cutthroat hybrids. Spawning rainbow trout seek gravel bars in streams in the spring when water temperatures reach 50°F. The female digs a redd in the gravel by turning on her side and beating her tail up and down. In this way the gravel is cleaned and a pit excavated that is longer and deeper than her body. Redd building takes place day and night. When the female is ready to spawn, she rests near the bottom, at the center of the redd, then the dominant male moves into position parallel to her. Both bodies are pressed together and the eggs and milt are released in a few seconds. The male courts the digging female and aggressively tries to drive other males away from the redd. There is generally more than one male spawning with each female. As soon as the female has spawned, she immediately moves upstream to the edge of the nest and begins displacing gravel to cover the eggs. Scott and Crossman (1973) state females may dig and spawn in several redds with one or more males. Chapman questions this, believing the defense of a redd is a key adaptive mechanism and multiple redds are maladaptive (Don Chapman, personal communication, 1983).

Eggs usually hatch in four to seven weeks, and alevins take an additional three to seven days to absorb the yolk before becoming free swimming. At a water temperature of 50° F, eggs hatch in about thirty-one days (Leitritz and Lewis 1980).

The average age at first spawning is two to three years; some hatchery rainbow spawn at age one and some wild fish do not spawn for the first time until they are age five. A high percentage of some strains of hatchery rainbow do not spawn in the wild. Many others are caught and some do not adapt to the environment. Rainbow and cutthroat trout that spawn in the same area may hybridize.

According to Scott and Crossman (1973) individual rainbow have been known to spawn in as many as five successive years. The survival rate for repeat spawners, however, is often very low, probably less than 10 percent. Spawning mortality is close to 100 percent for spawning steelhead in Idaho (Simpson and Wallace 1978).

Habitat, Ecology, and Behavior. The rainbow trout has adapted to and prospers in a wide range of aquatic habitats, including large, deep lakes and small farm ponds. It lives in some of the largest rivers of North America and in small creeks with a flow of only a few cubic feet per second. Some strains of rainbow trout in lakes tend to stay close to shore, rarely moving into deep water except to avoid high temperatures. Other strains are far ranging and pelagic.

Optimum temperatures are 54 to 56°F for reproduction and 60°F or a few degrees above for growth. At low temperatures the rainbow can withstand low oxygen concentrations, if it is inactive. At high temperatures it requires oxygen levels near saturation. It survives in lakes ranging in pH from 5.8 to 9.6. Best growth is achieved in alkaline water of pH 7.2 to 8.4.

Stream-dwelling rainbow trout tend to be aggressive, establishing feeding territories which are defended against intruders. This territoriality is not evident in lake populations. In lakes, rainbow trout form schools and move about in a more or less systematic fashion in search of food and optimum temperature habitats. Generally, the area of movement is small. The area inhabited by stream-dwelling rainbow may be only a few hundred yards, or in some cases, it may be confined to one or two pools and the riffles just above them. Steelhead, in contrast to resident rainbow trout, are highly migratory. Some stocks of "resident" rainbow trout which are descendant of anadromous stock may migrate intermediate distances.

Management. The preservation of the major forms of rainbow trout can best be discussed separately. The maintenance of native runs of the anadromous steelhead trout is dependent on such habitat factors as dams, flows, water quality, quality spawning substrate, and rearing areas. Kamloops trout generally prosper in large lakes where there is an abundance of forage fish. It needs tributary streams with adequate physical and chemical characteristics for spawning. The Eagle Lake rainbow trout is both unique and has a restricted habitat. Measures to preserve this species for further study should be implemented. The remaining forms of rainbow can be lumped into two groups: the nonanadromous trout that reproduce in the wild and the many strains that are produced and stocked by hatcheries.

All forms of rainbow need an acceptable habitat, legal protection from excessive exploitation, and at times supplemental stocking. Some strains of hatchery-reared rainbow are stocked to be caught in a relatively short time. Overwinter mortality of these fish in streams is generally high and generally less in lakes. In this put-and-take type of management, it is not preservation but rather the opposite that is in order.

Largemouth Bass *Micropterus salmoides* (Lacepède)*

Importance/Status. The largemouth bass is highly prized and is the most popular warmwater sport fish in the United States with experienced anglers. Over all of its natural and introduced range, it more than makes up in size what

---

*Adapted from Sigler and Sigler 1987.

it may questionably lose to the smallmouth in sport quality. It was, along with the smallmouth, an important commercial species in Canada until 1936 when harvesting was restricted to sport fishing. It tolerates high temperatures, slightly turbid waters, and prospers in a wide range of habitats from large cool reservoirs to warm farm ponds.

Range and Distribution. The original range of the largemouth bass includes most of the eastern half of the United States and north to southern Quebec and Ontario. This includes the lower Great Lakes states, the central part of the Mississippi River system south to the Gulf of Mexico. It is native to Florida and north along the Atlantic Coast to Virginia. Through extensive stocking it now occurs over virtually the entire Atlantic Coast in fresh waters from Maine to Florida, west to Texas and northern Mexico, north through the eastern parts of New Mexico to North Dakota, and east across southern Canada to western New York. It has also been introduced in many parts of the western United States. It has been introduced in England, Scotland, Germany, France, South Africa, Hong Kong, the Phillipines, and Brazil (Lee et al. 1980).

Taxonomy-Morphology and Genetics. The dorsal surface and head of large-mouth bass are bright green to olive, and, in large fish, the sides are almost as dark. The ventral surface is milk white to yellow. A well-defined, wide, solid black lateral band sometimes extends continuously from snout to the posterior margin of the opercle in young; it is broken or inconspicuous in older fish. The sides of the head are olive to golden green with some scattered black pigment. The inside of the mouth, as well as the belly, is milky white. The eyes are brownish. Both dorsal and caudal fins are opaque green to olive, the anal and pelvic fins green to olive with some white. The pectoral fins are amber and clear (Simpson and Wallace 1978; Scott and Crossman 1973; Sigler and Miller 1963). After yolk sac absorption the young is pale green, in contrast to smallmouth bass young which is black. The caudal fin of the young is like that of the adults; bright colors are absent (Scott and Crossman).

The largemouth is moderately large and robust with an ovate body that is less laterally compressed and deeper than the smallmouth. The head is large, long, and deep, its length from 26.6 to 31.7 percent of total body length (Scott and Crossman 1973). It has a long, deep notch extending over both eyes. The opercle is bony to the margin and pointed. The mouth is large, terminal, and wide with the lower jaw reaching past the center of the eye in adults, a characteristic distinguishing it from smallmouth bass. Fine brushlike teeth occur on palatines, both jaws, vomer, and sometimes the tongue.

The first dorsal fin has ten spines and is deeply separated from the soft ray portion, another characteristic distinguishing it from the smallmouth. The pelvic fins are thoracic in position with one spine that originates under the first dorsal fin. The pectoral fins are rather short and broad with rounded tips, and thirteen to fifteen rays. The anal fin has three spines. The caudal fin is slightly forked and not long, but it is broad with rounded tips. Largemouth have ctenoid scales which are larger than those of smallmouth bass, with eight rows from the lateral line to the dorsal origin and fourteen to eighteen rows from the lateral line to the anal fin insertion. The lateral line of largemouth is complete, high, and only slightly arched. There are fifty-five to sixty-nine scales in the lateral series. The peritoneum is silvery and the intestine is well differentiated (Moyle 1976; Scott and Crossman 1973; Sigler and Miller 1963; La Rivers 1962). At times it may be confused with the spotted bass.

Age and Growth. The largemouth bass is fast growing as well as long lived. It is the largest of the sunfishes. Yearly growth rates vary with locale; they are higher in warmer, southern climates. Cold waters produce interruptions in growth. Growth is rapid after hatching from the initial size of about 0.1 inch. Available invertebrate food in appropriate sizes and water temperature affect the size reached the first year and have an effect on overwinter survival. In the southern edge of its range, it may grow year around. Largemouth bass in lower Snake River reservoirs (Bennett et al. 1983) have mean total lengths of 3.3, 5.8, 9.1, 11.5, 14.1, 16.5, and 17.4 inches for fish ages one to seven. Fish in colder climates grow slower and live longer. La Rivers (1962) states fish ages three to six years from Ruby Marsh, Nevada, are 7.0, 8.8, 12.8, and 15.8 inches respectively. Moyle (1976) states the maximum size is 30 inches and the maximum age sixteen years. The length at the end of each year for Lake Simcoe, Ontario, largemouth is 4.0, 8.0, 10.0, 12.0, 13.5, 14.5, 16.0, 17.0, 17.5, 18.0, 19.0, 19.8, 20.4, 21.0, and 21.4 inches for fish ages one to fifteen (MacCrimmon and Skobe 1970). In Cache Valley, Utah, the length, in inches, at the end of each year is 3.0, 5.6, 7.6, 10.4, 13.4, 15.5, 16.9, and 18.6 for fish ages one to eight (Sigler and Miller 1963).

Morbidity and Mortality. Largemouth bass embryos and fry are food for other predacious fish such as other sunfishes, walleye, yellow perch, and northern pike. It is also preyed upon by birds such as bittern, heron, and kingfisher. Even crayfish, dragonfly larvae, and predacious diving beetle larvae prey on young largemouth. Adverse water temperatures during spawning, intense wave action, nest desertion, fluctuating water levels, parasite-caused sterility, and food availability for fry are important decimating factors (Scott and Crossman 1973). Food availability for fry may be the most important factor creating strong and weak year classes, which are eventually reflected in the harvest.

Food and Feeding Habits. Adult largemouth bass are piscivorous. Food preferences change as size increases from primarily zooplankton to insects, to fish, crayfish, and frogs. In Lake Opinicon, Ontario, Keast and Webb (1966) report largemouth food habits for 1.2-to-2.0-inch fish as cladocerans, mayfly nymphs, amphipods, chironomid larvae, and other items such as copepods, waterbugs, and caddisfly nymphs. Largemouth bass 2 to 3.8 inches long eat 40 percent mayfly nymphs, 20 percent dragonfly and damselfly nymphs, 20 percent crayfish nymphs, and a few amphipods, chironomid larvae, and small fish. Over 3 inches, the preferred diet is 50 to 90 percent small fishes and 10 to 40 percent crayfish.

Food is taken at the surface morning and evening, but during midday largemouth feed in the water column and near the bottom. It is a sight feeder, often in schools near shore and close to vegetation. At water temperatures below 50°F, and during spawning and in winter, feeding is reduced. About four to five pounds of food is required to produce one pound of fish flesh. Largemouth bass eat such fish as carp, gizzard shad, bluntnose minnow, golden shiner, silvery minnow, yellow perch, pumpkinseed, bluegill, and to a lesser extent, largemouth bass. It can be considered a predatory omnivore (Scott and Crossman 1973). It readily eats small mammals that fall into the water and occasionally, ducklings.

Reproduction. Largemouth nests are generally shallow depressions fanned out by the male in sand-, gravel-, or debris-littered bottoms at depths of three to seven feet. Nests are often built next to cover. The largemouth spawns from late spring to midsummer (sometimes as late as August), with the peak of spawning in early to mid-June in Canada (Scott and Crossman 1973). In California, Moyle (1976) reports spawning activity in April when water temperatures reach approximately 59° F; Sigler and Miller (1963) report 62°F for northern Utah. It spawns for the first time in its second or third spring at seven inches or more. Spawning activity is similar to that of smallmouth, but the male is less vigorous in defense of the nest. Each female lays eggs in one to several nests, the total number ranging from 2,000 to 90,000, depending on her size. The eggs are adhesive and hatch in two to ten days. Sac fry spend five to eight days in the nest or nearby. Broods may be formed by fry from several nests and are protected to varying degrees by a male for about two weeks beyond swimup.

Habitat, Ecology, and Behavior. Largemouth bass inhabit the upper warm-water layers in small, shallow lakes or ponds, the shallow bays of large lakes, and, in some cases, large, slow rivers. It occurs in reservoirs over most of its range. It is generally found in association with soft bottoms, stumps, and extensive growths of a variety of emergent and submergent vegetation. Rarely is largemouth bass found in rocky situations which smallmouth bass typically inhabit. Movement is not extensive, usually less than five miles, and summer territories are smaller. It moves to the bottom in winter but is more active than the smallmouth bass and may provide an under-ice fishery. In the spring, previous spawning areas and summer territories may be reestablished. Largemouth bass can tolerate higher water temperatures than smallmouth bass, sometimes as high as 80°F. At temperatures in excess of 80°F, it becomes inactive, resting in shaded areas. It does not prosper in low oxygen concentrations (Moyle 1976; Scott and Crossman 1973; Sigler and Miller 1963).

Management. Stable water levels during spawning and reduction of fish competing with young largemouth will improve yearly production. Since it is an aggressive feeder, it is subject to overfishing and may on occasion need the protection of minimum slot length and/or number limits.

Various slot lengths (e.g., 15–18 inches protected) are frequently used in reservoirs where fishing pressure is heavy. Minimum lengths are in order where reproduction or early survival is a limiting factor. Often only a few (two to three) large fish (e.g., 24 inches or more) may be taken. Stocking is rarely necessary once an adequate brood stock is established in acceptable habitat. Members of bass clubs catch large numbers of largemouth bass, but they frequently return most or all of the catch. Their interest is somewhat different than that of the average bass angler in that they keep few fish and are interested mainly in large ones.

Literature Cited

Anderson, R. O. 1975. Optimum Sustainable Yield in Inland Recreational Fisheries Management. Pp. 29–38 in P. M. Roedel, ed., *Optimum Sustainable Yield as a Concept in Fisheries Management, Proceedings of a Symposium at the 104th Annual Meeting of the American Fisheries Society, September 9, 1974, Honolulu, HI.* Washington, D.C.: American Fisheries Society. Special Publication 9.

Behnke, R. J. 1981. Systematic and Zoogeographical Interpretation of Great Basin Trouts. Pp. 95–124 in R. J. Naiman and D. L. Soltz, eds., *Fishes in North American Deserts.* New York: John Wiley and Sons.

Bennett, D. H., P. M. Bratovich, W. Knox, D. Palmer, and H. Hansel. 1983. *Status of* the Warmwater Fishery and the Potential of Improving Warmwater Fish Habitat in Lower Snake Reservoirs. Completion Report for Contract Number DACW68–79–0057. Walla Walla, Wash.: U.S. Army Corps of Engineers. 451 pp.

Bennett, G. W. 1962. *Management of Artificial Lakes and Ponds*. New York: Reinhold Publishing Corporation. 266 pp.

Black, E. C. 1953. Upper Lethal Temperatures of Some British Columbia Freshwater Fishes. *Journal of the Fisheries Research Board of Canada* 10(4):196–210.

Buck, H., and F. Cross. 1952. *Early Limnological and Fish Population Conditions of Canton Reservoir, Oklahoma, and Fishery Management Recommendations*. Report to the Oklahoma Fish and Game Council. The Research Foundation, Oklahoma A & M College. 110 pp.

Cairns, J., Jr. 1975. Critical Species, Including Man, within the Biosphere. *Die Naturwissenschaften* 62:193–99.

Everhart, W. H., and W. D. Youngs. 1981. *Principles of Fishery Science*. Second Edition. Ithaca and London: Comstock Publishing Associates. 350 pp.

Haskell, D. C. 1965. Are We Looking in the Right Direction in Fishery Research? *Progressive Fish-Culturist* 27(2):105–8.

Johannes, R. E., and P. A. Larkin. 1961. Competition for Food between Redside Shiners (*Richardsonius balteatus*) and Rainbow Trout (*Salmo gairdneri*) in two British Columbia Lakes. *Journal of the Fisheries Research Board of Canada* 18(2): 203–20.

Joseph, T., W. J. A. Sinning, R. J. Behnke, and P. B. Holden. 1977. An Evaluation of the Status, Life History, and Habitat Requirements of Endangered and Threatened Fishes of the Upper Colorado River System. FWS/OBS–77/62. Contract performed for Western Energy and Land Use Team. Fort Collins, Colo.: U.S. Fish and Wildlife Service. 184 pp.

Keast, A., and D. Webb. 1966. Mouth and Body Form Relative to Feeding Ecology in the Fish Fauna of a Small Lake, Lake Opinicon, Ontario. *Journal of the Fisheries Research Board of Canada* 23(12):1845–67.

Koster, W. J. 1955. Outline for an Ecological Life History Study of a Fish. *Ecology* 36(1):141–53.

Kramer, R. H. 1969. *A Preliminary Bibliography on Extent and Causes of Early Mortality in Freshwater Fish*. FAO Fisheries Circular 307. 20 pp.

Kutz, R. 1982. *Freshwater Angling Records, Official-world, USA, and State*. Hayward, Wisc.: National Freshwater Fishing Hall of Fame. 57 pp.

La Rivers, I. 1962. *Fishes and Fisheries of Nevada*. Reno: Nevada State Fish and Game Commission. 782 pp.

Larkin, P. A. 1980. Objectives of Management. Pp. 245–62 in R. T. Lackey and L. A. Nielsen, eds., *Fishery Management*. New York, Toronto: John Wiley and Sons.

Lee, D. S., C. R. Gilbert, C. H. Hocutt, R. E. Jenkins, D. E. McAllister, and J. R. Stauffer, Jr. 1980. *Atlas of North American Freshwater Fishes*. Raleigh: North Carolina State Museum of Natural History. 854 pp.

Leitritz, E., and R. C. Lewis. 1980. *Trout and Salmon Culture*. Bulletin No. 164. Sacramento: California Department of Fish and Game. 197 pp.

MacCrimmon, H. R., and E. Skobe. 1970. *The Fisheries of Lake Simcoe*. Toronto: Ontario Department of Lands and Forests. 140 pp.

McMullin, S. L. 1979. The Food Habits and Distribution of Rainbow Trout and Cutthroat Trout in Lake Koocanusa, Montana. M.S. thesis. Department of Fisheries, University of Idaho, Moscow. 80 pp.

Moyle, P. B. 1976. *Inland Fishes of California*. Berkeley, Los Angeles, London: University of California Press. 405 pp.

Nikolsky, G. V. 1963. *The Ecology of Fishes*. Translated from Russian by L. Birkett. London and New York: Academic Press. 352 pp.

Pister, E. P. 1976. A Rationale for the Management of Nongame Fish and Wildlife. *Fisheries* 1(1):11–14.

Prentice, J. A., and R. D. Clark, Jr. 1978. Walleye Fishery Management Programs in Texas—A Systems Approach. Pp. 408–16 in R. L. Kendall, ed., *Selected Coolwater Fishes of North America*. Bethesda, Md.: American Fisheries Society. Special Publication 11.

Reiser, D. W., and T. C. Bjornn. 1979. Habitat Requirements of Anadromous Salmonids. No. 1 in a series by W. R. Meehan, ed., *Influence of Forest and Rangeland Management on Anadromous Fish Habitat in the Western United States and Canada*. Portland, Oreg.: U.S. Department of Agriculture, Pacific Northwest Forest and Range Experiment Station, General Technical Report PNW–96. 54 pp.

Reiser, D. W., and R. G. White. 1981a. *Influence of Streamflow Reductions on Salmonid Embryo Development and Fry Quality*. Research Technique Completion Report, Project A–058–IDA. Moscow: Idaho Water and Energy Resources Research Institute, University of Idaho. 154 pp.

———. 1981b. *Effects of Flow Fluctuation and Redd Dewatering on Salmonid Embryo Development and Fry Quality*. Research Technique Completion Report, Contract No. DE–AC79–79BP10848. Moscow: Idaho Water and Energy Resources Research Institute, University of Idaho. 85 pp.

Robins, R. C., R. M. Bailey, C. E. Bond, J. R. Brooker, E. A. Lachner, R. N. Lea, and W. B. Scott. 1980. *A List of Common and Scientific Names of Fishes from the United States and Canada*. Bethesda, Md.: American Fisheries Society. 174 pp. Special Publication 12.

Rosa, H. 1962. *Preparation of Synopses on the Biology of Species of Living Aquatic Organisms*. FAO Fisheries Biology Synopsis, No. 1. FP/S1 SAST-General. Rome: Fisheries Division Biology Branch, Food and Agriculture Organization of the United Nations. 16 pp.

Scott, W. B., and E. J. Crossman. 1973. *Freshwater Fishes of Canada*. Ottawa: Fisheries Research Board of Canada. 966 pp.

Sigler, W. F., and R. R. Miller. 1963. *Fishes of Utah*. Salt Lake City: Utah State Department of Fish and Game. 203 pp.

Sigler, W. F., and J. W. Sigler. 1987. *Fishes of the Great Basin*. Reno: University of Nevada Press. 425 pp.

Simpson, E. H. 1949. Measurement of Diversity. *Nature* 163:688.

Simpson, J. C., and R. C. Wallace. 1978. *Fishes of Idaho*. Moscow: University of Idaho Press. 237 pp.

Starrett, W. C., and A. W. Fritz. 1965. A Biological Investigation of the Fishes of Lake Chautauqua, Illinois. *Illinois Natural History Survey Bulletin* 29(1):1–93.

Vigg, S. C. 1981. Species Composition and Relative Abundance of Adult Fish in Pyramid Lake. *Great Basin Naturalist* 41(4):395–408.

Voitland, M. P., and M. W. Duttweiler. 1984. Where's the Humanity? A Challenge and Opportunity for the Fisheries Community. *Fisheries* 9(4):10–12.

Williams, J. D. 1981. Threatened Desert Fishes and the Endangered Species Act. Pp. 447–75 in R. J. Naiman and D. L. Soltz, eds., *Fishes in the North American Deserts*. New York: John Wiley and Sons.

Wydoski, R. S., and R. R. Whitney. 1979. *Inland Fishes of Washington*. Seattle: University of Washington Press. 220 pp.

Appendix A
Common and Scientific Names of Fishes*

Order Petromyzontiformes

Petromyzontidae—lampreys

sea lamprey   *Petromyzon marinus* Linnaeus

Order Squaliformes

Rhincodontidae—whale sharks

whale shark   *Rhincodon typus* Smith

Lamnidae—mackerel sharks

basking shark   *Cetorhinus maximus* (Gunnerus)

Order Acipenseriformes

Acipenseridae—sturgeons

white sturgeon   *Acipenser transmontanus* Richardson

Order Semionotiformes

Lepisosteidae—gars

shortnose gar   *Lepisosteus platostomus* Rafinesque

Order Amiiformes

Amiidae—bowfins

bowfin   *Amia calva* Linnaeus

Order Anguilliformes

Anguillidae—freshwater eels

American eel   *Anguilla rostrata* (Lesueur)

*Following Robins et al. 1980. *A List of Common and Scientific Names of Fishes from the United States and Canada* (Modified).

Osmeridae—smelts

| surf smelt | *Hypomesus pretiosus* (Girard) |
| rainbow smelt | *Osmerus mordax* (Mitchill) |

Esocidae—pikes

| northern pike | *Esox lucius* Linnaeus |
| muskellunge | *Esox masquinongy* Mitchill |

Order Cypriniformes

Cyprinidae—carps and minnows

chiselmouth	*Acrocheilus alutaceus* Agassiz and Pickering
goldfish	*Carassius auratus* (Linnaeus)
grass carp	*Ctenopharyngodon idella* (Valenciennes)
common carp	*Cyprinus carpio* Linnaeus
Utah chub	*Gila atraria* (Girard)
tui chub	*Gila bicolor* (Girard)
humpback chub	*Gila cypha* Miller
bonytail	*Gila elegans* Baird and Girard
least chub	*Iotichthys phlegethontis* (Cope)
golden shiner	*Notemigonus crysoleucas* (Mitchill)
common shiner	*Notropis cornutus* (Mitchill)
bluntnose minnow	*Pimephales notatus* (Rafinesque)
fathead minnow	*Pimephales promelas* Rafinesque
Colorado squawfish	*Ptychocheilus lucius* Girard
northern squawfish	*Ptychocheilus oregonensis* (Richardson)
roach	*Rutilus rutilus* (Linnaeus)
creek chub	*Semotilus atromaculatus* (Mitchill)
tench	*Tinca tinca* (Linnaeus)

Catostomidae—suckers

Utah sucker	*Catostomus ardens* Jordan and Gilbert
longnose sucker	*Catostomus catostomus* (Forster)
white sucker	*Catostomus commersoni* (Lacepède)
mountain sucker	*Catostomus platyrhynchus* (Cope)
cui-ui	*Chasmistes cujus* Cope
June sucker	*Chasmistes liorus mictus* Miller and Smith
blue sucker	*Cycleptus elongatus* (Lesueur)
lake chubsucker	*Erimyzon sucetta* (Lacepède)
bigmouth buffalo	*Ictiobus cyprinellus* (Valenciennes)
black buffalo	*Ictiobus niger* (Rafinesque)

Order Siluriformes

Ictaluridae—North American catfishes

| black bullhead | *Ameiurus melas* (Rafinesque) |
| yellow bullhead | *Ameiurus natalis* (Lesueur) |

brown bullhead	*Ameiurus nebulosus* (Lesueur)
channel catfish	*Ictalurus punctatus* (Rafinesque)
flathead catfish	*Pylodictis olivaris* (Rafinesque)

Clariidae—labyrinth catfishes

| walking catfish | *Clarias batrachus* (Linnaeus) |

Order Clupeiformes

Clupeidae—herrings

alewife	*Alosa pseudoharengus* (Wilson)
Atlantic menhaden	*Brevoortia tyrannus* (Latrobe)
Atlantic herring	*Clupea harengus harengus* Linnaeus
Pacific herring	*Clupea harengus pallasi* Valenciennes
gizzard shad	*Dorosoma cepedianum* (Lesueur)
threadfin shad	*Dorosoma petenense* (Günther)
Pacific sardine	*Sardinops sagax* (Jenyns)

Order Salmoniformes

Salmonidae—trouts

lake herring	*Coregonus artedii* Lesueur
lake whitefish	*Coregonus clupeaformis* (Mitchill)
sockeye salmon (kokanee)	*Oncorhynchus nerka* (Walbaum)
chinook salmon	*Oncorhynchus tshawytscha* (Walbaum)
Bonneville cisco	*Prosopium gemmiferum* (Snyder)
mountain whitefish	*Prosopium williamsoni* (Girard)
golden trout	*Oncorhynchus aguabonita* (Jordan)
cutthroat trout	*O. clarki* (Richardson)
Lahontan cutthroat trout	*O. c. henshawi* (Gill and Jordan)
rainbow trout (including steelhead)	*O. mykiss* (Richardson)
Atlantic salmon	*Salmo salar* Linnaeus
brown trout	*Salmo trutta* Linnaeus
bull trout	*Salvelinus confluentus* (Suckley)
brook trout	*Salvelinus fontinalis* (Mitchill)
Dolly varden	*Salvelinus malma* (Walbaum)
lake trout	*Salvelinus namaycush* (Walbaum)
Arctic grayling	*Thymallus arcticus* (Pallas)

Order Gadiformes

Gadidae—codfishes

Pacific cod	*Gadus macrocephalus* Tilesius
Atlantic cod	*Gadus morhua* Linnaeus
Pacific hake	*Merluccius productus* (Ayres)
pollock	*Pollachius virens* (Linnaeus)

Order Atheriniformes

Exocoetidae—flying fishes

California flying fish   *Cypselurus californicus* (Cooper)

Cyprinodontidae—killifishes

Devils Hole pupfish   *Cyprinodon diabolis* Wales

Poeciliidae—live-bearers

western mosquitofish   *Gambusia speciosa* (Baird and Girard)

guppy   *Poecilia reticulata* Peters

Atherinidae—silversides

California grunion   *Leuresthes tenuis* (Ayres)

Order Perciformes

Percichthyidae—temperate basses

white bass   *Morone chrysops* (Rafinesque)

yellow bass   *Morone mississippiensis* Jordan and Eigenmann

striped bass   *Morone saxatilis* (Walbaum)

Centrarchidae—sunfishes

green sunfish   *Lepomis cyanellus* Rafinesque

pumpkinseed   *Lepomis gibbosus* (Linnaeus)

warmouth   *Lepomis gulosus* (Cuvier)

bluegill   *Lepomis macrochirus* Rafinesque

redear sunfish   *Lepomis microlophus* (Günther)

smallmouth bass   *Micropterus dolomieui* Lacepède

largemouth bass   *Micropterus salmoides* (Lacepède)

white crappie   *Pomoxis annularis* Rafinesque

black crappie   *Pomoxis nigromaculatus* (Lesueur)

Percidae—perches

rainbow darter   *Etheostoma caeruleum* Storer

fantail darter   *Etheostoma flabellare* Rafinesque

least darter   *Etheostoma microperca* Jordan and Gilbert

johnny darter   *Etheostoma nigrum* Rafinesque

yellow perch   *Perca flavescens* (Mitchill)

snail darter   *Percina tanasi* Etnier

walleye   *Stizostedion vitreum vitreum* (Mitchill)

blue pike   *Stizostedion vitreum glaucum* Hubbs

Sparidae—porgies

sea bream   *Archosargus rhomboidalis* (Linnaeus)

Sciaenidae—drums

freshwater drum   *Aplodinotus grunniens* Rafinesque

Mugilidae—mullets

striped mullet   *Mugil cephalus* Linnaeus

Sphyraenidae—barracudas

Pacific barracuda   *Sphyraena argentea* Girard

Chaenichthyidae—icefish

icefish   *Chaenocephalus aceratus* (Lonnberg)

Scombridae—mackerels

skipjack tuna   *Euthynnus pelamis* (Linnaeus)
Atlantic mackerel   *Scomber scombrus* Linnaeus
albacore   *Thunnus alalunga* (Bonnaterre)
bluefin tuna   *Thunnus thynnus* (Linnaeus)

Xiphiidae—swordfishes

Atlantic swordfish   *Xiphias gladius* Linnaeus

Istiophoridae—billfishes

sailfish   *Istiophorus platypterus* (Shaw and Nodder)
blue marlin   *Makaira nigricans* Lacepède

Cottidae—sculpins

mottled sculpin   *Cottus bairdi* Girard
Paiute sculpin   *Cottus beldingi* Eigenmann and Eigenmann
Potomac sculpin   *Cottus girardi* Robins
reticulate sculpin   *Cottus perplexus* Gilbert and Evermann
torrent sculpin   *Cottus rhotheus* (Smith)

Order Pleuronectiformes

Pleuronectidae—righteye flounders

Arctic flounder   *Liopsetta glacialis* (Pallas)

Soleidae—soles

lined sole   *Achirus lineatus* (Linnaeus)

Appendix B
Techniques for Otolith Removal and Preparation

Removal Techniques

Removal of large otoliths from fish requires a vertical cut behind the eyes and removal of the otoliths with forceps (Radtke 1983; Williams and Bedford 1974) from the exposed cavity. Liew (1974) reports removing otoliths from eels by making a transverse incision through the ventral wall of the head region and a cut along the midline to the lower jaw to expose the roof of the mouth. Bone scissors are used to make a transverse cut on the lower side of the cranium and the cranium broken open to expose the auditory capsule. Temple, Price, and Murphy (1985) used a Dremel Moto-Tool® to split the dorsal surface of walleye skulls vertically from between the eyes to the back of the head.

Murie and Lavigne (1985) report on a novel method of obtaining otoliths from gut contents of piscivorous marine mammals. This limited data procedure may have application in some age and growth studies.

Storage

It may be possible to improve visibility of the otolith ring structure by storing them in alcohol, glycerine, or alcohol and glycerine mixtures. Formalin or other acid mediums should not be used as they may destroy the ring structure making them unreadable, and long-term storage in liquid may reduce clarity (Williams and Bedford 1974). Ethanol (95 percent) may be preferred, especially for juvenile or larval fishes. Jearld (1983) reports storage of sagittal otoliths in a 2:3 glycerine/alcohol solution for preservation and cleaning. Otoliths may be air dried and stored in labeled paper or plastic envelopes. Small otoliths are easily stored when mounted in resin on a microscope slide.

Preparation Techniques

The inner and outer surfaces of otoliths should be ground, washed in water, and bleached. They then may be etched in hydrochloric acid for two to four minutes depending on size, dehydrated in alcohol, cleaned in xylene, and mounted (Fagade 1980). Another approach is to preserve semicircular canals in 100 percent ethanol, then remove the otoliths, clean them in bleach (5.25 percent sodium hypochlorite), rinse them in xylene and 95 percent ethanol, and air dry them (Wilson and Dean 1982).

Sectioning

In many cases, whole otoliths are too thick and opaque to read and must be sectioned. The section can be made across any regular plane, but ease of handling necessitates either a lateral section across the length or a longitudinal section across the width (Williams and Bedford 1974). Breaking rather than cutting provides a more rapid solution when there are large numbers of otoliths. To avoid discrepancies in generally underestimating the age, the break must be through the center of the nucleus. Otoliths of some species are easier to interpret when the surface to be read has been ground flat. Clearing of the smooth surface can be accomplished with xylene, various oils, or creosote (Williams and Bedford).

An inexpensive method of sectioning walleye otoliths uses a Dremel Moto-Tool® for dissecting walleye skulls and for grinding the otoliths. They can then be embedded in a 4-ml clear, epoxy-bonding compound and allowed to harden for twenty-four hours. This results in an otolith in resin which can be sectioned using the Dremel Moto-Tool®. Two transverse cuts made through the epoxy and primordium of the otolith yield a 1.0-1.5-mm-thick section (Temple, Price, and Murphy 1985).

Crack and Burn

Burning otolith surfaces which have been broken may enhance readability by charring the boundary layer between the end of each translucent zone and the beginning of the next opaque zone (Christensen 1964). It is fairly easy to burn otoliths too severely, resulting in loss of part or all of the otolith. It is also necessary to burn the entire surface evenly. This technique requires breaking an otolith along a transverse plane through the primordium and charring the protein exposed on the broken surface area (Christensen). Campana (1984) in a test to compare whole otolith ages with those obtained from the crack-and-burn technique reports (for starry flounder) greater numbers of annuli on the prepared otoliths. The error difference was significant.

Burning of the broken surfaces in many species produces more distinct variations between the boundary of the opaque and hyaline zones (Williams and Bedford 1974).

Grinding

Tilapia otoliths can be prepared by grinding both inner and outer surfaces successively on glass plates treated with carborundum with grit sizes 400, 600, and 800 microns (Fagade 1980).

Grinding otoliths can also be accomplished with hand-held devices (Wilson and Larkin 1980; Taubert and Coble 1977; Panella 1971), but this method may result in an uneven plane through the otolith and loss of detail. An apparatus-assisted technique for grinding has been adopted to hold a microscope slide with otolith attached (Neilson and Geen 1980). This eliminates the potential for uneven planes and operates similar to a metallurgical jig used to polish metal surfaces. Atlantic swordfish sagittae embedded in epoxy resin can be sectioned in the transverse plane on a Buehler Isomet saw and polished to 0.5-mm thickness with 600 grit sandpaper and 0.3-micron alumina polish (Wilson and Dean 1982).

Whole Otolith

External or whole otolith readings are made along the long axis of cleaned sagittae under reflected light and against a black background. External observation of whole otoliths fails to take into account the asymmetric deposition of materials occurring in old fish (Campana 1984) and may result in significant underageing (Boehlert and Yoklavich 1984). Otoliths may be read with no processing. However, if they do not present a clear picture of the annuli, it is necessary to grind them until they present a flat surface. When an otolith is so heavy that light cannot penetrate it, sectioning with a small saw, such as a jewelers' saw, is necessary.

Mounting

Eel otoliths can be mounted on black depression plates 6 by 12 cm using 1-2 dichloro-ethane. These plastic plates can hold fifty depressions. Otoliths are removed from the plates by dissolving the plastic with ethane (Liew 1974). Nail polish can be used to mount otoliths on scanning electron microscope (SEM) observation stubs. It is redissolved with acetone to remove the otoliths (Radtke 1982).

Examination and Light Sources

Examination of otoliths involves the use of either light or scanning electron microscopy (Radtke 1982; Neilson and Geen 1980; Popper 1978). Lighting for reading with a light microscope can be either reflected on the surface to be read or transmitted through the surface.

Literature Cited

Boehlert, G. W., and M. M. Yoklavich. 1984. Variability in Age Estimates in *Sebastes* as a Function of Methodology, Different Readers, and Different Laboratories. *California Fish and Game* 70(4):210–24.

Campana, S. E. 1984. Comparison of Age Determination Methods for the Starry Flounder. *Transactions of the American Fisheries Society* 113(3):365–69.

Christensen, J. M. 1964. Burning of Otoliths, a Technique for Age Determination of Soles and Other Fish. *Journal of the Permanent International Council for the Exploration of the Sea* 29(1):73–81.

Fagade, S. O. 1980. The Structure of the Otoliths of Tilapia guineensis (Dumeril) and Their Use in Age Determination. *Hydrobiologia* 69(1–2):169–73.

Jearld, A., Jr. 1983. Age Determination. Pp. 301–24 in L. A. Nielsen and D. L. Johnson, eds., *Fisheries Techniques*. Bethesda, Md.: American Fisheries Society.

Liew, P. K. L. 1974. Age Determination of American Eels Based on the Structure of Their Otoliths. Pp. 124–36 in T. B. Bagenal, ed., *Ageing of Fish*, Proceedings of an International Symposium, European Inland Fisheries Advisory Commission of FAO. Old Woking, Surrey, England: Unwin Brothers Limited, Gresham Press.

Murie, D. J., and D. M. Lavigne. 1985. A Technique for the Recovery of Otoliths from Stomach Contents of Piscivorous Pennepeds. *Journal of Wildlife Management* 49(4):910–12.

Neilson, J. D., and G. H. Geen. 1980. Method for Preparing Otoliths for Microstructure Examination. *Progressive Fish-Culturist* 43(2):90–91.

Panella, G. 1971. Fish Otoliths: Daily Growth Layers and Periodical Patterns. *Science* 173(4002):1124–27.

Popper, A. N. 1978. A Comparative Study of the Otolithic Organs in Fishes. *Scanning Electron Microscopy* 2:405–15.

Radtke, R. L. 1982. Istiophorid Otoliths: Extraction, Morphology, and Possible Use as Ageing Structures. Pp. 123–29 in E. D. Prince and L. M. Pulos, eds., *Proceedings of the International Workshop on Age Determination of Oceanic Pelagic Fishes: Tunas, Billfishes, and Sharks*. U.S. Department of Commerce, National Oceanic and Atmospheric Administration, National Marine Fisheries Service, Southeast Fisheries Center, Miami Laboratory, NOAA NMFS Technical Report No. 8.

Taubert, B., and D. W. Coble. 1977. Daily Rings in Otoliths of Three Species of *Lepomis* and *Tilapia mossambica*. *Journal of the Fisheries Research Board of Canada* 34(3):332–40.

Temple, A. J., D. J. Price, and B. R. Murphy. 1985. An Inexpensive Method for Sectioning Otoliths of Large Fish. *North American Journal of Fisheries Management* 5(4):612.

Williams, T., and B. C. Bedford. 1974. The Use of Otoliths for Age Determination. Pp. 114–23 in T. B. Bagenal, ed., *Ageing of Fish*, Proceedings of an International Symposium. European Inland Fisheries Advisory Commission of FAO. Old Woking, Surrey, England: Unwin Brothers Limited, Gresham Press.

Wilson, C. A., and J. M. Dean. 1982. The Potential Use of Sagittae for Estimating Age of Atlantic Swordfish, *Xiphias gladius*. Pp. 151–56 in E. D. Prince and L. M. Pulos, eds., *Proceedings of the International Workshop on Age Determination of Oceanic Pelagic Fishes: Tunas, Billfishes, and Sharks*. U.S. Department of Commerce, National Oceanic and Atmospheric Administration, National Marine Fisheries Service, Southeast Fisheries Center, Miami Laboratory, NOAA NMFS Technical Report No. 8.

Wilson, K. H. and P. A. Larkin. 1980. Daily Growth Rings in the Otoliths of Juvenile Sockeye Salmon (*Oncorhynchus nerka*) *Canadian Journal of Fisheries and Aquatic Sciences* 37(10):1495–98.

Appendix C
Chemical Formulas

Neutral Buffered Formalin

100 cc 37–40% formalin
900 cc DH_2O

4 grams $NaPo_4$ Monobasic (Sodium Phosphate
Monobasic)
6.5 grams $NaPo_4$ Dibasic Anhydrous

Bouins Solution

20 grams Picric Acid (saturated solution)
1500 cc DH_2O
500 cc Formalin
100 cc Glacial Acetic Acid

Deformalinizing Solution

Dissolve 1260 grams of $NaHSO_3$ and 840 grams Na_2SO_3 in 5 gallons of tap water to make the stock solution. Specimens removed from formalin solutions may be placed directly into this solution. The specimens should remain in the solution approximately 3 to 5 minutes. They may then be handled without danger. Before returning to formalin, specimens should be rinsed in water. This deformalinizing solution may be used several times.

Glossary

Accuracy—The closeness of an age estimate (based on one or more techniques) to the actual age of the specimen. Determination of accuracy requires each ageing technique be validated for that species or population.

Adult—A state in which the organism is able to reproduce; secondary sexual characteristics possessed by some species; fish which are about to spawn or which have spawned at least once. Fish which for some unexplained reason are large enough and old enough to be mature but which have never developed gonads.

Aflatoxins—A generic term referring to toxin produced by some strains of fungus. Specifically refers to toxins produced by *Aspergillus flavus*.

Age—A unit of time, expressed in days, weeks, months, years, or other units used to establish the relationship between present time and previous events.

Age-group—A group of fish of the same age, not the same as year class. Fish which have one annulus are known as one-year-old fish. They are also called yearlings. Those which have two annuli are termed two-year-old fish, and so forth.

Alevin—Larva of species in which postlarval stages are not recognized, that is, in which the yolk-bearing larva transforms directly into the juvenile (example, Salmonidae).

Allopatric—Originating or occurring in different geographical regions.

Amphidromous—Migrating from sea to fresh water or fresh water to sea at regularly definable stages not related to breeding.

Anadromous—A fish which spawns in fresh water and migrates to sea to complete most of its growth.

Angler—Any person who fishes for sport or noncommercial purposes.

Anguilliform—Eel-like.

Note: Some of the definitions used here dealing with age and growth are modifications of the glossary from R. F. Summerfelt and G. E. Hall, eds. 1987. *The Age and Growth of Fish*. Ames, Iowa: Iowa State University Press. 545 pp.

Annual Mark—A discernible structural feature on a hard body part which can be related to a yearly event.

Annuli—Plural of annulus.

Annulus—A structural concentric mark that may be used for age interpretation.

Benthic—Bottom-associated.

Benthophagic—Feeding on organisms that live on or near the bottom.

Bisexual—Sperm and eggs develop and are extruded by males and females.

Carangiform—Jacklike.

Carnivorous—Pertaining to animals that feed on other live animals.

Carrying Capacity—Maximum poundage of a given species or complex of species of fish that a limited and specifically defined aquatic habitat may support during a stated or defined interval of time.

Catadromous—Fish which spawns at sea and migrates to fresh or brackish water to complete most of its growth and maturity. It spends most of its life in fresh water and migrates to sea to breed.

Circulus—A concentric bony ridge laid down on the outer surface of a fish scale, or other bony part, by the addition of material.

Conductivity—Power of conducting electricity.

Contranatant—Migrations of fish against the current.

Core—Area of nonincremental growth material around an otolith primordium.

Current—The movement of electric charge from one position to another (assumed to be from the positive to the load and then to the negative).

Detritophagic—Pertaining to animals that feed on detritus.

Detritus—Organic material which normally occurs on the bottom of water bodies where current is slow or nonexistent.

Diadromous—Migratory between salt and fresh water, including anadromous and catadromous.

Diel—A regularly fluctuating, rhythmic activity, usually associated with one period of darkness and one period of light.

Duty Cycle—The proportion of time current flows in each second, essentially a measure of on-to-off time.

Egg—Female reproductive cell in the body or just extruded.

Electrotaxis—Fish swimming induced by any kind of electric current.

Electrotetany—Muscular rigidity induced by an electric field.

Embryo—A developing multicellular organism, the product of a fertilized egg.

Embryonic—The period of development from the moment of fertilization to the change-over to external feeding. This may be divided as follows: (a) when the development is taking place within the membrane, and (b) when the embryo is free living (pre-larvae), and development continues outside the membrane.

Epizootics—An outbreak of epizootic disease, affecting many animals of one species at the same time.

Equipotential—An area or surface which is connected in such a fashion that the electrical potential of the entire surface is equal.

Eury—Species which can survive in a wide range of a particular parameter.

Euryphagic—The act of feeding on a wide variety of foods.

Eurythermal—Species which can survive in a wide range of temperatures.

Extirpate—Make extinct, exterminate from large areas.

Fecundity—The ability to reproduce.

Galvanonarcosis—State of immobility induced by DC where fish are still and facing the anode.

Galvanotaxis—Artificial swimming induced by a new DC stimulus.

Herbivorous—Pertaining to an animal that eats vegetation.

Hermaphrodite—Both sexes are in one individual and may utilize self-fertilization.

Illiophagic—Literally meaning mud eating. Animals which are able to ingest large amounts of mud (bottom materials) along with detritus and other organic material; reportedly able to survive on bottom materials which are as high as 95 percent nonnutritive. The South American Sabalo is an example.

Immature—Having an external appearance similar to that of the adult but with gonadal development and sexual characteristics feeble or lacking.

Interspecific—Between species.

Intraspecific—Within species.

Joule—A unit of work or energy.

Juvenile—Young which are essentially similar to adults.

Larval Period—The time of feeding on external material; the external appearance and the internal structure are not similar to that of the adult.

Larvae—The stages of fish are generally divided into the prolarvae (larva still bearing yolk) or yolk-bearing stage, often called sac fry by fish culturists, and the postlarvae (larva following the time of absorption of yolk) stage which describes the fish after it has absorbed the yolk sac. The larvae generally differs from adults in morphology and structure; in some instances they are notably different than the adult. Developmental stages are well differentiated from the juvenile and intervening between the times of hatching and of transformation; commonly divisible into prolarva and postlarva.

Limnetic—Living away from edge of shore. Open water.

Lithophil—A fish which spawns on stony ground, usually in rivers and in the current or in the rocky shore areas of oligotrophic lakes. This group includes salmonids and sturgeons. Usually, though not always, it is in favorable respiratory conditions.

Littoral—Associated with near-shore areas.

Meniscus—The concave-shaped water surface in a cylinder.

Monophagic—The act of feeding on only a single type of food.

Mouth Positions—The mouth may be (1) dorsal (or superior), that is, lying above the body axis; (2) terminal, on the body axis; or (3) ventral (or inferior), lying on the underside of the body.

Narcosis—A state of immobility resulting from slackened muscles.

Narcotize—To render numb.

Oceanodromous—Migratory fish that remain within marine water.

Omnivores—Eating what is present, both plant and animal.

Opaque Zone—Zone in ageing material through which the passage of light is inhibited. The opaque zone is dark under transmitted light and bright under reflected light. Opposite of translucent zone.

Oscillotaxis—Artificial swimming motion induced by an alternating current.

Ostraciform—Trunkfishlike. Descriptive of a genus of boxfishes.

Ostracophil—A fish which spawns in the mantle cavity of mollusks or under the claws of crabs of other invertebrates. The eggs usually develop under conditions which are not particularly favorable from a respiratory standpoint.

Overfishing—A level of effort that prevents meeting management objectives, e.g., for fishing success.

Overharvest—A removal of more than the surplus from a stock that prevents meeting management objectives.

Overwintering—Living in a state of low activity with a low rate of metabolism and little or no feeding.

Oviparous—Embryos are hatched externally. Egg laying.

Ovoviviparous—Embryos receive internal nourishment but are extruded as free-swimming young. Live bearing.

Parthenogenesis—Development of young without fertilization by sperm.

Pelagic—Free swimming in the water column. Open water.

Pelagophil—A fish which spawns in the open water. The eggs and the free-living larvae develop in the water column, usually in highly favorable respiratory conditions. This group is composed of primarily marine fish.

Periphyton—That living material which is around and attached to fixed objects in the water.

Phytophil—A fish which spawns among plants often in stagnant or slow-moving water, on vegetation, or dead or dying plants. This group of fish includes common carp, perch, walleye, and sauger. Respiratory conditions may vary considerably.

Planktonic—Dependent on currents for movement. At the mercy of the waves.

Planktophagic—Feeding on plankton.

Potamodrous—Migratory fish that remain within fresh water.

Precision—Measure of the repeatability of an estimate. Not synonymous with accuracy. Used in connection with ageing technique verification, not validation.

Predacious—Pertaining to an animal that preys on, seeks out, pursues, and feeds on other animals.

Psammophil—A fish which spawns on sand, sometimes attaching the eggs to roots of plants, usually under favorable respiratory conditions.

Pulse—A short duration voltage between the generator terminals.

Pulse Rate—The number of complete pulses per second.

Senatant—Migrations of fish with the current.

Senility—The state of no longer being able to reproduce. Generally growth in either length or weight is extremely slow or lacking.

Steno—Species which have a relatively finely defined range for a particular characteristic.

Stenophagic—Pertaining to animals which feed on only a few types of food, narrowly limited in feeding activities.

Stenothermal—Species which can survive only in a relatively finely defined temperature range.

Subadult—A fish which has not spawned but is close enough to sexual maturity so that it may be reasonably assumed that it will spawn at the next natural spawning period.

Sympatric—Occurring in the same region without losing genetic identity.

Tetanus—Characterized by spasm and rigidity of the voluntary muscles.

Tetany—A state of muscular rigidity.

Translucent Zone—Zone in ageing material through which the passage of light is not inhibited. The translucent zone appears bright under transmitted light and dark under reflected light.

Two Year Old—Member of age-group II (or 2).

Verification—Used in ageing technique to signify that two or more readers agree on the number of zones in ageing material. Not synonymous with validation. Used in connection with ageing technique accuracy.

Viviparous—Embryos hatched internally and producing free-swimming young.

Volt—An electromotive force that has one ampere as a steady or constant current against a resistance of one ohm, thus expending one watt of power.

Watt—A unit of power.

Year-class—Fish which were spawned or hatched in any given year. Not the same as age class. See young-of-the-year.

Yearling—Member of age-group I, living in second calendar year.

Young-of-the-year—Any fish which is not old enough to have laid down an annulus is defined as a young, or a young-of-the-year fish (0 age-group). This period extends from hatching until a discernible annulus has been laid down. In practice it is generally assumed that young fish have one annulus as of January 1 in the Northern Hemisphere and July 1 in the Southern Hemisphere. Used as a synonym of calendar age.

Index

Page numbers in **bold** indicate words defined in the glossary. Major headings and subjects appear in CAPITAL letters.

About the Authors

Dr. William F. Sigler served as head of the Utah State University Wildlife Resources department from 1950 to 1974 and since then has worked as a consultant in natural resources and environmental planning. He is coauthor of *Fishes of Utah* and over a hundred other publications dealing with fish, fisheries, and wildlife. Dr. John W. Sigler has investigated fisheries and terrestrial ecology and has been associated with environmental impact assessment projects in several western states. He currently is manager of the western division of Spectrum Sciences and Software, a consulting firm with offices in Logan, Utah, and Fort Walton Beach, Florida. Together, this father and son team coauthored the book *Fishes of the Great Basin: A Natural History* published by the University of Nevada Press in 1987.